# A PRACTITIONER'S GUIDE TO FSA INVESTIGATIONS AND ENFORCEMENT

# A PRACTITIONER'S GUIDE TO FSA INVESTIGATIONS AND ENFORCEMENT

Consultant Editors
**Angela Hayes**
*Lawrence Graham LLP*
and
**Calum Burnett**
*Allen & Overy LLP*

## Second Edition

## City & Financial Publishing

**City & Financial Publishing**
8 Westminster Court, Hipley Street
Old Woking
Surrey GU22 9LG
United Kingdom
Tel: 00 44 (0)1483 720707 Fax: 00 44 (0)1483 727928
Web: www.cityandfinancial.com

This book has been compiled from the contributions of the named authors. The views expressed herein do not necessarily reflect the views of their respective firms. Further, since this book is intended as a general guide only, its application to specific situations will depend upon the particular circumstances involved and it should not be relied upon as a substitute for obtaining appropriate professional advice.

The law is stated as at 31 January 2007. Whilst all reasonable care has been taken in the preparation of this book, City & Financial Publishing and the authors do not accept responsibility for any errors it may contain or for any loss sustained by any person placing reliance on its contents.

ISBN 978 1905 121 137
© 2007 City & Financial Publishing and the named authors

British Library Cataloguing-in-Publication Data. A catalogue record for this book is available from the British Library.

*Typeset by Cambrian Typesetters, Camberley and printed and bound in Great Britain by Biddles Limited, King's Lynn.*

# Biographies

**Angela Hayes** is joint head of the Financial Services Group of Lawrence Graham LLP. She has extensive experience in advising financial services sector clients, listed companies and individual directors on investigations and proceedings by the Financial Services Authority, the UKLA and the Serious Fraud Office. These can cover compliance failures, market abuse, white collar crime and fraud. Angela is also an expert in financial litigation, in particular professional negligence actions involving fund management and financial advice. Angela's practice encompasses assisting clients on developing systems and controls to ensure regulatory compliance, including minimising the risks of market abuse, money laundering and fraud.

**Calum Burnett** is a partner in the Regulatory Investigations Group of Allen & Overy LLP. Calum has wide experience of acting for institutions and individuals in regulatory investigations by the principal UK financial regulators, including the FSA, the UKLA and the DTI, and of advising on cross-border investigations. He is also experienced in advising on criminal matters in the banking and finance spheres and in conducting internal investigations. Calum has spent time on secondment with the Fraud Division of the Crown Prosecution Service and the Enforcement Division of the Financial Services Authority.

**Margaret Cole** joined the FSA in July 2005 as Director of Enforcement. She is a solicitor with over 20 years' experience in private practice, specialising in commercial litigation with an emphasis on financial services. From 1990 to 1995 Margaret was a partner with Stephenson Harwood, where she was responsible for the recovery actions in relation to the Maxwell Pension Funds on behalf of the Pension Funds Trustee. In 1995 she joined the London Office of White & Case to found and head its Dispute Resolution Department. Notable cases at White & Case include representing RBC in proceedings in London and New York regarding an Enron-related $500 million swap transaction. On joining the FSA Margaret was responsible for the implementation of the recommendations from the Enforcement Process Review. Margaret is a member of ExCo, which discusses and makes decisions on the main strategic and operational issues faced by the FSA, and the FSA's Regulatory Policy Committee.

**Margaret Chamberlain** has been a partner with Travers Smith since 1991. She is head of its Financial Services and Markets Department, which advises on the law, practice and regulatory requirements relating to the financial services industry and the securities markets. Margaret is a member of the Council of the British Venture Capital Association ("BVCA"), Chairman of the BVCA Regulatory Committee and Chairman of the City of London Law Society Regulatory Sub-Committee. She was recently appointed by the European Commission to the European Securities Markets Expert Group ("ESME").

**Stephen Paget-Brown** joined Travers Smith in 1987, and became a partner in 1990. He has broad commercial litigation experience, with an emphasis on cases involving banking disputes, insurance disputes, fraud, regulatory misdemeanours, financial services disputes and investigations, judicial review and professional negligence. He is the lead partner on the firm's contentious work for one of the largest banks in Europe, and works for several other clients in the banking and financial services field, as well as one of the four big firms of accountants, and several listed companies. Stephen has managed several arbitrations and mediations, and has developed a significant practice handling FSA investigations.

**James Bagge** is a partner in the Dispute Resolution Department at Norton Rose. He specialises in fraud and the regulation of investment and banking business, in particular all forms of investigations, statutory or private, and associated legal proceedings involving the FSA, the SFO, the DTI and Revenue authorities. He has advised the corporate victims of fraud on investigation and recovery strategies and clients who are themselves the subject of disciplinary proceedings by regulators.

**Charles Evans** is a partner in the Norton Rose Dispute Resolution Department. His principal areas of practice are banking and financial services litigation. He has acted for clients in many regulatory investigations and enforcement proceedings involving the FSA, the SFO (as well as other regulatory bodies). He has also advised the regulators on their own investigations.

**Peter Bibby,** Group Head, Regulatory Group, Bingham McCutchen LLP, was Head of Regulatory Enforcement at the Financial Services Authority between 1998 and early 2002 with responsibility for regulation of the retail sector. He was author of FSA's Principles and Code for Approved Persons and was heavily involved in the development of the FSA's new approach to regulatory enforcement.

Prior to joining the FSA, Peter was a partner in private practice and led a number of high profile contentious regulatory cases including IMRO's enforcement cases in respect of pensions transfers, the Maxwell affair and Morgan Grenfell. During his time at the FSA, he was responsible for enforcement cases such as Royal Scottish Assurance, Royal London, United Friendly, Winterthur, Prudential and GAN. Peter also worked closely with the insurance directorate and general counsel on a number of difficult and novel cases relating to the insurance sector. Since leaving the FSA Peter has been appointed as a skilled person under s166 and has advised firms and individuals on major FSA enforcement cases.

**Simon Morris** joined Cameron McKenna in 1980, qualified as a solicitor in 1982 and has been a partner since 1988. He is a member of the firm's financial services group and advises financial institutions on commercial and regulatory matters. Simon has acted on many acquisitions and product launches, and has represented over 150 firms in regulatory and disciplinary proceedings brought by the FSA and its predecessors. Simon is author of *Financial Services: Regulating Investment Business* (third edition forthcoming) and contributed to the Centre for Policy Studies' recent publication *The Leviathan is still at large.* He was an adviser to HM Opposition's Treasury Team on the Financial Services and Markets Bill. He is a member of the City of London Law Society Regulatory Law Committee and has been a member of the FSA's Authorisation Manual Advisory Panel, With Profits Working Group and MiFID Lawyers' Consultative Group.

**Arun Srivastava** is a partner in Baker & McKenzie, London's Financial Services Group. He was seconded to the FSA between 1999 and 2000. He advises FSA authorised institutions on a broad range of regulatory issues relating to compliance, the Financial Services and Markets Act 2000 and the FSA's Handbook. He also represents firms and regulators in regulatory enforcement proceedings. Arun coordinates Baker & McKenzie's European Financial Services Practice Group.

**Stephen Gentle** is a partner in the criminal department of Kingsley Napley, specialising in financial crime and regulatory matters. He has a particular expertise in advising in money laundering investigations, corruption enquiries and cartel investigations. His regulatory experience is particularly directed at market abuse and market manipulation matters. He also has international criminal law expertise in the fields of extradition and mutual legal assistance.

**Tony Woodcock** has many years of experience in criminal and regulatory enforcement. He was a senior legal assistant with the DPP and the Treasury Solicitor where he was responsible for prosecuting serious criminal cases and representing the DPP in its submissions to bodies such as the Criminal Law Revision Committee and the Law Commission. In private practice he advised the Investment Management Regulatory Organisation (IMRO) on the membership, investigation and discipline chapters of its rulebook and sat as legal adviser to its disciplinary committee. Since N2 Tony has represented a number of individuals and institutions under investigation by the FSA and before the Regulatory Decisions Committee.

Tony is author (with David Kirk) of *"Serious Fraud – Investigation and Trial"* (Third Edition – 2003, Butterworths) and is a contributor to Butterworths Financial Law Service. He is a solicitor advocate (All Courts) and a deputy District Judge.

**David Scott** is a partner in Freshfields Bruckhaus Deringer's Financial Institutions Disputes Group. He specialises in banking and financial services litigation and regulatory proceedings and handles a wide range of disputes for numerous retail financial institutions and investment banks. David's work has included advising Legal & General in the Financial Services and Markets Tribunal proceedings against the FSA which triggered the FSA's Enforcement Process Review. He has also acted for fund managers involved in the FSA's investigations into the split capital investments trust industry and various financial institutions in connection with FSA investigations and enforcement proceedings and disputes before the Financial Ombudsman Service. He is co-author of *Freshfields Bruckhaus Deringer on Financial Services Investigations and Enforcement* (Tottel, 2005).

**Oliver Kerridge** is an associate in Freshfields Bruckhaus Deringer's Financial Institutions Disputes Group specialising in banking and financial services litigation and regulatory proceedings. He contributed to the second edition of *Freshfields Bruckhaus Deringer on Financial Services Investigations and Enforcement* (Tottel, 2005).

**Andrew Carnes** is a practising barrister at 4–5 Gray's Inn Square and formerly legal adviser to a major investment bank; he advises on all aspects of financial services law and regulation. Having conducted proceedings concerning market abuse, pensions misselling, split capital investment trusts, and analyst misconduct, he has recently successfully defended a significant financial services related money laundering trial, in 2004–5 brought to a successful conclusion regulatory action proposed against one of the principal fund managers in FSA's investigation into split capital trusts and provides regulatory advice on mergers and acquisitions and the capital markets. He also conducts disciplinary and advisory work in relation to other related professional disciplinary bodies. He is the editor of *Disciplinary and Regulatory Proceedings* (Jordans Publishing) now in its 4th Edition, co-author of *An Overview of Enforcement Processes of the FSA* (The Legal Practitioner 2005) and supervising editor of *Financial Markets & Securities Regulation* (JurisProductions).

**Saima Hanif** is a practising barrister at 4–5 Gray's Inn Square, called to the Bar in 2002. She specialises in financial services and other regulatory work, and has a strong public law practice. She was seconded to the Financial Services Authority for six months in 2004, giving her an expert understanding of this area. She frequently advises FSA authorised institutions and individuals, in respect of the full range of issues arising under the Financial Services and Markets Act 2000 and the FSA's Handbook.

**Charles Flint** QC is former joint head of Blackstone Chambers, (www.blackstonechambers.com). He specialises in financial services and regulatory work. He was called to the Bar in 1975 and became a Junior Counsel to the Crown in 1990. He is a member of the Lawyers Consultative Working Group established by the Financial Services Authority to advise on issues arising from the Financial Services and Markets Act 2000. He represented Legal & General in the first major challenge to the FSA Enforcement regime before the Financial Services and Markets Tribunal.

**Javan Herberg** is a barrister at Blackstone Chambers, called to the Bar in 1992. He specialises in financial services and other regulatory work, commercial law, and public/human rights law. He has appeared in a number of financial services disciplinary matters and judicial reviews, including *IMRO v. Morgan Grenfell (the Peter Young affair); SFA v. Archer (the "Flaming Ferraris" case); FSA v. Davidson and Tatham; FSA v. Shell/Sir Philip Watts; R (Davis) v. FSA* (2003, Court of Appeal), *R (Yukos) v. FSA* (2006, Administrative Court) and relating to split capital investment trusts and precipice bonds. He advises regularly on retail and wholesale regulatory matters under the Financial Services and Markets Act 2000.

**Andrew Lidbetter** is a solicitor advocate partner in Herbert Smith's litigation division who has considerable experience of dealing with a wide range of commercial disputes. He has a specialist public law practice including judicial review and professional regulation. He is the author of the 'judicial review' and 'human rights' chapters in *'Blackstone's Civil Practice'* and a book on DTI investigations. He is on the advisory board of *'JR'* (Judicial Review) and is listed as a leading public law and professional discipline practitioner in the legal directories.

# Contents

**9 How the FSA makes Disciplinary and Enforcement Decisions** 195

Tony Woodcock
*Partner*
*Stephenson Harwood*

**10 The Role of Mediation** 237

David Scott
*Partner*
Oliver Kerridge
*Associate*
*Freshfields Bruckhaus Deringer*

# Chapter 1

# Introduction and Overview

**Calum Burnett**

Partner
Allen & Overy LLP

**Angela Hayes**

Partner
Lawrence Graham LLP

## 1.1   Introduction

The implementation of the Financial Services and Markets Act 2000 ("FSMA 2000") and the creation of the Financial Services Authority ("FSA") were heralded as important and radical changes to the regulation of financial services in the UK. The FSA assumed the regulatory functions of a number of predecessor regulators and was also given responsibility for being the listing authority in respect of UK public companies, to create a single unified regulator.

This Guide focuses on the enforcement role of the FSA. It aims to draw on the knowledge and experience of leading practitioners in the field of financial regulatory enforcement to provide a practical, focused guide to help those involved in dealing with or advising on FSA enforcement issues to navigate the investigation and disciplinary process. This book is intended to reflect the position as at 31 January 2007. It does not seek to deal with the substantive statutory provisions and FSA rules which impose regulatory requirements as these are beyond its scope.

The FSMA 2000 requires the FSA to act in a way which is compatible with stated regulatory objectives and in a way that is most appropriate for the purpose of meeting those objectives. The four regulatory objectives are:

(a)   market confidence;
(b)   public awareness;
(c)   the protection of consumers; and
(d)   the reduction of financial crime.

These regulatory objectives now inform many of the FSA's decisions on its enforcement priorities and the seriousness with which it views different forms of misconduct.

The last two years have seen some dramatic developments in the FSA's Enforcement Division. On 19 July 2005, the FSA published the recommendations of its review of its enforcement process. The review had been commissioned by the FSA Board after aspects of its Enforcement process were criticised by the Financial Services and Markets Tribunal and because it was evident that many affected by enforcement actions had doubts about the fairness of the process. The review was led by David Strachan, director of retail firms, advised by Michael Brindle QC and David Pritchard, recently retired deputy chairman of Lloyds TSB. The Strachan review's 40 recommendations were accepted by the FSA Board and the Enforcement Division moved to immediate implementation.

The principal changes are that before an enforcement case is referred to the decision makers there should be a thorough legal review by lawyers in the Enforcement Division who are not part of the investigation team; and the administrative decision maker, the Regulatory Decisions Committee ("RDC"), is no longer to take legal advice from the Enforcement Division. A new function of Legal Adviser to the RDC has been created. Moreover, the Enforcement Division no longer has direct access to the RDC without the substance of such discussions being disclosed to the other party in the case.

To preserve the RDC's independence, a new settlement process has been created permitting settlement decisions to be made by the FSA Executive. Explicit incentives for early settlement have also been introduced.

The other major recent theme affecting all aspects of FSA regulation, not just enforcement, is the move to Principles Based Regulation ("PBR"). The Principles are a general statement of the fundamental

2

**Table 1.1**  *Principles for firms*

| | | |
|---|---|---|
| 1 | Integrity | A *firm* must conduct its business with integrity. |
| 2 | Skill, care and diligence | A *firm* must conduct its business with due skill, care and diligence. |
| 3 | Management and control | A *firm* must take reasonable care to organise and control its affairs responsibly and effectively, with adequate risk management systems. |
| 4 | Financial prudence | A *firm* must maintain adequate financial resources. |
| 5 | Market conduct | A *firm* must observe proper standards of market conduct. |
| 6 | Customers' interests | A *firm* must pay due regard to the interests of its *customers* and treat them fairly. |
| 7 | Communications with clients | A *firm* must pay due regard to the information needs of its *clients*, and communicate information to them in a way which is clear, fair and not misleading. |
| 8 | Conflicts of interest | A *firm* must manage conflicts of interest fairly, both between itself and its *customers* and between a *customer* and another *client*. |
| 9 | Customers: relationships of trust | A *firm* must take reasonable care to ensure the suitability of its advice and discretionary decisions for any *customer* who is entitled to rely upon its judgment. |
| 10 | Clients' assets | A *firm* must arrange adequate protection for *clients'* assets when it is responsible for them. |
| 11 | Relations with regulators | A *firm* must deal with its regulators in an open and cooperative way, and must disclose to the FSA appropriately anything relating to the *firm* of which the *FSA* would reasonably expect notice. |

obligations of firms under the regulatory system. They derive their authority from the FSA's rule-making powers as set out in the Financial Services and Markets Act 2000 and reflect the FSA's regulatory objectives.

The Principles are high level statements of ideal conduct. The Principles for firms are shown in Table 1.1.

There are similar principles which apply to approved persons.

As part of the FSA's move to a more principles-based approach, the FSA is looking to remove a significant volume of the detailed rules which have hitherto governed the regulated sector. The FSA's rule-book currently runs to some 8,000 pages. The FSA has already announced that it intends to implement a radical simplification of its Conduct of Business rules, its rules on financial promotions and rules on complaints handling.

The move to Principles Based Regulation has been tentatively welcomed by the industry and compared favourably with other, more prescriptive, regulatory regimes abroad, particularly that in the US. However, one area of residual concern, particularly to those alleged to have contravened a Principle, is the level of predictability under Principles Based Regulation in the absence of detailed rules and provisions. The FSA has stated that, where possible, it would prefer to provide predictability under the Principles and other high-level rules through various forms of guidance to firms, in particular through statements of good and poor practice and through case studies illustrating ways in which firms have successfully met its requirements. As a taste of what is to come, there has been a recent plethora of "Dear CEO" letters (so called because they are letters written by the FSA to the Chief Executive Officers of regulated firms), the purpose of which is to give a stong indication to the regulated community (or a relevant sector of it) of the conduct expected of a firm. The use of this mechanism has been perceived with some scepticism by firms as an attempt to legislate without following the consultation procedures set out in the statute. There has also been a concerning tendency to cite "Dear CEO" letters in enforcement actions brought by the FSA where a firm's conduct is percieved to have fallen short of the standards described in such a letter.

The major inhibition to a full Principles Based Regulatory regime is that many of the recent developments in regulatory law are the result of European legislation which still operates in a way that is compatible with a "rule book" system. However, many enforcement cases are now brought by the FSA on the basis of Principles contraventions alone and the FSA has expended considerable effort in explaining to the industry that this is the approach to be expected in the future.

## 1.2 The challenges faced by the FSA

The FSA is subject to considerable public and political scrutiny and criticism.

A challenge for the FSA in its early life has been the fact that it was created from staff from a number of different regulatory bodies. Those staff brought with them experience of a range of different approaches to regulation and regulatory enforcement. A considerable amount of time and FSA management effort has been required to overcome old divisions and methods to enable a more consistent "FSA approach" to emerge. The FSA has also struggled to devise the most efficient and workable internal structure, perhaps unsurprisingly given its broad range of responsibilities. From an enforcement perspective, the way that the FSA has internally organised itself has on occasion resulted in enforcement staff working on cases for which they lacked relevant experience, leading to concerns on the part of individuals and firms under enforcement that those investigating and bringing cases against them did not have the required product or industry knowledge. A high rate of staff turnover has hampered the establishment of a settled Enforcement Division. The Enforcement Division is currently undergoing a restructuring which is intended to create a leaner but more effective investigation and litigation function.

## 1.3 The role of enforcement

The FSA frequently states that it is not an enforcement-led regulator. It has consistently set great importance on the need for an open and effective supervisory relationship with the firms that it regulates. However, there is little doubt that enforcement is becoming a more prominent feature of the regulatory landscape and is an area of increasing concern for financial institutions.

The FSA is seen by many internationally, and particularly in the US, as being a more benign and flexible regulatory regime and there has been much comment on the impact on the competitiveness of the London markets as a result.

The FSA's approach has been to consider which regulatory messages it wishes to convey and to then target cases which it believes will convey those messages. It has also adopted a theme-based approach to enforcement cases, by which it identifies particular areas of concern and notifies the market that those are the areas upon which it intends to focus its enforcement resources for the forthcoming period, although not, of course, to the exclusion of pursuing other serious breaches of which it becomes aware. Recent examples of these enforcement themes have included payment protection insurance ("PPI"), pensions unlocking, mortgage endowments and breaches of the financial promotion rules, and the themes provide a useful barometer for firms of where regulatory risks might lie.

## 1.4   The level of FSA financial penalties

One of the recommendations of the Strachan Review was the introduction of reduced penalties for early settlement. Up to 30 per cent discount is available to firms who are prepared to admit the contravention at an early stage. This is a concept borrowed from criminal law where a reduction in sentence of up to a third is available to those who plead guilty at an early stage. The settlement process has also been formalised and "without prejudice" discussions are kept entirely from the RDC. The enforcement staff are given settlement parameters by two "Settlement Decision Makers" who are individuals of at least director level at the FSA. For the firm concerned it is often a question of balancing the advantages of an early settlement, when it has not had the opportunity to fully test and challenge the FSA's case, against the possibility that the case may develop quite differently to its benefit if not settled at such an early stage. It is likely that the FSA imperfectly understands its case at the early stages of an investigation. The firm will not have the advantage of full disclosure of the FSA's material which may well include material which assists the firm to assess the likely strength of the case made against it. The firm will not have had a legal review conducted by a more senior lawyer outside the investigation team.

One complicating factor in achieving settlement is the increased internationalisation of regulatory cases, which now often involve multiple regulators from a number of jurisdictions, and often criminal investigations as well, all arising from the same issue or event.

There are those who are sceptical as to whether engagement in the early settlement process actually does involve any reduction in penalty as there is no tariff and practically no guidance on the appropriate level of penalty for a given contravention. A 30 per cent reduction from an unquantifiable sum is not a particularly attractive incentive. The vast majority of enforcement cases have always been negotiated settlements. This limits their precedent value as usually a firm enters into the settlement process because of commercial imperatives and the level of fine imposed is often not as great a priority as limiting the adverse publicity which results from the publication of the FSA's findings. There is considerable scope for negotiating the language used in the FSA's Decision Notices as a result of the settlement process. An analysis of the fines imposed indicates very little consistency. One theme which does emerge, however, is that there may be a trade off between the level of fine imposed and the tone of the Final Notice, with high fines accompanying surprisingly benign Notices in a number of cases.

The level of fines imposed by the FSA are generally very low compared to the sanctions imposed by the US authorities and are more commonly in the hundreds of thousands rather than millions (although million-pound plus fines are not infrequent). In the case in which the FSA imposed its highest fine to date, a fine of £17 million imposed on Shell[1] for market abuse arising from the misreporting of its oil reserves, that fine was dwarfed by the $120 million fine levied on Shell by the Securities & Exchange Commission for the same misconduct.

Those opposed to higher fines say that they constitute a further cost to shareholders who may already have suffered a loss as a result of the misconduct and associated reputational damage. Those who support higher fines say that imposing a cost on shareholders in this way will result in pressure being brought to bear by them on senior management to achieve higher standards of compliance and corporate governance. The FSA's position is that fines should be set at a level which affects future behaviour and it has said that it will increase them if it considers that fines are being treated as a minor

---

[1] Final Notice, *The Shell Transport and Trading Company plc*, 24 August 2004.

cost of doing business. Senior FSA officials have also said that as the greatest deterrent to institutions is likely to be damage to their reputation and brand, one of the FSA's objectives in setting the level of penalties should be to set it at a level that will attract publicity and so adversely affect the brand value and reputation of the company in question.

It is important to bear in mind that the level of fines should not be viewed in isolation. The amount paid by firms in giving restitution or redress to their customers for losses resulting from misconduct is frequently far greater than the amount of fine imposed. That said, the FSA often states in such cases that, had the restitution or redress not been paid, the fine imposed would have been considerably higher.

A novel feature of the FSA enforcement regime has been the availability of mediation with the FSA to firms and individuals under enforcement. The FSA believes that it is the first financial services regulator to offer a formal mediation process as a means of resolving enforcement proceedings. Whilst there are certain tensions and difficulties which exist in applying mediation to the relationship between a regulated entity and a regulator with statutory duties, the scheme has met with some success and the FSA remains keen to encourage greater use of it in the future.

## 1.5   The FSA's use of its powers

A significant development under FSMA 2000 was the granting to the FSA of powers to prosecute certain market-related offences and offences for breaching the Money Laundering Regulations 2003. The FSA launched its first significant markets prosecution in May 2005 in the case of *Regina* v *Rigby and Bailey (AIT Group plc)*,[2] in which convictions were secured for an offence of making a misleading statement contrary to Section 397 of the FSMA 2000. There have been no subsequent prosecutions.

No criminal proceedings for offences under the Money Laundering Regulations 2003 had been commenced at the time of writing,

---

[2]  Verdict delivered on 16 August 2005.

although the FSA has brought a large number of regulatory enforcement proceedings in relation to what it considered to be significant breaches of the FSA's Money Laundering Sourcebook. These have constituted some of the largest fines imposed excepting those for market abuse.

On 4 September 2006 there was an indication that the Commons Treasury Select Committee is considering an investigation into insider trading amid fears that only a small proportion of perpetrators are caught and punished. This may well prompt the FSA to focus more on that area. There has yet to be a criminal prosecution for insider dealing brought by the FSA – an offence for which the FSA has been the statutory prosecutor since 2001. The FSA has so far pursued insider dealing-type cases under the market abuse regime, to which the civil standard of proof applies, rather than bringing a prosecution under Section 52 of the Criminal Justice Act 1993.

One reason for the FSA's disinclination to pursue more criminal prosecutions may be the enormity of the resource required. The FSA's costs in *Rigby and Bailey* were in the region of £2 million. Criminal prosecutions require a very large team and due to the difficulties of presenting complex financial information to a jury, they may take many months to be heard. The acquittal rate for white-collar crime is high.

Notwithstanding these concerns the FSA may simply feel it has no choice but to pursue more criminal cases and the recent recruitment of a number of criminal lawyers suggests that this is likely to happen in 2008/09.

## 1.6   Innovations in the enforcement process

Perhaps the most interesting enforcement case brought by the FSA to date has been that concerning a number of fund managers and brokers involved in the split capital investment trusts industry. The FSA instituted proceedings for market manipulation against the firms involved but, in parallel with pursuing those proceedings, sought to conclude a global settlement with the firms. This was achieved and 18 of the institutions agreed to contribute a total of £194 million to a fund established to compensate investors who had lost money, the first such arrangement entered into by the FSA, mimicking some of the industry-wide settlements brokered by US regulators in recent years. Also in common with many US settlements, the agreement involved no admission or finding of liability on the part of the firms. A "no admissions" settlement was also an interesting feature of the *Shell* case, even though the FSA's largest financial penalty was imposed.

## 1.7 Financial Services and Markets Tribunal

Circumstances do arise where it is not possible for the FSA and the person under enforcement to agree the outcome of enforcement proceedings. In those cases, the regulated person has the right to require the FSA to refer its case to an independent tribunal established under FSMA 2000, the Financial Services and Markets Tribunal ("FSMT").

The FSMT got off to a slow start, with few cases being referred to it initially. It was generally thought that firms would be reluctant to take enforcement matters to a FSMT hearing because of the risk that additional reputational damage would result from contested public proceedings with cross-examination of witnesses, although individuals faced with the loss of their livelihood would probably feel that they had less to lose by the additional publicity. However, as cases have begun to go through FSMT, it has repeatedly demonstrated its willingness to find against the FSA (as it did in the cases of *Baldwin*[3] and *Davidson*[4]) and to be an effective check on the FSA's enforcement powers. It has shown a willingness to reduce financial penalties imposed by the RDC but also ruled in *Jabre*[5] that it was not bound by the RDC's determination of the appropriate level of penalty and would reconsider the issue of the appropriate penalty in the light of all the material available to it, imposing such penalty as it saw fit, whether lower or higher. Subsequently, in *Parker*,[6] the FSMT indicated that this discretion would rarely be exercised to increase the level of penalty imposed by the RDC as it was accepted that this would act as a disincentive for an aggrieved party to make a reference.

---

[3] FSMT decision dated 5 April 2006.
[4] FSMT decisions dated 16 May 2006 and 11 October 2006 (costs).
[5] FSMT decision dated 10 July 2006.
[6] FSMT decision dated 11 May 2006.

The FSMT not infrequently criticises the approach of the enforcement division. An example of this was the case of *Hoodless and Blackwell*,[7] in which the FSMT decided that the conclusions reached in the FSA's decision notice went substantially beyond those that were justified by the evidence presented to the FSMT. The FSMT also imposed a high evidential burden on the FSA, in particular attaching less significance to the contents of transcripts of telephone conversations than the FSA did. The tribunal cautioned that it is easy to be misled by such transcripts and that it was important to distinguish between "brokers' banter" and things meant more seriously.

More recently, in a prominent misselling case brought by the FSA against Legal & General,[8] the tribunal concluded that whilst the FSA had proved some of the alleged instances of misselling, the evidence relied upon by the FSA did not support the extent of the misselling that was alleged. The tribunal said that the RDC, which decided to bring the proceedings, was in error in its approach and reached conclusions that were not justified by the material before it. The experience of *Legal & General* and *Hoodless and Blackwell* will encourage the FSA to consider more closely the adequacy of the evidence that it relies upon to bring enforcement proceedings.

## 1.8 Overview

### 1.8.1 Structure of this book

This Guide begins with a chapter written by Margaret Cole, the FSA's Head of Enforcement, which describes some of the key issues relating to FSA enforcement, as seen from the FSA's perspective, and highlights some key enforcement themes for the FSA (Chapter 2). Thereafter, this Guide has been structured to take the reader through relevant issues in an FSA investigation or enforcement action in the order in time in which they are likely to be encountered. For example, it is likely that most firms that are directly regulated by the FSA will at some time be asked to provide information or other assistance voluntarily to the FSA at a stage before a formal investigation has

---

[7] Final Notice, *Hoodless Brennan and Partners plc*, 17 December 2003.
[8] FSMT decision, *Legal and General Assurance Society Limited*, 13 January 2005.

been initiated. The first substantive chapter (Chapter 3), therefore, concentrates on general principles that apply to dealing with FSA requests for information in circumstances where a formal FSA investigation has not been launched. In the following chapter (Chapter 4) we give guidance on what a firm should do when it discovers that it has a regulatory problem, in particular notifications to the FSA and internal investigations. Remedial action and skilled persons reports are dealt with early on (Chapters 5 and 6) because if a firm discovers that it has breached FSA rules and this has disadvantaged customers, the nature and scope of potential remediation is one of the first things a firm should consider. A skilled person's report may be needed to assess the extent of the problem, recommend solutions, and identify customers that need to be compensated. Chapters 7 and 8 move on to an explanation of the FSA's formal investigation powers and how a firm should handle an FSA investigation. This is followed by a discussion of how the FSA makes regulatory decisions and the factors it takes into account in deciding on sanctions (Chapters 9, 10 and 11). The review of the enforcement process is completed by explaining how a firm can challenge an adverse FSA decision in the FSMT or in the courts or by other avenues (Chapters 12 and 13). The Guide ends by considering the challenges that firms and individuals face when investigations or proceedings by other agencies or prosecutors or in the civil courts are running in parallel with those of the FSA (Chapter 14).

Another aim of this overview is to provide a route map to particular topics, so that readers can go straight to the Chapter covering a particular topic of interest. Therefore, below is a brief indication of the ground covered by each Chapter.

### 1.8.2 *Chapter 2 – The FSA Perspective*

Chapter 2 provides an insight into the FSA's perspective on investigations and enforcement action. It focuses on current and future priorities and key trends for the Enforcement Division. The Chapter describes how Enforcement is integrated with the FSA's supervisory work and how cases are selected for investigation and possible enforcement action. The Chapter then provides some FSA observations on the enforcement process review and the role of the Tribunal, before concluding with an overview of some key trends, including the current handbook review, which will affect the current Enforcement and Decision making manuals.

### 1.8.3 Chapter 3 – FSA requests for information – general principles

This Chapter considers how a firm or individual might respond to a request by the FSA for information where there is no formal FSA investigation, looking at the FSA's powers and the limitations on them. Care should be taken because once information is released it cannot be retracted, and a firm could be exposing itself to liability to third parties by going further than it strictly needs to in providing assistance to the FSA.

The considerations that should be taken into account by authorised firms (and approved persons within them) differ from unauthorised entities and individuals. For example, an authorised firm has a duty to be open and cooperative with the FSA under Principle 11 of the Principles for Businesses. Nevertheless, the firm is entitled to consider whether the scope of the request is reasonable, whether the material sought is relevant, whether the firm may be restricted from disclosing the information by duties of confidentiality owed to third parties, and the extent to which a firm can withhold information covered by legal privilege. For firms and individuals that are not FSA authorised, there is no duty to cooperate but cooperation may nevertheless be appropriate.

### 1.8.4 Chapter 4 – Notifying the FSA of regulatory problems and conducting internal investigations

Sometimes a request by the FSA for information may be the first indication a firm receives that it has a regulatory problem, but there are a variety of other ways that regulatory problems can come to light, for example through customer complaints or internal audit. If the problem is significant a firm may be under a duty to notify the FSA of the problem immediately. However, it is likely that a firm will need to carry out an internal investigation to assess the nature and extent of the problem and to establish whether any remedial action is appropriate. If it can be demonstrated to the FSA at an early stage that a responsible approach is being taken to conducting an internal investigation, the FSA will often be prepared to await the outcome of the internal investigation rather than immediately launching its own formal investigation. A firm's duties to notify the FSA of regulatory problems, the approach to doing so and practical guidance on how to deal with internal investigations are discussed in depth.

### 1.8.5 Chapter 5 – Skilled persons reports

If the FSA is concerned about leaving the handling of a regulatory problem in the hands of the firm concerned, the FSA may require an authorised firm to obtain and provide to the FSA a report drawn up by a "skilled person". This is a person who has the skills necessary to make a report on the matter concerned and who is either nominated or approved by the FSA. This is a tempting route for the FSA to follow given its own limited resources for enforcement action. However, there can be disadvantages for a firm in acquiescing to an FSA request that a skilled person should be appointed. The costs are likely to be higher than appointing the same professional on a bilateral basis and firms can lose control of the process of dealing with the regulatory problem. It is important for firms faced with the possibility of a skilled person appointment to understand the likely terms of the appointment, the powers that the skilled person will have and the firm's duty to cooperate, and the limited capacity that a firm will have to influence the exercise once the skilled person is appointed. The Chapter also considers arguments a firm can raise to persuade the FSA that the involvement of a skilled person is unnecessary in particular circumstances.

### 1.8.6 Chapter 6 – Remedial action under FSMA 2000

Firms carry out most remedial action voluntarily. Most firms that identify a problem value their customers and would want to take any remedial steps that are appropriate promptly. Demonstrating to the FSA that appropriate remediation has been carried out is also an important way of persuading the FSA not to bring enforcement action or, if it does decide to proceed with enforcement action, that a lesser penalty is appropriate. This Chapter considers in detail the FSA's powers to require a firm to conduct remedial action and also the nature of remedial action that a firm should be considering and how to manage it within the context of a potential enforcement case.

### 1.8.7   Chapters 7 and 8 – Formal FSA investigations

If the FSA nevertheless considers that enforcement action is appropriate, it will appoint investigators and the firm is then in a new phase of responding to a formal FSA investigation. The correct approach for dealing with a criminal investigation or a market abuse investigation differs in significant respects from the general approach to responding to civil investigations by the FSA. Chapter 7 deals with formal civil investigations by the FSA. Chapter 8 deals with formal criminal investigations and market abuse investigations. These Chapters look in detail at the FSA's compulsory powers to obtain information and documents, and how to respond to such compulsory requests, and the FSA's approach to using compulsory and voluntary interviews of individuals as suspects and potential witnesses.

### 1.8.8   Chapter 9 – How the FSA makes disciplinary and enforcement decisions

Chapter 9 considers in detail how the FSA makes disciplinary and enforcement decisions following the review of its enforcement process in 2005. It explains the structure and practical workings of the RDC in detail, and describes its relationship with Enforcement under the new structure imposed after the Strachan review. The Chapter describes how decisions are made under executive procedures, the statutory notices process and the approach to making representations to the RDC. It concludes by discussing the settlement of enforcement actions.

### 1.8.9   Chapter 10 – The role of mediation

A large number of cases end in an agreed settlement. So far this has in most cases been achieved through informal, without prejudice discussions between firms and individuals and the FSA. However, as discussed in the introduction, an important option is the availability of mediation and it is a settlement tool that the FSA is eager to make greater use of. Critics of the FSA mediation process say that in reality it is little more than structured plea bargaining, with little possibility that the FSA will be persuaded to accept that there has been no breach and that it is expensive. The FSA's role as a statutory regulator bound by its regulatory objectives means that a "deal" in the ordinary commercial sense cannot be struck. Advocates of mediation mention cases where mediation has resulted in a significant change in outcomes, though because mediation is a confidential process objective data is hard to find. Chapter 10 focuses on the practical issues that arise in attempting to use mediation with the FSA to reach a favourable outcome.

### 1.8.10 Chapter 11 – Disciplinary sanctions and other enforcement options

As the title suggests, this Chapter examines the disciplinary sanctions and other enforcement options available to the FSA and the factors that the FSA takes into account in deciding what sanction to apply including the level of any financial penalty. The Chapter also considers some of the principles that can be drawn from the considerable body of published enforcement decisions that has now built up. A detailed understanding of how the FSA weighs particular factors in deciding whether to take disciplinary or enforcement action, and in determining the type of sanction and level of financial penalty, is vital to preparing representations to the FSA at RDC stage and in conducting negotiations with the FSA throughout the enforcement process.

### 1.8.11 Chapters 12 and 13 – Challenging FSA decisions

If the FSA reaches an adverse decision a firm may wish to challenge it. Chapter 12 looks at the mechanism for challenging FSA decisions in the FSMT, which will in most cases be the appropriate forum. The FSMT has shown itself to be robust in its consideration of disputed FSA decisions. This Chapter considers in depth the jurisdiction and procedures of the FSMT, including how to make a reference to that Tribunal, the FSA's formal Statement of Case and preparing a reply to it, the rules about disclosure of documents to be relied upon, and the conduct of hearings. Importantly, the FSMT's role is not limited to a review of FSA decisions. The Tribunal considers the matter afresh in light of all the evidence before it, which can include fresh evidence not taken into account by the FSA in reaching its original decision, and has the power to consider directing penalties more severe than those contemplated in the FSA notice being challenged.

Chapter 13 looks at other options for challenging FSA decisions, in particular the extent to which judicial review in the High Court may be available. The impact of the Human Rights Act 1998 is considered. The possibility of bringing claims against the FSA for negligence, breach of statutory duty or misfeasance in public office is also examined.

### 1.8.12 *Chapter 14 – Interface with other investigations and proceedings*

Finally, Chapter 14 looks at the pressures and practical difficulties that a firm can face if it is dealing with an FSA investigation and, at the same time, with parallel investigations by other investigatory or prosecuting bodies or legal action in the courts. The FSA's recognition of the potential collateral damage that a firm can face as a result of legal action by investors in the civil courts, in particular threatened "class" actions, has driven a new willingness of the FSA to consider entering into settlements of enforcement action that expressly involve "no admission" of breach by the firms or individuals involved. This leaves firms in a position where they may still be able to defend court action successfully. The practical issues that will arise in managing and responding to multiple investigations and proceedings are discussed.

# Chapter 2

# The FSA Perspective

**Margaret Cole**
Director of Enforcement
Financial Services Authority

## 2.1 Introduction

The objective of this chapter is to provide an insight into the FSA's perspective on its investigations and enforcement action. Rather than covering all of the aspects of the enforcement and decision-making processes that are discussed in detail in subsequent chapters of this book, this chapter focuses on current and future priorities and key trends for the Enforcement Division. It also looks at issues arising from the role of the Financial Services and Markets Tribunal, particularly the impact that its decisions have on the work of enforcement, and the changes that the FSA made in the wake of the Enforcement Process Review 2005.

The Enforcement Division's guiding philosophy is to be "bold and resolute". This philosophy influences and guides all enforcement activity. In this context, the FSA is committed to the effective use of the enforcement tool to assist in achieving the FSA's strategic aims and objectives. The FSA believes that a firm and confident approach to its enforcement activity is an essential part of that commitment. The Enforcement Division intends that its outcomes should demonstrate this approach.

## 2.2 Enforcement priorities and integration

The Enforcement Division exists to conduct timely, fair investigations and, where appropriate, take disciplinary or other action. Viewed strategically the enforcement tool exists to support the FSA's objectives and is used as part of the FSA's overall risk-based supervisory strategy.

In short, consistent with the way it undertakes all of its activities, the FSA takes a risk-based approach towards its use of the enforcement tool. This includes considering the FSA's regulatory objectives and principles of good regulation in the context of current stated priorities. The FSA considers carefully what course of action would be a proportionate response, exercises a common standard of fairness in the use of its powers and acts in a manner consistent with the Human Rights Act 1998. In addition, the FSA monitors closely and, where necessary, seeks to influence, legislative developments, such as the Regulatory Reform Bill, that it considers may impact on the way it conducts its enforcement activities.

The FSA does not have a set of enforcement priorities that are distinct from the priorities of the FSA as a whole. The Enforcement Division does not devise its own strategies, priorities and objectives but instead aligns its activity with the FSA's overall priorities. Therefore, the Division's priorities are necessarily a subset of the FSA's overall priorities. Ultimately, the objective is to ensure that the Enforcement Division operates at the heart of the FSA as a fully integrated tool focused on the delivery of the FSA's aims and objectives.

To reinforce this, in the 2007/08 FSA Business Plan, the Enforcement Division has not listed a separate set of enforcement priorities. Rather the FSA took this opportunity to re-emphasise its commitment to the effective use of enforcement in areas which pose the greatest risk to the FSA's statutory objectives.

To achieve this, the Enforcement Division is closely aligned with the FSA Wholesale and Retail Business Units. Priorities identified in this Business Plan include in the wholesale area, wholesale insurance, routine insurance, market abuse and market misconduct, particularly the area of systemic and organised insider dealing. In the retail area, the priorities include general insurance, the Treating Customers Fairly agenda, payment protection insurance, equity release and mortgage endowment complaints handling.

This does not mean that enforcement action will only happen in the FSA's priority strategic areas. There will always be particularly egregious cases where enforcement action is necessary, ad hoc cases where consumer protection is a key issue, or cases that are necessary in the interests of achieving effective deterrence. These cases could arise in a context that has not specifically been identified as one of the FSA's current priority areas.

Nevertheless, the FSA has already restructured the Enforcement Division to align with the FSA's Wholesale/Retail Business Unit model. This enables the Enforcement Division to focus its efforts, skills and resources so that it can better deliver the FSA strategic aims of promoting efficient, orderly and fair markets, helping retail customers achieve a fair deal, and improving its business capability and effectiveness.

## 2.3   Case selection

The FSA's approach to its regulatory responsibilities has to be sufficiently flexible to deal with the very different types and sizes of firms and markets that it regulates. The approach ranges from large firms having a dedicated supervision team and close and continuous supervision, through medium-sized firms who have a relationship manager but will not receive 100 per cent of that individual's attention, to small firms with individually low impact on the FSA's statutory objectives and whose relationship with the FSA may be primarily through the Firm Contact Centre. The FSA also seeks to address cross-cutting industry issues across all sizes of firms through thematic work where firms operating in a particular industry or offering a certain product might be selected for a thematic visit. Themes are, in general, selected to enable the FSA to improve its understanding of particular industry areas or to assess the validity of concerns it has about risks that those areas may present to the statutory objectives.

It is clear from the number of Final Notices issued by the FSA that the vast majority of transgressions identified are not addressed by the FSA taking disciplinary action. The FSA's risk-based approach means that not every matter in which a possible breach has been identified will be suitable for investigation by the Enforcement Division.

When considering whether to refer a matter for investigation by the Enforcement Division, supervisors will take into account a range of factors. These will include issues such as:

(a) whether the matter is one of significance to the FSA, that is, whether it poses a threat to the statutory objectives of the FSA, whether it is widespread and so on;

(b) what the potential impact of a disciplinary outcome at the end of an investigation would be, that is, whether it would encourage others to improve their behaviour or encourage consumers to take more responsibility for their decisions;

(c) how much the FSA believes it needs to achieve a deterrent effect in a particular area and whether the FSA is clear about who it is trying to deter;

(d) whether the desired effect – which may be industry-wide or firm specific – can be achieved by using other tools;

(e) what the cost and resource implications of pursuing particular areas are.

In line with this risk-based approach, the FSA devotes far more of its supervisory resources to high-impact firms. Accordingly it is more likely that problems in those firms will be identified through day-to-day supervision work. Additionally, given the nature and size of some of those firms, where such problems are identified, the potential impact can be of great significance. Accordingly, an enforcement investigation with a possible disciplinary outcome may be appropriate. That is not to say that simply the fact that a firm is large or high impact will by itself be a reason for contemplating enforcement action as a tool to address a particular issue rather than any other supervisory tool.

Alongside supervision, the other major source of referrals to the Enforcement Division is the thematic work that the FSA undertakes. In this regard, the reality again is that work is undertaken in areas which the FSA thinks are important and which potentially present risks to its statutory objectives. There is no presumption that some or all of any sample of firms visited as part of a theme will necessarily be referred to Enforcement. However, where issues are identified in firms which are visited as part of a theme, these will be considered for referral to enforcement as they would if they had been discovered in any other circumstance. And, by definition, the fact that they are in areas that are of importance to the FSA means that, following the risk-based approach through, they are proportionately more likely to result in the FSA determining that an investigation should be carried out by the Enforcement Division than issues in lower-priority areas.

Supervision and FSA themes are not the only means by which cases are referred to Enforcement. The press, members of the public and industry all regularly bring matters to the Enforcement Division's attention, particularly where it looks like somebody may be conducting regulated activities without appropriate authorisation from the FSA. Enforcement also receives referrals from other UK enforcement agencies, such as the Serious Fraud Office and the Department of Trade and Industry, as well as its counterparts in other jurisdictions. The same factors will be taken into account when considering whether to investigate matters referred from external sources, but an essential preliminary consideration will be to determine whether the FSA has jurisdiction over the matter at hand.

It is important to note that the fact that an investigation is commenced under Part XI of the Financial Services and Markets Act 2000 ("FSMA 2000"), does not in any way mean that a formal disciplinary outcome is inevitable. Excluding threshold conditions cases, in 2005/2006 37 per cent of matters investigated by Enforcement concluded with no formal disciplinary action being taken. In a further 9 per cent of cases, private warnings were issued. The FSA commences its investigations with an open mind and with a view to establishing the facts. It does not pursue disciplinary action at any cost.

Consistency in the way the FSA assesses which cases should be investigated by Enforcement is important. The process must also be fair. However, the FSA does not accept that fairness requires that no firm is ever investigated unless every other firm meeting the same criteria is also investigated. Nor does the FSA accept that its choice to use investigation by Enforcement and appoint investigators rather than use a supervisory tool in a particular area is a matter which goes to the question of fairness. Rather, the FSA sees this as a question of how the FSA puts into practice its risk-based approach, how it uses its resources effectively and efficiently and how it ensures that it is an effective regulator rather than just an effective enforcer. In short, the FSA's view is that efficiency and fairness are not opposing forces but forces that pull together to make the FSA as effective as possible.

## 2.4 Enforcement Process Review 2005

The FSA's key aim for the enforcement process is that it should not only be fair but it should be seen to be fair. To that end, following the Enforcement Process Review 2005, the FSA introduced a number of changes to the enforcement process.

The FSA's aim is to make sure that, however much firms and individuals dislike being involved in enforcement action, they will nevertheless consider that they have been treated fairly. From the FSA's perspective, this is equally important. The FSA does not intend to be diverted from its task (i.e. of obtaining efficient, speedy and robust outcomes in the interests of protecting the integrity of the markets and ensuring a fair deal for consumers) by fundamentally unproductive debates about processes. Now that the FSA has reviewed its processes carefully and implemented significant change following due consultation, it is important that firms and individuals (together with their advisers) focus on the real issues in cases rather than engaging in tactical process-driven skirmishes. It is necessary for firms and individuals to work with the FSA in order to achieve prompt, practical, proportionate and businesslike outcomes. This is what the FSA has been told that firms and individuals wish to achieve.

The key issues of process that used to trouble the regulated community have now been dealt with. The foremost of these were transparency and separation. There is no longer any special access for the enforcement team to the Regulatory Decisions Committee ("RDC"), and any significant communications between the enforcement team and the RDC are disclosed.

Oral representation meetings before the RDC have become more interactive and it is important that these are conducted in an atmosphere of informality. The FSA is opposed to any judicialisation of the RDC and is committed to maintaining a considerable degree of informality in the way it operates. Experience has shown that the RDC, in deciding what action it is appropriate for the FSA to take, finds it invaluable to hear from someone, such as the CEO of a firm, who is close to the business and qualified to talk about what happened, why it happened and what, if any, remedial steps have been taken. This is invariably far more helpful to the RDC than hearing lengthy legal submissions, however eloquently they are delivered.

It is worth remembering that the RDC is a committee of the FSA Board, and although the FSA Board cannot review individual RDC decisions, the RDC is accountable to the Board. As the Enforcement Process Review recognised, the FSA must, under the FSMA 2000, make regulatory decisions itself and cannot confer such decisions on a wholly independent body. The RDC, as a committee of the FSA Board, is the body that decides whether to issue warning and decision notices in contested cases. However, the RDC is not intended to resemble a court or tribunal or have a quasi-judicial function. The RDC does not set FSA policy, rather its role is to implement that policy taking into account the facts and matters before it. Accordingly, the RDC will make its decisions by applying the relevant statutory tests, and by having full regard for the FSA's settled policies (including on matters of legal interpretation).

One of the key recommendations of the Enforcement Process Review was that before being submitted to the RDC, cases should be reviewed by a lawyer who had not previously been part of the investigation team. In order to enable this to take place in the most efficient way possible, the Enforcement Division has set up a new department, Litigation and Legal Review. Although these reviews happened previously in many cases, adoption of this recommendation has enabled Enforcement to create a consistent framework for stress-testing cases. It enables a dispassionate review of the way a case is put and whether it is supported by sufficient evidence. This is designed to counter concerns that Enforcement adopts a "prosecution mindset". It is important to realise that the role of the RDC legal adviser is different from that of the Enforcement legal reviewer. Some concerns have been expressed about delays in the process caused by this legal review within the Enforcement Division, coupled with the advisory role of the RDC legal adviser. The FSA is working to ensure that timescales are minimised, and it was with this in mind that the new Litigation and Legal Review team was set up.

Another key change resulting from the Enforcement Process Review is the way that settlement decisions are now made entirely separately from the RDC in order to protect the integrity of the RDC in contested cases. Settlement decisions are discussed in further detail at 2.6.4 below.

## 2.5   Tribunal

The Financial Services and Markets Tribunal (the "Tribunal") is an essential part of the statutory framework set up by the FSMA 2000. The FSA itself must make decisions in enforcement cases rather than referring them to an independent body. However, in order to provide the right to a fair trial before an independent and impartial tribunal conferred by Article 6 of the European Convention on Human Rights, the FSMA 2000 establishes such a tribunal to hear cases where the subject of enforcement action is aggrieved as to the FSA's decisions. In view of the large number of regulatory decisions made by the FSA that could have been referred to the Tribunal, comparatively few references have been made.

The nature of the Tribunal process is very different from the FSA's internal decision-making process and in particular the procedures before the RDC. In contrast to the RDC, the Tribunal hears from live witnesses who are subject to cross-examination. Even complex cases before the RDC take a matter of hours, but equivalent cases before the Tribunal can take days or weeks. In view of the different nature of the process, it is not surprising that the Tribunal has sometimes disagreed with the FSA, even if no criticism can be made of the RDC decision in view of the material that was then before it. There may also be some issues of law where the Tribunal might take a different view from the FSA. The Tribunal may also take a different view on a conflict of evidence. If the FSA won every single case that was referred to the Tribunal, the FSA could be criticised for only bringing cases that it was bound to win. The FSA will continue to bring difficult cases. Naturally, this does not mean that the FSA will bring cases where it does not believe it has a reasonable prospect of success, nor does it demonstrate that the FSA has a "win at all costs" attitude.

The Tribunal is a true first instance Tribunal. It is tempting to believe, when the FSA has a relatively elaborate representations procedure before the RDC, that the Tribunal considers "appeals" from FSA decisions. However many times this message is repeated, the public perception is that the Tribunal does hear appeals, and this is certainly the way it is always portrayed in the press. However, the jurisdiction exercised by the Tribunal is a first instance Tribunal where the case is considered afresh and matters can proceed in a very different way from how they were considered before the RDC.

Although it was widely accepted that the Tribunal had a first instance jurisdiction, there remained scope for some argument as to the extent of that jurisdiction. The Tribunal must consider what the appropriate action is for the FSA to take in relation to the "matter" referred to it. There has been considerable argument as to what the "matter referred" is. This point has been settled by the *Jabre* decision[1] which held that the "matter referred" was very wide and not restricted to the four corners of the decision notice. The result of this is that subject to certain statutory restrictions, the Tribunal is able to consider remedies that were not considered, or were considered and rejected by the FSA at the decision-making stage. It is important that since the Tribunal is a first instance tribunal, it is not unnecessarily fettered by what has happened at the RDC stage.

When considering the Tribunal's decisions as precedents, it is important to bear in mind that rulings in previous cases are not binding on the Tribunal in subsequent cases, although they are of considerable persuasive value. Appeals from the Tribunal are on points of law only to the Court of Appeal, and at the time of writing there had been no substantive hearings in the Court of Appeal. Appeals are also limited to decisions of the Tribunal that dispose of the reference, that is, there appears to be no basis for an appeal to the Court of Appeal on an interlocutory ruling on a point of law. In any event, in order to appeal, permission of the Tribunal or the Court of Appeal is required. In practical terms, the FSA anticipates that permission will only be given and that the appeal will only have a reasonable prospect of success where the point of law was determinative of the outcome of the case.

This presents a dilemma for the FSA. Where the FSA believes that the Tribunal has erred in its interpretation of the law on a particular issue

---

[1] *Philippe Jabre v The Financial Services Authority* (Financial Services and Markets Tribunal case 035).

but, even if they had not done, the outcome of the case would not change, neither the FSA nor the other party are able to appeal. There is a clear interest, both for the FSA and for those against whom disciplinary action might be taken, to have clear, consistent and predictable interpretation of the law from the Tribunal. Until there is a clear weight of authority from higher courts, there may well be cases where the FSA or the opposing party may seek to ask the Tribunal to depart from previous rulings. Although this is to some extent unattractive, the FSA does not regard itself as precluded from doing so.

Another part of the Tribunal's jurisprudence that has received considerable recent attention has been the provisions relating to costs. Under the previous regulatory regime, some of the self regulatory organisations ("SROs") were routinely able to recover their costs in enforcement action, and many of the Tribunals established under that system also followed a rule whereby costs followed the event. It was widely considered that this was a significant disincentive to firms and individuals to challenge enforcement action. The FSMA 2000 contains provisions similar to many tribunals whereby costs do not follow the event but may only be awarded where a party has behaved vexatiously, frivolously or unreasonably. In addition, there is a special provision in the FSMA 2000 whereby a party may recover costs if the FSA decision which is the subject of the reference was itself unreasonable. This means the applicant must establish more than that the FSA's decision was wrong. There has been some disquiet that those who are cleared by the Tribunal following an FSA decision are not entitled to their costs, but this was essentially a political decision taken at the time of the legislation. There may have been even more of an outcry if the FSA was able to recover its costs in the greater number of cases where the FSA succeeds in, often very expensive, proceedings before the Tribunal. Any costs awarded against the FSA are ultimately costs that will be borne by the industry through the payment of fees.

## 2.6 Key trends

### 2.6.1 *Effective deterrence*

A key issue for the FSA for now and in the future is deterrence – in other words, how to use the enforcement tool effectively as a way to achieve behavioural change. Enforcement is only one of a number of regulatory tools available to the FSA and it is not the most widely used. Enforcement is a small but nonetheless important part of the regulatory relationship.

This is because the potential impact of enforcement action is significant. Enforcement activity generates more publicity about the FSA than any other single issue. Enforcement outcomes can therefore play a very significant role in educating the industry and consumers about issues of concern and the FSA's approach to them. It can also be a very powerful way of changing behaviour. The FSA expects enforcement action to encourage and promote high standards of behaviour, both in terms of its market integrity and protection of consumers' objectives.

The FSA will actively look for new ways to make sure its penalties bring about the deterrent effect that the FSA want to achieve. This means considering not only the types and levels of penalties that the FSA impose, but making sure that the penalties impact upon the right people. It also means acting with confidence and resolutely taking enforcement action where appropriate to convince wrongdoers that there is a real risk that they will be caught and proceeded against.

### 2.6.2 *Senior management responsibility*

Senior management responsibility remains high on the FSA's agenda. The FSA expects senior management to take responsibility for ensuring that firms identify risks, develop appropriate systems and controls to manage those risks, and ensure that the systems and controls mitigate the risks in practice. Failure to manage risks properly is now, more then ever, likely to result in disciplinary action being brought against individuals as well as firms. Senior managers need to understand this and ensure that they are taking appropriate action to identify and mitigate risks to protect their firm and increasingly themselves.

The FSA recognises that cases against individuals are very different in their nature from cases against firms. Firms and companies have a different business imperative – often they wish to resolve cases quickly to limit commercial damage to their ongoing business and corporate reputation. An individual faces greater risks from a successful enforcement action in terms of financial implications, reputation and livelihood. Generally, cases against individuals are hard fought, and at many practical levels they are harder to prove, take longer to resolve and are less likely to be settled. Nonetheless, the FSA is committed to ensuring that appropriate cases against senior management are pursued robustly and with sufficient resource.

The FSA's intention is to be resolute in this regard. This means that difficult cases will be taken on, including some cases where the FSA recognises, from the beginning, that it might be difficult to obtain a disciplinary outcome. These cases are likely to be cases which are of significant individual seriousness as well as strategic importance.

### 2.6.3 Penalties

To achieve effective deterrence, wrongdoers must not only realise that they face a real and tangible risk that they will be held to account, but they must expect a significant penalty. The FSA will seek to ensure that the sanctions that it imposes, including financial penalties, are fixed at levels that are sufficient to deter potential wrongdoers, and where necessary it will increase penalties to achieve this. The FSA intends to be bold in its approach particularly in cases where the regulatory requirements have been clear for some time and where the FSA need to ensure that regulatory fines are not simply regarded as just another cost of doing business. One example of this is in the area of market misconduct.

Given that the appropriate standards of market behaviour have been clearly set out since 2001, the FSA view very seriously conduct which falls below the standards set out in the FSMA 2000 or which contravene their Principles. Where the FSA considers that behaviour justifies criminal rather than civil penalties, it will be prepared to pursue such cases through the criminal courts. The FSA's commitment and ability to do so was demonstrated in 2005 by their successful prosecution of the directors of AIT for providing false and misleading statements to the market.

### 2.6.4   Settlement and mediation

The FSA considers that it is in the public interest for matters to settle (and settle early) if possible. This includes settlement via mediation.

Settlement decisions are now made on behalf of the FSA by two decision makers of at least director status. The director of the Enforcement Division will usually be one of the decision makers, the second being allocated as appropriate. This approach is proving to be an efficient and effective way of concluding settlements promptly. It has the advantage of involving FSA senior management in the decision-making process and facilitates close interaction between the Enforcement Division and the Wholesale and Retail Markets Business Units which will ensure consistency of approach to settlements and impact of outcomes.

The FSA recognises the importance of achieving consistency in the approach to penalties between RDC decisions in contested cases and Executive Settlement Decisions. The FSA considers that cases which result from Executive Settlement Decisions in settlement or mediation have equal precedent value to cases that are resolved via the RDC. Although the RDC and the Enforcement Division are separate, there is regular liaison between them at a policy level to ensure consistency of approach and to make sure that the RDC is fully briefed on the factors the FSA considers are important for penalty setting. All parties, including the RDC, Enforcement and firms, are able to discuss the detail of the rationale for penalties in concluded and published cases. It is in no one's interests for there to be forum shopping between the RDC and Executive Settlement Decision Makers.

Key aspects of the FSA's settlement philosophy are as follows. It is important to the FSA to achieve early settlements, including settlement via mediation. Such settlements facilitate prompt redress in consumer-related cases and enable the FSA to achieve swift and effective outcomes so that the FSA can utilise their resource more efficiently and move on to the next important issue. However, the FSA is only interested in getting the right settlements – ones which are justified on the basis of the law, the principles and the facts. The FSA will not compromise the integrity of its decisions and outcomes by rushing to finalise settlements on bases which are not appropriate. FSA

31

settlement discussions involve different considerations than apply to resolve a commercial transaction.

The FSA also intend to be time sensitive in settlement situations. In the past, the Enforcement Division have had concerns that settlement negotiations have drifted and been delayed for extended periods. If settlements with the FSA are to be successful then all parties must be prompt and cooperative in moving the matter towards resolution. In the intersts of efficiency and effectiveness, the FSA are intending to put stricter time limits on settlement negotiations. As an incentive to those engaged in settlement discussions with the FSA, and following recommendations in the Enforcement Process Review 2005, the FSA operates a discount scheme whereby a reduction in financial penalty of up to 30 per cent (at the pre Warning Notice stage) can be obtained.

### 2.6.5 *Principles*

A combination of two factors will lead to an increased focus on Principle-based enforcement cases:

(a) the FSA as a whole is moving towards more Principle-based regulation where the FSA will rely on general Principles rather than detailed rules whenever it can;

(b) as enforcement is a fully integrated tool for implementing FSA strategy, this long-term policy approach is likely to lead to increased focus on Principle-based enforcement cases. Enforcement's role is to support the objectives of the FSA, and Enforcement has moved with the rest of the FSA and will ensure that cases support the more Principle-based approach.

Currently the FSA's approach to regulation is a hybrid of high-level principles and detailed rules and guidance. While this broad structure is both necessary and desirable, the FSA aims where it can to change the balance significantly towards a more Principle-based approach. More Principle-based regulation is a key part of the FSA's Better Regulation Agenda and of the FSA's vision for the development of regulation. The FSA believes that this is the right approach to maintain the current constructive environment for mobile capital, and at the same time achieve better outcomes for retail customers.

The FSA considers that more Principle-based regulation provides better-quality regulation than simply a mass of detailed rules. The FSA believes that providing firms with the flexibility to decide for themselves what business processes and controls should operate so that compliance with the Principles is secured, will better align good regulation with good business practice. By taking a more overtly risk-based approach to the FSA's assessment of whether firms are operating in line with these Principles, the FSA intends to create incentives for firms to focus on compliance in return for a regulatory dividend – that is, less regulatory intervention.

This approach does not represent a radical change of direction for the FSA – the FSA has been advocating a more Principle-based approach to regulation for some time. The 11 high-level Principles for Businesses have been in place since 2001. They set overarching requirements for all financial services firms. They focus on what the FSA is trying to achieve and are therefore expressed in terms of outcomes rather than processes or procedures.

Where appropriate, the FSA can and does take enforcement action on the basis of principles alone. In 1999, in a letter to the London Investment Banking Association, the FSA set out the circumstances in which it might take Principle-based enforcement action where there are a number of cumulative rule breaches which call into question compliance with a Principle or where there are no detailed rules concerning the conduct but where it clearly contravenes a Principle. The FSA stated that it would expect the number of cases for a breach of a Principle alone to be small. This is no longer the FSA's position. Where appropriate, the FSA intends increasingly to take enforcement action on the basis of Principles alone.[2]

The concept of predictability is vital in this regard. In order for consequences legitimately to be attached to the breach of a Principle it must be possible to predict, at the time of the action concerned, whether or not it would be in breach of a Principle. As long as the action or actions in respect of which discipline is being brought could reasonably be predicted to be in breach of the Principle, the FSA does not

---

[2] John Tiner, keynote address, Enforcement Law Conference 16 June 2006 (http://www.fsa.gov.uk/pages/library/communication/speeches/2006/0616_jt.shtml)

consider that there is anything unfair about taking enforcement action for the breach of Principles. In other words where the requirement of predictability is met, it is legitimate for consequences to follow even though the principle is expressed in general terms.

### 2.6.6 *Handbook review*

The FSA's Handbook of Rules and Guidance (the Handbook) presents the standards it expects of regulated firms and is a key vehicle for communicating those standards to the outside world. Since the FSA assumed its powers in 2001, the Handbook has become an extremely long and sometimes very detailed document, bringing together a legacy of rules and principles from the FSA's predecessor organisations. In some key areas it has been extensively reformed since 2001.

For a number of years the FSA has publicly committed itself to making itself easier to do business with and an essential element of that commitment is to convey messages in as simple and accessible a way as possible. In 2005 the FSA launched a review of the Handbook aimed at ensuring that both its substance and form reflect the FSA's vision and values. Clearly the most essential role of the review was to ensure that the Handbook remained accurate and was a proper reflection of FSA priorities, such as the greater emphasis on Principles-based regulation, that had emerged in recent years. However, another important aspect of the review was to see whether the Handbook could be made more user friendly, not least by reducing its size.

The two most important parts of the Handbook affecting the work of enforcement are the Enforcement Manual (ENF) and the Decision-making Manual (DEC), and naturally their contents came within the scope of the review. The purpose was not to make wholesale changes to the FSA's enforcement policy but rather to produce guidance that was shorter and more focused than the existing manuals and fully up to date. In January 2007 the FSA published its proposals arising from the review of ENF and DEC.

It is fair to note that in the course of the review some areas, such as settlement, the criteria for fining and the use of prohibitions, were identified as in need of adjustment or clarification. However, the majority of the proposed changes reflect a shift in the FSA's approach to the giving of guidance on its enforcement and decision-making policy and a desire to improve how such guidance is communicated.

For example, while DEC used to be framed as a general explanation of the FSA's approach to decision making, the FSA now proposes that it be confined to a statement of the procedure to be followed in relation to the giving of statutory notices. Similarly, the only parts of ENF that the FSA proposes should remain in the Handbook are the policies which are formally required by the FSMA 2000, such as the statement of policy required under Section 210 in respect of financial penalties imposed on firms.

However, the FSA proposes that, in addition to those policies, there should be a new Enforcement Guide which is accessible through a link on the enforcement home page of the FSA website. This Guide will contain detailed descriptions of how the FSA goes about the various aspects of the enforcement process. The FSA will continue to consult on important changes to the Guide, but that will not be subject to the formal consultation discipline of the Handbook itself. As a result it will be easier to keep the Guide fully up to date and ensure that it is as useful as possible to all stakeholders.

Also, when looking at both DEC and ENF, the FSA realised that there was a great deal of extraneous text which it felt needed to be stripped out. So, for instance, it is proposed that sections which do little more than repeat sections of the FSMA 2000 should go. If these changes are made, the new Enforcement Guide will be able to provide much fuller substantive descriptions of the FSA's approach to enforcement than before and still be less than half the size of ENF.

The FSA considers that these changes will produce guidance on its approach to enforcement and decision making that is more streamlined and user friendly than before and more informative.

# Chapter 3

# FSA Requests for Information – General Principles

**Margaret Chamberlain and Stephen Paget-Brown**

Partners
Travers Smith

## 3.1 Introduction

The obtaining of information is a prerequisite to enabling the Financial Services Authority ("FSA") to determine whether an investigation is appropriate or, if an investigation has already started, to bring the investigation to a fair and apposite conclusion. The FSA and its appointed investigators have wide powers to request information not only from authorised persons, but also from those who do not need, or do not have, authorisation from the FSA to carry on their business.

Persons in receipt of a request from the FSA for information should consider the request carefully before complying with it, taking into account in particular its nature (voluntary or compulsory), the scope of the request and whether compliance may affect third parties. It should not be assumed that it is always necessary (or advisable) to comply with the FSA's requests. This is not to suggest that an unhelpful approach should be adopted, but care certainly should be taken. Once information is released it cannot be retracted; if more information is given than has been requested or required, then a firm may face difficulties on other fronts as a result of not having taken enough care in assessing and complying with the request.

A request for information may be made in the course of a routine or themed supervisory visit, as a precursor to a formal investigation, or as part of an investigation into the recipient of the request or into a third party, or at the request of a foreign regulator. Indeed, the purpose of the request may not have anything to do with the FSA disciplinary procedure.

The FSA may seek information or request documents by telephone, at meetings or in writing, including by electronic communication. It may ask an individual to attend an interview to provide information orally, or it may ask to be sent copies of relevant documents and records whether these are in paper form, electronically stored or kept in any other medium upon which information is recorded (such as audio tapes).

The request may be to provide information or documents, or to attend an interview, on a voluntary basis; or the request may be made pursuant to the FSA's statutory powers to compel the production of information and documents or to conduct compulsory interviews.

This chapter focuses on how to deal with FSA requests for information in circumstances where a formal FSA investigation has not been launched and, therefore, at that time no FSA investigators have been appointed under statutory powers. Such requests for information outside a formal investigation can arise in a number of contexts, for example to aid the FSA's supervisory work or to enable the FSA to decide whether circumstances warrant a formal investigation. However, the general principles discussed in this chapter are also relevant to information requests made in the context of a formal investigation. *See* Chapters 7 and 8 which cover formal FSA investigations and the FSA's information gathering powers during such investigations. (Where appropriate, Chapters 7 and 8 refer back to some of the principles discussed in this chapter.)

The FSA Handbook's Enforcement Manual, Chapter 2 ("ENF 2") deals with information gathering and investigation powers and various provisions of that chapter are referred to below. Chapter 2 of the FSA Handbook's Supervision Manual ("SUP 2") deals with information gathering by the FSA as part of the *supervision* process. Again, this is referred to below.

## 3.2 Compulsory or voluntary?

In December 2003, the FSA announced a change to its pre-existing practice regarding the use of its powers of compulsion. The regulator stated that from that time onwards it would, as a matter of course, utilise its statutory powers of compulsion rather than rely on voluntary cooperation where an enforcement investigation has been launched. In the context of a formal enforcement investigation, therefore, the use of its powers to compel attendance at interviews and to compel the production of documents is now standard procedure. However, requests for voluntary assistance are still used where a decision to launch a formal enforcement investigation has not yet been made, which for authorised firms will include in a supervisory context. The distinction between the use by the FSA of compulsory as opposed to voluntary powers in the context of formal FSA investigations is discussed in Chapters 7 and 8 below.

## 3.3 Voluntary requests for information – authorised firms and approved persons

The FSA's power to make and enforce a voluntary request for information is derived from Principle 11 of the Principles for Business ("Principle 11") and so is specifically relevant to authorised firms. Principle 11 states that a firm must "deal with its regulators in an open and cooperative way and must disclose to the FSA appropriately anything relating to the firm of which the FSA would reasonably expect notice". (Approved persons as individuals are subject to a similar duty to cooperate with the regulator under Principle 4 of the Statements of Principle for Approved Persons.) Principle 11 applies to unregulated activities carried on by an authorised firm as well as regulated activities and takes into account the activities of other members of a group. A failure to comply with Principle 11, whilst not exposing the offender to criminal sanctions, does nevertheless expose him to potential (and potentially serious) regulatory sanctions.

The firm's obligation to comply with Principle 11 underpins everything in Section 2.3 of SUP 2 which deals with *methods* of information gathering by the FSA requiring cooperation by authorised persons.

The FSA's guidance in SUP 2.3.3 provides greater detail on the level of cooperation the FSA considers is necessary under Principle 11 to satisfy an FSA request for information or access. A firm should:

"(1) make itself readily available for meetings with representatives or appointees of the FSA as reasonably requested;

(2) give representatives or appointees of the FSA reasonable access to any records, files, tapes or computer systems, which are within the firm's possession or control, and provide any facilities which the representatives or appointees may reasonably request;

(3) produce to representatives or appointees of the FSA specified documents, files, tapes, computer data or other material in the firm's possession or control as reasonably requested;

(4) print information in the firm's possession or control which is held on computer or on microfilm or otherwise convert it into a readily legible document or any other record which the FSA may reasonably request;

(5) permit representatives or appointees of the FSA to copy documents or other material on the premises of the firm at the firm's reasonable expense and to remove copies and hold them elsewhere, or provide any copies, as reasonably requested; and

(6) answer truthfully, fully and promptly all questions which are reasonably put to it by representatives or appointees of the FSA."

Furthermore, it should be noted that SUP 2.3.5R provides that a firm must permit the FSA's representatives or appointees to have access during reasonable business hours to any of the firm's business premises. The rule provides that such access must be granted whether or not the FSA has given notice. Guidance states that the FSA "normally" expects to give reasonable notice of a visit but that, on rare occasions, the FSA may seek access to premises without notice (SUP 2.3.6G and SUP 2.3.2G).

Thus an authorised firm is expected to provide a great deal of assistance in dealing with voluntary requests and, depending on the scope of the request, this may be costly in terms of the time involved and the resources allocated to the matter. A firm should consider whether, in each case, the FSA's request for information or access to documents is reasonable (bearing in mind that the requirement to allow the FSA access to the firm's premises is not subject to the reasonableness qualification).

The fact that an FSA request for information may put a firm to a considerable degree of inconvenience does not, of itself, make the request unreasonable. However, it is possible that a request, whilst not wholly objectionable, may in some respects go beyond the scope of what is reasonable. That is, it may ask for certain information that the firm is entitled, for some reason, to withhold (*see* below) or it may ask for a significant volume of information to be provided in an unrealistically tight timeframe. It may therefore be necessary to make representations to the FSA to attempt to narrow the scope of disclosure or to allow additional time in appropriate cases.

Although authorised firms cannot refuse to allow the FSA access to their premises (*see* above), there may be circumstances in which a firm would want to try to persuade the FSA to exercise its right of access in a circumspect fashion. For instance, where the FSA announces that it wants access to business premises to look at computer systems or listen to audio tapes but the firm does not wish to alert certain members of staff to an FSA visit, the FSA might be persuaded to visit out of hours or to receive the relevant information without visiting.

Circumstances where it may be reasonable for the firm to withhold disclosure are discussed in more detail below (*see* 3.6).

## 3.4 Voluntary requests for information – unauthorised firms and individuals

Because the FSA's power to make and enforce voluntary requests for information derives from Principle 11 (*see* 3.3 above), *unauthorised* firms and individuals are under no obligation to comply with such a request. Despite this fact, such a firm or individual should give the matter some thought before refusing to comply with a voluntary request on this ground. Willingness to cooperate may be a factor that causes the FSA to be favourably disposed and resolve a matter without launching a formal investigation. For example, where the FSA suspects that a firm has been carrying on a regulated activity or activities without authorisation, prompt and open explanation may enable the FSA to see that its suspicions are unfounded. However, where, as in this example, the sanctions for any wrongdoing are potentially criminal in nature, cooperation should be weighed carefully against the risk of self-incrimination (*see* below). Care should also be taken when considering disclosure of confidential documents or information that may constitute personal data under the Data Protection Act 1998 (*see* 3.6.2 below). In some circumstances, it may be preferable for the unauthorised firm or individual to advise the FSA that, whilst it might be happy to cooperate, it is unable to do so unless compelled because otherwise it risks breaching its duties to third parties.

Where the FSA is seeking information from an individual who, at the time of the events that the regulator is interested in, was an approved person but who no longer has that status, then the individual is no longer bound by Principle 4 of the Statements of Principle for Approved Persons. As an unauthorised individual, therefore, he is under no obligation to comply with a voluntary request (*see* above). (Note that it is likely that the FSA would be able to compel the individual to provide information and documents under Financial Services and Markets Act 2000 ("FSMA 2000"), Section 165 by virtue of the fact that, at the relevant time, he was connected to the authorised firm, for example as an employee (*see* 3.5 below)).

## 3.5   Section 165 – power to require information and documents outside an investigation

Section 165 FSMA 2000 gives the FSA and investigators authorised by the FSA power to serve a written notice on an authorised person compelling it to provide specified information or information of a specified description, or to produce specified documents or documents of a particular description, within a reasonable period. The FSA has stated that the powers under Section 165 to require information and documents will often be used in support of both its supervisory function and its enforcement function.

The notice compelling someone to produce information and/or documents pursuant to Section 165 FSMA 2000 may be served not just on an authorised person, but also on any person who is "connected with an authorised person" and certain other categories of person not themselves specifically authorised (such as a recognised investment exchange). Persons who are "connected" to the authorised person include persons who are – *or who at any relevant time have been* – members of the same group, controllers of the firm and officers, managers, employees and agents. So the FSA could compel not only current employees, but also ex-employees provided they were employed at the time of the events that the FSA is interested in.

Before responding, a recipient of a request under Section 165 should ensure that he does indeed fall within one of the categories of person who, in the circumstances of the particular case, the FSA is entitled to compel.

## 3.6 Dealing with an information request – grounds for withholding disclosure

If, whether during the course of a visit or otherwise, particular information is requested, careful consideration should be given to the nature of the request (i.e. whether it is compulsory or voluntary), the scope of the request, its implications and whether there may be any specific reason or grounds for certain material to be withheld from production. It should not be assumed that the FSA is automatically entitled to everything it has requested, even where the firm is an authorised firm and therefore subject to Principle 11. Each document should be reviewed in its entirety to decide whether there are valid grounds for withholding the whole document or for redacting part of it.

For instance, the FSA will not seek or expect the *voluntary* production of information pursuant to Principle 11 if it would not be able to obtain that particular information were it exercising its *compulsory* powers under FSMA 2000 instead. Irrelevant material need not be disclosed voluntarily (although in practice relevance can be difficult to determine (*see* 3.6.1 below)). Also, as noted below, breach of confidentiality may be a basis for not disclosing voluntarily in certain circumstances. The grounds upon which one might be able to withhold requested material in response to a *compulsory* request (irrelevance, banking confidentiality and legal privilege) are also addressed below. Anyone receiving a request for information should consider whether the request is part of a voluntary or compulsory procedure and whether there are any grounds for refusing the request in part or in whole.

The disclosure of information in circumstances where there is no obligation to disclose, could, if the information relates to third parties, give rise to liabilities to such persons (*see* 3.6.2 below, which also touches on the scope of the FSA's own duty of confidentiality and the risk that despite this duty, information may still make its way into the public domain). In addition, the voluntary disclosure of information that constitutes "personal data" could (absent the data subject's consent or an available exemption) breach the Data Protection Act 1998 (*see* 3.6.2.5 below).

There are only limited circumstances in which it would be legitimate for authorised firms to withhold requested material.

### 3.6.1 Relevance

Whether a disclosure is voluntary or compulsory, material should only be provided if it is relevant to the subject matter of the request or to the matter(s) being investigated. However, this can be a difficult issue to decide. What seems irrelevant to the provider may be relevant to the investigator because of other information in his possession. Advice on the particular situation should be taken before too readily relying on this ground to avoid disclosure, particularly in response to a compulsory request. However, depending upon the circumstances it may be possible to discuss with the FSA whether all of the information it has requested is relevant and to agree a more limited request which is focused more closely on the particular information sought by the FSA.

### 3.6.2 Confidentiality

#### 3.6.2.1 Banking confidentiality
If a firm has a banker's duty of confidentiality in relation to particular information, it would seem that, on balance, the firm could justifiably choose not to disclose to the FSA in response to a *voluntary* request on the basis that the duty outweighs the Principle 11 duty to disclose. A firm that chooses not to acquiesce to a voluntary request because it has a banker's duty of confidentiality should notify the FSA that its refusal is for that reason. The FSA then has the choice of imposing a specific compulsory information requirement, such as under Section 165 FSMA 2000.

Where confidentiality issues arise in the context of *compulsory* requests, however, there is less scope to resist disclosure. This is because the concept of banking confidentiality as a ground for non-disclosure is heavily limited in the context of *compulsory* investigations under Section 175(5) FSMA 2000. This provides that no person may be required to disclose information or produce a document in respect of which he owes an obligation of confidence by virtue of carrying on the business of banking *unless*:

(a)  the recipient of the request is the person under investigation or a member of that person's group; or

(b)  where the person to whom the obligation of confidence is owed is the person under investigation or a member of that person's group; or

(c)  the person to whom the obligation of confidence is owed consents to the disclosure; or

(d)  the investigating authority has specifically authorised the imposing on him of a requirement with respect to such information.

In practice, therefore, banks may be obliged to respond to requests made on a compulsory basis notwithstanding their duty of confidentiality under the general law and find themselves having to disclose confidential information about clients. Banks that receive a compulsory document request from the FSA must consider carefully how Section 175 may apply in the particular circumstances. In particular, it is necessary to be clear about the nature of the investigation in connection with which the document request is made in order to be in a position to determine whether the bank is entitled not to disclose any particular information in response to the request. If necessary this issue should be clarified with the FSA, although in doing so care should be taken not to indicate the nature and extent of any confidential material which might be legitimately withheld pursuant to Section 175. Moreover, it may be that only part of the information requested falls within the protection afforded by this provision, in which case the parts falling within the protection should be removed, but the remainder disclosed.

### 3.6.2.2   *"Ordinary" confidentiality*

It should be noted that a duty of "ordinary" (as opposed to banking) confidentiality will *not* be sufficient to justify withholding material from the FSA, or an investigator appointed by it, where they are exercising FSMA 2000 powers to compel or require production. Since disclosure under compulsion by the FSA would be required by law, it would appear that an English court would not uphold a claim for breach of confidentiality brought against the person disclosing such material. However, in circumstances where the disclosure of confidential material to the FSA would result in an exposure to a claim brought outside the UK, then the position is not so clear and the disclosing party may be faced with an irreconcilable conflict. Furthermore, even in the English courts, a firm might face an argument that the disclosure of a particular piece of confidential information in response to a compulsory request went beyond what the FSA had specifically requested and the firm was therefore in breach of its duty. Firms should therefore try to protect themselves against such legal risks in advance through the use of a contractual consent in customer and other contracts. Such a provision would permit disclosure by the firm to regulators – firms considering such a provision need to decide if they wish to have consent to voluntary or only compulsory disclosure. Anyone considering inserting such a provision should also consider whether such a clause is effective and lawful in the relevant jurisdiction.

In the context of a *voluntary* disclosure, it is not clear whether an English court would uphold a claim for breach of ordinary confidentiality and this is an area that, at the time of writing, has not been determined in the courts. In the case of unauthorised firms and individuals making voluntary disclosures to the FSA, it seems likely (but by no means certain) that the court *would* uphold a claim for breach of ordinary confidentiality on the grounds that the firm/individual was not governed by the general principle to be open and cooperative with the regulator and consequently nothing outweighed the duty of confidentiality. In the case of authorised firms making voluntary disclosure the position is even less clear. Whilst the court might well be swayed not to uphold a claim for breach of confidentiality on the grounds of public policy (given the FSA's status as a creature of statute and the fact that Principle 11 is a rule promulgated under its statutory rule-making powers), a firm's obligation of disclosure under Principle 11 (although wide-ranging) is not limitless in that it attaches to anything *relating to the firm* of which the firm would *reasonably* expect notice. As mentioned above, each of the disclosures and obligations referred to in SUP 2.3.3 are as the FSA "may *reasonably* request". Consequently, in respect of voluntary disclosures by authorised firms, a claimant might have an argument that it is not reasonable of the FSA to expect disclosure under Principle 11 and SUP 2.3.3 in circumstances where such disclosure has the effect of placing the firm in breach of confidentiality. If this argument were to succeed, the court might well conclude that the firm should not be protected from a claim where it has made such a disclosure voluntarily.

Thus, the duty to be open and cooperative with the regulator under Principle 11 would need to be weighed on a case-by-case basis with any relevant duty of confidentiality. Faced with this dilemma and the legal uncertainty as to how the English courts would react, it may be advisable to notify the FSA that the firm would be happy to cooperate on a voluntary basis but, due to the risk of breaching its duties of confidentiality to a third party, is unable to do so unless the FSA makes its request using compulsory powers. Prudence would appear to dictate that this approach should be adopted by any firm that is in receipt of a *voluntary* request for information and which is subject to a duty of confidentiality in respect of that information, regardless of whether it is a banker's duty or an "ordinary" duty.

Whether confidential information is provided to the FSA voluntarily or not, the FSA is itself under a statutory obligation to treat that information as confidential (Section 348 FSMA 2000) unless the person from whom the information was obtained or, if different, the person to whom it relates, has consented to its disclosure. However, this obligation is diluted by a number of exceptions in subordinate legislation[1] under which the FSA is entitled to make disclosure of information. This enables the FSA to disclose information obtained by it to, for example, the police. It also enables the FSA to use the information in civil and criminal proceedings and for the purposes of disciplinary action. By those means information could ultimately come into the public domain. Although *prima facie* these confidentiality restrictions would prevent the FSA from disclosing information to another firm or individual, the information may be required to be disclosed to

---

[1] The Financial Services and Markets Act 2000 (Disclosure of Confidential Information) Regulations 2001 (SI 2001/2188), which permits the FSA to disclose confidential information for the purpose of, for example, a criminal investigation.

them for the purposes of criminal or regulatory proceedings that the FSA is bringing against that other firm or individual.

### 3.6.2.3 Legal privilege

Under Section 413 FSMA 2000 (protected items), no person may be required under FSMA 2000 to produce, disclose or permit the inspection of "protected items". This provision applies to both compulsory and voluntary requests for information. The phrase "protected items" is defined in FSMA 2000 as, broadly, covering communications between a professional legal adviser and his client or any person representing his client, which is made:

(a)   in connection with the giving of legal advice to the client; or

(b)   in connection with, or in contemplation of, legal proceedings and for the purposes of those proceedings.

Essentially, this definition was intended to cover the two limbs of legal privilege – "legal advice" privilege on the one hand and "litigation" privilege on the other, although there is not an identity of coverage.

Where the FSA has made a request for information to be provided either voluntarily or under Section 165, legal advice privilege will usually be the relevant head of privilege to consider. It is necessary to examine carefully documents which are, in terms of their relevance, susceptible to the request, in order to determine whether it can properly be said that they are "made", "in connection with the giving of legal advice". The scope of legal advice privilege was the subject of a decision of the House of Lords in the *Three Rivers District Council* case.[2] This confirmed that "legal advice is not confined to telling the client the law; it must include advice as to what should prudently and sensibly be done in the relevant legal context". On that basis the Lords held that advice given by lawyers to the Bank of England about how to present evidence to the Bingham enquiry was covered by legal advice privilege. This was a non-adversarial enquiry and as such it was accepted that litigation privilege did not apply.

---

[2] *Three Rivers District Council and others* v *Governor and Company of the Bank of England (No. 10)* [2004] UKHL 48.

There is authority in the cases of *Gotha City* v *Sotheby's (No. 1)*[3] and *USP Strategies plc and another* v *London General Holdings Limited and others*[4] for the argument that privilege in solicitors' reports or other privileged documents that are voluntarily disclosed to the FSA is *not* automatically waived as against third parties – so that such third parties would not be able to obtain discovery of the documents disclosed to the FSA as part of litigation against the regulated firm.

The decisions in *Gotha* and *USP Strategies* were based on the underlying *confidentiality* of the communication as between the owner of the privilege and the third party. In *Kaufmann & Ors* v *Credit Lyonnais Bank*,[5] Arden J made some comments that may be of concern in this regard (although it should be noted that the case did not relate to legal professional privilege but concerned the question of whether there was public interest immunity in reports and documents prepared by Credit Lyonnais' solicitors and auditors which were then forwarded to the Securities and Futures Authority ("SFA")). Arden J noted that there was no suggestion in the evidence to suggest that Credit Lyonnais had sought an assurance of confidentiality from the SFA in respect of the information disclosed and indeed the SFA could not have provided such assurance, as it may have been required to disclose the information to the Securities and Investments Board which, in itself, may have made further disclosures. Therefore, the documents in question were not provided on the understanding that they would be entirely confidential to the SFA.

Based on the comments of Arden J in *Kaufmann*, a third party might seek to run the argument that documents provided to the FSA should be disclosed on the basis that they were not provided to the FSA "on the understanding that they would be entirely confidential" and therefore privilege was waived. Although Section 348 FSMA 2000 provides that the FSA may not disclose confidential information provided to it without the provider's consent, Section 349 provides various exceptions to this rule.

---

[3] [1998] 1 WLR. 114.
[4] [2004] EWHC 373 (Ch).
[5] [1995] CLC 300.

A Privy Council case, *B and others* v *Auckland District Law Society and others*[6] (the *Russell McVeagh* case) addresses the question of whether privilege is lost or waived if limited disclosure is made. The case concerned the disclosure by a New Zealand law firm, Russell McVeagh McKenzie Bartleet & Co., of certain documents to the Auckland District Law Society. The documents were subject to privilege but Russell McVeagh agreed to disclose them to counsel appointed by the law society, *subject to their use being restricted and privilege not being waived*. The law society subsequently appointed a new counsel, but he was not informed of the arrangements relating to the privileged documents and some of them were disclosed to the law society itself. Russell McVeagh sought the return of the documents.

The Privy Council held that legal professional privilege was not waived generally because a privileged document was disclosed for a limited purpose only: the documents were both confidential and privileged and, except in respect of the agreed and limited use of the documents, privilege had been expressly reserved in this case.

With all of the above in mind, great caution should be exercised in the face of any request from the FSA to hand over documents that might be protected by privilege, whether on a voluntary basis or a compulsory basis. If documents are subject to privilege the starting point should be to refuse disclosure to the FSA – *see* Section 413 FSMA 2000 and the *Three Rivers District Council* case. Furthermore, despite the authority in *Gotha* and *USP Strategies*, the prudent course would be not to disclose privileged documents voluntarily. The *Russell McVeagh* case may suggest that it should be possible, in theory at least, to agree with the FSA that disclosure will be made on a limited basis only and that the documentation will remain confidential and privileged as against third parties – but again, the starting point should be not to disclose.

### 3.6.2.4   *Privilege against self-incrimination*
In brief, the general principle is that a person is entitled to assert that he should not be required to answer a question if to do so would tend to incriminate him. In the context of civil proceedings this privilege is

---

[6] [2003] UKPC 38.

limited to self-incrimination in respect of criminal offences and penalties under the laws of the UK (which has been held to include penalties under European legislation which forms part of the laws of the UK). The privilege would apply in the context of compulsory interviews but not in the context of voluntary interviews (*see* 3.6.3 below).

### 3.6.2.5 *The Data Protection Act 1998*

Any request for information which involves disclosing information about individuals ("personal data") has to be considered in the light of the Data Protection Act 1998 ("DPA 1998"). Not all information about individuals is "personal data" – generally speaking, personal data can be seen as "information affecting a person's privacy whether in his personal or family life, business or professional capacity", but must be more than simply recording a person's involvement with the issue in question. If the DPA 1998 applies, then, unless certain exemptions referred to below are fulfilled, the firm will have to obtain the consent of the individual concerned ("data subject") before passing the information to the FSA. The nature of the consent is also defined in the DPA 1998. Particular caution is needed if the data is "sensitive personal data" for purposes of the DPA 1998 (e.g. as to state of health, or as to the alleged commission of any offence).

It will frequently be necessary to inform the data subject of the disclosure in any event, under the DPA 1998.

Where actual consent has not been obtained the question of whether disclosure can be made to the FSA should be considered in each case against the specific exemptions. In broad terms it may be possible to disclose under the DPA 1998 without consent where:

(a) such disclosure is necessary for compliance with any legal obligation to which the holder is subject, for example where the FSA's request for information is made under powers conferred by legislation. (Where the FSA request is mandatory and addressed to a regulated firm it will therefore generally not be possible to use the DPA 1998 as a barrier to disclosure); or
(b) such disclosure is necessary for the exercise of any functions conferred on any person by or under any enactment.

Other exemptions may be available under the terms of the DPA 1998, depending on circumstances.

Of course not all requests for information made by the FSA are mandatory. Where the firm in question is not regulated, the FSA has no statutory powers to make that request and as a consequence there is no legal obligation on the part of the firm to provide the requested information. In this instance, the consent of any relevant data subject will be needed before the data could be supplied, unless the firm is keen to cooperate and the circumstances fit any other exemption under the DPA 1998.

Where the FSA makes a voluntary request to a regulated firm it is unclear as to whether the firm can make disclosure of personal data without breaching the DPA 1998. As referred to above, a regulated firm has a duty to be open and cooperative with the FSA under Principle 11 – which has the status and force of a rule, promulgated under the FSA's statutory rule-making powers. It may therefore be possible to argue that the firm's disclosure of personal data in response to a voluntary request should be exempt from the DPA 1998 on the grounds that such disclosure is necessary in order for the firm to comply with its "legal obligation" under Principle 11. However, since it is far from clear as to whether the "compliance with law" exemption would be available in these circumstances, the prudent approach would be for the firm to notify the FSA that it would be happy to cooperate with the voluntary request but, due to concerns over breaching the DPA 1998, is unable to do so unless the FSA makes its request using its compulsory powers.

The FSA itself is subject to the DPA 1998 and can only use the information obtained in a limited way.

### 3.6.3   Voluntary interviews

As mentioned above, voluntary interviews (not under caution) are relatively uncommon these days. Nevertheless, they do happen and the FSA has made it clear that if a person chooses not to attend a voluntary interview, or attends but refuses to answer any questions at such an interview, then this will not expose that person to any kind of penalty or to an allegation of breach of Principle 11 of the Principles for Business or Statement of Principle 4 for Approved Persons. Despite this, it is obvious that a refusal to attend a voluntary interview will be regarded by the FSA as significant. As the participant in a voluntary interview is not protected by privilege against self-incrimination, a refusal to attend may suggest to the FSA that the individual is concerned about self-incrimination. This may therefore move the FSA either to compel attendance or to redouble its efforts to find relevant evidence elsewhere. Very careful thought is needed before deciding not to attend a voluntary interview and in deciding how to communicate the refusal. Furthermore, if a person chooses to provide answers to questions at a voluntary interview, then this may mean that he is given credit for cooperation should he ultimately become the subject of an adverse finding.

As interviews are more likely to be conducted where a formal investigation is underway, further detail on the conduct of interviews, whether voluntary under caution or pursuant to compulsory powers, is given in Chapters 7 and 8 below on formal FSA investigations.

# Chapter 4

# Notifying the FSA of Regulatory Problems and Conducting Internal Investigations

**James Bagge and Charles Evans**

Partners
Norton Rose

## 4.1   Introduction

Whenever a regulatory problem arises, a firm needs to ensure that it responds by taking appropriate, effective and timely action. This action should be calculated to identify the problem and its possible implications in order to minimise its regulatory impact and to maintain good relations with the regulator.

This chapter examines the practical steps that a firm should take once a regulatory problem has arisen, when the FSA should be notified and how to conduct an effective internal investigation.

### 4.1.1   What is a regulatory problem?

Broadly, regulatory problems are matters which impact on the financial stability and integrity of the markets (wholesale and retail) and which concern the Financial Services Authority ("FSA") in fulfilling its statutory objectives, such as the promotion of market confidence, protection of consumers and reduction of financial crime. The kinds of regulatory problems that may need to be notified to the FSA cover a wide range of issues, including market misconduct, issues going to the fitness and propriety of approved persons, and systems and controls failures.

### 4.1.2 How regulatory problems emerge

Regulatory problems usually emerge as a result of:

(a) "tip-offs", such as a customer's complaint, whistleblowing by an employee, anonymous letters or market rumour;
(b) internal audit or compliance checks;
(c) inquiries carried out as part of the firm's audit;
(d) a supervision visit by the FSA or other domestic or overseas regulator;
(e) an investigation carried out by the FSA or other domestic or overseas regulator; or
(f) findings relayed by another regulator to the FSA.

Self-evidently, if the FSA has discovered a problem as a result of a supervision visit, it will already be aware of the problem and the surrounding circumstances. From the firm's perspective, it is preferable for a problem to be identified internally, in good time, through the operation of its own systems and controls, rather than being brought to its attention by an external source.

A failure to detect a problem may, of itself, constitute a breach of the requirement to establish and maintain appropriate systems and controls in some circumstances.[1] Furthermore, a firm will lose the opportunity to take forthright action to deal with the problem and thereby potentially remove the need for an investigation by the FSA and mitigate any associated legal action, such as claims by market counterparties or investors.

### 4.1.3 First steps on discovery of the problem

#### 4.1.3.1 Carrying out a preliminary assessment
Upon the discovery of a regulatory problem, a firm needs to establish what has happened and who was involved. This information needs to be acquired quickly so that the firm can determine whether a notifiable event has occurred, assess whether there is an ongoing breach that immediately needs to be addressed and take appropriate action

---

[1] *See* SYSC 3.1.1R and Principles for Businesses 2 and 3.

to prevent any further damage being caused to the firm and its customers (such as the removal or suspension of relevant individuals from sensitive positions and restricting their access to documents).

Despite the preliminary nature of this assessment, a firm should ensure that:[2]

(a)   all relevant records and documents are secured from the outset;

(b)   the individuals carrying out the assessment are not implicated in the regulatory problem (whether by being involved in the events in question or because of a potential management failure on their part); and

(c)   the assessment is kept confidential.

### 4.1.3.2   *Notifying the FSA*

Once the preliminary assessment is complete, the firm should consider whether:

(a)   a formal notification to the FSA is required (*see* below); or

(b)   an informal notification should be made to the firm's usual supervisory contact, pending discovery of further facts, and the contact informed that a formal notification will follow (again, if required).

Firms are required formally to notify the FSA if there are circumstances which suggest that certain prescribed events may have happened, so that the FSA can carry out its responsibilities under the Financial Services and Markets Act 2000 ("FSMA 2000") to monitor the firm's compliance with its regulatory obligations.[3] The notification requirements, set out in Principle 11[4] of the FSA's Principles for Businesses and Chapter 15 of the Supervision Manual, are examined in detail in 4.2 below. An auditor appointed under or as a result of a statutory provision also has a duty to communicate matters to the FSA.[5]

---

[2] *See* further 4.3.

[3] SUP 15.2.1G.

[4] A firm must deal with its regulators in an open and cooperative way, and must disclose to the FSA appropriately anything relating to the firm of which the FSA would reasonably expect notice.

[5] *See* Section 342 FSMA 2000 and the Financial Services and Markets Act 2000 (Communications by Auditors) Regulations 2001.

A failure to notify, or a significant delay in making a notification, may constitute a regulatory breach. In addition, in determining whether to take disciplinary action, the FSA will take into account how quickly the firm, or approved person, brought the matter to its attention.[6] Whilst a firm is entitled to make appropriate enquiries to establish whether a notification should be made, it is not permitted to delay making a notification until it has established all of the relevant facts.

## 4.2 Notification of regulatory problems[7]

A distinction must be drawn between specific and general notification requirements. The specific notification requirements are governed by rules and guidance in Chapter 15 of the Supervision Manual, whilst the general notification requirement arises under Principle 11.

### 4.2.1 Specific notification requirements

#### 4.2.1.1 Breaches of rules and other requirements in or under the Act, including a Principle or a Statement of Principle for Approved Persons[8]

A firm must notify the FSA immediately it becomes aware, or has information which reasonably suggests, that a significant breach has occurred, may have occurred or may occur in the foreseeable future by the firm or any of its directors, officers, employees, approved persons or appointed representatives in relation to:

(a) an FSA rule, Principle or Statement of Principle for Approved Persons;
(b) any requirement imposed by the FSMA 2000 or by regulations or an order made under FSMA 2000 by the Treasury; or
(c) the bringing of a prosecution for, or a conviction of, any offence under FSMA 2000.

---

[6] *See* ENF 11.4.1(2)(a)G.
[7] *See* Figure 4.1 for a quick-reference flowchart of the considerations and steps relevant to a particular regulatory breach.
[8] *See* SUP 15.3.11R.

In recognition of the privilege against self-incrimination, SUP 15.3.11 only requires a firm to notify the FSA of the fact that a prosecution has been brought, or a conviction secured, against the firm; it does not require a firm to notify the FSA of the fact that the firm has or may have committed a criminal offence.[9] From a practical perspective, however, a firm is still required to notify the FSA immediately of circumstances which call into question the fitness and propriety of Approved Persons. On this basis, the protection against self-incrimination may be illusory.

### 4.2.1.2   *Civil, criminal or disciplinary proceedings against a firm*[10]

A firm must notify the FSA immediately if any civil proceedings are brought against it and the amount of the claim is significant in relation to the firm's financial resources or its reputation. A firm must also notify the FSA of actions for damages under Sections 71 and 150 FSMA 2000[11] regardless of the size of the claim, or where a disciplinary measure or sanction is imposed on the firm by a statutory or regulatory body other than the FSA or a professional organisation or trade body.

As above, a firm is not required to notify the FSA of the fact that it has committed or may have committed an offence involving fraud or dishonesty. The notification requirement is triggered only where the firm is prosecuted for, or convicted of, such offence, or if any penalties are imposed on it for tax evasion.[12] In practice however, a firm is likely to have to notify the FSA immediately of fraudulent or dishonest behaviour on the part of one or more of its employees[13] as well as for possible related systems and controls failures.[14]

---

[9] This is also in line with Principle 11, which requires a firm to disclose to the FSA anything relating to the firm *of which the FSA would reasonably expect notice*, as it is unlikely that the FSA would reasonably expect a firm to provide self-incriminating information. But *see* 4.2.1.3.

[10] *See* SUP 15.3.15R.

[11] Section 71 FSMA 2000 provides that an action may be brought by a person, whether private or otherwise, who suffers loss as a result of a contravention of Section 56(6) or Section 59(1), (2) FSMA 2000, subject to the defences and other incidents applying to actions for breach of statutory duty. To avoid liability, an authorised person must take reasonable care to ensure that no regulated function of his is performed by a person who is prohibited from performing that function and that no controlled function of his is performed by another person unless the FSA gives its approval. Similarly, liability under Section 150 may arise where an authorised person contravenes any rule made by the FSA under FSMA 2000.

[12] SUP 15.3.15(4)R.

[13] SUP 15.3.17R.

[14] SYSC 3.2.6R and SUP 15.3.11R.

### 4.2.1.3   Fraud, errors and other irregularities[15]
A firm must notify the FSA immediately if:

(a)   it becomes aware that a fraud has been committed against one of its customers by one of its employees, or against the firm by any person; or

(b)   it considers that anyone is acting with intent to commit a fraud against it; or

(c)   it identifies irregularities in its accounting or other records, whether or not there is evidence of fraud; or

(d)   it suspects that one of its employees may be guilty of serious misconduct, concerning his honesty or integrity; and

the event in question is significant.

In determining whether a matter or event is significant, a firm will have to consider the size of any monetary loss or potential monetary loss to itself or its customers as well as the risk of reputational loss to the firm and whether the incident or pattern of incidents reflects weaknesses in the firm's internal controls.[16]

The FSA states that it needs to be aware of the types of fraudulent and irregular activity which are being attempted, as well as undertaken, and to act, if necessary, to prevent effects on consumers and other firms.[17] The FSA's stance on matters involving fraud is understandable given its statutory objectives. However, the strict approach also means that a firm is required to whistleblow on its employees in the circumstances, *inter alia*, where an employee *may* have committed serious misconduct.[18] The firm may thereby potentially incriminate itself in the process if the employee's conduct can, as a matter of law, be attributed to the firm for the purposes of a criminal prosecution.

### 4.2.1.4   Insolvency, bankruptcy and winding up[19]
A firm must notify the FSA immediately of any of the events in SUP 15.3.21R, including winding up, a composition or arrangement with

---

[15] *See* SUP 15.3.17R.
[16] *See* SUP 15.3.18G.
[17] SUP 15.3.19G.
[18] *See* SUP 15.3.17(5)R.
[19] *See* SUP 15.3.21R.

the firm's creditors, the appointment of a receiver, the appointment of an administrator or a trustee in bankruptcy, or an application to dissolve the firm or strike it off the Register of Companies.

### 4.2.1.5 *Matters having a serious regulatory impact*[20]

A firm must notify the FSA immediately it becomes aware, or has information which reasonably suggests, that any of the following has occurred, may have occurred or may occur in the foreseeable future:

(a) a failure to satisfy one or more of the threshold conditions;[21]
(b) any matter which could have a significant adverse impact on the firm's reputation;
(c) any matter which could affect the firm's ability to continue to provide adequate services to its customers and which could result in "serious detriment" to a customer of the firm;[22] or
(d) any matter in respect of the firm which could result in serious financial consequences to the financial system or other firms.

This notification requirement captures a wide range of matters. The key theme is that the matter in question must have a serious regulatory impact. Furthermore, a firm must notify the FSA if it receives information which reasonably suggests that a notifiable event may occur in the foreseeable future. It may be difficult enough to gauge whether an event has had serious regulatory impact, let alone assess whether an event which may occur in the foreseeable future could have such an impact. The firm will need to consider properly all potential consequences, the likelihood of the event occurring and the severity of the outcome should it occur.[23] In practical terms, consideration should also be given to the potentially wide-ranging impact on the firm's reputation which may include loss of market share and decreased customer satisfaction.

### 4.2.1.6 *Suspicious transactions (market abuse)*

A firm which arranges or executes a transaction in a qualifying investment admitted to trading on one of the prescribed markets and

---

[20] *See* SUP 15.3.1R.
[21] *See* COND.
[22] "Serious detriment" to a customer is not defined in the FSA Handbook. The expression is left deliberately vague but would potentially include customers who have lost the whole or a substantially large proportion of their investment.
[23] SUP 15.3.2G.

which reasonably suspects that a transaction might constitute market abuse must notify the FSA without delay.[24]

An investment firm or credit institution must assess on a case-by-case basis whether there are reasonable grounds for suspecting that a transaction involves market abuse, and if it becomes aware of a fact or information that gives reasonable grounds for suspicion concerning a transaction it must notify the FSA without delay.[25]

An investment firm or a credit institution which notifies the FSA of a suspicious transaction (market abuse) must not inform any other person, in particular the persons on behalf of whom the relevant transaction has been carried out or parties related to those persons, of the FSA notification, except in accordance with an obligation imposed by or under statute.[26]

### 4.2.2  General notification requirements under Principle 11

Notification pursuant to Principle 11 is an even more broadly defined duty. It requires that the FSA be notified of any matter of which it would reasonably expect notice. This includes, but is not limited to:

(a)   any proposed restructuring, reorganisation or business expansion, which can have a significant impact on the firm's risk profile or resources;

(b)   any significant failure in the firm's systems or controls, including those reported to the firm by the firm's auditors; or

(c)   any action which the firm proposes to take which would result in a material change in its capital adequacy or solvency.

This catch-all duty to notify should always be borne in mind when considering whether to notify the FSA of a particular problem. Even if a notification is not required under any of the specific rules in SUP 15, examined in 4.2.1 above, it may be required under Principle 11.

---

[24]  SUP 15.10.2R.
[25]  SUP 15.10.3R and SUP 15.10.5R.
[26]  SUP 15.10.9R. A notification made under SUP 15.10 will not constitute a breach of any restriction on disclosure of information imposed by the FSA Handbook of Rules and Guidance (SUP 15.10.9(2)R).

More often than not, a regulatory problem arises as a result of a fail-ure in a firm's systems and controls. If the failure is significant, it will constitute a notifiable event under Principle 11. It should also be remembered that the list of matters above is non-exhaustive. The test is that the FSA should be notified of any matter of which it would reasonably expect notice.

### 4.2.3  Form and method of notification

#### 4.2.3.1  Contents of written notification

Firms must ensure that matters are properly and clearly communi-cated to the FSA and that the information provided in relation to them is accurate and complete.[27] In particular, notification of breaches of rules and other requirements under the Act should include:

(a)  information about relevant circumstances;
(b)  identification of the rule, requirement or offence; and
(c)  information about steps which a firm or other person has taken or intends to take to rectify or remedy the breach or prevent any future potential occurrence.[28]

Notification of civil, criminal or disciplinary proceedings against a firm should include details of the matter and an estimate of the likely financial consequences, if any.[29] Notification of fraud, errors and other irregularities should provide all relevant and significant details of the incident, or suspected incident, of which the firm is aware.[30]

Notification of a suspicion that a transaction might constitute market abuse must contain a description of the transaction, including the type of order (such as limit order, market order or other characteristic of the order) and the type of trading market (such as block trade) and the reasons for suspicion. In addition, the FSA must, as soon as possi-ble, also be provided with:

---

[27] SUP 15.3.10G.
[28] *See* SUP 15.3.14G.
[29] SUP 15.3.16G.
[30] SUP 15.3.19G.

(a) the means to identify the persons on behalf of whom the transaction has been carried out, and other persons involved in the
transaction;

(b) the capacity in which the firm operates; and

(c) any other significant information.[31]

Notification of a suspicion that a transaction might constitute market
abuse may be made to the Market Conduct Team at the FSA.[32]

### 4.2.3.2 Written or oral

Notifications must be in writing[33] unless, having regard to the
urgency and significance of a matter, it is more appropriate to notify
the firm's usual supervisory contact at the FSA by telephone or by
other prompt means of communication before submitting a written
notification.[34] This would be warranted where, for example, the
matter appears to be serious but little is known at the time, making it
impossible to submit a written notification.[35]

The value of developing a good relationship with the firm's supervisory contact – with whom a firm could discuss issues at an early stage
without a risk of overreaction on the part of the FSA – should not be
underestimated. In practice, it is of vital importance to be able to
present a remedial plan and proposal for conducting an investigation
either internally or with the assistance of external advisers. If the FSA
can be persuaded that the firm is dealing with the problem effectively
and responding appropriately, the prospect of the FSA launching its
own investigation is substantially decreased.

Very careful consideration needs to be given to the creation of new
documents which may be disclosable in any litigation. There is a
constant tension between providing the FSA with adequate information on the one hand and not creating documents which may be
damaging to the firm on the other.

---

[31] SUP 15.10.6R
[32] SUP 15.10.7R
[33] *See* SUP 15.7.1R, which provides that the notification must be in writing, in English and must give the firm's FSA Firm Reference Number.
[34] SUP 15.7.2G.
[35] In such circumstances the FSA may request a written confirmation of the matter, *see* SUP 15.3.9G.

### 4.2.3.3   Oral notification requirements

An oral notification left with another person or left on a voicemail or other automatic messaging service is unlikely to have been given appropriately.[36] A record should be kept of any information provided orally to the FSA in case a dispute should arise at a later stage about what information was or was not provided. Notification by email should be sufficient if a firm then follows it up with a telephone call directly to the supervisory contact to confirm that the email has been received.

## 4.2.4   When to notify

The decision to make a notification requires judgement on the part of the firm as to the seriousness of the matter, having regard to all the circumstances, and whether it has sufficient facts to hand to make a notification as required.

The following factors may indicate that the breach is serious:

(a)   potential serious financial consequences to the firm and its customers;[37]

(b)   frequency of the breach and implications to the firm's systems and controls;[38]

(c)   delays in identifying or rectifying the breach;[39]

(d)   any fraud, dishonesty, commission of serious misconduct;[40] or

(e)   risk of significant reputational loss to the firm.[41]

However little is known of the detailed facts at the time, if the matter is serious, for example if fraud is suspected, the sooner the FSA is notified, the better. Obviously, the firm's suspicions must be well founded. If, for example, a firm receives an anonymous letter claiming that one of its employees is guilty of fraud, it is likely that the firm would want to notify the FSA only once it has satisfied itself that the allegations have reasonable foundation. If insufficient information is

---

[36] SUP 15.7.2G.
[37] *See* SUP 15.3.1(3)(4)R, SUP 15.3.12G, SUP 15.3.18(1)G and SUP 15.3.20G.
[38] *See* SUP 15.3.8(2)G, SUP 15.3.12G, SUP 15.3.18(3)G and SUP 15.3.20G.
[39] *See* SUP 15.3.12G.
[40] SUP 15.3.17R.
[41] *See* SUP 15.3.1(1)R, 15.3.18(2)G.

available to notify the FSA fully in writing, it is likely to be appropriate to make an oral notification rather than wait until the end of the investigation to present the FSA with the full report on a matter which it has not heard of before.

Care should be taken in drafting any written notification to ensure that the notification accurately reflects the information available to the firm at the time. In particular, if there is doubt as to whether a regulatory problem has occurred at all, the notification should make this clear and should explain that information is being gathered to establish the true position. Firms must also take care when referring to third parties or other individuals in any written notification so as to reduce the risk of liability to these parties or individuals if it subsequently emerges that they were not, in fact, engaged in any wrongdoing.

The appropriate response to each event will depend on the circumstances of each case. The decision-making process must be logical, flexible and well reasoned. A firm should bear in mind the possibility that, in determining whether it has failed to comply with its notification obligations, it may be judged with the benefit of hindsight. With this in mind, firms may consider it appropriate to document the reasons behind a decision *not* to notify the FSA of a particular incident or group of incidents. These reasons may include a need to guard against potential third-party claims where allegations are yet to be substantiated. A record of the firm's consideration of the relevant factors would therefore be available and might constitute grounds for mitigation should the matter subsequently be the subject of an FSA investigation. On the other hand, firms should be mindful of the fact that the documents produced may be disclosable in subsequent litigation. Furthermore, the FSA may take action against the firm for failing to notify within a reasonable period in breach of SUP 15. Firms must therefore consider all of the implications of the problem that has arisen and, if in doubt, notify.

### 4.2.5 *Who should notify*

While strictly speaking any member of the firm is entitled to make a notification, firms should establish and encourage the use of a reporting protocol to ensure there is a sensibly coordinated, consistent reporting process. A firm should consider nominating appropriate employees and ensure that only they make notifications to the FSA on its behalf.

An employee may "blow the whistle" under the Public Interest Disclosure Act 1998 ("PIDA 1998") in a variety of circumstances, including where there has been the commission of a criminal offence or a failure to comply with any legal obligations. Whilst the issue may or may not constitute a notifiable event under Chapter 15, under Section 2 PIDA 1998 the employee will enjoy statutory protection as regards the disclosure made. The protection gives the employee the right not to be subjected to any detriment by any act, or any deliberate failure to act, by his employer as a reaction to the disclosure made.

The FSA also has a separate policy on the treatment of whistleblowers.[42] Firms are encouraged to consider adopting appropriate internal procedures which will encourage employees with concerns to report matters internally which are relevant to the functions of the FSA. Firms should also consider informing employees that they can report matters to the FSA. The FSA would regard as a serious matter any evidence that a firm had acted to the detriment of an employee because he had made a protected disclosure about matters which are relevant to the functions of the FSA.[43] Such evidence could call into question the fitness and propriety of the firm or relevant members of its staff and could also affect the firm's continuing satisfaction of the threshold conditions[44] or an individual's status as an approved person.

It is also worth adding that an auditor (to whom Sections 342 or 343 FSMA 2000 apply[45]) is under a duty to report certain matters to the FSA.[46] Sections 342(3) and 343(3) FSMA 2000 provide that an auditor does not contravene any duty by giving information or expressing an

---

[42] *See* SYSC 18: Guidance on Public Interest Disclosure Act: Whistleblowing.
[43] *See* SYSC 18.2.3G.
[44] In particular, Threshold Condition 5: Suitability.
[45] An auditor of a firm appointed under or as a result of a statutory provision, or an auditor of a person who has close links with the firm.
[46] These include a significant contravention of any relevant requirement that applies to the firm and which may be of material significance to the FSA in determining whether to exercise its functions in relation to that firm. *See* Financial Services and Markets Act 2000 (Communications by Auditors) Regulations 2001.

opinion to the FSA if he is acting in good faith and he reasonably believes that the information or opinion is relevant to any functions of the FSA. It is also worth noting in this regard that Section 346 FSMA 2000 makes it a specific criminal offence to provide false or misleading information to a statutory auditor.

# 4.3   Internal investigations

After a preliminary assessment has been made of a regulatory problem, a firm should set up an investigation team as soon as possible. An initial meeting should be held to discuss practical questions, such as organisation and process of the investigation.

### 4.3.1   The purposes of an investigation

Carrying out an internal investigation is vital to secure the following aims:

(a)   to identify, preserve and assess the relevant evidence;

(b)   to establish the facts, to address any failure in internal systems and controls, to ensure failings and concerns do not continue and to prevent the problems arising in the future;

(c)   to limit the need for a subsequent FSA investigation[47] and to mitigate any penalty;[48]

(d)   to ascertain whether any employees have engaged in wrongdoing and enable the firm to invoke its disciplinary processes, if appropriate;

(e)   to mitigate potential legal exposure in subsequent criminal and/or civil proceedings;

(f)   to enable management and the board of directors properly to discharge their responsibilities under the approved persons regime; and

(g)   to enable the firm to be able to confirm that it is dealing with the matter proactively, should it become public.

---

[47] *See* ENF 11.4.1(2)G.
[48] *See* ENF 13.3.3(5)G.

Ignoring allegations of wrongdoing will not improve the situation and may lead to very serious consequences if the regulator becomes involved and discovers that the firm was aware of the problem but did nothing about it. Equally, an ineffectual investigation, which results in only part of the problem being identified and disclosed to the FSA can exacerbate a problem should the FSA later become aware that the information which has been reported to it was incomplete.

### 4.3.2   Investigation team

The composition of any investigation team is important. First, it must be independent and uninvolved with the matters which are under investigation. In effect, this means that any person in a management position who may be implicated must not be part of the investigation team. Second, the team must have access to the right resources including legal, accounting and IT, as well as relevant expertise in the affected business or product area. Third, a decision must be taken at an early stage as to whether it is appropriate or necessary for the work product of the team to be covered by legal professional privilege.

### 4.3.3   Evidence

#### 4.3.3.1   *Gathering and preserving evidence*
From the beginning of the investigation, steps must be taken as soon as possible to preserve all relevant evidence. The discovery of the destruction of evidence, a failure to adhere to the full record retention period or any unexplained gaps in documentation will often give rise to considerable problems.

Not only is the destruction of documents in certain circumstances a criminal office,[49] in any subsequent legal proceedings, a court or a tribunal could draw negative inferences from the gaps in documentation. A firm may therefore want to consider imposing an absolute ban on the destruction of potentially relevant documents during the investigation.

---

[49] *See* Section 177 FSMA 2000, which states that it is a criminal offence for an individual to, *inter alia*, destroy a document when he knows or suspects that an investigation is being or is likely to be conducted.

#### 4.3.3.2 *Electronic documents*

Electronic documents and particularly emails can greatly increase the practical difficulties involved in gathering and preserving relevant information, mainly because of their huge volume.

Generally, more emails are sent than letters, memoranda and other paper documents. Moreover, it is virtually impossible to delete emails or other electronic documents. A firm must ensure that its IT systems are capable of searching for, and storing safely, all relevant electronic documents. It may be necessary to appoint a forensic computer expert to take responsibility for locating and preserving any computer records so that the evidence which is obtained is admissible in any subsequent proceedings.

Another issue to consider is the preservation of metadata if it could be relevant to the investigation. Metadata is information contained within the electronic version of a document that may not be apparent in a printout of the same document (such as the date the document was created, the identity of the author and the history of editorial changes). The metadata can be preserved by imaging the hard drive of a PC or other device, or converting all of the files into a special format, such as TIF or PDF. This would allow the document to be searched without the metadata or any other part of the document being altered. Again, it may be necessary to appoint a forensic computer expert to undertake this exercise.

#### 4.3.3.3 *Paper documents*

Paper documents can be requested from specified individuals, or sometimes it will be necessary to carry out an unannounced inspection to examine the documents in their location and remove all the relevant ones, especially where the individuals in question are unlikely to cooperate.[50]

#### 4.3.3.4 *Other types of evidence*

Recordings of telephone conversations and telephone logs (including mobile telephone logs) can be of important evidential value and must be preserved. Other types of evidence which can be relevant include

---

[50] However, *see* 4.3.6.

diaries, expense forms, PowerPoint presentations, Bloomberg messages and internal "chat" systems. Security system logs can also, if available, show who had access to specific areas and when.

### 4.3.3.5   Document handling and storage

All of the information that is collected must be stored safely to ensure that it is not tampered with. It is important to preserve not only the original documents but also the order of the documents and to keep a record of where, when and from whom, the evidence was obtained.

It may be appropriate to take photocopies of all the paper documents and snapshots of the electronic documents that have been collected, to ensure that no documents are altered.

All the documents collected should be reviewed and analysed. On the basis of these findings, the investigators should be in a position to establish their next course of action.

### 4.3.4   Retaining privilege

Legal professional privilege has been described by the House of Lords as a "fundamental human right" and consists of two limbs: litigation privilege and legal advice privilege. Litigation privilege attaches to confidential communications between a lawyer and his client or a lawyer and a third party which come into existence with the sole or dominant purpose of being used in aid of pending or contemplated litigation. The rationale is to allow a litigant to prepare for litigation without the danger of any documents produced for that purpose, and any documents which give an insight into the advice given by the lawyer or the way in which the client's case is being conducted, from being disclosable to the other party. Legal advice privilege protects from production confidential communications between a client and his lawyer which are created for the purpose of seeking or giving legal advice. Unlike litigation privilege, legal advice privilege does not protect communications between the client or his lawyer and a third party, such as a witness or an expert.

Under Section 413 FSMA 2000, a person may not be required to produce, disclose or permit the inspection of a "protected item". The definition of a protected item is slightly broader than legal professional privilege under the common law. The following communications are protected when made in connection with the giving of legal advice to the client or in connection with, or in contemplation of, legal proceedings and for the purposes of those proceedings:

(a)    communications between a professional legal adviser and his client or any person representing his client;
(b)    communications between a professional legal adviser, his client or any person representing his client and any other person; and
(c)    items which are enclosed with, or referred to in, such communications and are in the possession of a person entitled to possession of them.

The investigation team needs to distinguish between those documents which existed prior to the start of the investigation and those which have been created as part of the investigation.

As far as the first category is concerned, the privileged documents need to be identified and marked as such. Care must be taken not to waive privilege inadvertently by disclosing these documents to third parties or to the FSA. It may be that a decision is taken to waive privilege over those documents in order to assist the FSA with its investigation. If this is done, careful consideration should be given to such disclosure being restricted expressly for those purposes thereby enhancing the chances of retaining privilege in those documents for other purposes.[51] However, the FSA may be reluctant to accept documents on this basis as it may fetter the use of such documents.

As far as the second category is concerned, considerable care and thought should be given to the generation of new (potentially unhelpful) material. Where litigation is not ensuing, or is not in reasonable contemplation, documents will only attract privilege if they represent legal advice or are created for the purpose of, or in

---

[51] *See British Coal Corporation v Dennis Rye Ltd* [1998] 1 WLR 1113, where it was decided that the documents which came into existence for the purpose of civil proceedings and thus were privileged, remained privileged when disclosed for the limited purpose of assisting in the conduct of a criminal investigation. *See also Russell McVeagh McKenzie Barleet & Co. and others v Auckland District Law Society and another* [2003] UKPC 38 in which the Privy Council held that privileged documents could be disclosed to another party without waiving privilege generally, if it was made clear that the privilege was not waived and the documents remained confidential.

connection with, the giving or receiving of legal advice. The House of Lords in *Three Rivers*[52] held that communications recording a lawyer's strategic advice on how clients should present their cases to judicial or other fact-finding inquiries will normally be covered by legal advice privilege.

Where litigation is ensuing or is in reasonable contemplation,[53] privilege will extend to documents created (whether by the client or third parties) with the dominant purpose of obtaining advice on the litigation or the gathering of evidence for use in the litigation. In the context of FSA enforcement proceedings, there is considerable uncertainty as to the point at which litigation can be said to be in reasonable contemplation. It is arguable that litigation can only be said to be in contemplation after a Warning Notice has been issued (or even later). Once the Warning Notice is issued, there is a possibility of a reference being made to the Financial Services and Markets Tribunal and litigation can be said to be in contemplation. Accordingly, during the usually sensitive investigatory period, authorised firms and approved persons may have to rely on legal advice privilege.

There will be certain pros and cons to the production of a written report recording details of incidents which may have regulatory consequences. On the one hand, a firm will be able to point to written material in mitigation should the FSA find that a breach has occurred. On the other hand, a firm will need to have regard to the use to which a written report may be put in regulatory proceedings or in litigation. For example, in the US, regulatory problems frequently give rise to class action litigation and the current practice in the US is not to produce a written report. From a practical perspective, it should be noted that where a report is to be produced, it is important that it is drafted with care and without drawing needless conclusions or using unnecessary critical language.

---

[52] *See Three Rivers District Council and others* v *Governor and Company of the Bank of England* [2004] UKHL 48.

[53] There is no definitive law as far as regulatory investigations threatened or actual are concerned on this point. *See* Henderson A (2003) "FSA proceedings and legal professional privilege revisited in the light of *Three Rivers DC* v *Bank of England (No. 5)*". *Journal of International Banking Law and Regulation*, 488.

### 4.3.5 Interviewing witnesses/employees

#### 4.3.5.1 Preliminary considerations

Having reviewed relevant documents, investigators should be in a position to identify who needs to be interviewed and in relation to which issues. While it is usually better for the interviewer to prepare for an interview by reading the relevant documents, this is not always the case. There may be occasions when it is more appropriate to talk to those involved at an early stage. But care should be exercised in respect of seemingly plausible explanations which subsequently do not "stack up" with the documents.

Any risk of non-cooperation by the employees during internal investigations can largely be pre-empted by outlining a disciplinary procedure in the staff handbook or contract of employment. The provisions in the handbook or employment contract should include an obligation to attend interviews, if requested, as well as to answer questions, reasonably pertinent to an investigation. A failure to do so can then be regarded as misconduct.

#### 4.3.5.2 Conduct of the interview

The purpose of any investigatory interview is to obtain information. The person who must be encouraged to do the most talking is the interviewee and not the interviewer! As a general rule, the more comfortable and less threatened the interviewee is made to feel, the more information they will divulge. For internal investigation purposes (which are not part of any disciplinary process) there is no need to "caution" the interviewee, nor is it necessary that they be accompanied by a lawyer or a friend. However, a firm should consider its response to a request from an interviewee to have a lawyer or friend present and weigh up whether to cover the cost of such a request. It may depend to a large extent on the purpose of the interview and whether the evidence given could subsequently be used against the employee in question. In such circumstances, it would be difficult to envisage grounds for refusing a request to have a lawyer or friend present.

If an individual employee is part of a firm-wide FSA investigation, the firm is more likely to cover the employee's costs in this regard. If costs are covered by the firm, the employee in question is expected to cooperate fully with the fact-gathering process. The firm may also consider offering an indemnity or insurance in return for assistance and cooperation. However, the firm should be careful not to offer employees anything which the FSA might consider may act as a discouragement to individuals within the firm to report misconduct or "blow the whistle". Offering the employee insurance to defend proceedings would generally be acceptable with the proviso that insurance monies will not be applied should the employee be found to have acted dishonestly.[54]

It is important to ensure that, at some stage during the interview process, the salient points or allegations under investigation are explained to the interviewee and that the interviewee is given an opportunity to answer them. In order to avoid a hostile or defensive environment, it is often the case that this takes place at a second or third interview and probably towards the end of that interview. The investigation team should also consider whether to provide relevant documents before the interview or confront the interviewee with them during the interview. The decision will depend on the particular circumstances of the case. The interviewee should always be asked at the end whether they have anything further that they would like to add.

It is important to have an accurate note (not necessarily a full transcript) of what has been said and so it is preferable to have at least two people conduct the interview. Their notes should be finalised soon after the interview.

It will usually be prudent to ask the interviewee to agree and sign the notes, but it is preferable that they are not given a copy of the notes to keep so that the investigation team maintains control of the documents.

### 4.3.5.3 Securing privilege[55]
In light of the decision of the House of Lords in *Three Rivers*, it is evident that if privilege is to attach to the record of the interview in

---

[54] The firm may seek an undertaking or charge from the employee to reimburse monies in the event that he is found to be dishonest.
[55] Also *see* 4.3.4.

circumstances where litigation is not in reasonable contemplation, the communication must fall within the requirements of legal advice privilege.

### 4.3.6 The European Convention on Human Rights ("the Convention")

There is a risk that an employee may claim that their right to privacy under Article 8 of the Convention has been infringed in some way during the information gathering process, for example as a result of an unannounced inspection and retrieval of documents.

Although an individual may not directly rely on a Convention right against another individual, an employee may seek to rely on this right in a subsequent court or tribunal hearing to challenge his dismissal,[56] or disciplinary action taken by the FSA, which, as a public body, is subject to the Human Rights Act 1998.

The right is not absolute and can be overridden if the interference is carried out in accordance with law for a legitimate aim and is proportionate and necessary in a democratic society. Whether the justification for the interference is made out will very much depend on the factual circumstances of the case, but the firm must be careful to ensure that the means employed in gathering information and intercepting employees' communications are proportionate to the aim of the investigation.

It is important to include a provision in the employment contract and/or the staff handbook that the employer may, in certain circumstances, gain access to the employee's desks, cupboards and computer hard drives and monitor communications, so that there should be no expectations of privacy.

### 4.3.7 Data protection legislation

A firm should also ensure that it complies with any applicable data protection laws governing the storage, use and disclosure of any

---

[56] Under Section 6 of the Human Rights Act 1998 a court or a tribunal is required to act in a way which is compatible with the provisions of the Convention.

"personal data" contained in any communications and documents that have been gathered. However, the extent to which the Data Protection Act 1998 ("DPA 1998") applies to internal investigations is uncertain. In *Durant* v *Financial Services Authority*,[57] the Court of Appeal restricted the definition of "personal data" to that which "affects [the individual's] privacy, whether in his personal or family life, business or professional capacity". The difficulty therefore arises in assessing the extent to which the data affects the privacy of the individual in question.

Unless and until there is a resolution of this problem, advisers must proceed on the basis that any data concerning an individual may be caught by the DPA 1998. In particular, regard should be had to the UK Information Commissioner's Code of Practice to employers, which is indicative of the Commissioner's approach to the DPA. This states, *inter alia*, that companies must be up front about their monitoring activities and covert monitoring is unlikely to be permissible except as a last resort and in prescribed circumstances.

### 4.3.8 Insurance

Another matter to be considered on discovering a problem and which can sometimes be overlooked is insurance. The firm may have insurance cover for some, or all, of the losses or costs involved during the investigation. For example, the directors and officers insurance policy may cover expenses incurred by directors in liaising with the investigators. There may also be other relevant insurance policies, for example fidelity or business interruption cover.

The insurers in question must be notified and any further investigation steps may need to comply with relevant terms of the insurance policy.

## 4.4 Post-investigation steps

Following the investigation, conclusions have to be reached as to whether a notifiable event has occurred (if a notification has not

---

[57] [2003] EWCA Civ 1746.

already been made) and, if so, consideration given as to the form and content of a notification. If a notification has already been made, consideration should be given to whether that notification should be updated in light of further information that has emerged from the investigation. It may be that any report that is produced should be presented to the FSA together with the relevant documentation uncovered (maintaining privilege wherever possible).

### 4.4.1 Suspension

Provided the contract of employment provides for suspension, where an employee is suspected of a criminal offence or a breach of regulatory requirements, a firm may want to suspend them from work (on full pay and benefits[58]) pending resolution of the investigation. Whilst there is no need to establish that the employee is guilty of misconduct, there must be reasonable grounds to believe that the employee has been involved in misconduct or alleged misconduct of sufficient seriousness to warrant suspension.

Suspending an employee can often assist an investigation in that the integrity of evidence can be better preserved and witnesses, who otherwise might be disinclined to provide evidence, may be more willing to come forward. Additionally, where the alleged breach or misconduct has come to light as a result of a whistleblowing disclosure by a third party, suspending the employee should assist the employer in complying with its obligations under PIDA 1998 and the FSA's SYSC 4 to ensure that the whistleblower suffers no detriment. The suspension, which should be kept as confidential as possible, should only be for a reasonable time which, in practice, is usually as long as is necessary to undertake the investigation. If an employer suspends an employee for an unreasonably long period of time, this could give the employee grounds to claim unfair or constructive dismissal. As another option, the firm should consider whether it is necessary to take employees out of controlled functions if doubts exist over their fitness and propriety.

---

[58] If an employee is suspended without full pay and benefits, the suspension will count as a disciplinary matter and the suspension must accord with the statutory minimum disciplinary procedure. If the employee is suspended on full pay and benefits, the suspension will not count as a disciplinary matter and the statutory minimum disciplinary procedure will not be engaged.

### 4.4.2   Subsequent action

At the conclusion of the investigation, the firm may wish to take disciplinary action internally against employees or the FSA may well decide to take its own action. Subsequent action of this nature is dealt with in detail in other chapters.

### 4.4.3   Notification to other authorities/regulators

If the regulatory problem involves the commission of a crime, a firm should consider notifying the police. If it is decided to notify the police, careful consideration needs to be given as to the timing of such notification. The involvement of any external party may disrupt the firm's investigation and divert resources. A criminal prosecution may also create damaging publicity.

However, a firm should notify the police where:

(a)   it believes that third parties may be affected by the criminal activities concerned; or

(b)   police intervention is required to assist in obtaining asset freezing and asset recovery orders or to search the suspect's home for evidence.

Under the Proceeds of Crime Act 2002, notification to the Serious Organised Crime Agency is required where money laundering is suspected.

## 4.5   Conclusion

Ideally, regulatory problems will never arise. Experience suggests otherwise and any firm can be affected. However, by carrying out an effective internal investigation, making timely notification to the FSA and implementing necessary improvements to the firm's systems and controls, the firm can mitigate the damage.

**Figure 4.1**  Notifications to the FSA

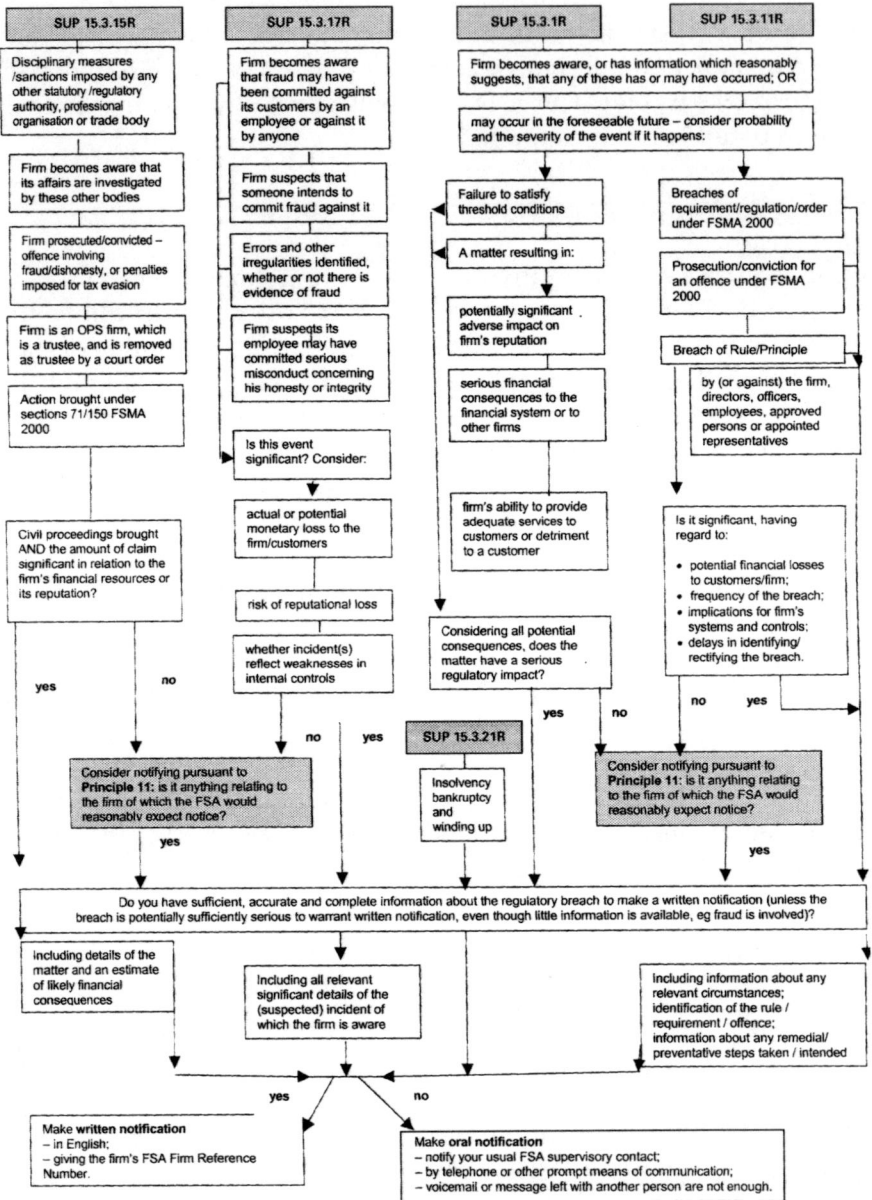

# Chapter 5

# Skilled Persons Reports

**Peter Bibby**
Partner and Head of Financial Regulatory Group
Bingham McCutchen LLP

## 5.1 Introduction – the FSA's power under Section 166 FSMA 2000

### 5.1.1 Overview of the power

Financial Services and Markets Act 2000 ("FSMA 2000") Section 166 gives the Financial Services Authority ("FSA") the power to require authorised persons (and certain other persons connected to them) to provide a report to the FSA from a "skilled person". A skilled person is someone that appears to the FSA to have the skills necessary to make a report on the matter concerned and who is either nominated or approved by the FSA. The report can be on any matter in respect of which the FSA could have required information or documents under its general information-gathering power in Section 165 FSMA 2000, namely any information or documents the FSA reasonably requires in conducting its functions conferred under the FSMA 2000. This is therefore a very wide power.

The cost of the appointment will be borne wholly by the appointing firm, not by the FSA. It is easy to see, therefore, given the FSA's own limited financial resources, that a skilled person appointment is a tempting route for the FSA to follow. In the financial year to 31 March 2004 the FSA used its power to appoint a skilled person 28 times. In the financial year to 31 March 2003 the FSA used the power 31 times. The cost to firms was estimated at £7.05 million in 2003/2004 and £10.75 million in 2002/2003. The cost range for skilled persons reports over the two years was from £13,000 to £4 million. In the financial years ending 31 March 2005 and 31 March 2006 the FSA used the power 19 times and 17 times respectively. The use of skilled person appointments has reduced, despite the extension of the FSA's remit into new sectors such as general insurance and mortgage regulation. Further, costs have also been falling. The cost to firms was estimated at £6.5 million in 2004/2005 and £3.7 million in 2005/2006. The cost range for a skilled persons report for that period was between £400 and £1.15 million.

Although it is a powerful tool for the FSA, for an authorised firm appointment of a skilled person pursuant to the Section 166 power will usually be something best avoided. Such an appointment will mean that the firm loses control of the process in dealing with a potential issue which has been identified. The cost is also likely to be higher than the appointment of the same professional adviser by way of a bilateral contract. It is therefore important for firms, when faced with the possibility of a skilled person appointment, to come up with alternatives to satisfy the FSA's concerns. Firms will therefore need to be aware of their rights and obligations and the factors which are relevant to the FSA's decision to appoint a skilled person. Where they are required to appoint a skilled person they will need to take significant care in managing relationships in order to keep costs and scope under control.

The purpose of this chapter is to set out in more detail the FSA's policy relating to the use of this power and a firm's obligations and rights when facing exercise of it by the FSA. The FSMA 2000 gives no right of challenge or appeal against the FSA in respect of the appointment of a skilled person. However, a firm would be able to seek a judicial review of the FSA's decision to appoint a skilled person if the FSA acted in an unreasonable manner. In practice, establishing that the FSA has acted unreasonably in making such an appointment is likely to be very difficult.

### 5.1.2 Scope of the power

The FSA can have free and unfettered access to the working papers of the skilled person and can insist on terms in the contract between the skilled person and the appointer to exclude any duty of confidentiality which may otherwise be owed by the skilled person to the appointer. This is something that the FSA do in practice. The FSA can and do dictate the timetable, the precise scope of the report and also the form in which the report is made.

### 5.1.3 *Examples of circumstances when the FSA will use a skilled person*

The power is used in both a supervisory and an enforcement context. The FSA has set out a detailed policy on the factors it will take into account in determining whether to use this tool and these are set out in more detail in this chapter. Examples where the FSA has used the power in the past have included:

(a) a review of complaints-handling processes;
(b) oversight of a past business review;
(c) reporting on a firm's financial resources.

The decision in the *Legal & General* case[1] and the finding that the Regulatory Decisions Committee ("RDC") did not have sufficient evidence on which to base a decision that there had been widespread misselling is likely to mean that where the Section 166 tool is used to review a sample of past sales in order to show systemic misselling, this sample will need to be statistically significant resulting in greater cost to a firm.

The FSA has tended to use its Section 166 power for information gathering purposes. However, it has recently proposed using the power for consumer protection purposes in relation to firms who are exempt from statutory audit requirements by reason of being a small company under the Companies Act 1985. The inclusion of FSA regulated firms in this exemption is new and the FSA has proposed to select annually 50 small firms (both randomly and targeted) to be subject to a review by a skilled person. The intention is to minimise the risks of a reduction in the standards of a firm's internal controls as the firm will know they could be subject to a detailed inspection by an external auditor or FSA staff.

## 5.2 Detailed ambit of the Section 166 power

### 5.2.1 *Requirements imposed on a range of people*

The power can be exercised in relation to a very wide range of businesses. It is not limited to authorised entities but extends to a wide range of connected parties.

---

[1] *Legal & General Assurance Society Ltd* v *Financial Services Authority* [2005] UKFSM FSM002 (18 January 2005).

The FSA may by notice in writing require a person to provide it with a report on any matter about which it has required or could require the provision of information or production of documents under Section 165. The effect is that the FSA can require a skilled person to report on any matter on which it reasonably requires information in connection with the exercise by the FSA of functions conferred on it by or under the FSMA 2000. It could therefore ask for a report examining not only authorised activities but also, for instance, looking into the ownership or control of a business.

Section 166 reports can be required from a range of people provided they have the necessary connection with the authorised person. Reports can be required by the FSA from:

(a)    an authorised person;

(b)    any other member of the authorised person's group;[2]

---

[2] The authorised person's group for this purpose is defined under Section 421 FSMA 2000 as follows:

(a) a parent undertaking of the firm;

(b) a subsidiary undertaking of the firm;

(c) a subsidiary undertaking of a parent undertaking of the firm (i.e. a sister company);

(d) a parent undertaking in a subsidiary undertaking of the firm;

(e) an undertaking of which the firm or any of the above has a participating interest;

(f) if the firm is a building society then an associated undertaking of that building society; or

(g) if the firm or undertaking in (a) to (d) above is an incorporated friendly society, a body corporate of which that friendly society has joint control.

**Parent undertaking and subsidiary undertaking**
A parent undertaking for the purposes of Section 166 is defined by Part VII of the Companies Act 1985 as a company which:

(a) holds the majority of the voting rights in the authorised person;

(b) is a member of the authorised person and has the right to appoint or remove a majority of its board of directors;

(c) has the right to exercise a dominant influence over the authorised person:

    (i) by virtue of provisions contained in the authorised person's Memorandum or Articles, or

    (ii) by virtue of a control contract;

(d) is a member of the authorised person and controls alone, pursuant to an agreement with other shareholders or members, a majority of the voting rights in the firm.

An undertaking will be treated as a member of the authorised person if it is a shareholder in the authorised person or if:

(a) any of the subsidiaries of the undertaking is a member of the authorised person; or

(b) any shares in the authorised person are held by a person acting on behalf of the undertaking or any of its subsidiary undertakings.

(c)    a partnership of which the authorised person is a member; or
(d)    a person who has at any relevant time been a person falling within paragraph (a), (b) or (c) above.

The impact of the definition of "group" for these purposes under the FSMA 2000 is that companies which are higher up in the corporate structure of a group of which the authorised firm is a part or are lower down in the corporate structure can be required to appoint a skilled person to report to the FSA.

The person from whom the report is required must be, or have been at the relevant time, carrying on a business. The FSA cannot therefore require a skilled person report from an entity which was dormant at the time of the events to which the report relates.

### 5.2.2   The identity of the skilled person

The FSA must either nominate or approve the person who is appointed as a skilled person. The FSA may provide the appointer with a shortlist from which to choose. The FSA will, however, normally leave it to the firm to put forward names of suggested skilled persons. In its Handbook at SUP 5.4.8G the FSA has set out the matters which it will take into account when deciding whether to nominate or approve a skilled person. It will consider:

(a)    the skills necessary to make a report on the matters concerned. It may be that the particular skills are skills which are only to be found in an accountant, a lawyer, an actuary or a person with relevant business technical or technological skills. In that case it will only be prepared to accept the appointment of such a person. The FSA will consider proposals for skilled persons on a

---

In addition, an undertaking will be a parent undertaking in relation to the authorised person if it has a participating interest in the authorised person and:
(a) actually exercises a dominant influence over it; or
(b) the authorised person and the undertaking are managed on a unified basis.

A participating interest is an interest in the shares of the authorised person which are held on a long-term basis for the purpose of securing a contribution to the activities of the parent by the exercise of control or influence arising from or related to that interest. A holding of 20 per cent or more of the shares of the authorised person shall be presumed to be a participating interest unless the contrary is shown.

case-by-case basis. Whilst the FSA does not keep a central list of skilled persons it is prepared to approve, it will of course gain experience from previous appointments and this will influence how prepared the FSA will be to accept a particular nomination;

(b) the ability to complete the report within the time expected by the FSA. The FSA will take into account the resources that may be available to the skilled person and whether the skilled person is likely to be able to deliver on time and in the format that the FSA has required;

(c) any relevant specialised knowledge. It may be that the FSA will be aware of a particular person who has specialised in a specific area or alternatively that knowledge of the particular business carried on by the appointer is necessary in order to produce the report;

(d) any professional difficulty or potential conflict of interest that a person may have in reviewing the matters to be reported on. In many cases the appointer may wish to use existing professional advisers. Often this will reduce the costs as the existing advisers will have a better knowledge and understanding of the business. However, those existing professional advisers may have advised on the matters which are to be covered by the skilled persons report or may even have carried out certain tasks which are then to be reviewed as part of the skilled persons report. The FSA recognises that it may be cost effective to nominate or approve the appointment of a skilled person who has previously acted for or advised the appointer. However, it will need to be certain that there is not a potential conflict of interest for that person;

(e) where there is an existing professional or commercial relationship the FSA will consider whether the potential skilled person is sufficiently detached to give an objective opinion on the matters concerned. This will be particularly important in the context of a disciplinary or other enforcement action where it is likely that the report of the skilled person could be used as evidence in those proceedings and the skilled person himself could be called as a witness.

### 5.2.3 Requirement to cooperate with the skilled person

Any provider of services to the appointer must give the skilled person all assistance that the skilled person may reasonably require

(Section 166(5) FSMA 2000). The duty on the service provider can be enforced by the FSA by an injunction, or in Scotland an order for specific performance of the obligation. Obligations of confidentiality will be overridden. However, whilst legal advisers will be required to cooperate with a person appointed as a skilled person, they cannot be required to deliver up legally privileged documentation. Under Section 413 FSMA 2000, legally privileged material counts as a "protected item" and no person may be required under the FSMA 2000 to produce, disclose or permit the inspection of protected items. Where the appointer wishes to provide access to legally privileged material to the skilled person then steps should be taken to try to minimise the extent to which legal privilege more generally is waived. It should be made clear that the confidentiality in the legally privileged material is intended to be maintained subject only to this limited disclosure.

There is no formal mechanism for challenging a request from a skilled person where the firm views it as unreasonable. However, the enquiries undertaken by the skilled person and the activities carried out by it will need to be referable to the terms of reference of the skilled person. It will therefore be important for the skilled person to be able to show why he requires information or to interview a particular person when considered against the terms of reference under which he has been appointed. If the skilled person's requests are viewed by the appointer as unreasonable then the appointer should raise this in the first instance with the skilled person and obtain an explanation of why the information or activity is necessary. If the appointer is not satisfied with the response from the skilled person and the skilled person persists in his request then it would be appropriate for the appointer to raise the matter with the FSA. The FSA is unlikely to wish to second guess the approach by the skilled person but will want to be sure that the skilled person is acting reasonably. The FSA will be conscious that the firm is paying for the skilled person and therefore if the FSA approves work which is unreasonable in scope or extent then it could potentially face criticism.

### 5.2.4 Failure to cooperate with the FSA

A failure to appoint a skilled person where required by the FSA under Section 166 can be treated as a contempt of court (Section 177 FSMA

2000). It will be a defence for the person to show he had a reasonable excuse for failing to appoint. There are no examples of what amounts to a reasonable excuse and it will be a matter for the court to decide. When considering whether a requirement to appoint a skilled person is unreasonable, the court will assess the proposals made by the firm to deal with the matter against the FSA policy set out in the Enforcement or Supervision Manual. It is possible to envisage a circumstance where a court would find it unreasonable for the FSA to require the appointment of a skilled person if the firm could show that it has a necessary skill or expertise to carry out a task and there are no grounds on which to believe the firm will not report objectively. For instance, if the task involves the review of a database where the firm had the necessary expertise and where there were no reasons to suggest that the firm may not be objective in its review.

## 5.3 The FSA's policy on the appointment of skilled persons

### 5.3.1 Relevant sections of the Handbook

The main sections of the FSA Handbook which are relevant to the appointment of a skilled person are the Supervision Manual and the Enforcement Manual. SUP 5 provides the detailed policy and rules relating to the appointment of a skilled person. ENF 2.3 and 2.5 set out the additional policy for the use of a skilled person in an enforcement context.

### 5.3.2 When the FSA will use its skilled person power

The FSA's policy on the use of a skilled person is set out at SUP 5.3.1G. It may be used for the following purposes:

(a)   for diagnostic purposes, to identify, assess and measure risk. The relevant risk here will be the indirect risk to the FSA's statutory objectives (i.e. to enable the FSA to understand the extent of any risks which may exist and to do so by receiving a report from someone who is skilled in relation to the particular issue). The report should assist the FSA to determine whether steps are needed to mitigate the risk or to determine whether there has been a rule breach. The FSA may for instance have a concern about the quality of systems and controls or the implications or consequences of incomplete customer files. For example, the FSA may appoint a skilled person to determine whether a failure by a firm's investment advisers to recommend suitable products to a customer is hidden by the incomplete files;

(b)    for monitoring purposes, to track the development of identified risks, wherever these arise. The tool would be used in this circumstance to keep under review an identified risk. An in-depth report may be commissioned to look at a particular aspect of a firm's business when the FSA considers that it is material to the risk profile of the firm;

(c)    in the context of preventative action, to limit or reduce identified risks and so prevent them from crystallising or increasing. In this context the FSA will commission the report from the skilled person to assist the firm to manage and mitigate any risks which already exist. For instance, a skilled person may be appointed to report on the effectiveness of improvements to monitoring procedures implemented by the firm where the FSA may be considering whether it is necessary to take action to vary a permission and so limit the business which the firm can undertake;

(d)    for remedial action, to respond to risks when they have crystallised. Where a firm is undertaking a past business review a skilled person will often be appointed. The skilled person's role will be to oversee and report to the FSA on the past business review. The FSA will be seeking comfort that the review covers all relevant cases; that the methodology is appropriate to identify cases where there has been a regulatory breach; and that the method for delivering compensation will provide the appropriate recompense to investors.

### 5.3.3   *Matters the FSA will take into account when deciding whether to require a report by a skilled person*

SUP 5.3.3G sets out the matters to which the FSA will have regard. Whilst this list appears in the Supervision Manual, the FSA has stated that it will also take account of these factors in an enforcement context. The list is very important as it provides the basis for any challenge to an FSA direction to appoint a skilled person:

(a) Circumstances relating to the firm, in particular:

    (i)    whether the firm is being cooperative (i.e. is it able and willing to provide the information itself);

    (ii)    whether there is a history of similar issues at the firm. The FSA will assess whether the firm has a history of problems which, despite its own efforts, it has failed to put right. This will indicate that an independent skilled person report may be required in order to adequately report on the matter;

    (iii)    the quality of the firm's systems and records. Are the firm's systems and records such that it can provide the information needed, or is it necessary to involve a skilled person in order to obtain the information from the systems? This situation can arise where, for example, the FSA requires information from a computer system in a particular format and the firm does not have the necessary in-house skill or expertise to interrogate its databases in the manner required;

    (iv)    the objectivity of the firm and whether the FSA has confidence in the firm's willingness and ability to deliver an objective report. The FSA may be concerned that the firm will not be able to provide an objective report if the results may lead to the firm facing potential disciplinary action;

    (v)    conflicts of interest and the knowledge or expertise available to the firm. Where the appointer does not have the necessary expertise, for instance in designing a past business review where the compensation methodology may require legal input and analysis, then a skilled person appointment may be appropriate.

(b) Alternative tools available to the FSA. The FSA will have regard to whether the information could be provided on an informal basis; in an enforcement context the FSA will consider whether it could be provided under Section 165 FSMA 2000, or whether an investigation would be more appropriate under Section 167 or Section 168 of the Act.

(c) Legal and procedural requirements. The FSA will consider whether it is desirable to obtain an authoritative and independent report for use in any subsequent proceedings. This consideration will apply in both a supervision and enforcement context but is most likely to be relevant in an enforcement case where there is suspicion that there has been a rule breach.

(d) The objectives of the FSA enquiries. The FSA will assess whether historic information or evidence is required, in which case it is more likely to use information-gathering powers and investigation powers.

(e) Cost considerations. The FSA will consider whether the firm will derive some benefit from the work carried out and recommendations made by the skilled person (*see* 5.4 below).

The FSA will also take into account its own availability of resources and whether it has the necessary expertise to carry out the work itself. It will consider whether the resources required to produce the report or to make enquiries are available within the FSA and whether the use of those resources would be the best use of the FSA's resources at the time.

### 5.3.4 Uses of Section 166 in an enforcement context

The FSA may use its skilled person tool where it has decided that it is appropriate to make further enquiries in an enforcement context where a firm potentially faces disciplinary proceedings. Such an appointment will normally occur after the firm has been notified of the appointment of investigators. The FSA has stated that it cannot list exhaustively the circumstances which may cause it to make further enquiries. ENF 2.5.5 of the FSA Handbook gives the following examples of situations in which the FSA may make further enquiries:

(a) a firm or an approved person within a firm may have acted in a way which prejudiced the interests of consumers;

(b) a firm or an approved person within a firm may have acted in breach of the requirements of the FSMA 2000 or the rules;

(c) a firm may no longer meet the threshold conditions or an approved person within a firm may not be a fit and proper person to perform a controlled function;

(d) a firm may have been used or may be deemed used for the purposes of financial crime including money laundering;

(e) the FSA is concerned about the ownership or control of a firm, including whether a person who has acquired influence over the firm meets the requirements of the FSA;

(f)     the conduct of certain types of regulated activities in which a firm is involved are a cause of serious public concern.

At ENF 2.5.6 the FSA has given examples of when it may use its power to appoint a skilled person in an enforcement context and when it may consider that it is more appropriate to use its investigation powers to gather the necessary information. The FSA has stated that if its objectives are limited to gathering historic information or evidence for determining whether enforcement action may be appropriate then its powers under Section 165 and its investigation powers under Sections 167–175 may be more effective and more appropriate powers to use than its power under Section 166. While the use of Section 166 to gather evidence in an enforcement context is clearly contemplated by both the FSMA 2000 and its own guidance, the FSA makes relatively sparing use of skilled persons reports in an enforcement context and this has continued following the *Legal & General* case.

The Section 166 appointment is likely to complement the ongoing investigation and bring additional skills and expertise which the investigation team need to carry out the investigation.

If the FSA's objectives include obtaining expert analysis or considering or receiving recommendations for remedial action, the power under Section 166 may be appropriate to use instead of or in conjunction with the FSA's other available powers.

## 5.4     The cost of the skilled person appointment

The basic position is that the costs of the skilled person report will be borne by the person required to appoint the skilled person. The costs can range from the tens of thousands to millions of pounds depending upon the nature of the appointment, the issue under consideration and the requirements imposed on the skilled person by the FSA. When deciding whether to use a skilled person rather than using alternative methods to obtain information such as visits, the FSA will take account of a number of relevant factors relating to the costs. These will include:

(a)   the extent to which the firm may derive benefit from the work carried out and recommendations made by the skilled person. It may assist the firm to have a better understanding of its business and its risk profile or the operation of its information system or improvements to its systems and controls;

(b)   whether the firm should have already carried out the work, or whether it should have already been done by persons instructed by the firm on its own initiative. For instance, this could include a compliance review or the development of new systems;

(c)   the extent to which the firm's record keeping and management information systems are so poor that the required documents are not readily available or an analysis of the required information cannot readily be performed without expert assistance;

(d)   if the firm appears to have breached regulatory requirements or put consumers at risk and whether it is unable or unwilling to review and remedy the matters of concern or the FSA considers that it cannot rely on the firm to do so; and

(e)   the likelihood and seriousness of possible future breaches of regulatory requirements and the possible need for further action.

The costs incurred in a skilled person appointment are very likely to be greater than the costs which would be incurred by a firm if it was to commission the report itself outside the terms of Section 166. This is because of the terms which the FSA requires in the appointment between the skilled person and the appointer. These terms require the skilled person to report matters to the FSA both on a formal and informal basis. The skilled person is therefore serving two different masters (the FSA and the appointer). The skilled person will need to be sure that it can satisfy itself that its findings as reported to the FSA are fully justifiable and supported by all relevant records as these findings may subsequently be used against the appointer in regulatory proceedings.

## 5.5   Avoiding the appointment of a skilled person

A firm may avoid the appointment of a skilled person if it can convince the FSA that its policy would not be met by such an appointment. This will often involve the firm volunteering to appoint professional advisers to carry out an investigation or review a matter which would otherwise be the subject of a skilled person appointment. The FSA will be receptive to this approach if the professional adviser has the necessary skills and expertise and if there are no reasons to believe that the report will not be objective. Where, however, the proposal is in the context of a disciplinary case and there are indications that the firm has failed to address or report matters in the past, then the FSA may feel it needs the comfort of a truly independent report. The FSA's attitude to avoiding Section 166 will also depend on the identity of the professional adviser which the firm proposes to appoint. If it is an adviser that the FSA regularly comes into contact with and which has detailed regulatory knowledge, the FSA is more likely to be persuaded than if it is less well known. The FSA will take account of arguments about cost but these will not outweigh the other policy considerations which the FSA has listed.

## 5.6  The appointment of a skilled person

### 5.6.1  *The scope of the report*

The scope of any report to be produced by the skilled person will be driven initially by the FSA. The FSA has stated at SUP 5.4.2 that it will normally discuss its needs with the appointer before finalising its decision to require a report by a skilled person. However, in the context of an enforcement case it is often the situation that the FSA will have decided that a skilled person appointment is necessary and will provide the formal notice before discussion with the person under investigation. The person may still come up with reasons why it may be possible to carry out the tasks without the appointment of a skilled person. However, the FSA is unlikely to be persuaded at this stage that the person should carry out the work on its own and is likely to require the involvement of the skilled person, as an independent third party, in preparing a response to the FSA's queries.

The written notification given by the FSA will set out the purpose of the report, its scope, the timetable for completion and other relevant matters. The FSA should make clear, both to the firm and the skilled person, the nature of the concerns that have given rise to the decision to appoint a skilled person and the possible use of the results of the report. The FSA will expect to see a detailed timetable for the production of the report to be produced by the skilled person and it is likely that there will be a meeting between the appointer, the skilled person and the FSA prior to the finalisation and conclusion of the terms. This will enable discussion to be held, before the work begins, about the record-keeping and evidence needed to support the conclusions of the report. This is particularly important where the output may be used in enforcement proceedings.

Although a report may be commissioned for supervisory purposes, issues may be identified that could lead to enforcement proceedings. Therefore, while work on a skilled persons report is in progress, there should be regular liaison meetings between the firm, skilled person and the FSA to identify any material new information which might affect the future direction of the work, consistent with SUP 5.5.4G.

In an enforcement context the appointment of a skilled person will have been driven by the belief that there has been a rule or requirement breach. The firm will not be dealing with its normal supervisors but with enforcement staff with whom it does not have an ongoing relationship. Enforcement on its part is therefore likely to feel less comfortable about trusting the firm than normal supervisory contacts may. In these circumstances Enforcement will place great store on the fact that it will be able to trust the skilled person to produce an objective and reliable report based on sound evidence. It will also wish to ensure that anybody who is appointed will be prepared to report matters to the FSA as and when required and will be credible as a witness if called to give evidence.

### 5.6.2 Selection of the skilled person

The person who makes the report must be a person who is either nominated or approved by the FSA. It must also appear to the FSA that the person has the skills necessary to make a report on the matter concerned. The FSA will normally expect the firm to come up with proposals for who should be the skilled person. The FSA will be prepared to listen to any proposals provided the proposed skilled person has the necessary skills and expertise. Whilst the FSA will have greater experience of the big four accounting firms and some of the major legal firms, it will be prepared to listen to proposals for second tier accountants and less well-known legal firms. As part of the selection process the FSA will expect to meet with the skilled person to discuss the resources available, the approach that the skilled person would take and the expertise that the skilled person has. The FSA will possibly wish to take up references and will certainly wish to receive CVs of those individuals who will have the key roles in carrying out the skilled person appointment.

### 5.6.3 *The reporting process*

When the FSA requires a firm to appoint a skilled person it is looking for a report which it can rely on. Therefore in most circumstances it will expect the skilled person to produce a report, which is discussed with the appointer before it is provided to the FSA. To the extent that issues are raised by the appointer then the skilled person will need to consider those and, if appropriate, amend the report before finalisation and provision to the FSA. The FSA will expect the skilled person to keep all drafts of the report and these will be available to the FSA to review should that be necessary.

## 5.7 Terms of appointment

In agreeing the terms of reference for the skilled person it is also very important to agree precisely what will be looked at and the role that the skilled person will have. Given the responsibility of the appointer to meet the costs, a clearly defined set of tasks and objectives should be agreed with the skilled person and the FSA in advance. If the appointer considers that the costs of the skilled person are unreasonable for the work that is being carried out then it should first raise the matter with the skilled person but should also be prepared to raise the issue with the FSA if it has evidence of work which does not appear to be necessary or which has been done to an inadequate standard.

The FSA will require particular terms in the appointment of the skilled person. SUP 5.5.1R requires the contract between the appointer and the skilled person to include the following terms:

(a)   the skilled person is required to cooperate with the FSA both during and after the course of his appointment in the discharge of the FSA's function under the FSMA 2000 in relation to the appointer. The effect of this is that the skilled person will be required to give evidence on behalf of the FSA should that prove necessary. The skilled person will also be required to provide further information to the FSA and an explanation of any of its work should that be necessary. The cost of this additional assistance will of course be borne by the appointer;

(b)   to notify the FSA if the skilled person reasonably believes that the firm may have contravened a relevant requirement and the contravention may be of material significance to the FSA in determining whether to take regulatory action. The impact of this is that the skilled person is not required to report every breach of a relevant requirement but is required to consider whether that breach would be such that the FSA would consider taking action against the firm. The FSA will therefore expect a detailed appreciation of regulatory requirements on the part of the skilled person. The skilled person will be expected to apply an approach similar to that in Chapter 15 of the Supervision Manual concerning notification to FSA. There is no requirement for the skilled person to notify the firm that he is making such a disclosure to the FSA and there is no requirement on the skilled person to discuss it with the firm in advance. The skilled person will need to consider in all cases what the most appropriate approach would be. If the failure goes to the integrity of the appointer then the notification is likely to be made without reference to the appointer;

(c)   to notify the FSA if the skilled person reasonably believes that there are matters which may be of material significance to the FSA in determining whether the firm continues to satisfy the threshold conditions. A skilled person may find himself in this position if he considers that there is information which has come to light which suggests that the firm is no longer fit and proper or that it is connected to a person who will render it impossible for the FSA to properly supervise the firm. Again, there is no requirement on the skilled person to discuss the matter in advance with the appointer;

(d)   the skilled person reasonably believes that the firm is not or may cease to be a going concern. Such information is likely to come to the attention of the skilled person if he has been appointed to report on the financial resources of the appointer. Again, the skilled person will be under no duty to discuss the matter with the firm in advance;

(e)    the skilled person will be required to prepare a report as notified to the firm by the FSA within the time specified by the FSA.

The FSA has stated that the terms in the contract will need to reflect what the FSA requires in terms of reporting from the skilled person. Therefore, the contract should require the skilled person to provide the following if the FSA has requested:

(a)    interim reports;
(b)    source data, documents and working papers;
(c)    copies of any draft reports given to the firm; and
(d)    specific information about the planning and progress of the work to be undertaken. This may include project plans and progress reports.

Prior to requiring the provision of source data and working papers the FSA will consider what benefit it may derive from the information. It has stated that it will only seek working papers and other information where it believes that information is relevant to an investigation it may conduct or action it may need to consider taking against the firm. However, a skilled person will be fully aware of the possibility that the FSA may wish to review its working papers and therefore will need to ensure that a full audit trail has been retained justifying its findings and conclusions. Given that the appointer of a skilled person is required to cooperate with the skilled person, the skilled person will often seek to include a statement that it cannot be held liable for inaccuracies in information provided to it. Skilled persons will also seek to include their normal terms of business in any appointment and this will often limit their liability in damages.

### 5.7.1   Confidentiality

The FSA will require the terms of contract to include a waiver of any duty of confidentiality owed by the skilled person to the firm which might limit the provision of information or opinion by the skilled person to the FSA.

Where a lawyer is appointed as a skilled person then the FSA will require the firm to waive legal professional privilege in respect of the lawyer's work as a skilled person. In such circumstances, the lawyer would not be able to continue to advise the appointer since any advice which he gave to the appointer about his legal position would not be covered by legal professional privilege. An appointer in such circumstances would be wise to have separate legal advice over which he could continue to claim legal professional privilege. It is common for firms to take separate legal advice on the findings of a skilled person. The legal adviser can have access to all information provided by the skilled person and can advise the appointer on the possible implications of the skilled person's findings. This advice will be legally privileged and will be important in directing the appointer's response to the skilled persons report.

### 5.7.2   Other terms of the contract

The FSA has also stated that the contract must be governed by the laws of the UK.

The contract must also provide the FSA with a right to enforce the provisions set out above even though it is not party to the contract.

If the contract includes an arbitration agreement then the FSA is not to be bound by that arbitration agreement.

Finally, and most importantly, the specified provisions required by the FSA in the contract must be irrevocable and may not be varied or rescinded without the FSA's consent.

### 5.7.3   Review of the draft contract

At SUP 5.5.7G the FSA has stated that where it considers appropriate, it may request a firm to give it a copy of the draft contract before it is made with the skilled person. In practice, the FSA is likely to wish to see the draft contract and to agree the terms of the contract in all significant appointments. Firms which are commonly appointed as skilled persons will have already gone through the process of agreeing basic terms with the FSA on other appointments and therefore it is likely to prove to be less time consuming and more cost effective to appoint a firm which has experience of acting as a skilled person. Given that the appointment is a commercial contract between the appointer and the skilled person, the FSA will expect the parties to agree a form of words which it can then comment on.

## 5.8 Appointed representatives and auditors

Under SUP 5.5.9R the firm is required to provide all reasonable assistance to a skilled person.

The FSA has specifically provided that this includes the firm requiring each of its appointed representatives to waive any duty of confidentiality and provide reasonable assistance as though the rule applied directly to the appointed representatives.

Reasonable assistance is stated to include access to accounting and other records, the provision of information and explanation as reasonably required. This includes the right for the skilled person to obtain information directly from the firm's auditor.

## 5.9 Commenting on a draft skilled person's report

The normal process will be for a skilled person to produce a report for comment to the appointer. The report (dependent on the circumstances) will usually contain a facts section and an opinion section. The normal approach will be to analyse the facts in order to achieve a consensus that they are a fair reflection and then to discuss whether any changes to the facts impact on the opinions. From the skilled person's perspective it will be important to bear in mind that the FSA will have access to all drafts of the report. The skilled person will need to keep an audit trail of any changes which are made (in particular to the opinions) and will need to be able to justify to the FSA the reasons for any such changes.

## 5.10 Conclusion

The power to appoint a skilled person is a major tool in the FSA's armoury. It enables the FSA to get an independent and objective report on a matter of concern at the cost of the firm. From a firm's point of view it is expensive, and may result in a report which will be used against the firm in subsequent proceedings. The terms of reference, scope and handling of the appointment need to be carefully managed in order to minimise cost and ensure focus of the work. Where a firm suspects that a skilled person may be appointed it should consider what it can do to set the FSA's mind at rest and in that regard it should focus its effort on addressing the issues raised in the FSA's stated policy.

# Chapter 6

# Remedial Action under FSMA 2000

**Simon Morris**
Partner
CMS Cameron McKenna

## 6.1 Introduction

This chapter examines remedial action that may be taken by, or be ordered to be taken by, a person authorised to carry on regulated activities under the Financial Services and Markets Act 2000 ("FSMA 2000") (a "firm") or an individually approved person working for a firm.

The concept of remedial action is central to the financial services regime. Investor protection is achieved by prescribing standards to be observed and, if these are breached, then it is clear that corrective action should be commenced. However, there is no definition of "remedial action" contained in the FSMA 2000, nor is there a Financial Services Authority ("FSA") Handbook devoted to this topic.[1] The FSA has no single overriding power to require firms to take remedial action and, while there are some sections in FSMA 2000 concerned with remedial action, these are rarely used and may be considered as being reserve powers. There is, thus, no single power to require remedial action, and the provisions that may be relied upon to require a firm to take this action are fragmented, some scattered throughout FSMA 2000 while others are to be implied from the wording of the FSA Handbook. A further characteristic of this topic is that in most cases the FSA has not needed to invoke its formal powers of remedial action as firms usually recognise their duty to offer redress,

---

[1] All references to Sections in this part refer to Sections of FSMA 2000 unless otherwise stated.

when appropriate, either on their own initiative or when prompted by the FSA. These powers are thus only rarely exercised.

For the purposes of this chapter "remedial action" will be regarded as action, positive or negative, that a firm or an individual registered with the FSA (an "approved person") may take on their own initiative, or may be required or recommended to take by the FSA or by the Financial Ombudsman Service ("FOS"), in order to ensure that their conduct conforms with the requirements of the FSA and FOS. In other words, remedial action is what a firm does to either resume compliance or, if it has not complied in the first place, to begin complying with the rules. This may take the form of altering its procedures, introducing additional systems and controls or engaging additional or replacement staff. Where customers have been disadvantaged as a consequence of the non-compliance, the firm will be expected to offer appropriate redress that, in the case of financial loss, will typically take the form of compensation. Most firms will periodically take remedial action to remain compliant, and the need to provide compensation is not restricted to circumstances when required by the FSA. Instead, for the reasons already mentioned, it is most often self-identified and self-implemented.

This chapter examines the following points:

(a)   the basis of the FSA's power to require a firm to take remedial action is considered at 6.2;
(b)   the ways that the need to take remedial action may come to light are considered at 6.3;
(c)   a firm needs to take remedial action when its conduct falls below the required standard, so the key standards against which the firm's conduct is judged are examined at 6.4;
(d)   where a firm refuses to take necessary remedial action the FSA may need to exercise formal powers and these are discussed at 6.5;
(e)   particular aspects of remedial action are considered at 6.6: publicity, the availability of funds and the position of individuals;
(f)   the extent of financial remedial action is reviewed briefly at 6.7;
(g)   at 6.8 there are some suggestions of how a firm faced with taking remedial action could discharge its responsibilities.

## 6.2 The basis of the FSA's power to require firms to take remedial action

In this section we consider in turn:

(a)   the FSA's statutory objectives and the Principles of Good Regulation that govern the FSA's overall approach to requiring that a firm take remedial action;
(b)   the FSA's general powers granted in FSMA 2000 that are relevant to requiring a firm to take remedial action; and
(c)   the specific powers of remedial action contained in FSMA 2000.

### 6.2.1   The FSA's statutory objectives

The starting point for consideration of this subject is the FSA's statutory objectives (Section 2(1)), of which three are especially relevant. These set out the expectation that firms will take remedial action when appropriate and form the basis of the FSA's power to require them to do so when necessary.

(a)   Maintaining confidence in the financial system (Section 3). This objective underlies the expectation that firms will take remedial action when failure to do so might undermine either investors' or the market's confidence. Where firms have failed to take such action this objective may justify the FSA requiring them to take action. Examples of circumstances that might undermine confidence, and thus when remedial action may be required, include where an investment exchange is failing to settle transactions, or where firms are widely mismarketing a retail product.
(b)   Securing an appropriate degree of consumer protection (Section 5). This objective requires firms to take remedial action in circumstances where their acts or omissions would otherwise fail to secure this objective. An example of this is where an adviser has given incorrect advice to an investor, then his firm is expected to offer appropriate redress to that investor.
(c)   Reduction of financial crime (Section 6). Where a firm has failed to take appropriate measures to prevent or monitor for offences involving market misconduct, fraud, dishonesty or money laundering, it may be required to take remedial action pursuant to

this objective, for example by strengthening systems or reviewing past transactions.

### 6.2.2 *The Principles of Good Regulation*

Both the FSA's decision to request a firm to take remedial action and its exercise of powers to enforce that action should a firm decline to cooperate are constrained by the Principles of Good Regulation. These are the seven items listed at Section 2(3) to which the FSA must have regard when discharging its general functions of making rules, issuing codes, giving general (i.e. not firm-specific) guidance and determining general policy and principles (Section 2(4)). Thus, while not expressly applicable to a decision that the FSA may make with regard to the need for an individual firm to take remedial action, the FSA is nonetheless guided by these principles in reaching such a decision. The three key principles relevant to this topic are:

(a) Efficient use of resources (Section 2(3)(a)). The FSA will not needlessly devote its resources to require firms to take unnecessary remedial action. The FSA will therefore tend to concentrate on circumstances where significant market or investor detriment might otherwise go uncorrected.

(b) The responsibility of each firm's management to ensure that the firm is run compliantly (Section 2(3)(b)). A cornerstone of FSMA 2000 is that a firm's management is responsible for running its business, which includes identifying the need to take remedial action and then carrying it to an appropriate conclusion. This principle indicates that the FSA should only intervene if it appears that a firm is reluctant to, or will not, take appropriate action itself.

(c) The burden of regulation should be proportionate to its benefits (Section 2(3)(c)). This principle constrains the FSA from requiring that a firm take remedial action where, for example, investor detriment is minimal or the remedial cost disproportionately burdensome.

### 6.2.3 *The FSA's general powers relevant to remedial action*

The FSA's statutory objectives and the Principles of Good Regulation determine the extent and general exercise of its powers. The specific powers conferred on the FSA by FSMA 2000 especially relevant to remedial action are as follows:

(a) Making rules (Sections 138 to 147). These rules, together with the FSA's Principles for Business and Principles for Approved Persons, form the yardstick against which conduct is judged and any need for remedial action is assessed.
(b) Requiring firms to provide information (Sections 165 and 166) and investigating firms (Sections 167 to 168). These powers enable the FSA to obtain information about a firm's or individual's conduct as a preliminary to determining if its requirements have been breached and whether any remedial action is necessary.
(c) Taking disciplinary action against a firm (Sections 205 to 224). While separate from the requirement for a firm to take remedial action, the FSA's ability to take disciplinary action against a firm or an individual can be used to give impetus to a requirement for a firm (or an individual) to take remedial action on his own or a firm's behalf.
(d) Taking action against individuals. The FSA's power to discipline an approved individual for misconduct (Section 66), to withdraw an individual's approval (Section 63) or to prohibit any individual (Section 56) are actions that the FSA can take in relation to an individual who has refused to implement remedial action.
(e) Cancelling a firm's permission. If a firm refuses to take appropriate remedial action it can, as a last resort, be de-authorised by the FSA (Sections 42, 44 and 45).

### 6.2.4 *Specific powers of remedial action*

There are six circumstances in which the FSA or an investor is expressly empowered to take or seek remedial action under FSMA 2000. It is noteworthy that none of them directly underlies the most usual occurrence of remedial action, which is a firm recognising that it has fallen short of the FSA's requirements, or the FSA pointing this out to it, and the firm responding accordingly. The seven circumstances are as follows.

#### 6.2.4.1 *Empowering the FSA to require remedial action is taken*
Section 404 FSMA 2000 empowers the Treasury to require the FSA to establish a scheme to investigate wrongdoing and compensate

investors where widespread non-compliance may have led to loss for private investors. The Treasury can exercise this power if it is satisfied that there is evidence suggesting:

(a)  that there has been a widespread or regular failure on the part of authorised persons to comply with rules relating to a particular kind of activity; and

(b)  that, as a result, private persons have suffered or will suffer loss in respect of which authorised persons are or will be liable to make compensation payments.

In those circumstances the Treasury can make an order authorising the FSA to establish and operate a scheme for:

(a)  determining the nature and extent of the failure;

(b)  establishing the liability of authorised persons to make compensation payments; and

(c)  determining the amounts payable by way of compensation payments.

This provision was added towards the end of the passage of the Bill as a result of a minority opposition amendment. It did not form part of the original overall scheme of FSMA 2000 and it is difficult to see how it adds to the FSA's other powers. It requires a positive resolution by statutory instrument to establish a scheme, and to date this power has only been implemented to continue the pre-FSMA 2000 review of personal pensions widely sold by firms between 1988 and 1994.[2]

### 6.2.4.2   *The FSA's remedial action on an unapproved change of control*

The FSA is empowered to require a person who has failed to obtain the FSA approval to acquire shares in a firm to take remedial action. Section 189 enables the FSA to issue a restriction notice, which has the effect of freezing[3] shares that were acquired in breach of the provisions of FSMA 2000.

---

[2]  Transitional Provisions (Reviews of Pensions Business) Order (2001/2512).

[3]  The FSA can use this power to avoid the transfer of shares, to restrict the holder of the shares from exercising their voting rights or from acquiring further shares or from receiving payment of any sums due on the shares.

### 6.2.4.3   *Investors' remedial action for unauthorised investment business and financial promotions*

Sections 26 to 30 FSMA 2000 empower individual investors to take their own remedial action when they have dealt with a person acting in breach of either of the two key restrictions of FSMA 2000:

(a)   the need to obtain authorisation; and
(b)   the requirement that financial promotions are issued or approved by an authorised person.

These Sections provide that agreements made by or through a person carrying on a regulated activity in breach of FSMA 2000 (i.e. without authorisation), or in consequence of the issue of an unapproved financial promotion, may be unenforceable. Where this is the case, the other party may be able to apply to the court to claim restitution and compensation. The court has discretion to allow the agreement to be enforced if it is satisfied that it is just and equitable to do so.

### 6.2.4.4   *Investors' remedial action for breach of the FSA rules*

A private investor who suffers loss in consequence of a firm's breach of certain of the FSA's rules – notably for breaches of the Conduct of Business Rules – can bring a claim against that firm for damages pursuant to Section 150. Private investors rarely invoke this Section because of the time and expense involved in bringing court proceedings. Instead, they will normally complain to the firm in question and, if still dissatisfied, will take their complaint to FOS.

### 6.2.4.5   *Financial Services Compensation Scheme*

An investor who suffers loss at the hands of a firm that becomes insolvent, or which is otherwise unable to satisfy claims, may be able to obtain redress in the form of financial compensation through the operation of the Financial Services Compensation Scheme established under Part XV of FSMA 2000.

### 6.2.4.6   *The FSA's power to seek an order for remedial action*

The FSA has the power under Section 380(2) FSMA 2000 to apply to the court for an order that anyone who has contravened FSMA 2000 and certain other provisions, or who has been knowingly concerned in a breach of a requirement imposed by or under FSMA 2000, shall take appropriate remedial steps. This power is potentially applicable to any person – a firm or an individual whether or not authorised by the FSA, individually approved or otherwise.

The meaning of "knowingly concerned" was considered in the case of *Securities and Investments Board* v *Pantell*[4] where this phrase was used in a similar section of the Financial Services Act 1986.[5] In *Pantell* the question was whether solicitors who had acted in a fraudulent share sale could be held liable as being "knowingly concerned" in the transaction and therefore liable to pay compensation to the wronged investors. Although the correct construction of the term "knowingly concerned" was not directly addressed in this case, it was held that in authorising the transfer of sums paid by investors into the second defendants' account, in making arrangements for the collection of monies from investors and in attempting to set up a bank account for the defendant company, the solicitors were "knowingly concerned" in the breach and therefore liable under the Act. This was despite several issues being raised by the defendants as to the interpretation of the relevant provisions of the Financial Services Act 1986 relating to the payment of compensation and whether this was restricted to actual contraveners only. The meaning of this expression as used in FSMA 2000 has been considered in the recent case of *Financial Services Authority* v *Martin*[6] where it was held that the former solicitors of an individual in breach of Section 3 of the Financial Services Act 1986 had, in circumstances similar to those in *Pantell*, been knowingly concerned in that breach and that under Section 380(2) FSMA 2000 the court therefore had power to make an order against the solicitors even though they were not the actual contraveners.

A further example of when the FSA may use Section 380(2) is where a firm has failed to observe the applicable Conduct of Business Rules and in consequence customers have suffered, or will suffer, detriment. In such circumstances the FSA may request the firm to take remedial action and, if it indicates that it will refuse to do so, the FSA may then threaten to use this Section in order to compel the firm to take that action.

---

[4] SA (No. 2) [1993] Ch. 256.
[5] Section 6 Financial Services Act 1986.
[6] (Ch D) 21 December 2004 (unreported).

There are three types of order that the court can make under Section 380:[7]

(a)    to restrain a contravention;
(b)    to take steps to remedy a contravention;
(c)    to secure assets.

The FSA states in ENF 6.6 that it will take into account matters including the following:

(a)    the nature and seriousness of the contravention, whether the losses suffered or assets at risk are substantial and whether the number of consumers who have suffered loss or at risk are substantial;
(b)    whether the contravening conduct has stopped or is likely to stop and whether any steps have been taken to ensure the interests of consumers are adequately protected;
(c)    whether there is a danger of assets being dissipated;
(d)    whether there are remedial steps that could be taken;
(e)    the costs of enforcing any remedial action.

### 6.2.4.7    *The FSA's power to seek an order for restitution*

Where a person has made profits, or others have suffered loss, because of the breach of FSMA 2000 and certain other provisions then, under Section 382 FSMA 2000, the FSA may seek a court order regarding the distribution of profits or award of compensation for loss to affected persons. There is a corresponding provision relating to market abuse in Section 383 FSMA 2000. The FSA may act directly against an authorised person under Section 384.

Section 382 empowers the court to order that those who may have been wronged by a contravention of FSMA 2000 will be compensated. An order under this Section can require the contravener to pay to the FSA such sums as the court may find just, having regard to the amount of profit that may have been accrued and/or any loss that may have been suffered. It is then for the FSA to distribute these monies to those persons whom the court has directed to be paid –

---

[7] Similar provisions in Section 381 relate to where there has been or is likely to be market abuse.

those who suffered loss or other adverse effect or to whom the profits were attributable.

The FSA's policy in relation to the exercise of its powers under this Section is set out in the FSA's Enforcement Sourcebook ("ENF") rule 9.6, which states that the FSA may seek a restitution order where:

(a)   there are quantifiable profits or identifiable losses;
(b)   there are significant losses, or losses for a large number of people;
(c)   other remedies, such as through litigation or the FOS, are unavailable or inappropriate; or
(d)   the exercise of another of the FSA's powers, such as in relation to insolvency, is not more appropriate.

Under Section 384 the FSA may of its own accord, without recourse to the courts, make an administrative order against an authorised person.[8] Such an order can be made requiring an authorised person to pay or distribute such amounts as are considered appropriate by the FSA where it is satisfied that one or more events has taken place. These are where an authorised person has contravened a requirement of FSMA 2000 or has been knowingly concerned in such contravention, has engaged in market abuse or encouraged another person to do so, and in any such case profits have accrued as a result, or one or more persons have suffered loss or have been otherwise adversely affected.

On discovery that there has been a contravention of FSMA 2000, the FSA therefore has the option of exercising its own administrative powers under Section 384 to obtain redress from firms or to apply to the court to exercise the powers under Sections 382 and 383. Generally, the FSA will employ its own administrative powers before applying to the court to take action. However, this may not always be considered the most appropriate action and there may be cases where the FSA will seek a court order under Sections 382 and 383 in the first instance. Examples of when this might occur are contained in ENF 9.7 as follows:

---

[8] Unlike the powers of the court under Section 380(2), administrative orders made by the FSA can only be made against authorised persons.

(a) where the FSA want to combine an order for restitution with other court action such as for an injunction;
(b) where the FSA wishes to bring related court proceedings against an unauthorised person where the factual basis is likely to be the same as the restitution claim;
(c) where the FSA suspects that the firm may not comply with an administrative requirement to give restitution and feels that a court order may be needed to ensure compliance.

## 6.3 Identifying the requirement to take remedial action

This section examines the different ways that the requirement to take remedial action may be identified by a firm or by the FSA.

### 6.3.1 *Identified by the firm*

The need to take remedial action may be identified by a firm on its own initiative or as a result of a complaint. The firm may need to disclose this to the FSA, which expects a firm to provide information voluntarily, including communicating circumstances where significant remedial action is required. Specifically, firms are expected to cooperate with the FSA under Principle 11 and freely disclose information to it, and are additionally required under the FSA Supervision Sourcebook ("SUP") rule 15 to provide certain specified notifications to the FSA.[9]

If concerns arise, the FSA may perform an investigation and, in complex or detailed cases, appoint a skilled person under Section 166 FSMA 2000. The terms of appointment of a skilled person may include the requirement to identify appropriate remedial action and supervise its performance.[10]

### 6.3.2 *Identified by the FSA – supervisory visit*

Alternatively, the need to take remedial action may be identified by the FSA as a result of a supervisory visit. The FSA's approach to

[9] Described further in Chapter 4 above.
[10] The use of skilled persons is dealt with in detail in Chapter 5 above.

supervision involves obtaining information by inspection visits and other means about a firm, its controllers, its financial standing, the people it deals with, and the investments and sectors in which it operates. The FSA then analyses the risk that the firm presents in light of that information – risk of breaches of rules or principles, possible customer detriment and risk to the FSA's objectives.[11] The FSA may – and often does – require that a firm take remedial action on the basis of information obtained in this way.

### 6.3.3 Identified by the FSA – ARROW visit

The need to take remedial action may also arise in consequence of an ARROW visit. ARROW is the FSA's risk-based approach for assessing material risks incurred by individual firms.[12] The FSA has carried out risk assessments on most firms that it considers are potentially high risk or high impact. At the conclusion of the visit the FSA will usually provide the firm with a Risk Mitigation Programme. This is intended to be proportionate to the risk posed by the firm and will take into account the strength (or otherwise) of its internal controls. It usually comprises a number of outcome-specific regulatory actions to be taken by the firm, and may thus be viewed as a series of required remedial actions.

## 6.4 The key standards that underlie the requirement to take remedial action

It is not practicable to provide a complete list of all the FSA rules of which breach can result in a firm being required to take remedial action because, in principle, nearly every rule is capable of having this effect. Nevertheless, practical experience of the FSA's operations during the first few years of its existence has indicated a number of key areas, which are discussed below.

### 6.4.1 The FSA's Principles for Business

The FSA's Principles for Business are intended to be a general statement of the fundamental obligations that a firm must observe. The

---

[11] *See* SUP 1 and Consultation Paper ("CP") 30.
[12] The FSA's risk-based regulatory approach, February 2003.

FSA's requirement to take remedial action is frequently based upon failure to observe these principles. Five principles upon which a requirement to take remedial action is often based are discussed below, together with examples of the remedial action that the FSA has required to be taken where they are not observed:

(a)   A firm must conduct its business with skill, care and diligence (Principle 2). Where, for example, a custodian had inadequate systems and controls and in consequence failed to administer customers' accounts properly, the FSA required it to compensate its customers for the resulting losses.

(b)   A firm must maintain adequate financial resources (Principle 4). The FSA may, by way of example, require a firm to increase its capital, maintain a margin above required capital, or refrain from certain transactions in circumstances where the FSA does not consider that it is maintaining adequate capital resources.

(c)   A firm must treat customers fairly (Principle 6). Breach of this principle frequently underlies the requirement to take remedial action. The FSA interprets this principle widely, considering that "fairness" includes fulfilling legitimate expectations.[13] For example, if pre-sale material suggests that a product or service will have certain characteristics, the FSA may require a firm to fulfil the description. Where a firm's marketing material included the statement that, if a fund grew at X per cent per annum then it would be worth £Y after 10 years, then even though this was inconsistent with the terms of the contract, the FSA considered that it should be treated as a term of the contract in view of its prominence in the marketing material because to do otherwise would not be treating customers fairly.

(d)   A firm must manage conflicts fairly (Principle 8). By way of example, the FSA will require a fund manager to compensate customers who have been disadvantaged because the firm failed to manage the conflict between its own and its customers' interests fairly in relation to the allocation of proprietary and customer trades in the same securities.

(e)   A firm must ensure suitability of advice (Principle 9). Failure to observe this requirement, which is principally relevant to retail

---

[13] Treating Customers Fairly, Discussion Paper June 2001.

sales, is probably the most frequent cause of the need to take remedial action. This may take the form of varying the investment product to take into account the investor's requirements, returning the investment monies or, where neither of these is appropriate, providing compensation.

### 6.4.2   Other parts of the FSA Handbook

Aside from the Principles, duties arising under other parts of the FSA Handbook commonly underlie the requirement that a firm takes remedial action, and they are often used together with the Principles for this purpose.

#### 6.4.2.1   Financial promotions

The FSA's fundamental requirement is that a firm's financial promotions are clear, fair and not misleading. This rule is derived from Principle 7 which calls for clear customer communications. Given that financial promotions, other than to private investors, are "exempt promotions" to which detailed Conduct of Business Rules do not apply, most remedial action for breach of this requirement has been taken by firms in relation to retail advertising. The FSA focuses on lack of balance in the description of benefits; misleading claims that create unrealistic expectations; and important information hidden in small print.[14] The FSA often requires firms to take remedial action over misleading advertisements. Between October 2002 and March 2003 it received over 2,000 complaints in relation to financial promotions; in 82 cases it required the firm to withdraw or change its advertising and on eight occasions the firm was required to write to its customers, point out further risks, and offer a refund.[15] In December 2004 the FSA reported that since enlarging the department and setting up a dedicated hotline in July 2004, it had investigated 397 cases, of which 60 were pursued with various outcomes, including getting the promotion amended or remedial action offered. Sixty-four were not pursued and 162 were ongoing. Of the 115 reports received via the hotline, 47 were for mortgages and 68 for investment products.[16]

---

[14] The FSA's Approach to Financial Promotions, April 2002.
[15] The FSA's press release "FSA takes action on poor advertising", July 2003.
[16] FSA Financial Promotions Consumer Bulletin, December 2004.

### 6.4.2.2 *Fair dealing*

These rules are associated with Principle 6 – treating customers fairly. The FSA's rules impose a requirement that, when dealing in equities on an advisory basis or acting as discretionary manager, transactions must be in the customer's best interest, together with a requirement to achieve best and timely execution and fair allocation. When these rules apply, failure to observe these duties may result in a firm being required to reverse an improper transaction, refund inappropriate charges or to compensate where, for instance, a transaction was not executed on a timely basis and resulted in a customer suffering loss.

### 6.4.2.3 *Client assets*

These rules are based upon Principle 10, which requires firms to safeguard client assets. Failure to segregate clients' funds or investments from those of the firm or of other clients in accordance with the FSA's custody or client money requirements frequently underlies a requirement to perform remedial action.

### 6.4.2.4 *Money laundering*

A failure to carry out the requisite know-your-customer identification checks at point of client take-on may result in the FSA requiring that these actions are performed at a later date.

### 6.4.2.5 *Collective investments*

There are a number of detailed requirements that firms occasionally breach under the FSA's Collective Investment Schemes Sourcebook ("CIS"), typically failing to price units correctly or perform the necessary reconciliations, and the FSA will require a firm to take remedial action accordingly.

### 6.4.2.6 *Systems and controls*

The FSA attaches considerable importance to a firm maintaining adequate systems and controls to control the risks to which it is exposed. This is based on Principle 2, which requires firms to operate competently. Some examples of remedial action that the FSA may require firms to take in order to enhance their systems and controls include the following, which show the breadth of duties arising under this heading:

(a)  to enhance the quality and contents of management information;
(b)  to exercise increased control over outsourcing;

(c)     to appoint additional experienced non-executive directors to the board;
(d)     to improve anti-money laundering systems; or
(e)     to clarify the responsibility of joint chief executives.

Each of these requirements is derived from the FSA's Systems and Controls Sourcebook ("SYSC").

### 6.4.2.7    Senior management responsibility

The FSA's Sourcebook for Approved Persons ("APER") contains the Principles for Senior Management. These require that an individual working for a firm and approved by the FSA in a senior management position must control the part of the business for which he is responsible, and ensure that it is compliant. Examples of remedial action that the FSA can require where these obligations are breached include:

(a)     improving reporting lines so that senior management receives adequate reports from subordinates;
(b)     ensuring that a manager's key staff are sufficiently qualified and experienced;
(c)     requiring that a manager properly supervises his delegates; and
(d)     ensuring that staff have proper job descriptions and are regularly held to account.

It will be noted these remedial actions are similar to those that may be required in relation to a firm's systems and controls, and in practice the two often overlap.

### 6.4.2.8    Financial requirements

The FSA will require a firm to take remedial action over the adequacy of its financial resources. A firm may be obliged to increase its financial resources to meet or, occasionally, exceed regulatory requirements, or to refrain from undertaking certain transactions that may have the effect of weakening its financial stability.

## 6.5    How the FSA enforces remedial action

The FSA's fundamental position is that a firm's management is responsible for ensuring that it is compliant, and the FSA therefore looks to management to identify the need for, and implement, remedial action. However, where management has not taken or (relatively unusually) will not agree to take remedial action, the FSA has appropriate reserve powers.

### 6.5.1 To discipline

The FSA has power to take disciplinary action against a firm or an individual, although the result of discipline is restricted to fining or issuing a public statement or, in very serious cases, removing a firm's authorisation or an individual's approved person status. However, the FSA can and does use its ability to take disciplinary action as an incentive for firms to take remedial action. In particular, a private warning addressed to a firm or an individual, which the FSA may issue when it considers that rules may have been breached but formal disciplinary action is not justified, may be used to convey the required remedial action. It is common for final notices to record the fact that, in addition to whatever sanction has been imposed, a firm has, or has agreed to, take remedial action.[17]

### 6.5.2 To injunct

In addition to the FSA's powers to seek orders from the court for remedial action and restitution, it can also seek an injunction under Section 380(1) FSMA 2000 to prevent an ongoing or anticipated breach. Section 381(1) provides a similar power in cases of market abuse.

The FSA policy on the use of injunctions is contained in ENF 6.6 and includes their use where the matter in question would otherwise go unremedied. The FSA is prepared to use this power to require a firm to take remedial action by ceasing, or refraining from committing, a breach that it is otherwise refusing to take.

---

[17] For example, the final notice issued to Lloyds TSB Bank plc 24 September 2003 referred not only to the fine of £1.9 million which was imposed but also to the fact that Lloyds had agreed to pay £98 million in compensation to those investors that had suffered loss or been adversely affected.

A Practitioner's Guide to FSA Investigations and Enforcement

### 6.5.3 To issue a supervisory notice

The FSA can require a firm to take remedial action by altering its Part IV permission.[18] This process is commenced by the issue of a supervisory notice, and enables the FSA to insert into a firm's permissions a requirement that it takes, or refrains from taking, any given action. A firm that fails to obey this variation to its permission may then be subjected to the exercise of the FSA's other remedial powers discussed in this chapter. Section 45 establishes the criteria for the exercise of this power.

It enables the FSA to exercise this power if it appears to it that a firm is failing, or is likely to fail, to satisfy the threshold conditions or it is desirable to exercise the power in order to protect the interests of consumers or potential consumers.

This Section makes it clear that the exercise of this power may be triggered by two events. The first is failure to satisfy the threshold conditions, which includes having adequate resources and being fit and proper. The second is where it is desirable to protect the interests of consumers, which is equally wide.

Section 44 states the methods by which a Part IV permission can be varied. These are:

(a) adding a regulated activity to those for which it gives permission;
(b) removing a regulated activity from those for which it gives permission;
(c) varying the description of a regulated activity for which it gives permission;
(d) cancelling a requirement imposed under Section 43; or
(e) varying such a requirement.

Section 43 indicates that the requirement imposed in the Part IV permission may be positive or negative. That is to say they may require the person concerned to take specified action or refrain from taking specified action.

---

[18] The situations when a supervisory notice may be issued include (Section 395(13)) the variation of a Part IV permission on the FSA's own initiative (Section 53(4), (7) and (8)(b)).

The FSA's procedures for the issue of a supervisory notice are contained in the FSA's Decision Making Sourcebook ("DEC") rule 3 and provide that the notice must:

(a)   be in writing;
(b)   give the FSA's reasons;
(c)   inform the recipient that they may make representations to the FSA; and
(d)   inform the recipient that they may refer the matter to the Tribunal.

## 6.6   Particular aspects of remedial action

This section reviews three particular aspects of the FSA's powers to require remedial action: whether the FSA seeks publicity, whether the required extent of remedial action may be constrained by shortage of funds, and the application of remedial action to individuals.

### 6.6.1   Publicity

In contrast to the FSA's exercise of its powers of discipline, where its policy is almost invariably to give publicity to the taking of disciplinary action, the FSA does not necessarily require that publicity be given when a firm takes, or it requires a firm to take, remedial action.[19] In the first place, there will be no need for publicity for minor or routine remedial action. However, where a firm takes or is required to take major remedial action, perhaps involving contacting many thousands of customers and offering compensation, then the FSA may require that this is publicised. There are two reasons for this. The first is where the publicity is needed to bring the availability of the redress to the attention of affected customers. This may arise where the firm does not have a full list of its customers. Second, the FSA may wish to publicise that it has required a firm to undertake major remedial work where this is indicative of the exercise of its powers of investor protection, particularly where the remedial action forms part of a disciplinary settlement. However, this is by no means a fixed rule and there have been circumstances where firms have offered significant redress to large classes of customer at the FSA's behest and in

---

[19]  ENF 2.

respect of serious rule breaches where the FSA has not required the issue of any public statement. The FSA states at ENF 6.11 that, where it has taken successful action through the courts (e.g. under Section 382 or Section 383), it will generally feel it appropriate to publish the details of such action. This is particularly true for example where the court has ordered an injunction to prohibit further illegal activity as this will prevent consumers from inadvertently dealing with the person that is the subject of the injunction. However, it is not necessarily the case that the FSA will publish all successful court actions. In all cases the FSA will give due regard to whether such publication could damage confidence in the financial system or undermine market integrity to the detriment of consumers.

### 6.6.2   Availability of funds

In principle, the requirement to take remedial action is not determined by the availability of funds. The FSA will not allow a firm with inadequate systems to continue in operation simply because it cannot afford to replace them. Similarly, where a customer has suffered, or is prospectively likely to suffer, some detriment as a result of a firm's failure to comply with the FSA's requirements, it is not acceptable for that firm to take no action on grounds of cost. If a firm has inadequate available assets, the FSA will expect it to look within its group for further assets, to its shareholders or to its insurers or, where the detriment is attributable to the default of some third party, to recover its loss by litigation. Ultimately, if insufficient funds are available and the firm becomes insolvent, then it is the responsibility of the Financial Services Compensation Scheme to offer the possibility of compensation to affected investors.

In practice though, the FSA is prepared to take a pragmatic stance. Although there is no specific rule determining this approach, current experience is that the FSA is prepared to work with a resource-constrained firm to identify ways of it providing redress without making the firm insolvent. This is conducive to achievement of two of the FSA's statutory objectives and Principles of Good Regulation. First, by enabling the firm to stay in business, the FSA is ensuring that the service that it provides to its other customers is not disrupted. Also, where the firm forms a major part of the financial system, then its failure might give rise to systemic risk. Second, by assisting the firm to prioritise and stagger the making of redress, perhaps over several years, the FSA would view itself as acting proportionately.

### 6.6.3 *Individuals*

Remedial action is most often taken by, or required of, firms. This may be action that a firm has to take in relation to an individual, for example that:

(a)  a senior manager be replaced because he is insufficiently skilled;
(b)  an individual with stated experience be added to strengthen the Board; or
(c)  a manager's reporting lines are altered.

However, there are instances where the remedial action will be directed at an approved individual, for instance:

(a)  that he re-train;[20]
(b)  that he changes his duties so that he has no unsupervised contact with investors; or
(c)  that he ceases performing any regulated function.

These occasions are relatively unusual, and the examples given occurred in the context of the settlement of disciplinary action where they were conveyed to the individuals in private warnings.

## 6.7  The extent of financial remedial action

There are two principal types of financial remedial action that a firm may take in order to provide redress to a financially disadvantaged customer.

---

[20] In the press release issued by the FSA on 24 December 2004 relating to the Split Capital Investment Trust settlement it was noted that private warnings to certain individuals had been given by the FSA and that those individuals agreed to undertake remedial measures including: redeployment/removal of supervision responsibilities; refresher training; increased supervision; and/or undertakings not to perform particular controlled functions/work in the financial services industry for specified periods.

The first is based upon the contractual measure of damages, which is applicable where a firm has failed, or stated that it will fail, to implement a promise that it has made to a customer. This promise may be, for example, that the return on an investment will be 5 per cent per annum or growth will equal 30 per cent after four years. However, under the principle of treating customers fairly, the promise may be implied by the FSA from the wording of the contractual or pre-contractual material. A particular example is where the FSA extrapolated a contractual promise from a pre-sale illustration provided to purchasers of mortgage endowment policies. This document gave three rates of return, one stating "if the funds grow at 9 per cent then this will pay off your mortgage" and the FSA has required affected firms to treat this statement as a promise and to implement it.

The second is based upon the tortious measure of compensation. This is effectively to put the customer back in the position he would have been had he been properly advised. This is the measure of compensation awarded by FOS and offered by firms where there is no specific breach of promise. It also equates to the measure of damages for breach of statutory duty arising under Section 150 FSMA 2000 were an investor to take action against a firm on the basis of a rule breach, although this is a rare occurrence because the matter more often forms the subject of a complaint to the firm or to FOS, neither of which involves legal expenses or the requirement to argue one's case in any great detail. The extent of tortious redress awarded depends upon the circumstances. At its simplest it may be a return of the investment, often with interest determined at the generous FOS (and court) rate of 8 per cent per annum. Where an unsuitable investment was sold, and the customer should have been offered another, such as a repayment mortgage instead of an interest only mortgage, or where the investor should have been advised to invest in gilts rather than in a higher-risk investment, then the award may be the sum of money that the customer's investment would now be worth had they received such advice.

## 6.8  Managing remedial action

In view of the great number of different situations that can underlie the need for a firm to take remedial action, it is not practicable to lay down any hard and fast rules of how a firm should approach the task. It is nonetheless possible to offer some suggestions based upon current experience of how firms have handled this and how the FSA has reacted. In the following paragraphs it is assumed, as is usually the case, that the firm is voluntarily undertaking remedial action and is not being compelled to do so by the FSA in exercise of the powers described elsewhere in this chapter.

### 6.8.1  Scoping the issue

The firm's first task should be to scope the matter that has caused the problem. It should swiftly, but thoroughly, investigate the matter to ascertain what has gone wrong, how many investors have been affected and to what extent. Any urgent remedial action, for example to stem further losses or to repair an obvious system fault, should be taken immediately.

### 6.8.2  Project plan

The firm should then prepare a project plan addressing the following aspects of the issue.

(a)  First, the firm should carry out a root cause analysis – what went wrong, why did it go wrong and what lessons can be learned? The purpose of this is to ensure that whatever caused the need to offer redress will not recur. This may call for an alteration to procedures, staff retraining or perhaps redesign of a product or service.

(b)  Next, the firm should take steps to confirm that its wider systems and controls are sufficiently robust to protect against the occurrence of events similar to, but not necessarily identical to, the specific problem in question.

(c)  Finally, the firm must determine whether to offer redress to affected investors and, if so, the method and amount of that redress.

### 6.8.3  Project management

The firm should ensure that it has adequate project management resources to handle the systems and remediation project. There should be a formal methodology with appropriate milestones and periodical reports. Senior management should be closely involved throughout the project. The project team must have the necessary skills to address the different aspects of root cause analysis, wider systems and controls, and remediation. If the team is made up internally, for example Compliance or Internal Audit, the firm must ensure that they operate to a protocol and standards that the FSA will find acceptable. Where outside resources are employed, the firm must keep close control over their work. In either case all reports must be robust and indicate that the firm is seeking to treat customers fairly as well as to protect its own commercial interests.

### 6.8.4    Contacting the FSA

The FSA should be notified of any material remedial action that a firm needs to take, especially when arising from a systemic weakness rather than an isolated cause. Such notification may arise under Principle for Business 11 or under one of the specific provisions of the Supervision Manual. While the FSA rightly expects to be informed as soon as a notifiable matter arises, it is advisable for a firm first to scope the matter and to identify the broad parameters of its remedial action so that, when making contact with the FSA, it can demonstrate that it has understood the fundamental aspects of the issue without needing the FSA to help it do so.

Regulatory tools available to the FSA at this juncture (in addition to the possibility of disciplinary action against the firm or approved individuals) are:

(a)    To investigate why the event that has given rise to the need for disciplinary action has occurred. The FSA is less likely to do this where it has confidence that the firm will itself carry out a proper analysis and identify what systems and controls require enhancement.

(b)    To appoint a skilled person under Section 166 FSMA 2000. This is typically done to perform, or to oversee the firm's performance of, the identification and compensation of affected investors. A firm that produces a robust plan and has adequate resources to discharge it – for which *see* 6.8.5 below – may satisfy the FSA that it can be trusted to perform this task without a skilled person being appointed.

Depending on the seriousness of the matter the FSA is likely to remain involved until it has been resolved. In any case the FSA is likely to require the submission of periodical progress reports until the remediation project has been completed.

### 6.8.5   *Investor compensation exercise*

Where investors have suffered loss because of the firm's act or omission, then they may be due redress. Where financial compensation is due, the FSA will expect the firm to take steps to ensure that appropriate compensation is received within a suitable period. In such circumstances the firm should:

(a)   Ensure that it has correctly identified affected investors, including those who have become, or ceased to be, investors during the affected period.

(b)   Determine a formula for quantifying investors' losses and, if appropriate, agree this with the FSA.

(c)   Prepare a form of communication notifying investors of the compensation that is being provided. The FSA may require that this makes clear what has taken place, and may also require that investors be reminded of their right to complain to the Financial Ombudsman Service. Where it is necessary for the investor to claim compensation rather than have a cash injection made into the product, then an initial contact letter will usually need to be followed by two reminders one month apart.

(d)   Manage the investor contact and remediation exercise fairly and efficiently. Steps should be taken to trace investors for whom a current address is not held; compensation should be paid quickly; and any complaints or queries should be properly investigated and fairly resolved.

# Chapter 7

# Formal FSA Investigations: Civil Investigations

**Arun Srivastava**
Partner
Baker & McKenzie

## 7.1 Introduction

This chapter examines the investigation powers available to the Financial Services Authority ("FSA") when an investigation is formally launched by the FSA's appointment of investigators and considers how a firm should respond to the use of such powers. It covers:

(a) the circumstances in which the FSA may use its investigation powers;
(b) the nature of those powers and how the FSA may exercise them;
(c) the FSA's powers to enforce cooperation with an investigation;
(d) the limits on the FSA's investigation powers;
(e) how firms and individuals should respond to a formal investigation.

The FSA's investigation powers contained in Part XI of the Financial Services and Markets Act 2000 ("FSMA 2000") are similar in nature to the powers exercised by the FSA's predecessor regulators but are broader. In particular, the FSMA 2000 has given the FSA much wider powers to gather information from those who are not regulated and to enforce their cooperation. The FSA's approach to the use of its investigation powers is set out in the Enforcement Manual, which forms part of the FSA's Handbook of Rules and Guidance. It is likely that the Enforcement Manual will be deleted from the FSA's Handbook of Rules and Guidance. In CP 07/2 the FSA has stated that it intends to replace the Enforcement Manual with a new

Enforcement Guide, which will not form part of the FSA's Handbook of Rules and Guidance. Reference is made below to the draft text of the Enforcement Guide. At the time of writing, this text was under consultation and therefore subject to change.

This chapter concentrates on "civil" investigations, that is investigations where the likely outcome is the use of civil rather than criminal sanctions by the FSA. Chapter 8 is a counterpart chapter, looking at formal investigations where criminal penalties may be the outcome. Market abuse investigations are dealt with in Chapter 8 because it is generally prudent for those under investigation and their advisers to treat such investigations, at least in the early stages, as though they could lead to criminal sanctions.

Some of the investigation powers given by Parliament to the FSA are also granted to the Secretary of State. This chapter does not specifically mention where investigation powers can also be exercised by the Secretary of State, and instead concentrates on the FSA's use of those powers.

## 7.2 The circumstances in which the FSA may use its powers of investigation and the nature of those powers

### 7.2.1 Background

The FSA's investigation powers should be considered in light of the FSA's statutory objectives found in Sections 2 to 6 FSMA 2000. These statutory objectives are:

(a)  maintaining confidence in the financial system;
(b)  promoting public awareness of the financial system;
(c)  securing an appropriate degree of protection for consumers; and
(d)  reducing the extent to which a business carried on by a regulated person or in breach of the general prohibition can be used for the purpose of financial crime.

These statutory objectives will inform the FSA's decision to use its investigation powers. For example, in deciding to launch an investigation into alleged misselling by an authorised person the FSA will have regard to its consumer protection objective and the objective of maintaining confidence in the financial system. In considering whether to investigate a possible breach of the general prohibition the FSA will have regard to its consumer protection objective and the objective of preventing financial crime.

Senior figures at the FSA have stated that the FSA is not an "enforcement-led" regulator. Although the FSA's Enforcement Division has a sizeable budget, it has finite resources with which to discharge its functions. Section 2(3)(a) FSMA 2000 provides that the FSA must have regard to the need to use its resources in the most efficient and economic way. These pressures mean that the FSA will not always seek to use its investigation powers where there are other methods of securing its regulatory objectives. For example, in relation to compliance issues that have arisen in respect of an FSA-authorised firm, a more expedient method of dealing with any problems may be the authorised firm investigating matters itself and reporting to its FSA supervisors on the scale of the problem. In such cases it is clearly important for firms to implement effective remedial action promptly, as if the firm does not do this the FSA is likely to take action in relation to the original breach.

The Report of the Strachan Review ("the Report") emphasised that the FSA is a risk-based regulator, meaning that its enforcement resources will be directed towards issues which are likely to have the greatest impact on the FSA's statutory objectives. The Report confirmed that cases were selected for enforcement based on their gravity and whether they fit with the FSA's overall priorities. The setting of enforcement priorities has led to criticism that the FSA may unfairly refer matters for enforcement in specified priority areas, while resolving other matters through its supervisory relationship with the firm concerned. The FSA have recognised this fact in the draft Enforcement Guide, in which the FSA state that certain cases will be subject to enforcement action and others not, even where they may be similar in nature or impact. Potential rule breaches in priority areas will therefore continue to take precedence over rule breaches in other areas in terms of allocating enforcement resources.

The draft Enforcement Guide contemplates distinct case selection criteria depending on whether the issues raised by the case concern a breach of the FSA's Threshold Conditions or not.

The FSA state that in cases involving a breach of the Threshold Conditions, enforcement action will be taken in all cases that come to the FSA's attention unless the breach can be resolved through the use of supervisory tools. Given that a breach of the Threshold Conditions, such as a failure to maintain required levels of regulatory capital, is a serious matter and implies that the firm is no longer fit and proper to be authorised, it is understandable why enforcement action will be taken where the firm does not make use of an opportunity to correct the breach by taking appropriate remedial action.

In other cases the FSA indicate that a two-stage process will be followed. The first stage will involve an assessment of the case in light of the FSA's strategic priorities. It should be noted that these are the FSA's general priorities as an organisation and not stand-alone enforcement priorities. This is consistent with the risk-based approach described above. The second stage of the process involves consideration on an individual case basis as to whether an enforcement investigation is appropriate. The FSA state in the draft Enforcement Guide that an assessment will be made as to whether the statutory requirements to found an investigation are met and also other relevant factors such as whether alternative tools are available.

The Enforcement Manual presently sets out the following non-exhaustive criteria that will influence the FSA's decision as to how to proceed:

(a)  whether there has been prejudice to the interests of consumers;
(b)  an authorised person may no longer meet the threshold conditions and therefore may need to have its Part IV permission removed;
(c)  an approved person may no longer be fit and proper to perform a controlled function;
(d)  the FSA should be concerned about the ownership or control of an authorised person;
(e)  a firm may have been used or may be being used for the purposes of financial crime, including money laundering;

(f)     the conduct of certain types of regulated activities in which a firm is involved are a cause of serious public concern;

(g)     confidentiality obligations mean that the FSA is unable to obtain all the information that it needs to identify the nature of any possible concerns.

A further important factor overlaying the above is the FSA's continued development of a principles-based model of regulation. The draft Enforcement Guide makes it clear that the FSA will rely on its Principles for Businesses as opposed to detailed rules wherever it can. To date the FSA has shown a reluctance to bring enforcement proceedings based purely on a breach of principle. However, the overall trend of the move towards a more principles-based approach, focusing on outcomes of actions, means that it is more likely that cases will be brought on this basis alone.

Before appointing investigators to investigate a particular matter in relation to an authorised person the FSA may use its information-gathering power set out in Section 165 FSMA 2000. This allows the FSA to request in writing from an authorised person specified information, information of a specified description, specified documents or documents of a specified description. The use of this power before investigators are appointed is discussed in detail in Chapter 5.

The Section 165 power is likely to be of more use to the FSA as part of its supervisory functions than as part of its enforcement functions.

The FSA may also use its power under Section 166 FSMA 2000 to require that a skilled person be appointed to report on any matter about which the FSA could itself require the provision of information or documents under its Section 165 powers. The FSA's use of this power is discussed in detail in Chapter 5. The power to require a skilled persons report is one that is more likely to be used by the FSA's supervisors than the FSA's enforcement department, although in principle it may be used in both an enforcement and a supervisory context. When the FSA originally consulted on its approach to requiring skilled persons reports there was some disquiet about the prospect of the FSA's enforcement department ordering such reports rather than investigating matters itself and incurring costs which could not be recovered from the firm under investigation in the event of successful enforcement action. The FSA made clear that it would not use its power to require skilled persons reports in substitution for an investigation. Nevertheless, the report itself may disclose concerns which will give rise to a need by the FSA to begin a formal investigation.

In the draft Enforcement Guide the FSA state that the factors that it will take into consideration in determining whether to require a report by skilled persons include:

(a) if the FSA is predominantly fact finding, that is, obtaining historic information to determine whether enforcement action is appropriate, the use of powers under Sections 167 and 168 FSMA 2000 are more likely to be appropriate;

(b) if the FSA's objectives include obtaining expert analysis or recommendations such as for the purpose of seeking remedial action, then the power under Section 166 may be appropriate, instead of or in conjunction with the exercise of other powers.

The FSA's formal investigation powers are dealt with below.

Once a matter has been accepted by the Enforcement Division, in cases involving the investigation of authorised firms or approved persons the Report recommended that the FSA should hold an initial scoping discussion as a matter of course, the purpose being to provide the firm or individual concerned with a clear indication of the scope of the investigation, the process that will be followed and evidence (individuals and documents) that the FSA's investigation team will need access to. This recommendation has been included in the draft Enforcement Guide which states that in cases involving firms or approved persons the FSA will generally hold scoping discussions with the firm or individual concerned close to the start of the investigation. The draft Enforcement Guide states that such a meeting may be held in other cases as well. Where the firm is relationship managed, the firm's supervisor may attend the initial scoping meeting. Firm's should expect the FSA to provide sufficient detail as to the nature of and reasons for the FSA's concerns and the reasons why the matter has been referred to Enforcement. It is important to use the initial scoping meeting as an opportunity to obtain as much information as possible about the scope of the investigation as this will assist the person under investigation to develop a proper under-standing of the FSA's concerns, the case it may need to meet and its response to that case. However, in practice, if the investigation is at an early stage, the amount of information that the FSA investigators are able or willing to provide may be limited. The Notice of Investigation may also be provided to the firm or individual at the meeting. However, this will only contain a very general description of the matters under investigation.

### 7.2.2  *General investigations – Section 167 FSMA 2000*

Section 167 FSMA 2000 gives the FSA power to conduct general inves-tigations in relation to:

(a)  the nature, conduct or state of business of an FSA-authorised person or appointed representative;
(b)  a particular aspect of that business;
(c)  the ownership or control of an FSA-authorised person.

FSA guidance in the Enforcement Manual states that the FSA will use its Section 167 power where the FSA has general concerns about a firm but the circumstances known to the FSA do not indicate a specific breach or contravention by the firm under investigation. After a Section 167 investigation the FSA may believe that there have been specific breaches committed by a firm. In those circumstances the FSA may proceed to investigate the firm using the powers under Section 168 of FSMA 2000, which give wider powers of investigation where specific contraventions are being investigated. The circum-stances in which the FSA may conduct an investigation under Section 168 are detailed in 7.2.3 below.

The person appointed by the FSA to conduct the investigation under Section 167 (an "investigator") is also able to supplement the investi-gation by investigating the business of a person who is or at any rele-vant time has been:

(a)  a member of the group of which the person under investigation is part; or
(b)  a partnership of which the person under investigation is a member.

The FSA's general investigation power under Section 167 may also be exercised in respect of a former FSA-authorised person or former appointed representative in respect of:

(a)  business carried on by him when he was an authorised person or an appointed representative;

(b)  the ownership or control of a former FSA-authorised person (but not an appointed representative) at any time when he was authorised.

The term "business" includes any part of a business even if it does not consist of regulated activities conducted by an authorised person or appointed representative.

Section 171 FSMA 2000 sets out the powers which are given to the person appointed by the FSA to conduct an investigation under Section 167. Such persons can:

(a)  require the person under investigation or any person connected with the person under investigation to attend before the investigator at a specified time and place and answer questions and also to provide such other information as the investigator may require;

(b)  require any person to produce at a specified time and place any specified document or documents of a specified description.

A person is connected with the person under investigation where it is a:

(a)  member of that person's group;
(b)  a controller of that person;
(c)  a partnership of which that person is a member;
(d)  (in broad terms) an officer, manager or agent of that person or the person's parent undertaking; or
(e)  (in broad terms) a person who is or was at the relevant time a partner, manager, employee, agent, appointed representative, banker, auditor, actuary, solicitor of that person, that person's parent undertaking, a subsidiary undertaking of that person, a subsidiary undertaking of a parent undertaking of that person or a parent undertaking of a subsidiary undertaking of that person.

### 7.2.3 Specific investigations under Section 168 FSMA 2000

The FSA has power to conduct specific investigations in the circumstances set out in Sections 168(1), (2) and (4). As mentioned above, an investigation under Section 168 confers on the FSA wider powers than those conferred on the FSA when it conducts a general investigation under Section 167. Further, within the context of Section 168 investigations, the FSA's powers differ depending on whether or not the investigation is conducted in the circumstances set out in Section 168(1) and (4) or the circumstances set out in Section 168(2). Broadly, Section 168(2) is concerned with investigations into more serious regulatory breaches under FSMA 2000 and criminal offences, and the FSA is given still wider information-gathering powers to enable it to tackle these more serious situations.

*7.2.3.1 Powers under Section 168(1) and (4)*
The FSA may conduct a civil investigation under Section 168(1) if it appears that a person may have contravened any regulations made by the Treasury in respect of the FSA's asset identification rules which apply to authorised insurers.[1]

The FSA may conduct a civil investigation under Section 168(4)[2] if it appears that there are circumstances suggesting that:

(a)    an authorised person may have contravened Section 20 FSMA 2000 by conducting a regulated activity for which he did not have the necessary permission;
(b)    an authorised person may have contravened a rule made by the FSA;
(c)    an individual may not be a fit and proper person to perform functions in relation to a regulated activity carried on by an authorised person or exempt person;
(d)    an individual may have performed or agreed to perform a function in breach of a prohibition order;

---

[1] Section 168(1) also applies where there are circumstances suggesting that criminal offences may have been committed under Sections 177, 191, 346 or 398(1) or under Schedule 4 to FSMA 2000 – *see* Chapter 8 for criminal investigations.
[2] Section 168(4) also applies where there are circumstances suggesting to the FSA that a person is guilty of a criminal offence under money laundering regulations – *see* Chapter 8 for criminal investigations.

(e)   an authorised or exempt person may have failed to comply with Section 56(6) FSMA 2000 (which obliges such persons to take reasonable care to prevent a person subject to a prohibition order carrying out a function in relation to a regulated activity);

(f)   an authorised person may not have complied with Section 59(1) or (2) FSMA 2000 (which obliges such a person to ensure that persons performing controlled functions on its behalf receive the FSA's prior approval);

(g)   an approved person may not be fit and proper to perform a controlled function; or

(h)   an approved person may be guilty of misconduct[3] under Section 66 FSMA 2000.

The FSA has the following powers (conferred by Section 172) when it conducts an investigation under Section 168(1) or (4):

(a)   the same powers granted to an investigator under Section 167 FSMA 2000 (on which *see* above); and

(b)   in addition, the power to require a person who is neither the person under investigation nor a person connected with the person under investigation to attend before the investigator at a specified time and place and answer questions or otherwise to provide such information as the investigator may require for the purposes of the investigation. However, such a requirement can only be imposed if the investigator is satisfied that the requirement is "necessary or expedient" for the purposes of the investigation. (A person who is not under investigation and not connected with a person under investigation might before complying, depending on the circumstances, properly question why the FSA is asking it to answer questions or provide information if the information is of a type that the FSA could obtain from an authorised firm under investigation direct. It will be appropriate to seek such clarification where it could be time consuming and costly to deal with the information request.)

---

[3] An approved person will be guilty of misconduct if, while an approved person, he has failed to comply with any of the Statements of Principle for Approved Persons or has been knowingly concerned in a contravention by the relevant authorised firm of a requirement imposed on that firm by or under FSMA 2000.

### 7.2.3.2   *Additional powers under Section 168(2)*
The FSA may conduct an investigation under Section 168(2)[4] if it appears that there are circumstances suggesting that:

(a)   there may have been a breach of the general prohibition against conducting regulated activities without authorisation or a person has been making false claims to be authorised or exempt from authorisation;
(b)   criminal offences of insider dealing (Part V Criminal Justice Act 1993) or misleading statements or practices (Section 397 FSMA 2000) may have been committed;
(c)   there may have been a breach of Section 21 FSMA 2000 (communicating a financial promotion in circumstances where the communicator is not authorised or the communication has not been approved by an authorised person);
(d)   there may have been a breach of Section 238 FSMA 2000 (promoting an unregulated collective investment scheme in circumstances outwith the FSMA 2000 (Promotion of Collective Investment Schemes) (Exemptions) Order 2001); or
(e)   market abuse as defined in Section 118 FSMA 2000 has taken place.

The FSA has the following powers (conferred by Section 173) when it conducts an investigation under Section 168(2) which are exercisable if the investigator considers that *any person* is or *may* be able to give information which is or *may be relevant* to the investigation:

(a)   the power to require any person to attend before the investigator at a specified time and place and answer questions or otherwise to provide such information as the investigator may require for the purposes of the investigation;
(b)   the power to require any person to produce at a specified time and place any required document or documents of a specified

---

[4] All of the contraventions to which Section 168(2) applies, save for market abuse under Section 118, attract criminal sanctions. Although criminal investigations are dealt with in Chapter 8, it is relevant to discuss the Section 168(2) powers here as many firms and individuals required to provide information or answer questions under these powers will not themselves be under investigation; further, at the commencement of the investigation using these powers the investigators may be looking at circumstances rather than specific individuals or firms that are suspected.

description which appear to the investigator to relate to any matter relevant to the investigation; and

(c) the power to require any person to give the investigator *all assistance* in connection with the investigation which the person is *reasonably* able to give.

This is a wide power directed at any person who may have relevant information, regardless of whether that person is a suspect. Investigators are given a wide discretion with no statutory "necessary or expedient" test that need be satisfied.

### 7.2.4 *Investigations in support of overseas regulators*

Section 169 FSMA 2000 gives the FSA power to conduct an investigation at the request of an overseas regulator. In those circumstances the FSA may ask an authorised person or connected person to provide information or documents using its Section 165 power, or appoint investigators to investigate any matter. Any investigator so appointed has the same powers as an investigator appointed under Section 168(1) (*see* above). This means that the investigators can exercise their powers in respect of persons who are not regulated by it if they are satisfied that it is necessary or expedient to do so.

The FSA is not bound to request information or investigate at the request of an overseas regulator. If the request has been made by a competent authority in another EU state then the FSA must decide whether or not the exercise of its investigative power is necessary to comply with a community obligation.

In relation to requests that have been made by regulators that are not made pursuant to an EU obligation, the FSA must take into account before deciding whether or not to exercise its investigation power the following matters:

(a) whether in the country or territory of the overseas regulator concerned, corresponding assistance would be given to a UK regulatory authority;

(b) whether the case concerns the breach of a law or other requirements which has no close parallel in the UK or involves the assertion of a jurisdiction not recognised by the UK;

(c)   the seriousness of the case and its importance to persons in the UK; and

(d)   whether it is otherwise appropriate in the public interest to give the assistance sought.

Further, the FSA may decide not to exercise its investigative powers unless the overseas regulator decides to make a contribution towards the costs of its exercise as the FSA considers appropriate.

In the case of requests made in relation to EU obligations which the FSA believes that it must comply with, the FSA is not bound to consider the circumstances set out above, nor to ask for a contribution to its investigative costs.

If the FSA decides to appoint an investigator in response to a request by an overseas regulator, it may direct the investigator to permit a representative of the overseas regulator to attend and take part in any interview conducted for the purposes of the investigation. However, such a direction will only be given where the FSA is satisfied that any information obtained by an overseas regulator as a result of the interview will be subject to confidentiality safeguards equivalent to those set out in Part XXIII of FSMA 2000.

In relation to attendance at an interview by an overseas regulator, the FSA has published a statement of its policy which has been approved by the Treasury. The FSA's policy contains the following elements:

(a)   The FSA will consider whether to direct an investigator to permit the attendance at the interview by an overseas regulator's representative at the same time that it considers the initial request, and also after it has appointed investigators.

(b)   Any direction will identify the representative of the overseas regulator permitted to attend an interview and the role he will play in the interview.

(c)   Notwithstanding the attendance at the interview by the overseas regulator's representative, the FSA's investigator will have conduct of the interview. This means that the FSA's investigator will instigate and conclude the interview, introduce everyone present and explain the procedures of the interview. The FSA's investigator will issue the appropriate warnings in relation to a refusal by the person interviewed to answer questions. It is for the FSA's investigator to determine the length of the interview and when any break should occur. The FSA's investigator will be responsible for making a record of the interview. The FSA's investigator can also suspend the interview and ask the overseas representative to leave.

(d) Notwithstanding the fact that the FSA will control the interview, the representative of the overseas regulator may assist in preparation for the interview. Further, the FSA may permit the representative to attend and ask questions of the interviewee in the course of the interview. In practice, the representative's involvement can be considerable.

(e) In relation to documents, the FSA's investigator will decide which documents need to be produced to the interviewee. If the overseas regulator's representative wishes to produce documents and ask questions on them, those documents can be inspected by the FSA's investigator who may suspend an interview if he has not previously had the opportunity to inspect them.

(f) Interviews will be conducted in English, notwithstanding the presence of any translators. All compulsory interviews will be tape recorded. The interviewee will be provided with a copy of the tapes of the interview, but not the transcripts unless he agrees to meet the cost of producing them.

(g) The interviewee may be accompanied at the interview by a legal adviser or non-legally qualified observer of his choice. The person attending with the interviewee can be a person familiar with the interviewee's home jurisdiction. However, the FSA reserves the right to continue with the interview if it is not possible to find such a person to attend that interview within a reasonable time.

### 7.2.5 Investigations in relation to collective investment schemes and open-ended investment companies

In addition to its investigative powers described above, the FSA has specific powers to appoint investigators to examine the affairs of any collective investment scheme or of the manager, operator, trustee or depositary of such a scheme,[5] and to investigate and report on the

---

[5] Section 284 FSMA 2000.

142

affairs of an open-ended investment company, or a director or depository of an open-ended investment company.[6]

These powers can be exercised if it appears to the FSA that it is in the interest of the collective investment scheme's participants or potential participants to do so, or it appears that it is in the interest of shareholders or potential shareholders of the open-ended investment company, or in either case, that there is a matter of public concern.

In the case of collective investment schemes and open-ended investment companies, the FSA's powers are very similar. The FSA's investigator can:

(a)   require a person to produce to the investigator any documents in his possession or under his control which appear to be relevant to the investigation;

(b)   require the person to attend before the FSA investigator; and

(c)   require the person to give the FSA investigator all assistance in connection with the investigation which that person is reasonably able to give.

## 7.3   The conduct of investigations

As shown in the paragraphs above, the FSA's powers of investigation are wide ranging. In a number of circumstances the powers can be exercised not just in relation to the regulated community but also to members of the general public. The methods that the FSA will use to conduct an investigation are in part a function of the powers granted by Parliament and partly a product of the policies it has set out in its Enforcement Manual. The FSA's investigation process can be broken down into a number of distinct phases once the FSA has decided to investigate:

(a)   the giving of the Notice of Investigation;

(b)   a decision as to whether or not to publicise the fact of an investigation;

(c)   the information-gathering stage;

---

[6] Regulation 30 of the Open-Ended Investment Companies Regulations 2001.

(d)   a review of the evidence obtained so far and, if appropriate, a preliminary findings letter.

### 7.3.1   Notice of investigation

Where the FSA appoints an investigator under Sections 167 or 168 FSMA 2000, the FSA must give written notice of the appointment of the investigator to the person who is the subject of the investigation. The notice (which is called a Memorandum of Appointment of Investigators) must specify the provisions under which, and as a result of which, the investigator was appointed and state the reason for his appointment. Experience suggests that such a notice will be couched in broad language, which although giving the person under investigation a general idea of the area which the FSA wishes to focus on, will not set out the FSA's specific concerns at such an early stage. The receipt of a Memorandum of Appointment of Investigators can cause considerable disquiet to the person under investigation. This is especially so where the person under investigation has not been previously made aware of any FSA concern. In those circumstances it becomes important to attempt to obtain from the FSA as much information as possible in relation to their concerns so as to allow the person under investigation to prepare appropriately for the investigation.[7] As indicated at 7.2.1 above, the initial scoping meeting with the FSA will provide an opportunity to obtain further information as to the nature of the investigation.

The FSA is not under an obligation to issue a written notice of the appointment of an investigator to the person under the investigation in the following circumstances:

(a)   where the investigator is appointed as a result of Section 168(1) or (4) and the FSA believes that a written notice would probably result in the investigation being frustrated; and

(b)   where the investigator is appointed as a result of Section 168(2).

---

[7] A written Memorandum of Appointment of Investigators should also be given in investigations connected with authorised unit trusts and/or open-ended investment companies. Similar considerations apply where the FSA believes that such a notice would lead to the investigation being frustrated.

If during the investigation there is a change in the scope or conduct of the investigation and in the opinion of the FSA the person subject to investigation is likely to be significantly prejudiced by not being made aware of it, that person must be given written notice of the change. However, such a notice need not be given where the FSA, in the case where the investigators were appointed under Section 168(1) or (4), believes that the notice would lead to the investigation being frustrated or where the investigator is appointed as a result of Section 168(2).

The FSA's Enforcement Manual gives an explanation of its policy on notification to the person under investigation under Section 168(2). It explains that in possible insider dealing, market abuse, misleading statements and practices offences or breaches of the general prohibition, the restriction on financial promotion or the prohibition on promoting collective investment schemes, the FSA may not know the identity of the offender at the outset of the investigation and may instead be looking into circumstances rather than investigating a particular person. The FSA has said that in those circumstances it will try to give an indication of the nature of the subject matter of its investigations to those who are required to provide information to assist with the investigation. The FSA's policy then goes on to state that when it becomes clear who the person under investigation is, the FSA will normally notify him of the fact when it decides to exercise its statutory powers to require information. However, the policy makes clear that it will not notify persons under investigation if that would prejudice the FSA's ability to conduct the investigation effectively.

### 7.3.2 Publicity

FSMA 2000 is silent on whether or not the FSA can publicise matters which are under investigation. There is no prohibition on the giving of such publicity although all concerned will be careful not to take action which could lead to contravention of Section 348 FSMA 2000 which restricts the disclosure of confidential information. The FSA's current policy is not normally to make public the fact that it is or is not investigating a particular matter, or to make public any other findings or conclusions of an investigation. However, there are exceptional circumstances which may make it necessary for the FSA to issue a public notice. The FSA has recently increased the number of press statements issued in respect of investigations.

The FSA's Enforcement Manual states that the exceptional circumstances which may give rise to the need to publicise the fact of an investigation are likely to occur where the matters under investigation have become the subject of public concern, speculation or rumour. The FSA states that it may be desirable for the FSA to make public the fact of its investigation in order to allay concern or contain the speculation or rumour. Further, a public announcement may help the investigation itself by bringing forward witnesses. This can often be the case in situations where a person has contravened the general prohibition by taking illegal deposits from members of the general public in circumstances where the full scale of the misconduct is not fully appreciated. Further, such a notice may prevent others transferring funds to unauthorised entities in circumstances where in the event of fraud or an insolvency the ability of the members of the public making the deposits to recover their losses will be restricted because recourse to the Financial Services Compensation Scheme is not available.

The FSA's policy suggests, however, that the circumstances in which an announcement of the results of an investigation will be made will be rarer. However, such announcements have been made in the past where, in relation to matters of public speculation, the FSA has found no evidence of misconduct and therefore has decided to publish that fact in order to quell any further undue speculation.

### 7.3.3   Information gathering

As can be seen from the FSA's powers of investigation detailed above, the FSA has wide powers to compel the production of documents and to require persons to attend interviews.

#### 7.3.3.1   The FSA's policy in requiring documents and interviews
Under Section 174 FSMA 2000, answers given to an investigator during a compulsory interview under Sections 171, 172 or 173 are not admissible in most criminal proceedings or proceedings for market abuse. However, answers given during a voluntary interview may be admissible, subject to the usual need to administer a caution at an appropriate part of the interview should there be reason to suspect the interviewee of having committed a criminal offence.

In relation to authorised persons and approved persons, the FSA initially appeared to adopt the practice of seeking production of documents and/or attendance at interviews on a voluntary basis. However, the interplay of the FSA's formal powers to compel the production of information and the need for authorised firms to cooperate with a regulator under Principle 11 of the FSA's Principles for Businesses[8] meant that there was some confusion about how the proper methods by which requests for information and interviews should be made by the FSA and responded to by the recipient of the request. It was frequently the case that the correct advice for an adviser to give an individual who was requested to attend for a voluntary interview when it was unclear whether the investigation might result in criminal or market abuse proceedings was that the individual should ask to be compelled to attend the interview in order to obtain the Section 174 protection. However, this was often an unattractive step for an approved person to take.

The FSA clarified its policy in a statement entitled "The Use of Statutory Powers in Investigations". The FSA has stated that its standard practice now is to use statutory powers to require the production of documents or the answering of questions in interview. The draft Enforcement Guide makes it clear that from the FSA's perspective a person who is required to attend an interview by the use of statutory powers has no entitlement to insist that the interview takes place voluntarily.

In relation to criminal or market abuse investigations the FSA is likely to prefer to question the person on a purely voluntary basis. Should the interviewee answer those questions in a voluntary interview then the answers could be used against him in subsequent proceedings including criminal or market abuse proceedings.

Further, the FSA would not seek to use its formal powers in relation to persons who have no connection with the financial services industry, such as the victims of an alleged fraud or misconduct. Individuals may also be asked to provide evidence on a voluntary basis where, for example, they are third-party witnesses who are not themselves

---

[8] And for approved persons to cooperate under Statement of Principle 4 for Approved Persons.

the subject of the investigation. In such circumstances, information may be sought voluntarily. Whether it is appropriate for the person concerned to attend voluntarily will depend at least in part on an assessment of whether the FSA is likely to ask questions about matters that are the subject of confidentiality obligations. If so, in order to avoid any allegation that the interviewee has breached such obligations, the interviewee may wish to be compelled by the FSA to attend and answer questions in the course of the interview.

The FSA state in the draft Enforcement Guide that a person asked to attend an interview on a purely voluntary basis is not entitled to insist that he be served with a requirement pursuant to the FSA's statutory powers of compulsion. Where a person is the subject of an investigation it is therefore unlikely that the FSA will agree to conduct an interview under powers of compulsion where the FSA has requested attendance on a voluntary basis. However, in the case of witnesses, where issues of admissability of statements are more limited, it is submitted that in appropriate cases the FSA will be prepared to consider requests that interviews take place on a compelled as opposed to a voluntary basis.

In relation to investigations conducted at the request of overseas regulators, the FSA may depart from its standard approach in order to apply the most appropriate method for obtaining evidence for use in the overseas regulator's country.

The FSA's policy statement clarifies that insofar as regulated firms and approved persons are concerned, a failure to comply with a request from the FSA to produce information or answer questions voluntarily will not be considered by the FSA to be a breach of Principle 11 of the Principles for Businesses and/or Statement of Principle 4 for Approved Persons. However, it is likely that a failure to provide information voluntarily will mean that the person under investigation will not receive the benefit of having been seen to give full cooperation to the FSA should a criminal or civil sanction be imposed.[9]

---

[9] *See* Chapter 11 below.

It is important to remember that the FSA can use information provided as a result of its compulsory powers in proceedings other than general criminal proceedings and/or market abuse proceedings. It will be admissible in, for example, disciplinary proceedings brought by the FSA against an authorised person or approved person for breaches of the FSA's Rules. It is also possible that the FSA will not accept that an authorised firm or approved person who declines a voluntary interview and asks instead that formal powers are used, will not be considered to have given full cooperation and therefore any credit for such cooperation may not be available.

### 7.3.3.2 Practical issues for firms and individuals facing information requirements

Considerable care needs to be taken in preparing for and responding to information requests. It is important to identify the legal and regulatory issues underlying a request for information at an early stage in order to ensure that the firm has a proper understanding of the context in which the request is being made. If necessary, clarification should be sought from the FSA. While this may not always be forthcoming, the request will at least put down a marker in case there is any subsequent issue as to the understanding of the basis of the request. A party involved in enforcement proceedings will want to ensure that it maintains a consistent position in relation to the case it is facing and it is therefore important that statements made at an early stage in an investigation are made on an informed basis taking into account the full facts (or at least as full as possible) and likely legal or regulatory concerns that the individual or firm is facing. The manner of dealing with an information request will vary depending on whether the person concerned is regarded as a witness or as a suspect. Clearly, a person in the position of a suspect will need to have in mind the fact that information provided may ultimately be used against it in enforcement proceedings.

Once an information request is received, steps should be taken to secure information and documents relating to the subject matter of the request, whether or not the information or documents have been specifically requested. Inadvertent destruction of relevant materials, for example in accordance with a standard document retention policy, may result in the loss of significant evidence. Continued use of computing equipment holding relevant information might also result in a loss of that information. Section 177 FSMA 2000 makes it an offence for a person to dispose of documents which that person knows or suspects would be relevant to an investigation. This offence can be committed both where a person knows that an investigation is being conducted and where he knows or suspects that the investigation is likely.

The scope of an information request may cause concerns. This could be because the request is ambiguous, it is drawn in extremely broad terms or compliance with the request could interrupt the ordinary running of the business. Where appropriate, these matters can be discussed with the FSA and agreement reached as to the scope of the request and timing of compliance with the request. The FSA's cooperation can be expected where there are genuine concerns on the part of the person subject to the request. It will often be appropriate to seek legal advice on compliance with an information request in order to ensure that the request is validly made, is not drafted in unnecessarily broad terms and does not seek the production of documents or information that might be legally privileged.

The fact that the FSA is conducting an investigation into a particular matter is likely to be confidential and the recipient of the request may well be asked by the FSA to maintain this confidentiality. Disclosure of confidential information communicated by the FSA might constitute an offence under Section 348 FSMA 2000. A firm may also wish to preserve confidentiality in order to ensure that wrongdoers are not "tipped off". The fact that an FSA investigation is taking place may also be price sensitive for a listed company. Compliance with more extensive information requests is likely to require the involvement of a team of individuals. Care therefore needs to be taken in establishing an appropriate team structure and controlling the disclosure of information relating to the FSA's request. When structuring a team to handle an information request or carry out an internal review of matters that are subject to investigation, care should be taken so that the structure adopted preserves legal privilege as far as possible. This will require the involvement of a lawyer in the process.

Issues of conflicts of interest might arise between a firm that has received an information request and individuals who have been involved in the subject matter of the request. It is not unusual for regulatory breaches to give rise to internal disciplinary issues for individuals concerned which might result in their suspension *or* dismissal while an FSA investigation is running in tandem. In such cases, where the firm holds certain individuals culpable for regulatory breaches being investigated by the FSA, the issue of conflicts is stark. In other cases there will be a unity of interest between the firm and individuals involved in alleged wrongdoing. In such cases there may be no need for separate representation of the firm and the individuals concerned, at least before any findings are issued by the FSA. However, the issue of conflicts should be monitored on an ongoing basis as the investigation progresses. A firm may in any event wish to offer individuals involved the opportunity to seek separate advice and representation, so as to avoid any issue being raised at a later stage in connection with the individual's representation.

When responding to a request it is important to ensure that all documents sought by the FSA are produced. Failure of a person to produce all requested documents or information may be regarded as non-compliance by the FSA with the request, and the person may expose himself to the risk of sanction in respect of this non-compliance (for example, as a contempt of court).

Where an individual is required to attend an interview with the FSA, steps should be taken to clarify with the FSA the matters to be covered in the course of the interview and in particular whether the FSA proposes to discuss particular documents in the course of that interview or whether it intends to play recordings of taped telephone conversations to the interviewee for comment. The FSA can be reticent in providing details of the matters to be covered in the course of the interview but will generally be amenable to providing a bundle of documents to be considered in the course of the interview and a description of the broad topics to be discussed.

A person attending an interview should prepare fully for this by familiarising himself with the matters under investigation. An interview is an opportunity to put forward the firm's or the individual's version of events and to clarify any misunderstandings. Preparation will generally involve the review of materials provided by the FSA and the firm's or individual's own documents and other materials. It is sensible to consult with internal or external legal advisers prior to

attending an interview, in order to ensure that the prospective interviewee is fully aware of the potential regulatory breaches under
investigation and potential legal liabilities. It is common for a legal
representative to attend an interview with the person under investigation. The FSA should not draw an adverse inference from the presence of the legal representative. The presence of a legal
representative helps to ensure fairness of the process and provides
general support to the interviewee. Interviewees should provide
succinct, direct answers to questions posed and avoid lengthy
responses or covering issues that they have not specifically been
asked to comment on. Clarification should be sought before responding to any ambiguous questions. Transcripts are prepared of some
but not all interviews depending on their relevance and importance.
Where a transcript is prepared, a copy will be provided in draft to
the interviewee who will have an opportunity to correct and
comment on the transcript.

### 7.3.4 Review of evidence and preliminary findings letter

In cases where regulatory action is proposed, the output of the investigation process will be the FSA Enforcement team's preliminary
investigation report, which will be sent to the Regulatory Decisions
Committee. The FSA's usual practice is to send the subject of the
investigation a preliminary findings letter which attaches a draft of
the preliminary investigation report. These documents will set out the
FSA's factual findings and proposals and the recipient will be invited
to comment on these matters.

This process assists, for example, in resolving factual inaccuracies and
providing the person under investigation with an opportunity to
comment on the matters that are the subject of contention. In the
course of the interview process, a person who is under investigation
is likely to be referred to evidence that the FSA has gathered in the
course of the investigation, particularly if the person under investigation is interviewed on more than one occasion, as is likely to be the
case. Accordingly, the person under investigation is likely to be familiar with the evidence obtained by the FSA. However, the preliminary
findings letter and the accompanying report will provide an opportunity to consider more generally the manner in which the FSA is
intending to present its case and the facts upon which the FSA relies.

The FSA may not provide a preliminary findings letter to a person under investigation in all cases. In particular, in cases of urgency or where the FSA has already disclosed its case and the subject of the investigation has already commented on it, the FSA may dispense with this stage of the process.

# 7.4 Limits on the FSA's investigation powers

## 7.4.1 Scope of powers

Chapter 3, in the context of FSA requests for information before investigators have been formally appointed, reviewed in detail limitations on the FSA's powers to request information under the following headings:

(a) relevance;
(b) confidentiality, including banking confidentiality; and
(c) legal privilege (including "protected items" under Section 413 FSMA 2000).

Those general principles are not repeated here, but they continue to be valid in assessing the proper scope of an FSA information requirement once a formal investigation has been commenced and investigators appointed. Any information requirement issued under the powers discussed in this chapter should therefore be reviewed bearing in mind these limitations on the FSA's investigation powers.

## 7.4.2 Privilege and protected items

On the topic of legal privilege/protected items, the following observation is made in the context of formal FSA investigations.

Section 413 FSMA 2000 provides that a person may not be required under FSMA 2000 to produce, disclose or permit an inspection of protected items. The definition of protected items broadly includes items which are subject to legal professional privilege. The first set of protected items are those communications between a professional legal adviser and his client which are made in connection with the giving of legal advice to the client. The second category of protected items are communications between a professional legal adviser, his client or any person representing his client and any other person which are made in connection with, or in contemplation of, legal proceedings and for the purposes of those proceedings.

There has been some uncertainty about when a person subject to an investigation can claim privilege in relation to communications between himself, his legal advisers and third parties. If the FSA is merely investigating matters, is it reasonable to contemplate or apprehend litigation when the FSA has made no decision to begin formal enforcement action before the FSA's Regulatory Decisions Committee? If an enquiry is received from the FSA, will advice from a lawyer as to the presentation of the client's position be covered by privilege?

In the case of *Three Rivers District Council* v *Governor and Company of the Bank of England* [2004] UKHL 48 the court was required to consider the issue of whether advice on the presentation of a party's position in the context of an enquiry could be subject to legal professional privilege. The court in that case held that it could, provided that the presentational advice was provided in a relevant legal context. This should include the backdrop of an FSA investigation. Accordingly, it seems clear that communications between a lawyer and a client in the context of an FSA investigation should be covered by legal professional privilege, even though the advice might be on the presentation of the position of the person under investigation as opposed to comprising legal advice in its own right. The issue remains, however, as to whether communications with third parties will be covered by litigation privilege at the investigation stage.

In circumstances where the FSA has issued to the person a notice of appointment of investigators looking at the conduct of named persons, it is the authors' view that a Tribunal should conclude that litigation is reasonably contemplated or apprehended. This is because the notice will point to broad areas of possible misconduct by the person to whom it is addressed. However, where no such notice is issued then it may not be reasonable to contemplate litigation and litigation privilege would not necessarily apply to communications between the person contacted by the FSA and third parties and legal advisers and third parties. This continues to be a difficult area on which firms and individuals taking legal advice about how to respond to an investigation should take care if privilege in that advice is to be maintained and disclosure of it to the FSA avoided.

## 7.5 The FSA's ability to enforce cooperation with investigation powers

### 7.5.1 Search warrants

The FSA can apply to a Justice of the Peace or, in Scotland, a sheriff for a search warrant providing it gives information or evidence on oath that demonstrates that there are reasonable grounds for believing that one of three conditions is satisfied. The three conditions are as follows:

(a)    that a person on whom an information requirement has been imposed has failed to comply with it and that on the premises specified in the warrant there are documents which have been required or there is information which has been required;

(b)    that the premises specified in the warrant are premises of an authorised person or an appointed representative; that there are on the premises documents or information in relation to which an information requirement could be imposed; and if such a requirement were to be imposed it would not be complied with; or the documents or information to which it related would be removed, tampered with or destroyed; or

(c)    that an offence mentioned in Section 168 for which the maximum sentence on indictment is two years or more has been (or is being) committed by a person; that there are on the premises specified in the warrant documents or information relevant to determining whether that event has been (or is being) committed; that an information requirement could be imposed in relation to the documents or information; and that if such a requirement were to be imposed it would not be complied with; or the documents or information to which it related would be removed, tampered with or destroyed.

Any search warrant is exercisable by a police constable. The FSA has said that it will seek to ensure that the FSA's investigator is named on the warrant and is entitled to accompany the constable on the search. The person on whom the warrant is being executed should carefully review the warrant and ensure that all steps taken to execute the warrant are in compliance with the scope of the warrant. The FSMA 2000 provides a protection for legally privileged items, under Section 413, where they are referred to as "protected items" and Section 413(1) provides that "a person may not be required under this Act to produce, disclose or permit the inspection of protected items". Consequently, issues may arise in relation to the protection of privileged items, for example, in relation to the removal of data stored electronically on a computer which may include some privileged materials.

### 7.5.2   Contempt of court

Under Section 177 FSMA 2000, the FSA may, in circumstances where there has been a failure to comply with an information requirement, certify that fact in writing to the court. If the court is satisfied that the defaulter failed without reasonable excuse to comply with the requirement, it may deal with the defaulter as if he were in contempt. The court's power extends to any director or officer of a body corporate which includes a member of a limited liability partnership. The wording in Section 177(2) FSMA 2000 is broad in scope and provides that sanctions for contempt may be imposed on any director or officer of the company concerned. Given that the general position under the criminal law is that directors are not *ex officio* liable for the acts of the company and that personal culpability is required for liability to arise, it is suggested that notwithstanding the wide terms in which Section 177 is drafted, sanctions for contempt are likely to be imposed only on directors or officers with some personal involvement in the matters giving rise to the failure to comply. This would be consistent with a purposive interpretation of Section 177, which is designed to ensure compliance with the requirements imposed by the FSA.

A sanction for contempt may only be imposed where there has been a failure to comply without reasonable excuse. Practical difficulties in complying with a requirement imposed by the FSA, for example because of an unreasonable timing requirement, absence of particular individuals or a legitimate need to obtain legal advice on the scope of a request, are all matters which may constitute reasonable excuses.

The court ultimately retains a discretion as to whether to impose a sanction for contempt given that Section 177(2) provides that the court "may" deal with a defaulter as if the defaulter was in contempt. It is unlikely therefore that the FSA will resort to this remedy unless there has been a persistent failure to comply with the FSA's request or there is an urgency to the matter. Most practical difficulties in complying with an FSA requirement are likely to be able to be resolved with the FSA by agreement and it is therefore only the more deliberate cases of default that are likely to come before the courts. In the case of *Financial Services Authority* v *Christopher Westcott* (9 October 2003) the High Court sentenced a person who failed to cooperate with a FSA investigation to 28 days' imprisonment which was suspended for 12 months on condition that the Defendant cooperated with the FSA investigators. This case concerned the failure of the Defendant to comply with requests to attend an interview. The Defendant failed to attend for a number of months in spite of the FSA making numerous requests. The Court found that the Defendant's default was serious notwithstanding that some 14 months after the original requirement was imposed the Defendant did attend an interview and provide certain information. The Court appears to have suspended the sentence on the basis that an immediate custodial sentence may have prejudiced the efficacy of the FSA's investigation.

### 7.5.3   Offences

Any person who knows or suspects that an investigation is being or is likely to be conducted is guilty of an offence if he falsifies, conceals, destroys or otherwise disposes of a document which he knows or suspects would be relevant to such an investigation or if he causes or permits the falsification, concealment, destruction or disposal of such a document. It is, however, a defence for the person to show he had no intention of concealing facts disclosed by the documents to the investigator.

Further, a person who in purported compliance with a requirement imposed by the FSA provides information which he knows to be false or misleading in a material particular or recklessly provides information which is false or misleading in a material particular is guilty of an offence. The penalty for committing either of these offences on summary conviction is imprisonment for a period not exceeding six months or a fine not exceeding the statutory maximum or both, or upon conviction on indictment to imprisonment for a term not exceeding two years or a fine or both.

Finally, any person who intentionally obstructs the exercise of any rights conferred by a warrant under Section 176 is guilty of an offence and liable on summary conviction to imprisonment for a term not exceeding three months or a fine not exceeding level 5 on the standard scale (i.e. £5,000) or both.

# Chapter 8

# Formal FSA Investigations: Criminal Investigations

**Stephen Gentle**
Partner
Kingsley Napley

## 8.1   Introduction

The reduction of financial crime is one of the four statutory functions given to the Financial Services Authority ("FSA") by the Financial Services and Markets Act 2000 ("FSMA 2000"). Financial crime has been broadly defined[1] and includes conduct involving fraud or dishonesty, market manipulation, the misuse of market information, market misconduct or handling the proceeds of crime, that is, money laundering. In addition to this broad statutory objective, the FSMA 2000 creates a number of specific criminal offences which the FSA may prosecute and also confers on the FSA the power to prosecute offences under certain other legislation (*see* 8.2 below).

In order to enable the FSA to meet its statutory objectives including that of combating financial crime, the FSMA 2000 has given it a broad range of powers which enable it to use investigative methods more normally associated with the police or Serious Fraud Office. Unlike those bodies, however, in many of its cases the FSA will also have available to it regulatory enforcement tools which it may decide to use instead of, or alongside, its criminal powers (*see* Chapter 2 of the Enforcement Guide ("EG")). As a consequence, it is important to appreciate that having received a report of, or information suggesting, criminal conduct, usually the FSA will not start immediately what might be termed a "criminal investigation" if the nature of the alleged misconduct is such that the FSA may also have available non-criminal

---

[1] Section 6(3) FSMA 2000.

159

enforcement tools. The FSA will instead commence an investigation using the full range of its enforcement powers, some of which may be more common in the criminal sphere, such as search and seizure of documents and interviews under caution. Even if these tools are used, this does not mean that a criminal prosecution will ensue if evidence of wrongdoing is uncovered. On the contrary, to date, the FSA has preferred to adopt the regulatory proceedings route for sanctions at the conclusion of an investigation rather than dealing with misconduct in a criminal court. However, in any case in which criminal proceedings are a possibility, the FSA will be mindful of the need to collect evidence of the standard required for a criminal prosecution. The decision as to which route to adopt is dealt with below at 8.12.

## 8.2 Designated criminal offences

Section 401 FSMA 2000 gives the FSA power (although not the exclusive power) to prosecute a number of offences under the FSMA 2000, and Section 402 gives it the power to prosecute certain offences under other legislation. A full list of these offences is contained in Table 8.1 below. Some of the most important are:

- carrying on or purporting to carry on a regulated activity without authorisation or exemption (under Section 23);
- making false claims to be authorised or exempt (under Section 24);
- communicating an invitation or inducement to engage in investment activity in breach of the restrictions on financial promotion (under Section 25);
- performing or agreeing to perform functions in breach of a prohibition order (under Section 56(4));
- offences relating to breaches of listing rules, including that of offering new securities to the public in the UK before publishing a prospectus if required by listing rules made under Section 84 FSMA 2000 (Section 85(2));
- failing to cooperate with, or giving false information to, FSA-appointed investigators or interfering with documentation to conceal facts from the investigation (under Section 177);
- failing to comply with provisions about notification or control over authorised persons (under Section 191);

- providing false or misleading information to an auditor or actuary (under Section 345);
- misleading statements and practices offences (under Section 397);
- misleading the FSA (under Section 398);
- insider dealing under Part V of the Criminal Justice Act 1993;
- breaches of prescribed regulations relating to money laundering.

## 8.3   Who may incur criminal liability?

The FSA may prosecute individuals or corporations for most offences under the FSMA 2000. There are some exceptions, for example, an individual cannot be prosecuted for a breach of paragraph 21 of Schedule 3 to the FSMA 2000 (dealing with EEA passport rights) and, perhaps most importantly, a corporation cannot be prosecuted for insider dealing under Part V of the Criminal Justice Act 1993. Such proceedings can only be taken against an individual.

Offences under the FSMA 2000 fall into two categories: those requiring a mental element on the part of the offender (i.e. some knowledge, intention or recklessness) and, secondly, those where no such element is necessary (so-called strict liability offences).

Where an individual is being prosecuted, this distinction is generally non-problematic. However, if a corporate entity is being prosecuted, this does not obviate the need for the FSA to prove to the criminal standard any requisite mental element. Since corporations are legal constructs, this mental element must be attributed to one or more natural persons. Although a corporation may carry out the relevant criminal acts through its employees or agents, an individual identified as being a controlling or directing mind representing the will of the company must be proved to have the necessary control and direction of those acts in order for the mental element to be made out in a criminal prosecution. Clearly, this identification may be relatively straightforward in a small company but in a large corporation, the directing mind may be remote from the criminal acts complained of. In such cases, therefore, a criminal prosecution against a corporate entity is less likely. Identifying who is the directing mind of a company is made more complicated by the fact that this may vary depending on the nature of the offence in question. Whilst it is often an officer or director of a company who will have to be proved to have had the required *mens rea*, this is not always the case and the courts will construe the relevant statutory provisions to determine what level of employee constitutes the company's controlling mind for a particular offence.

If an offence by a body corporate is shown to have been committed with the consent or connivance of an officer, or be attributable to any neglect on his part, the officer, as well as the body corporate, is guilty of the offence and liable to be proceeded against and punished accordingly (*see* Section 400(1) FSMA 2000). An officer is broadly defined to include a director, member of the Committee of Management, Chief Executive, Manager, Company Secretary or other similar officer of the body (or a person purporting to act in such a capacity) or an individual who is a controller of the body (*see* Section 400(5) FSMA 2000). This means that practitioners should have regard to the function of the individual concerned within the relevant organisation, rather than simply using his title as a guide to whether a prosecution may take place.

There are similar provisions attributing criminal liability to members who run corporate bodies, partners and officers of unincorporated associations.

In order to prove consent, the relevant person must have knowledge of the acts constituting the criminal behaviour (although not necessarily that the acts themselves are criminal) and either explicitly or implicitly consent to those acts taking place. To connive in the relevant activity is to maintain a form of Nelsonian blindness to it and, again, allow it to continue. To prove neglect, there must be a duty to supervise the conduct of the primary offender and evidence that the individual failed in that duty. Clearly, internal policies and the external FSA regime will provide a good framework for deciding whether the relevant duty was in fact complied with.

The FSA is primarily a regulatory, rather than a prosecuting body. Accordingly, it will only institute criminal proceedings in appropriate cases. Where the FSA takes the view that there has been a serious misleading of the market, damaging the interests of consumers, and the behaviour contains a substantial element of dishonesty, then a criminal prosecution is more likely to take place. At the time of writing, however, there has been only one FSA prosecution for an offence relating to market misconduct, brought under Section 397 FSMA 2000 and only three criminal prosecutions in total between 2002 and 2005. Equally, in cases of strict liability where there is no necessity to prove a mental element, again, a criminal prosecution may be appropriate since the evidential hurdles to overcome are relatively low and, for example, a magistrates' court prosecution may be cheaper and more effective than adopting a regulatory approach. It is worth noting that the cost of a criminal prosecution is sometimes given as an explicit reason in an investigation report for adopting a regulatory means of enforcement rather than a criminal prosecution. It is also of note that the Financial Services and Markets Tribunal stated in the *Davidson* decision on costs that it is "not reasonable to decide against criminal proceedings on the ground that a higher penalty could be imposed by a civil penalty".[2]

At the time of writing, there have been no prosecutions by the FSA for breach of money laundering regulations although there have been a number of significant fines following regulatory proceedings. For example, the Bank of Ireland was fined £375,000 for breach of anti-money laundering requirements in 2004, and in 2005 a fine of £30,000 (the highest so far) was imposed on an individual for failings in his firm's anti-money laundering procedures together with a £175,000 fine on the firm.[3]

## 8.4 Market abuse

As explained further below, sanctions for market abuse are not criminal in nature, at least from a UK law perspective. However, when the FSA commences a market abuse investigation it will generally keep its options open as to whether, depending on the nature of the evidence it gathers and other factors, it will prosecute the offender for the relevant criminal offence, usually insider dealing or market manipulation, or instead take civil market abuse proceedings. Indeed, the Memorandum of Appointment of Investigators will usually make

---

[2] In the Financial Services and Markets Tribunal, Paul Davidson and Ashley Tatham, 7 September 2006 at paragraph 65.

[3] Investment Services UK Ltd and Ram Melwani, 9 November 2005.

it clear that criminal offences are being investigated as well (commonly those set out in Part V of the Criminal Justice Act 1993 (insider dealing) and Section 397 of FSMA 2000 (market misleading offences)). It is prudent, therefore, for anyone who is the subject of a market abuse investigation and their advisers to approach the investigation as though it is a criminal investigation and that criminal proceedings may be the outcome, and to deal with the FSA accordingly. For this reason we have included market abuse in this chapter about criminal proceedings.

The introduction of a statutory regime designed to prevent, and if necessary punish, market abuse was one of the most significant features of FSMA 2000. In drafting the FSMA 2000, it was recognised that successful prosecutions of insider dealing under the Criminal Justice Act 1993 and market misconduct offences under the Financial Services Act 1986 were rare, yet it was generally believed that such behaviour was relatively widespread and represented a real threat to the reputation of the UK's financial markets. Accordingly, the FSMA 2000 created a new regulatory "offence" which sought to define a very broad range of punishable behaviour in relation to the market. The aim was both to deter such behaviour and increase the number of successful proceedings against those engaging in misconduct. This was to be achieved by lowering the standard of proof in the proceedings and removing the need to overcome the numerous legal hurdles required to be surmounted in order to prosecute an offender under the existing criminal legislation.

Market abuse is not a criminal offence under English law. It cannot he prosecuted in the criminal courts; the tribunal with jurisdiction over market abuse cases is the Financial Services and Markets Tribunal. The FSA adopts the same decision-making process in deciding whether to impose a sanction for market abuse as it does in relation to sanctions for other regulatory breaches. However, market abuse has certain unique features which reflect its hybrid character between a regulatory and criminal process. In particular, in recognition that market abuse is classified as a criminal offence from a European Convention on Human Rights perspective,[4] transcripts of a compulsory interview

---

[4] In the Financial Services and Markets Tribunal, Paul Davidson and Ashley Tatham, 16 May 2006 at paragraph 184.

of a suspect in a market abuse investigation cannot be relied upon by the FSA as evidence against that individual in subsequent market abuse proceedings. This is a similar statutory protection against self incrimination to that provided to suspects in serious fraud investigations. By contrast, transcripts of FSA compulsory interviews can be used in evidence in disciplinary proceedings under FSMA 2000.

## 8.5   Market abuse – definition

The definition of market abuse and the penalties for it are set out in Section 118 FSMA 2000 as amended by the Financial Services and Markets Act (Market Abuse) Regulations 2005 (SI 2005/381) implementing the EU Market Abuse Directive. In addition, the FSA's Code of Market Conduct[5] issued under Section 119 FSMA 2000 includes descriptions of behaviour which the FSA may deem to constitute, or not constitute, market abuse.

Market abuse covers three broad types of behaviour: misuse of information, creating false or misleading impressions in the financial markets, and distorting the financial markets. The amendments to Section 118 FSMA 2000 implementing the Market Abuse Directive added extra detail and complexity to the statutory definition of market abuse.

An examination of the constituent elements of market abuse is beyond the scope of this work.

Although not a criminal offence, the market abuse regime applies to the public at large and not only to the regulated sector. The sanctions which may be imposed following a finding of market abuse are very severe, albeit that it is not punishable by imprisonment. Wrongdoers may face unlimited financial penalties (fines of £750,000 each were levied on GLG LP (a hedge fund) and its managing director, Philippe Jabre, in 2006) and, if they work in the financial services industry, they may have their livelihood removed by having their authorisation/ approval withdrawn or a prohibition order made against them. A decision that a person engaged in market abuse will be made public.

---

[5] MAR 1.

It is easy to see why on occasion market abuse is described as a civil offence rather than a "regulatory breach".

The decision-making process which the FSA adopts in deciding whether to bring proceedings for market abuse is the same statutory notice procedure used in respect of other regulatory breaches.

## 8.6 Information gathering: general outline

When the FSA receives information suggesting that potentially criminal conduct has occurred, it does not designate its subsequent investigation as "criminal" or "regulatory". Chapters 5 and 6 of the Enforcement Guide set out the FSA policy on the use of its information and investigation powers and the conduct of investigations. Consequently, in a case where both criminal and regulatory sanctions are available relevant to the same conduct, it will usually be unclear at the start of an investigation whether the FSA will pursue the matters criminally. For example, in cases of suspected market misconduct it is common for the memorandum of appointment of investigators to describe the investigation as being into suspected market abuse, insider dealing, Section 397 FSMA 2000 and breaches of the FSA Principles. The Enforcement Division of the FSA will use whatever powers it deems appropriate to perform its statutory function to investigate the alleged misconduct. For example, a suspect may be interviewed by the FSA using its compulsory powers under Sections 171–173 FSMA 2000 (where, broadly, responses given in the interview cannot be used in evidence against the suspect in subsequent criminal proceedings) and subsequently interviewed under caution (where responses can be used in evidence). Documents may be obtained from the suspect using compulsory powers and then he or she may be interviewed as to their contents under caution. Advisers should recognise that the FSA will always adopt what it believes to be the most effective means of gathering information rather than proceeding down a particular regulatory or criminal route.

### 8.6.1 Interviews (EG 6.18–EG 6.28)

Interviews may be of three types, namely voluntary and not under caution, voluntary under caution and compulsory. In all interviews the FSA will allow a person to be accompanied by a legal adviser (EG 6.21).

### 8.6.1.1   *Voluntary interviews (EG 6.20)*
ENF 2.11.2G states that investigators may not always believe it necessary to use their statutory powers and will occasionally conduct interviews on a voluntary basis. In an update to its website in December 2003, the FSA gave examples of situations when such interviews may be conducted including interviews with victims of financial misconduct and some investigations conducted by overseas investigators. If a voluntary interview takes place which is not under caution, and the interviewee incriminates himself and criminal proceedings ensue, it is possible that the defendant would make an application for the incriminating statements to be excluded from a criminal trial under Section 78 of the Police and Criminal Evidence Act 1984 ("PACE") on the basis that they had been unfairly obtained.

It is important that professional advisers ensure that the FSA identifies the reason for an interview and confirms the status of the interviewee before the interview takes place. If the FSA is requesting a voluntary interview and it is clear that the interviewee is being regarded as a suspect, then the correct advice may be to refuse a voluntary interview and leave it to the FSA to decide whether to request a voluntary interview under caution, compel the individual to attend an interview or have them arrested and then interviewed under caution (as to which *see* below).

### 8.6.1.2   *Voluntary interviews under caution (EG 6.22)*
A caution should be administered "to a person whom there are grounds to suspect of an offence". There must be some reasonable objective grounds for the suspicion based on known facts or information which is relevant to the likelihood the offence has been committed and the person to be questioned committed it. A caution should always be given before any questions or further questions are put to the suspect "regarding his involvement in that offence if his answers or his silence may be given in evidence to a court" (*see* PACE Codes of Practice Code C, paragraph 10.1 and Note 10A).

It would be extremely rare for someone suspected of a criminal offence to volunteer to be interviewed without the protection of a caution or without having been compelled to attend an interview pursuant to the FSA's statutory powers. The most likely scenario is for the suspect to be interviewed voluntarily under caution. A voluntary interview under caution will generally be carried out at the FSA's offices. As would be the case with any criminal investigation, advisers should ensure that they understand the nature of the allegation and request advance copies of any documentation that is to be used in interview. Although there is no obligation to provide such material, failure to do so may impact on the admissibility of the interview in any future criminal proceedings and indeed, particularly if the suspect has been arrested, may justify a refusal to answer questions altogether. This is because a jury may not be given a direction by the judge that it may draw an adverse inference from a defendant's failure to answer questions in an interview under caution if proper disclosure of the case against the defendant was not provided prior to interview. Any interview under caution will be conducted according to the provisions of PACE and, in particular, Code C which deals with the detention and questioning of suspects.

Prior to a voluntary interview under caution, the suspect will be informed of his right to leave the interview at any time (since he is not under arrest) and his right to legal advice. As regards the latter, a suspect in a voluntary interview under caution has the same right to legal advice as if he were detained at a police station (PACE Code C, Note 1A).

The interview will, obviously, be tape recorded and at its commencement, the terms of the caution will be read to the suspect. The caution states:

> "You do not have to say anything, but it may harm your defence if you fail to mention when questioned something which you later rely on in court. Anything you do say may be given in evidence."

The effect of the caution is threefold. It encapsulates the right to silence of those facing criminal allegations. It provides that any answers given in response to questions under caution may be used in evidence. Finally, and most controversially, it allows a court to direct a jury to draw an adverse inference from the failure of a suspect to mention a fact in interview (or in a written statement given under caution – *see* below) that he later relies on in his defence at trial. The inferences that may be drawn include that the suspect had no answer which he could have given, that is, that any answer would tend to have incriminated him or that the defence given at trial is based on "recent fabrication" – that the defendant had waited for the case against him to be made explicit following charge and tailored his defence accordingly.

In preference to answering questions orally, a prepared written statement may be read out on tape. Questions may then not be answered by the suspect. This has the advantage of ensuring a degree of control over the structure and content of a suspect's response to an allegation and will prevent the drawing of an adverse inference provided the statement contains the facts that the defendant later relies on at trial and these were facts which should reasonably have been mentioned in response to questions. However, advisers should be aware that if a matter proceeds to a criminal trial or regulatory hearing, the suspect may be asked his reasons for preferring to give a written statement rather than answer questions. In addition, giving a written statement does not prevent investigators asking questions on its contents in interview.

Advisers should be aware that in order to ensure suspects understand the terms of the caution, experienced investigators may ask a suspect to repeat back the terms of the caution in their own words since, if at a later stage, a suspect can show he did not understand the caution, the admissibility of the interview may be called into question. Advisers must therefore be very clear in their explanation of the terms of a caution.

Those representing the suspect being interviewed under caution should adopt a proactive role in interview in identifying the areas of relevance and concern and, in particular, seeking to identify the evidence upon which the FSA is relying. This is important since advisers may wish to make representations to the FSA prior to the investigation report being drafted and, possibly, a warning notice being issued by the Regulatory Decisions Committee. Advisers should not be shy in intervening in interviews where appropriate, forcing the investigators to justify questions and narrowing the ambit of any enquiries. Equally, advisers should be robust in advice given to suspects, particularly as to whether a voluntary interview should be attended at all or whether it should be curtailed at any time.

Advisers may wish to advise a client to refuse to answer questions for a number of reasons. If a suspect will make admissions to a criminal offence or offences, it will generally be unwise for him to answer, unless the evidence against him is overwhelming and a guilty plea has already been decided upon. In those circumstances, admissions in interview may be useful mitigation. At the opposite end of the scale, if there is no, or very little, admissible evidence against a suspect, a "no comment" interview may be appropriate. Lack of disclosure or a suspect's mental or physical ill health may also justify advice to answer no questions.

If advice is given not to answer questions, it is possible that in future proceedings, subject to a waiver of privilege, advisers may be asked to explain the reasons for their advice in order, generally, to contest any adverse inference being drawn. It is essential, therefore, that detailed notes are kept of any such advice.

Interviews are to enable investigators "to obtain evidence by questioning" (PACE Code C). That evidence is generally sought to prosecute the suspect. Advisers should always therefore ensure that questions are relevant, clear and not misleading. If a suspect does not understand questions or wishes to consult his solicitor, the solicitor should have no hesitation in suspending the interview for consultation.

If a suspect has already been interviewed by the FSA under its compulsory powers, before he is interviewed under caution the investigators will give him a transcript or other record of the compulsory interview and an explanation of the difference between the two types of interview (EG 6.23). They will also tell the individual about the limited use that can be made of his previous answers in criminal proceedings or in the proceedings in which the FSA seek a penalty for market abuse (*see* 8.6.1.3) Where a suspect has been interviewed under caution and the FSA subsequently wishes to conduct a compulsory interview with him, the FSA will again explain the difference between the types of interview and will notify the individual of the limited use that can be made of his answers in a compulsory interview (EG 6.24).

A refusal to attend a voluntary interview under caution will not expose the suspect to any kind of penalty although if there were to be criminal proceedings, adverse inferences might be drawn if no answers are given in a subsequent interview following an arrest. The fact that a suspect might be an approved person or otherwise representing an authorised firm imposes no separate obligation on the individual concerned to attend voluntarily and answer questions. The requirement in statement in Principle 4 for approved persons should not be read as requiring an approved person to attend an interview at which he may incriminate himself. APER 4.4.9E states that failing to attend an interview without good reason breaches Principle 4 but prospective self incrimination would provide the necessary good reason to prevent proceedings for breach. Although rare, a suspect may attend at a voluntary interview under caution and answer no questions. The primary reason for this would be to avoid an arrest and interview at a police station (*see* below), as this would generally result in a suspect being bailed and, effectively, entering the formal criminal investigative process. Although no conditions can be placed on bail at this stage, the fact of the arrest will be recorded and may cause problems, for example in obtaining overseas visas.

FSA investigators do not have the power of arrest. If it is believed that to request the attendance of a suspect on a voluntary basis might prejudice an investigation (for example by enabling the destruction of documents to take place) or that the suspect will not attend on a voluntary basis, the assistance of the police will be called for to arrest the suspect. Once the suspect has been arrested and is in custody, they can be interviewed and adverse inferences can be drawn from a refusal to answer questions. If this route is adopted, the usual PACE 1984 procedures will be followed in the police station and the interview will be conducted there (EG 6.25).

A memorandum of understanding has been entered into between the City of London Police and the FSA which sets out the agreed best practice for the arrest and questioning of suspects where the police and the FSA have reasonable grounds to suspect that an individual has committed an offence. PACE Code G sets out a number of bases upon which the police may arrest. The most important of these is that the arrest must be "necessary and proportionate". Circumstances have arisen where the FSA has requested the assistance of the City of

London Police; suspects have subsequently been arrested and interviewed at a police station.

### 8.6.1.3 *Compulsory interviews*

Compulsory interviews may be conducted by the FSA under Sections 171–173 FSMA 2000 and there is nothing to prevent the FSA conducting such interviews with those whom they suspect of having committed criminal offences. It is not proposed to deal with this aspect of information gathering here since it is extensively covered in Chapter 3 above. Although compulsory interviews form a key part of investigations of potential criminal conduct as well as investigation into what might be termed more regulatory malpractice, Section 174 FSMA 2000 explicitly prevents the use in criminal proceedings of statements given to an investigator in compliance with "an information requirement", that is, in response to questions in an interview conducted under Sections 171–173.

The answers given may, however, be used in proceedings against the suspect by the FSA in a prosecution under Section 177 (failure to comply with a requirement imposed by the FSMA 2000) or Section 398 (misleading the FSA). The FSA has also made it clear that it will use its powers of compulsion as an investigative tool to obtain other admissible evidence.

In addition, advisers should be aware that the fetters on the use of compelled answers only apply to the prosecution. If, for example, the transcript of an interview under Section 171 is provided to a co-defendant in a criminal prosecution (as would invariably be the case) there is nothing to prevent the use of that transcript in cross-examination of the suspect.

## 8.7 Powers to obtain documents: compulsory powers

The power of the FSA to obtain documents under its compulsory powers is set out in Sections 165, 171 and 172 FSMA 2000. Readers are invited to refer to Chapter 6 for a full description of these powers. However, in brief, Section 165 FSMA 2000 allows the FSA to require, by notice in writing, an authorised person to provide specified information and documentation in relation to a specified matter that falls within the remit of the FSA as set out in the FSMA 2000. The information or documentation must be provided or produced within a specified reasonable period of time and at a specified location. The FSA can also require persons or entities connected with the authorised person to disclose documentation or information.

Once Inspectors have been appointed under Section 167 or Section 168 FSMA 2000, they have the power to require the production of documents under Section 171 and Section 172 FSMA 2000.

Failure to comply with such requirement is punishable as a contempt of court. It should be noted that although statements given under compulsion cannot be used by the FSA in criminal proceedings against an accused, this protection does not extend to documents obtained by compulsion.[6]

## 8.8   Powers to obtain documents: search and seizure

The FSA and its investigators may apply to a magistrate for a warrant to search for and seize documents or information under Section 176 FSMA 2000 (EG 6.29 and EG 6.30). The court may issue a warrant if it is satisfied that there are reasonable grounds for believing that:

(a)   a person has failed to comply with the requirement to provide information or produce documents and that the required documents or information are on the premises specified in the warrant (Section 176(2)); or

(b)   the premises specified in the warrant are those of a firm or an appointed representative and that there are documents or information on the premises which could be the object of an information requirement and that the requirement would not be complied with or the documents or information would be removed, tampered with or destroyed if such a requirement were made (Section 176(3)); or

---

[6] *See* A-G reference (No. 7 of 2000 [2001] EWCA Crim 888).

(c)   an offence mentioned in Section 168[7] for which the maximum sentence on conviction on indictment is two years or more has been, or is being, committed and that the documents or information relevant to that offence are on the specified premises, and that an information requirement could be imposed on those documents or that information and that the requirement would not be complied with, or the documents or information would be removed, tampered with or destroyed (Section 176(4)).

## 8.9   Search and seizure, practical guidance

A detailed discussion as to the law relating to search and seizure is beyond the scope of this work, but certain practical points may be of assistance to regulated firms and individuals faced with a search warrant. The first of these is to ensure that the warrant itself is correctly drawn. It must be signed and dated and contain a description of the nature of the documentation which is sought. If documentation is requested beyond the scope of the warrant then this point should be made to those executing the warrant. In extreme cases an injunction can be sought to prevent further execution of the warrant and, if that is not an option, the warrant itself may be the subject of a judicial review application at a later stage.

A full list of those in attendance at the search should be obtained, including details of the capacity in which they are attending.

Disclosure of the search and the warrant to third parties should be carefully considered as such disclosure could in some circumstances be a breach of the "tipping off" and "prejudicing an investigation" provisions of the Proceeds of Crime Act 2002.

Although the FSA will have a responsibility to list documents which are being seized, an independent list should be kept by those who are subject to the search. At the conclusion of the search, a request should be made for a copy of the search record.

One of the most difficult areas to address in searches is that of the extent to which computer material may be seized when it may contain items

---

[7] Relevant offences under Section 168 are offences under Sections 177, 191(5), 346, 398(1) and 397 FSMA 2000 or Part V Criminal Justice Act 1993.

which are outside the scope of the warrant, confidential in themselves and, potentially, the subject of legal professional privilege. The power to seize such material (or the lack of such power) is now regulated by Sections 50–66 of the Criminal Justice and Police Act 2001 ("CJPA 2001"). Essentially, the FSA is entitled to seize what is known as "inextricably linked material", even if such material is subject to legal privilege. However, privileged material cannot be examined other than for the purposes of identifying it as such (Section 53(2) CJPA 2001) and, if the person from whom the material is being seized or anyone with a "relevant interest" in the property gives notice to the appropriate judicial authority (usually the local Crown Court) then the FSA must retain the material and not examine it pending determination of whether they are entitled to retain the relevant material or whether it must be returned.[8] This process is carried out by an independent lawyer, it is arranged by the FSA and generally takes place either at the lawyer's offices/ chambers or at the offices of the FSA in the presence of the suspect's lawyers. FSA personnel will not be present at the examination.

In general terms, those advising on searches should ensure that warrants are complied with as far as is necessary and, as with interviews, give appropriate and sometimes robust advice where necessary.

## 8.10 Intrusive powers

The FSA is a relevant body under Sections 28 and 29 of the Regulation of Investigatory Powers Act 2000. This allows it to conduct surveillance and use covert human intelligence sources ("CHISs"), that is informants, in performing its statutory objective of reducing financial crime provided it is proportionate to do so. It does not, however, have the power to intercept communications, whether postal or via the telecommunications network.

---

[8] Sections 50–51 CJPA 2001 limits the power to seize, *inter alia*, privileged material to circumstances where it is not reasonably practicable to determine on the premises whether it is privileged material and it is not practicable to separate such material from seizable material.

The subject of the search is entitled to a Notice setting out what has been seized (Section 52 CJPA 2001). If an application is to be made to the court for return of the seized material (Section 59 CJPA 2001), the FSA must secure the property (Section 60 CJPA 2001) and must not examine it pending a determination of the issue by the court (Section 61 CJPA 2001).

There is an obligation to return all material which is identified as being privileged (Section 54 CJPA 2001).

## 8.11 Criminal investigations: the international aspects

A significant proportion of information received by the FSA in relation to market misconduct comes from overseas regulators, particularly from Europe and the US. The recent memorandum of understanding with the Securities and Exchange Commission relating to consultation, cooperation and exchange of information is a concrete example of this cooperation. Subject to any use limitation which the overseas authorities have placed upon the information and the relevant Memorandum of Understanding, the FSA may use this information as it sees fit in its investigations.

In addition, Section 169 FSMA 2000 gives the FSA power to conduct investigations to assist an overseas regulator (EG 5.12). As at October 2006, requests for assistance were running at about 20 a month although there have been as many as 56 in a month. The FSA may use its powers to require the production of documents or information under Section 165 or to appoint inspectors to investigate the relevant matters. In deciding whether or not to assist an overseas authority, the FSA will take into account factors such as whether reciprocal assistance will be offered by the overseas authority, the seriousness of the case and its importance to citizens in the UK, and whether it is otherwise appropriate in the public interest to give the assistance sought. Interestingly, in contrast to other criminal investigating and prosecuting agencies such as the Serious Fraud Office, the FSA may decide not to exercise its powers unless a financial contribution to the cost of doing so is made by the requesting authorities.

Representatives of the overseas authorities may attend at interviews as long as the FSA is satisfied that the information which is provided will be subject to the safeguards detailed in Part XXIII FSMA 2000, which imposes restriction on the disclosure and use of confidential information. Regarding US requests, these are increasingly resulting in interviews at the US Embassy where US law will apply – including the Fifth Amendment right to silence. Evidence obtained under compulsion will not be admissible in US proceedings.

The other investigating and prosecuting agencies who use compulsory powers of information gathering, such as the Serious Fraud Office or the Department of Trade and Industry, will require an undertaking from an overseas authority when providing information to it that the information being provided will not be used for the prosecution of the individual who was the subject of the exercise of the compulsory powers. In other words, the overseas authority may not use the information in a way which is contrary to the way in which it could be used in the UK. In recent cases, the FSA has disputed this restriction and has maintained that it is entirely appropriate for it to provide information to overseas authorities which has been obtained as a result of the use of its compulsory powers but without requiring any use limitation from the overseas jurisdiction. It remains to be seen whether this will be challenged as contrary to Article 6 of the European Convention on Human Rights protections and the guidance followed by other agencies following the *Saunders* case[9] in the European Court. Certainly, the FSA does appear to be out of step with other agencies in this regard.[10]

The Law Policy and International Cooperation Department, which is part of the Enforcement Division, deals with incoming and outgoing requests for assistance.

## 8.12   The decision to prosecute

The FSA's published policy is "to pursue through the criminal justice system all those cases where criminal prosecution is appropriate" (EG 12.2). It will apply the Code for Crown Prosecutors[11] – that is the template used by all prosecution agencies in deciding whether to prosecute.

The Code contains a two-stage test. First, the FSA must be satisfied that there is sufficient evidence to provide a realistic prospect of conviction, that is that a jury, properly directed in accordance with the law, is more likely than not to convict the defendant of the charge alleged ("the evidential test"). In deciding whether the evidential threshold is passed, the FSA will look at factors such as the reliability of the evidence and the nature of the defence which is likely to be advanced. There is no exhaustive list of evidential matters which must be examined.

---

[9] *Saunders* v *United Kingdom* (1996) EHRR 313.
[10] *See* Chapter 13 for a more detailed discussion of the role of the ECHR in FSA investigations and proceedings generally.
[11] To be found at www.cps.gov.uk/publications/docs/code2004english.pdf.

If the evidential test is passed, the FSA must then consider whether it is in the public interest to prosecute. In 1951, Lord Shawcross, who was then the Attorney General, gave the classic statement on public interest, which has been supported by Attorneys General ever since: "It has never been the rule in this country – I hope it never will be – that suspected criminal offences must automatically be the subject of prosecution".

Experience suggests that the FSA will examine matters such as the proportionality of a criminal prosecution and the cost and speed of criminal prosecutions compared with pursuing a regulatory sanction. There may indeed be specific reference in an investigation report as to why a regulatory route for dealing with misconduct is being adopted rather than a criminal prosecution.

If a decision is taken to prosecute, then the process is the same as for any other criminal prosecution, a description of which is outside the scope of this work.

Paragraphs 12.7 to 12.10 of the Enforcement Guide set out the policy to be adopted in cases of market abuse. A number of specific factors are set out which the FSA will consider in deciding whether to prosecute the relevant activity in the criminal courts as insider dealing or one of the offences under Section 397 FSMA 2000, or whether to choose a regulatory route for sanction and deal with the behaviour as market abuse under Section 118. The factors include the seriousness of the misconduct and the losses to victims. As one would expect, conduct which involves dishonesty or abuse of trust is more likely to lead to criminal prosecution.

Advisers faced with situations where the conduct in question is on the borderline of being dealt with by the criminal courts may wish to make written representations to the FSA that a regulatory route should be preferred. Such representations are relatively common in other spheres of criminal prosecution and the FSA would be required to examine such representations when deciding whether or not to prosecute an individual or corporate entity. Alternatively, of course, in cases where it is clear that a criminal prosecution is likely, advisers may wish to avoid any such engagement with the FSA since any points made on behalf of the prospective defendant may ultimately be used against them in a criminal prosecution. For example, if admissions were made by lawyers on behalf of clients in correspondence then clearly it may be difficult for a defendant to defend those admissions in the criminal courts.

## 8.13 Cooperation with other agencies

For cases where particular conduct may be of interest and concern to other agencies, such as the Serious Fraud Office, the Department of Trade and Industry or the Crown Prosecution Service, Annex 2 of the Enforcement Guide sets out broad principles as to which agency should deal with a particular instance of financial crime or market misconduct. The aim of this framework is to avoid duplication and prevent unfairness to the subject of the investigation as well as to facilitate cooperation between agencies.

There is an extent to which this cooperation is more apparent than real. Defendants are frequently enmeshed in parallel proceedings and the FSA has not shown itself to be enthusiastic in allowing, for example, a criminal process against a defendant to take precedence over regulatory proceedings. The Government's Fraud Review, published in 2006, identified parallel proceedings as increasing the cost and complexity of dealing with fraud – not to mention the obvious burdens on a defendant.

Generally speaking, the FSA will investigate and take proceedings against those whose behaviour has an impact on consumers or affects the integrity of the financial markets or where the subject of the investigation is an FSA-regulated individual or entity. The availability of market expertise in the FSA is also a consideration.

## 8.14 Conclusion

Combating financial crime is becoming an increasingly crowded area for law enforcement involving the police, the Serious Fraud Office, the terrorism orientated intelligence gathering of the Security Service and, from 2006, the financial crime remit of the Serious and Organised Crime Agency. The FSA is busy seeking to mark out its territory as the principal UK authority in this crowded field. Certainly, the powers it has are extensive and should enable it to investigate financial crime effectively. These powers have to date been used almost without exception to sanction individuals within the regulatory framework rather than in the criminal courts. However, it would be naïve not to envisage an increased number of criminal prosecutions in the future – focusing particularly on institutional offences and insider dealing rings. Indeed, in her speech to the School of Law at Fordham University on 17 October 2006, Margaret Cole specifically stated that "we expect to bring more criminal cases going forward".

The recent convictions of former AIT directors for offences contrary to Section 397(1)(a) and (c) are indicative of the approach of both the FSA and the court to such offences. Sentences of two years' and three-and-a-half years' imprisonment were handed down at first instance, later reduced to nine months and 18 months. Confiscation, compensation and costs orders were also sought by the FSA. Confiscation orders were later quashed on appeal. It is possible that in the future powers to restrain suspect's assets may be exercised. However, the FSA is likely to remain primarily a regulator which exercises enforcement sanctions in the civil sphere rather than a criminal prosecution agency. Certainly, overseas financial regulators rarely have criminal powers of prosecution and, where they do, even more rarely are they exercised. The close cooperation between the FSA and sister bodies in the International Organisation of Security Commissions ("IOSCO") perhaps emphasises where the FSA lies in the geography of world financial regulation.

For practitioners, the key point to grasp in dealing with FSA investigations is not to maintain a rigid view of prospective outcomes based on the tools that are used by investigators on a given case. The FSA has made plain both publicly and in private that it does not regard itself as constrained in its use of powers by the likely ultimate outcome of an investigation. Certainly, this sometimes leads to a lack of transparency in investigations since advisers cannot ever be sure whether, at least in the early stages, an investigation is a criminal one at all in the sense in which that term is commonly understood. The only way to ensure that the rights of those subject to an investigation are protected is to ensure that the FSA's preference for a flexible approach to investigation does not result in a lack of transparency as to the nature of the investigation, the processes being adopted and the ultimate outcome.

*Table 8.1*  *Designated criminal offences*

| Section | Offence | Sentence after summary conviction | Sentence after conviction on indictment | Other details |
|---------|---------|-----------------------------------|-----------------------------------------|---------------|
| 23 | Breach of Section 19(1) – the "general prohibition": "No person may carry on a regulated activity in the United Kingdom, or purport to do so, unless he is– (a) an authorised person; or (b) an exempt person" | Imprisonment not exceeding 6 months, or a fine not exceeding the statutory maximum, or both | Imprisonment not exceeding 2 years, or a fine, or both | |
| 24 | False claims to be authorised or exempt | Imprisonment for a term not exceeding 6 months or a fine not exceeding level 5 on the standard scale, or both | | If the offence involved public display of any material the maximum fine is multiplied by the number of days for which the display continued |
| 25 | Breach of Section 21(1): "A person ('A') must not, in the course of business, communicate an invitation or inducement to engage in investment activity" | Imprisonment not exceeding 6 months, or fine not exceeding the statutory maximum, or both | Imprisonment not exceeding 2 years, or a fine, or both | |
| 48(9) | Breach of Section 48(6): "no assets held by a person as trustee in accordance with the requirement [mentioned in Section 3(b)] may, while the requirement is in force, be released or dealt with except with the consent of the Authority" | A fine not exceeding level 5 on the standard scale | | |

**Table 8.1** *continued*

| Section | Offence | Sentence after summary conviction | Sentence after conviction on indictment | Other details |
|---|---|---|---|---|
| 56(4) | Breaches of a prohibition order: "An individual who performs or agrees to perform a function in breach of a prohibition order is guilty of an offence" | A fine not exceeding level 5 on the standard scale | | |
| 83 | Failure to register a copy of listing particulars on or before publication under Section 83(3): "On or before the date on which listing particulars are published as required by listing rules, a copy of the particulars must be delivered for registration to the registrar of companies" | A fine not exceeding the statutory maximum | A fine | The offence can be committed by the issuer of the securities in question and any person who is party to the publication and aware of the failure. |
| 85(2) | Admitting new securities to the official list prior to the publication of a prospectus, if required: "if listing rules made under Section 84 require a prospectus to be published before particular new securities are admitted to the official list it is unlawful for any of those securities to be offered to the public in the United Kingdom before the required prospectus is published" | Imprisonment not exceeding 3 months, or a fine not exceeding level 5 on the standard scale | Imprisonment not exceeding 2 years, or a fine, or both | |
| 98 | Requirement to submit advertisements: | A fine not exceeding the statutory maximum | Imprisonment not exceeding 2 years, or a fine, or both | |

| | | |
|---|---|---|
| | "If listing particulars are, or are to be, published in connection with an application for listing, no advertisement or other information of a kind specified by listing rules may be issued in the United Kingdom unless the contents of the advertisement or other information have been submitted to the competent authority and that the authority has – (a) approved those contents; or (b) authorised the issue of the advertisement or information without such approval" | |
| 142(5) | Breach of regulations under Section 142(1): "The Treasury may make regulations for the purpose of preventing a person who is not an authorised person but who – (a) is a parent undertaking of an authorised person who has permission to effect or carry out contracts of insurance, and (b) falls within a prescribed class from doing anything to lessen the effectiveness of asset identification rules." **No regulations in force** | |
| 177(2) | Failure to comply with a requirement under Part XI (Information gathering and Investigations) | To be treated as if in contempt (High Court). Imprisonment not exceeding 2 years, or a fine, or both |

183

**Table 8.1** *continued*

| Section | Offence | Sentence after summary conviction | Sentence after conviction on indictment | Other details |
|---------|---------|-----------------------------------|------------------------------------------|---------------|
| 177(3) | Falsification / concealment of documents: "A person who knows or suspects that an investigation is being or is likely to be conducted under this Part is guilty of an offence if – (a) he falsifies, conceals or destroys or otherwise disposes of a document which he knows or suspects is or would be relevant to such an investigation, or (b) he causes or permits the falsification, concealment, destruction or disposal of such a document" | Imprisonment not exceeding 6 months, or a fine not exceeding the statutory maximum, or both | | |
| 177(4) | Providing false information: "A person who, in purported compliance with a requirement imposed on him under this Part – (a) provides information which he knows to be false or misleading in a material particular, or (b) recklessly provides information which is false or misleading in a material particular, is guilty of an offence" | Imprisonment not exceeding 6 months, or a fine not exceeding the statutory maximum, or both | Imprisonment not exceeding 2 years, or a fine, or both | |
| 177(6) | Obstruction of the exercise of a search warrant: "Any person who intentionally obstructs the exercise of any | Imprisonment not exceeding 3 months, or a fine not exceeding level 5 on the standard scale, or both | | |

| | Offence | Penalty | Relevant provision |
|---|---|---|---|
| | rights conferred by a warrant under Section 176 is guilty of an offence" | | |
| 191(1) | Failure to notify the FSA of changes in control: "A person who fails to comply with the duty to notify the Authority imposed on him by Section 178(1) . . . is guilty of an offence" | A fine not exceeding level 5 on the standard scale | Section 178(1): "If a step which a person proposes to take would result in his acquiring (a) control over a UK authorised person, (b) an additional kind of control over a UK authorised person, or (c) an increase in a relevant kind of control which he already has over a UK authorised person, he must notify the Authority of his proposal" |
| 191(1) | "A person who fails to comply with the duty to notify the Authority imposed on him by . . . Section 190(1) is guilty of an offence" | A fine not exceeding level 5 on the standard scale | 190(1): "If a step which a controller of a UK authorised person proposes to take would result in his – (a) ceasing to have control of a relevant kind over the authorised person, or (b) reducing a relevant control over that person, he must notify the Authority of his proposal" |
| 191(2) | "A person who fails to comply with the duty to notify the Authority imposed on him by Section 178(2) . . . is guilty of an offence" | A fine not exceeding level 5 on the standard scale | 178(2): "A person who, without himself taking any such step acquires any such control or additional or increased control must notify" |

**Table 8.1** *continued*

| Section | Offence | Sentence after summary conviction | Sentence after conviction on indictment | Other details |
|---|---|---|---|---|
| | | | | the Authority before the end of the period of 14 days beginning with the day on which he first becomes aware that he has acquired it" |
| 191(2) | "A person who fails to comply with the duty to notify the Authority imposed on him by ... Section 190(2) is guilty of an offence" | A fine not exceeding level 5 on the standard scale | | 190(2) "A controller of a UK authorised person who, without himself taking any such step, ceases to have that control or reduces that control must notify the Authority before the end of the period of 14 days beginning with the day on which he first becomes aware that (a) he has ceased to have the control in question; or (b) he has reduced that control" |
| 191(3) | "If a person who has given notice of control to the Authority carries out the proposal to which the notice relates, he is guilty of an offence if – (a) the period of three months beginning with the date on which the Authority received the notice is still running; and (b) the Authority has not responded to the notice by either giving its approval or giving him a warning notice under Section 183(3) or 185(3)" | A fine not exceeding level 5 on the standard scale | | |

| | | |
|---|---|---|
| 191(4) | "A person to whom the Authority has given a warning notice under Section 183(3) is guilty of an offence if he carries out the proposal to which the notice relates before the Authority has decided whether to give him a notice of objection" | A fine not exceeding level 5 on the standard scale | 183(3):"If the Authority proposed to give the person concerned a notice of objection under Section 186(1), it must give him a warning notice"<br><br>186(1): "On considering a notice of control, the Authority may give a decision notice under this section to the person acquiring control ('the acquirer') unless it is satisfied that the approval requirements are met" |
| 191(5) | "A person to whom a notice of objection has been given is guilty of an offence if he acquires the control to which the notice applies at a time when the notice is still in force" | A fine not exceeding the statutory maximum or, under Section 198(8), a fine not exceeding one-tenth of the statutory maximum for each day on which the offence has been committed | Imprisonment not exceeding 2 years, or a fine, or both |
| 191(11) | "A person who fails to comply with the duty to notify the Authority imposed by subsection (10) is guilty of an offence" | A fine not exceeding level 5 on the standard scale | 191(10):<br>"If a person – (a) was under the duty to notify the Authority imposed by Section 178(1) or 190(1) but had no knowledge of the act or circumstances by virtue of which that duty arose, but (b) subsequently becomes aware of that act or those circumstances, he must notify the Authority before the end of the period of 14 days |

*Table 8.1* continued

| Section | Offence | Sentence after summary conviction | Sentence after conviction on indictment | Other details |
|---|---|---|---|---|
| | | | | beginning with the day on which he first became so aware" |
| 203 | Breach of a prohibition on the carrying on of Consumer Credit Act business | A fine not exceeding the statutory maximum | Fine | |
| 204 | Breach of a restriction on the carrying on of Consumer Credit Act business | A fine not exceeding the statutory maximum | Fine | |
| 333(1)(a) | False claims to be a person to whom the general prohibition does not apply: "A person who (a) describes himself (in whatever terms) as a person to whom the general prohibition does not apply, in relation to a particular regulated activity, as a result of this part . . . is guilty of an offence if he is not such a person" | Imprisonment not exceeding 6 months, or a fine not exceeding level 5 on the standard scale, or both | | 333(4) "But where the conduct constituting the offence involved or included the public display of any material, the maximum fine for the offence is level 5 on the standard scale multiplied by the number of days for which the display continued" |
| 346 | Provision of false or misleading information to an auditor or actuary: "An authorised person who knowingly or recklessly gives an appointed auditor or actuary information which is false or misleading in a material particular is guilty of an offence" | Imprisonment not exceeding 6 months, or a fine not exceeding the statutory maximum, or both | Imprisonment for a term not exceeding 2 years, or a fine, or both | |

| | | | |
|---|---|---|---|
| 352(1) | Disclosure of confidential information: "A person who discloses information in contravention of Section 348 . . . is guilty of an offence" | Imprisonment not exceeding 3 months, or a fine not exceeding the statutory maximum, or both | Imprisonment not exceeding 2 years, or a fine, or both | 348(1): "Confidential information must not be disclosed by a primary recipient, or by any person obtaining the information directly or indirectly from a primary recipient, without the consent of – (a) the person from whom the primary recipient obtained the information; and (b) if different, the person to whom it relates" |
| 352(1) | Disclosure of Revenue information without authority: "A person who discloses information in contravention of Section . . . 350(5) is guilty of an offence" | Imprisonment not exceeding 3 months, or a fine not exceeding the statutory maximum, or both | Imprisonment not exceeding 2 years, or a fine, or both | 350(5): "Information obtained as a result of subsection (1) may not be disclosed except – (a) by or under the authority of the Commissioner of Inland Revenue; (b) in proceedings mentioned in subsection (4)(c) or (e) or with a view to their institution" |
| 352(3) | Use of unlawfully disclosed confidential information: "A person is guilty of an offence if, in contravention of any provision of regulations made under Section 349, he uses information which has been disclosed to him in accordance with the regulations" | Imprisonment not exceeding 3 months, or a fine not exceeding the level 5 on the standard scale, or both | | |

**Table 8.1** *continued*

| Section | Offence | Sentence after summary conviction | Sentence after conviction on indictment | Other details |
|---------|---------|-----------------------------------|------------------------------------------|---------------|
| 352(4) | Use of unlawfully obtained Revenue information: "A person is guilty of an offence, if in contravention of subsection (4) of Section 350, he uses information which has been disclosed to him in accordance with that Section" | Imprisonment not exceeding 3 months, or a fine not exceeding the level 5 on the standard scale, or both | | 350(4): "Information obtained as a result of subsection (1) may not be used except – (a) for the purpose of deciding whether to appoint an investigator under Section 168; (b) in the conduct of an investigation under Section 168; (c) in criminal proceedings against a person under this Act or the Criminal Justice Act 1993 as a result of an investigation under Section 163; (d) for the purpose of taking action under this Act against a person as a result of an investigation under Section 168; (e) in proceedings before the Tribunal as a result of action taken as mentioned in paragraph (d)" |
| 366(3) | Failure to notify the FSA of a meeting to wind up an insurer: "A person who fails to comply with subsection 2 is guilty of an offence" | A fine not exceeding level 5 on the standard scale | | 366(2): "If notice of a general meeting of such an insurer is given, specifying the intention to propose a resolution for voluntary winding up of the insurer, a director of the insurer must notify the Authority as soon as practicable after he becomes aware of it" |

| | | | | |
|---|---|---|---|---|
| 397(2) | False statements, promises or forecasts:<br><br>"A person to whom subsection (1) applies is guilty of an offence if he makes a statement, promise or forecast or conceals the facts for the purpose of inducing, or is reckless as to whether it may induce, another person (whether or not the person to whom the statement, promise or forecast is made) – (a) to enter or offer to enter into, or to refrain from entering or offering to enter into, a relevant agreement;" | Imprisonment not exceeding 6 months, or a fine not exceeding the statutory maximum, or both | Imprisonment not exceeding 7 years, or a fine, or both | 397(1):<br>This subsection applies to a person who – (a) makes a statement, promise or forecast which he knows to be misleading, false or deceptive in a material particular; (b) dishonestly conceals any material facts whether in connection with a statement, promise or forecast made by him or otherwise; (c) recklessly makes (dishonestly or otherwise) a statement, promise or forecast which is misleading, false or deceptive in a material particular |
| 397(1)(b) | Concealment of facts:<br>*see* Section 397(2) above, "Other details" | Imprisonment not exceeding 6 months, or a fine not exceeding the statutory maximum, or both | Imprisonment for a term not exceeding 7 years, or a fine, or both | |
| 397(3) | Creation of false impression:<br><br>"Any person who does any act or engages in any course of conduct which creates a false or misleading impression as to the market in or the price or values of any relevant investments is guilty of an offence if he does so for the purpose of creating that impression and of thereby inducing another person to acquire, dispose of, subscribe for or underwrite those investments | Imprisonment not exceeding 6 months, or a fine not exceeding the statutory maximum, or both | Imprisonment not exceeding 7 years, or a fine, or both | |

**Table 8.1** *continued*

| Section | Offence | Sentence after summary conviction | Sentence after conviction on indictment | Other details |
|---|---|---|---|---|
| | or to refrain from doing so or to exercise, or refrain from exercising any rights conferred by those investments" | | | |
| 398 | Misleading the FSA: "A person who, in purported compliance with any requirement imposed by or under this Act, knowingly or recklessly gives the Authority information which is false or misleading in a material particular is guilty of an offence" | A fine not exceeding the statutory maximum | A fine | |
| 402(1)(a) | Insider dealing: "Except in Scotland the Authority may institute proceedings for an offence under – (a) Part V of the Criminal Justice Act 1993 (insider dealing)" | | | |
| 402(1)(b) | Breaches of money laundering regulations: "Except in Scotland the Authority may institute proceedings for an offence under – (b) prescribed regulations relating to money laundering" | | | |
| Schedule 3 Para 21(1)(a) | Breach of EEA passport rights: "If a UK firm which is not an authorised person contravenes the prohibition imposed by (a) sub-paragraph (1) of paragraph 19 . . . it is guilty of an offence" | A fine not exceeding the statutory maximum | Fine | Schedule 3, para. 19(1): "A UK firm may not exercise an EEA right to establish a branch unless three conditions are satisfied" |

| | | | |
|---|---|---|---|
| Schedule 3, para. 21(1)(b) | "If a UK firm which is not an authorised person contravenes the prohibition imposed by (b) subparagraph (1) or (5) of paragraph 20 it is guilty of an offence" | A fine not exceeding the statutory maximum | Fine |
| Schedule 4, para. 6(1) | Exercise of Treaty rights: "A person who contravenes paragraph 5(2) is guilty of an offence." | A fine not exceeding the statutory maximum | A fine | Schedule 4, Para 5(2): "At least seven days before it begins to carry on such a regulated activity, the firm must give the Authority written notice of its intention to do so" |
| Schedule 13, para. 11(3)(a) | Failure to cooperate with the Tribunal: "A person who without reasonable excuse – (a) refuses or fails – (i) to attend following the issue of a summons by the Tribunal or (ii) to give evidence . . . is guilty of an offence" | A fine not exceeding the statutory maximum | A fine |
| Schedule 13, para. 11(3)(b) | Tampering with evidence: "A person who without reasonable excuse . . . (b)alters, suppresses, conceals or destroys, or refuses to produce a document which he may be required to produce for the purposes of proceedings before the Tribunal, is guilty of an offence" | A fine not exceeding the statutory maximum | Imprisonment not exceeding 2 years, or a fine, or both |

# Chapter 9

# How the FSA makes Disciplinary and Enforcement Decisions

**Tony Woodcock**
Partner
Stephenson Harwood

## 9.1   Introduction

### 9.1.1   The nature of the procedure

This chapter examines the mechanisms by which the Financial Services Authority ("FSA") makes disciplinary and enforcement decisions. The procedure was overhauled in the Enforcement Process Review ("the Review"), the recommendations of which the FSA accepted entirely. The process is undergoing a further review and, at the time of writing, consultation is taking place on a proposal to delete ENF and DEC and to replace them with the Decision Procedure and Penalties Manual ("DEPP") and a new regulatory handbook, the Enforcement Guide ("EG"). References in this chapter to firms include individuals unless otherwise stated.

Essential to understanding the decision-making process is the appreciation that the process is an administrative decision-making process rather than a judicial process, a characterisation that was reaffirmed in the Review[1] in July 2005.

---

[1] Enforcement Process Review (July 2005); CP 02/07 (which aims to consolidate and simplify the current enforcement and decision-making procedures) – references to the proposed new DEPP and EG provisions follow the references in these footnotes to the current DEC and ENF provisions where available.

In CP65,[2] it was summarised:

> "We have sought to develop a decision making procedure that is effective, fair and does not duplicate the function of the Financial Services and Markets Tribunal. Therefore, this procedure is not intended to provide a judicial hearing of the case, but rather to enable the principal issues to be identified, and, if possible, resolved, before a Tribunal hearing."

Though administrative, the procedure nevertheless provides for:

(a)   all enforcement and disciplinary decisions to be made independently of the FSA's investigators;[3]

(b)   access to the evidence upon which the FSA has relied in coming to its decision or which might undermine the FSA's decision;[4] and

(c)   an opportunity to make written and oral representations before the decision is finalised.[5] Forensic challenge is reserved for the Financial Services and Markets Tribunal ("the Tribunal").

The implementation of these features has changed significantly as a result of recommendations made in the Review.

The procedure enables the FSA to make enforcement decisions which can, without more, have binding effect. Unless the target of the enforcement action itself asks to put the matter before the Tribunal, the FSA's decision will stand. A consequence is that the FSA cannot refer the matter to the Tribunal; the decision maker is making the decision on the FSA's behalf and it cannot therefore challenge its own decision.

### 9.1.2   *What disciplinary and enforcement decisions are open to the FSA?*

In its discussion paper *A New Regulator for a New Millennium*,[6] the FSA confirmed that discipline and enforcement are just one of a range of

---

[2] Consultation Paper 65: The Enforcement Manual, paragraph 3.46 and Appendix A at paragraph A6 where the FSA describes itself as having "proposed an option more towards the administrative end".

[3] Section 395(2) FSMA 2000.

[4] Section 394 FSMA 2000.

[5] Section 387(2) FSMA 2000.

[6] January 2000.

"regulatory tools" to ensure compliance with regulatory requirements and to support pursuit of its statutory objectives. Other tools in
this context are, particularly, proactive supervision and monitoring of
firms and an expectation of swift remedial action where rule breaches
are found. The chairman of the FSA has reaffirmed that the FSA is not
an "enforcement-led" regulator. However, the FSA has indicated
through its Enforcement Manual (and, for the future, the Enforcement
Guide) the cases and circumstances in which it will opt for disciplinary action.[7] Broadly, the disciplinary options open to the FSA are:

(a)    criminal prosecution;
(b)    civil proceedings;
(c)    regulatory enforcement.

### 9.1.2.1    Decisions relating to criminal proceedings

The Financial Services and Markets Act 2000 ("FSMA 2000") creates
more than 30 criminal offences ranging from misleading the market[8]
to failing to give certain notices to the FSA.[9] It may also prosecute
certain other types of financial crime.[10] Criminal investigations and
proceedings, and the enforcement policies relating to them, are dealt
with in Chapter 8 of this Guide. There are cases, however, where the
alleged misconduct could amount to both a criminal offence and a
regulatory beach. Where criminal proceedings have been commenced
or will be commenced, the FSA will consider whether regulatory
action is also required.[11] The criminal proceedings may raise concerns
as to fitness and propriety to conduct regulated activities, in which
case the FSA may seek to withdraw the authorisation or vary or
cancel the Part IV permission of an authorised person, or withdraw
approval from an approved person, or seek an order prohibiting an

---

[7] *See* ENF 1.2.3G (EG). The FSA is required in some instances to prepare and publish statements of policy and procedures on the exercise of its enforcement powers: *see*, for example,
Section 69 (misconduct by approved persons); Section 124 (market abuse); Section 210 (imposition and amount of penalties). Specific provisions relating to enforcement policy are found
in ENF 11 (the FSA's general approach); ENF 12 (Public Censures and Public Statements);
ENF 13 (Financial Penalties); ENF 15 (Prosecution of Criminal Offences), which will be
carried through into EG.

[8] Section 397 FSMA 2000.

[9] For example, Schedule 4 paragraph 5 FSMA 2000.

[10] Section 402 FSMA 2000 permits the FSA to prosecute offences under Part V of the Criminal
Justice Act 1993 (insider dealing) and under the Money Laundering Regulation 2003 (*see*
Money Laundering Regulations 2000, regulation 1(3)).

[11] *See* ENF 15.4.3G (EG 12.4).

individual from carrying out functions in connection with regulated activities.[12] In determining whether to take regulatory action where criminal proceedings exist or are in contemplation, the FSA takes into account whether the action:

(a)   might unfairly prejudice the criminal prosecution;
(b)   might unfairly prejudice the defendants in the conduct of their defence;
(c)   is appropriate having regard to the scope of the criminal proceedings and the powers available to the criminal courts.[13]

There is no reason in principle for regulatory action to await the outcome of the criminal proceedings.[14]

In relation to offences under Section 397 FSMA 2000 (misleading statements and practices) and Part V of the Criminal Justice Act 1993 (insider dealing), where the FSA also has power to impose a sanction for market abuse, the FSA will consider what (if any) regulatory action is also appropriate.[15]

It is the FSA's policy not to impose a sanction for market abuse where a firm is being prosecuted for an offence relating to market misconduct or has finally been convicted or acquitted of market misconduct where the prosecution arises from substantially the same allegations. Equally, it is the FSA's policy not to commence a prosecution for a market misconduct offence where the FSA has brought or is seeking to bring disciplinary proceedings for market abuse arising out of the same facts.[16] However, where it takes criminal action, the FSA may take regulatory action to withdraw the approval of an approved person or to cancel the permission, or withdraw the authorisation, of an authorised person, or to prohibit an individual from carrying out functions in connection with regulated activities,[17] which courses are not open to a criminal court.

---

[12]  Section 56 FSMA 2000.
[13]  ENF 15.4.4G (EG 12.4).
[14]  *R (on the application of Nicholas Land)* v *Executive Council of the Joint Disciplinary Scheme* [2002] NLJR 1617; *R* v *Solicitors Disciplinary Tribunal ex parte Gallagher* 30 September 1991, unreported, CA (Civil Division).
[15]  ENF 15.4.2G (EG 12.4).
[16]  ENF 15.7.4G (EG 12.10).
[17]  ENF 15.7.5G (EG 12.4).

Specific guidance is given as to the factors which the FSA may consider when deciding whether to commence a criminal prosecution for market misconduct rather than to impose a sanction for market abuse.[18] These include, but are not limited to:

(a) the seriousness of the misconduct and the prospect of a significant sentence;

(b) whether or not there are victims who have suffered loss;

(c) the extent and nature of the loss suffered, including the number of victims;

(d) the effect of the conduct on the market, particularly where there is a significant distortion or disruption of the market or significant damage to market confidence;

(e) the gain made or the loss avoided by the miscreant;

(f) the risk of a recurrence of the misconduct;

(g) the miscreant's record;

(h) the extent (if any) of any steps to provide redress to the victims;

(i) the effect of proceedings on the solvency of a firm or individual insofar as it affects the prospect of securing redress for victims;

(j) the extent and cooperation with the FSA and the personal circumstances of the individual, including his honesty, any abuse of a position of trust and his culpability in comparison with the activities of others also involved.

A decision to prosecute for a criminal offence is taken by the Regulatory Decisions Committee ("RDC") chairman or, in an urgent case and if the chairman is not available, by a deputy chairman with another RDC member.[19] In cases of exceptional urgency, a decision to prosecute may be made by the Director of Enforcement or, if not available, at director of division level.[20] In less serious cases and less complex cases, the decision to prosecute may be taken at senior executive level.[21] These are various offences under the Building Societies Act 1986, the Friendly Societies Act 1974 and 1992, the Credit Unions Act 1971 and the Industrial and Provident Societies Act 1965. In reaching a decision to prosecute or to refer the case to another authority for

---

[18] ENF 15.7.2G (EG 12.8).

[19] DEC 4.6.1G.

[20] DEC 4.6.2G.

[21] DEC 4.6.2AG and 4.6.2BG.

prosecution, the FSA will apply the basic principles set out in the Code for Crown Prosecutors, namely: is the evidence sufficient to provide a realistic prospect of a conviction and, if so, is prosecution in the public interest?[22] The FSA may, instead, issue a formal caution where there is a reasonable prospect of a conviction, where the offence is admitted, and the offender understands the significance of a caution and gives informed consent.[23] The Secretary of State may also specify the FSA as a "relevant prosecutor" for the purposes of issuing "conditional cautions" under the Criminal Justice Act 2003 by which failure to comply with a condition imposed with a caution may lead to prosecution for the original offence.[24]

### 9.1.2.2    Civil proceedings

The civil law remedies available to the FSA are dealt with in Chapter 11 of this Guide. Many of the civil-law powers exercisable through the courts against any alleged miscreant are also directly enforceable by the FSA against authorised persons or approved persons through the FSA's internal disciplinary procedure.[25]

Where civil action is to be taken through the courts, the decision is taken in the same manner as for criminal proceedings, save that there is no provision for the use of executive procedures. Where the FSA seeks to exercise those powers itself it does so through the statutory notice procedure described below in relation to regulatory action.

### 9.1.2.3    Regulatory action

The remainder of this chapter focuses on how the FSA makes its disciplinary and enforcement decisions in relation to regulatory proceedings, and specifically on the process by which such decisions are reached. For this purpose, the chapter is confined to the procedure known as the warning notice and decision notice procedure where it is proposed to impose a fine, issue a public statement/censure, revoke certain authorisations, permissions or approvals, or order restitution.

---

[22] ENF 15.5; Code for Crown Prosecutors (November 2004) (EG 12.2; EG 12.7).
[23] ENF 15.6; Home Office Guidance on the Cautioning of Offenders: Home Office Circular 18/1994 (EG12.2).
[24] Part 3, Criminal Justice Act 2003.
[25] Sections 384 to 386 FSMA 2000 in relation to restitution, using the warning/decision notice procedure.

## 9.2 Regulatory enforcement

### 9.2.1 Overview

Where the FSA proposes to take formal enforcement action, it must do so using a statutory notice procedure. The type of notice will depend upon the type of enforcement action contemplated. Annex 1G to DEC 2 (DEPP 2 Annex 1) lists the enforcement action which is subject to the warning notice and decision notice procedure and states who the decision maker is in each case.

Part XXVI FSMA 2000 provides the statutory framework for the issue of:

(a) warning notices;
(b) decision notices;
(c) notices of discontinuance;
(d) final notices.

Part XXVI also deals with ancillary matters such as access to evidence, publicity and the right of third parties to have access to evidence and make representations as regards any disciplinary action which may prejudice them. These matters are known as "statutory notice associated decisions".

The legislation provides the target of proposed regulatory action with the right to be informed of the action being proposed and the reasons for it, having regard to the FSA's policy. There is a right within a reasonable time to make written and oral representations to a decision maker who is independent of the investigators. In most instances this will be before a body known as the Regulatory Decisions Committee ("RDC"). There are provisions enabling certain types of decision to be taken at senior executive level. The post-representation stage may lead to a confirmation, variation or withdrawal of the enforcement action proposed. Where the FSA has decided on enforcement action, there is a right to a judicial hearing before the Tribunal. Details of the decision-making procedure are found in the decision-making manual ("DEC" or "DEPP").

## 9.3 The decision maker

### 9.3.1 Introduction

Section 395 FSMA 2000 requires the FSA to establish and publish the procedure that it will follow in relation to giving warning notices and decision notices. The FSA must follow its published procedure and though failure to follow its procedure in a particular case does not affect the validity of a warning notice or a decision notice, the Tribunal may take any such failure into account when considering a matter referred to it.[26]

Section 395(2) provides that the procedures must ensure that the decision to give a notice is made by a person not directly involved in establishing the evidence on which the decision is based. The FSMA 2000 further provides that the FSA may make arrangements for any of its functions to be discharged by a committee, subcommittee, officer or other member of its staff. That is all that is prescribed by statute.[27] CP 65[28] set out the means through which this statutory requirement would be implemented. It proposed the establishment of a Regulatory Decisions Committee to make decisions on behalf of the FSA. Executive procedures, involving senior FSA staff, were proposed for less serious cases. The RDC would not be involved in the investigation of a case. The RDC is not referred to in FSMA 2000; its constitution and procedure are contained in Chapter 4 of DEC (DEPP 3).

DEC 4.1.4G (DEPP 2 Annex 1) lists the decisions which must be made by the RDC.[29] Other decisions can be made through executive procedures: examples are provided in DEC 4.1.8G. The allocation of cases as between the RDC and FSA staff was the subject of considerable discussion in the Review. In the event, DEC was amended only in the context of authorisation and approval decisions in that the warning notice decision would be made by FSA staff and the decision notice decision by the RDC.[30] This is unchanged by DEPP.

---

[26] Section 395(9) and (11).
[27] Paragraph 5(1) Schedule 1 FSMA 2000.
[28] Consultation Paper 65: The Enforcement Manual, at Annex A, paragraph A6.
[29] DEC 4.1.4G (DEPP 2 Annex 1).
[30] Enforcement Process Review, paragraphs 6.24–6.26; Policy Statement 05/11 paragraphs 2.3–2.8; DEC 4.1.4G (as amended in October 2005); 4.1.4AG and 4.1.4BG as promulgated in October 2005 (Enforcement (Settlement and other procedures) Instrument 2005) (DEPP 2).

Decisions in relation to enforcement remain with the RDC both as to the issue of a warning notice, a decision notice and a final notice, save that new provision has been made for decisions to be made in straightforward cases by the RDC chairman or deputy alone or with one other.[31]

## 9.3.2 *The Regulatory Decisions Committee*

The RDC is appointed by the FSA board to make decisions on the FSA's behalf relating to certain regulatory enforcement action. The RDC is accountable to the FSA board for its decisions.[32] It has a secretariat, now known as the "RDC office", which liaises between it and enforcement staff and provides other support functions to the RDC, notably the provision of legal advice.[33] The RDC consists of a chairman and several deputy chairmen. Though neither FSMA 2000 nor DEC (DEPP) require it, the chairman and the deputy chairmen appointed by the FSA to date have a legal background.[34] Although accountable to the FSA board for its decisions, the RDC is not part of the management structure of the FSA: only the chairman is an employee of the FSA and is salaried. He is appointed by the FSA board on the recommendation of an independent group established for that purpose; the group comprises a non-executive member of the FSA board and, for example, the chairman of the FSA's Consumer Panel. Deputy chairmen and other members are chosen by the FSA board on the recommendation of the chairman of the RDC.

The other members of the RDC are current or recently retired practitioners with financial services industry skills and knowledge, and non-practitioners,[35] such as academics and representatives of consumer groups. All represent the public interest, rather than the FSA or the interests which appoint them. The FSA recognised the difficulty in predicting the amount of work with which the RDC would be involved but planned to have a membership of 37, comprising the chairman, four deputy chairmen, 16 practitioner members

---

[31] *See* 9.3.4 below.
[32] DEC 4.2.1G (DEPP 3.1.1G).
[33] DEC 4.2.4G (DEPP 3.1.4G).
[34] It was the expectation of CP65 that the chairman would come from a legal background: *see* Annex D, paragraph D6.
[35] DEC 4.2.3G (DEPP 3.1.2(3)G).

and 16 other public interest members.[36] In fact, the number has been reduced. The Review reiterated that it is important that RDC members have enough work to gain experience of the RDC and its business. It recommended a reduction in membership, which would also reduce the risk of inconsistency in decision making.[37] Other than the salaried chairman, the members are paid an annual retainer and hourly rates for attendance and preparation. A member of the RDC may only be removed by the FSA for misconduct or incapacity.[38]

### 9.3.3   The RDC office

Prior to the Review, the RDC Secretariat provided purely administrative services to the RDC. It arranged meetings, liaised between the RDC and Enforcement, and liaised between the RDC and firms against which enforcement action was being taken. It did not provide legal advice to the RDC nor did it attempt to summarise the frequently bulky material that Enforcement presented to the RDC to support its application for the issue of a warning notice. The RDC received its legal advice from Enforcement. In response to the "considerable criticism" received in relation to the perceived partiality of the legal advice provided to the RDC, the Review recommended that the RDC should have its own small dedicated legal function which would assist the RDC to finalise draft warning notices and to draft decision notices, to ensure that any substantive communications between the RDC and Enforcement are recorded and disclosed to the firm, to assist the RDC in considering the case and the underlying material, and to provide any legal advice required.[39] These arrangements are in place. It is difficult to assess the impact of the change. The legal complement of the RDC office is small. Though the lawyers come from the General Counsel's team and are independent of Enforcement, it is difficult to see how they can still be anything other than very reliant upon Enforcement, particularly its lawyers. Legal professional privilege will serve to ensure that neither the quantity nor the quality of professional input from the RDC office to the RDC can be judged.

---

[36] Consultation Paper 65: The Enforcement Manual, Annex D, paragraph D16.
[37] Enforcement Process Review, paragraph 6.13.
[38] DEC 4.2.7G (DEPP 3.1.2G(2)).
[39] Enforcement Process Review, paragraphs 6.14–6.17.

### 9.3.4    The RDC's relationship with Enforcement

For the purposes of deciding to issue warning, decision and final notices, the RDC is the FSA. Its decisions are those of the FSA; neither the FSA board nor FSA staff can overrule it. The RDC can take a softer line or a harder line than that suggested by Enforcement dealing with a particular case. Enforcement carry out the investigation and the RDC, which makes the decisions, is not involved in establishing the evidence on which the decision is based. This is consistent with the administrative nature of the process and complies with FSMA 2000.[40] Nevertheless, the distinction between the two bodies and their functions was far from watertight. Enforcement had a considerable influence on the decision-making process. The process raised questions as to the independence of the RDC, the transparency of its decisions, the value it added, and the extent to which it was equipped to challenge staff decisions. This issue was raised starkly in the *Legal & General* case[41] where there was criticism of the RDC for simply adopting an expert report to establish that a case had been made in circumstances where the expert had qualified its report and accepted that it did not of itself establish the breaches complained of. This shortcoming caused practitioners to have considerable concern about the fairness of the process. The Review summarised the areas of criticism as follows:

(a)    the giving of confidential legal advice by Enforcement to the RDC (and the non-disclosure of the case review paper to the firm);

(b)    the non-disclosure of other communications between Enforcement and the RDC;

(c)    the discussions that take place between Enforcement and the RDC in the absence of the firm following oral representations; and

(d)    the lack of explanation in the decision notice as to how the RDC has dealt with the key points made by the firm or individual.

As a result of these criticisms, the relationship between Enforcement and the RDC has been considerably modified though the FSA did not

---

[40]    Section 395(2) FSMA 2000.
[41]    *FSA v Legal & General Assurance Company Limited*, 18 January 2005, paragraph 206.

concede that the existing process was not compliant with FSMA 2000. Reference has already been made to the establishment of the RDC office. The following recommendations of the Review have now been implemented (none required a change to ENF or DEC; they are a matter of internal practice). These are as follows:

(a) All substantive communications between Enforcement and the RDC (whether oral or written) should be disclosed to the firm. Plainly, legal advice within Enforcement is privileged (as is the legal advice provided from the RDC office to the RDC), but insofar as Enforcement makes legal submissions orally or in writing to the RDC for the purpose of supporting its application for the issue of a warning notice, such legal submissions must be disclosed to the firm.

(b) Enforcement are no longer to meet with the RDC following the oral representations meeting. It is assumed that this will include after the submission of written representations (whether or not oral representations follow the submission of written representations). It was a cause of considerable concern that, having made representations, Enforcement were entitled to remain with the RDC having heard the representations. It was rightly assumed that Enforcement would then participate in discussions with the RDC as to the value of the representations made and seek to persuade the RDC that the representations were, in whole or in part, without merit. This now ceases.

(c) It is envisaged that the oral representation stage should be conducted on a more interactive basis. Enforcement, particularly, will be required to contribute to the debate before the RDC.

One particular bone of contention in the past has been the provision to the RDC by Enforcement of a case review paper. Disclosure was refused to the firm either on the basis of privilege or public interest immunity. The Review has recommended that there will no longer be a non-disclosed review paper and that all legal and policy issues raised before the RDC will be disclosable, save for very sensitive material about performance or comparative penalty material which is not yet public.[42]

---

[42] Enforcement Process Review, paragraph 6.16.

### 9.3.5 *How the RDC works*

#### 9.3.5.1 *Panels*

The RDC may meet either as a full committee or in panels.[43] Each meeting of the RDC will include the chairman or a deputy chairman and at least two other members. There is no requirement that each of the other members should come from the practitioner group and the non-practitioner group respectively. The composition and size of panels, and the frequency of their meetings, will depend on the matters under consideration.[44] Prior to the Review the RDC was arranged in fixed standing groups, with eight members deciding on the issue of warning notices and a smaller panel (usually three) considering the issue of a decision notice, including hearing any oral representations. The Review concluded that a panel of eight for the issue of warning notices was too large. It recommended that the chairman or deputy chairman should determine the appropriate panel size at both stages.

The Review has modified the decision-making process in this regard in a further fundamental respect. It recommended that in "straight-forward cases" (such as simple cases involving threshold conditions) the decision should be made by the chairman or deputy chairman alone or with one other member. It was anticipated that, where representations are to be made, the decision notice panel would usually have two members in addition to the chairman or deputy chairman, but the ultimate decision on composition would be a matter for the chairman or deputy.[45] This modification (one of the few which required amendment to DEC) is found at DEC 4.5.16G (DEPP 3.2.9.G(1)). In the consultation process[46] there was concern that it would be for the chairman alone to make such decisions and to assess what was "straightforward". Consultees asked what would happen if there was a dispute between the firm and the FSA on whether the case was straightforward. It has now been accepted that if the firm makes representation to the RDC after the warning notice is issued, the matter will then be considered under full RDC procedures. As

---

[43] DEC 4.2.8G (DEPP 3.2.2G – the RDC may meet or deal with representations in writing or by telephone or email).
[44] DEC 4.2.9G (DEPP 3.2.3G).
[45] Enforcement Process Review, paragraph 6.23.
[46] Policy Statement 05/11 paragraph 2.2.

regards "straightforward", the FSA indicated that it would regularly publish the types of case being decided under this procedure. It envisages cases concerning firms that have not submitted regulatory returns or paid fees. The FSA does not expect the procedure to be used where there are significant issues in dispute. A requirement that the firm should consent before this procedure was adopted for the case was rejected on the basis that firms frequently fail to respond to the enforcement process. If these limits are maintained, little difficulty is anticipated. However, there is no effective means of challenging the decision to deal with a matter under the "straightforward" procedure short of taking the matter to the Tribunal thereafter. In reality, however, it is unlikely that this approach will cause any practical difficulties.

DEC (DEPP) provides a procedure for ensuring that members who have a conflict of interest in any matter before the RDC raise the conflict with the chairman and do not participate in the decision.[47]

Meetings of the RDC, including panels of the RDC in enforcement matters, take place in private. There is no mandatory procedure; proceedings are managed in the way the RDC or the panel considers suitable in order to enable it fairly to determine the issues before it.[48] Each member of the RDC present at the meeting may vote, and the chairman of the meeting will have a casting vote if there is a tie.[49]

### 9.3.5.2 *Considering the warning notice*
The initiative for bringing a matter before the RDC rests with Enforcement. Where Enforcement considers that action is appropriate, having regard to the information gathered in the course of the investigation and to the FSA's policies, they will recommend to the RDC that a warning notice of enforcement action be given.[50] There is no right at this stage for the firm targeted to have access to the staff recommendation or to make representations on it. A draft warning notice will be provided to the RDC containing the information

---

[47] DEC 4.2.10G (DEPP 3.2.4G).
[48] DEC 4.2.12G (DEPP 3.2.7G).
[49] DEC 4.2.13G. (DEPP 3.2.8G).
[50] DEC 2.2.1G. (DEPP 2.2.1G).

required by Section 387(1),[51] together with a copy of the Investigation Report and any analysis conducted by, and legal advice obtained by, Enforcement. The RDC may then decide not to take further action (with or without a private warning) or decide to give a warning notice.[52] Though DEC does not say, it is implicit that as the warning notice comes from the RDC, its terms may differ from those recommended by Enforcement and, in practice, the RDC does make changes to the terms of drafts submitted to it by Enforcement. No guidance is given as to how the RDC should exercise its discretion, though it would be expected to implement FSA policy[53] and reach some, if only a prima facie, view of the strength of the evidence. It may take into account the previous disciplinary record of the firm concerned in determining whether to take action and, if so, the level of any financial penalty, though not for the purpose of proving a later breach.[54] If the RDC decides to take enforcement action, the warning notice will be served on the firm.[55] It must also be served on any third party whose interest may be affected.[56] If the RDC decides to take no further action, and the FSA had previously informed the target that it intended to recommend action, the FSA will communicate the decision promptly to the person concerned.[57] Usually FSA staff will indicate, even if only on an informal basis, whether or not the matter is being referred to the RDC and, in due course, the decision. A warning notice will be served shortly after the decision to issue it has been reached.

Where an investigation is being conducted and where it becomes likely that enforcement action will be taken, a practice has developed under which a firm will seek to negotiate the terms of the warning notice with the FSA. This has the advantage of easing the process through the RDC and influencing the terms not only of the warning notice but also of the decision and final notices.

---

[51] *See* 9.4.1.
[52] DEC 2.2.2G. (DEPP 2.2.3G)
[53] For the reasons expressed in 9.3.3.
[54] DEC 4.2.15G (DEPP 6.2.1G(3)(a)).
[55] In accordance with the FSMA (Service of Notices) Regulations SI 2001/1420.
[56] Section 393 FSMA 2000; DEC 2.4.
[57] DEC 2.2.6G (DEPP 3.2.25G).

### 9.3.6 *Decisions made by FSA staff under executive procedures*

DEC provides that certain types of decision may be made by FSA staff under executive procedures.[58] These have historically related to authorisation and approval issues. If the FSA decide to grant applications for authorisation or approval, this is done at FSA staff level. Rejections, however, are dealt with by the RDC. The Review describes the procedure and its significant differences from enforcement cases. In order to improve the efficiency and fairness of the process in authorisation cases, it proposed that FSA staff should make the warning notice decision with the RDC considering an applicant's oral and written submissions and making the decision notice decision. Further, the material provided to the RDC should be disclosed to the applicant.

DEC 4.1 (DEPP 2) describes how decisions are now to be allocated between the RDC and FSA staff. FSA staff responsible for preparing and recommending action in individual cases allocate cases to the RDC or to executive procedures according to the criteria set out in DEC 4.1.4G and DEC 4.1.6G (DEPP 2.1.1.G Annex 1 and Annex 2).[59] DEC 4.1.4G (DEPP 2.1.1.G Annex 1) contains a list of decisions for which the RDC alone has responsibility. Decisions, for these purposes, include associated decisions:

(a)    to set or extend the period for making representations;
(b)    to send a notice to a third party and afford an opportunity to make representations;
(c)    to refuse access to FSA material;
(d)    and as to the information it is appropriate to publish relating to a final notice.

DEC 4.3 sets out the procedures to be followed where decisions are made by FSA staff, and the line management responsibilities. As required by Section 395(2) FSMA 2000, and consistently with the RDC process, the decision-maker will not have been involved in establishing the evidence.[60] Decisions may be made by individual FSA staff

---

[58]  DEC 1.2.6G (DEPP 1.2.5G).
[59]  DEC 4.1.3G (DEPP 2.1.1G).
[60]  DEC 4.3.3G (DEPP 1.2.1G).

members or by a senior staff committee.[61] There is no guidance in DEC (DEPP) as to how the decision-making process is allocated within the FSA staff structure. Individual staff decisions may be made only at the level of an executive director of the FSA board (or his delegate, who must be of at least the level of associate) on the recommendation of an FSA staff member of at least the level of associate and with legal advice from a staff member of at least the level of associate.[62] A senior staff committee is chosen by the FSA chairman's committee and may delegate decisions in particular cases or types of cases to sub-committees.[63] Any committee or sub-committee must have a chairman and at least two other members. It may act only on the recommendation of an FSA staff member of associate level and with legal advice from a staff member of associate level. There are provisions enabling FSA staff to seek a decision in an urgent case from a chairman or deputy chairman of the RDC or a director of division level.[64]

Notices served under executive procedures must comply with the Sections 387 to 390 FSMA 2000.[65] Representations may be made to the executive decision maker in the same manner as to the RDC.[66]

As the Review acknowledged, most enforcement cases settle, either before the issue of a warning notice, between warning and decision notice, or even during Tribunal proceedings. Prior to the Review, where a decision notice was required in respect of a settlement (i.e. in all enforcement cases), the RDC had to make that decision. In practice, the FSA staff would consult the RDC to obtain "settlement parameters" with a view to seeking settlement within those parameters. There was no provision that the RDC panel considering settlement should be debarred from considering the case on a fully contested basis if the settlement negotiations broke down. The Review recommended that the RDC should no longer make decisions on statutory

---

[61] DEC 4.3.1G (DEPP 4).
[62] DEC 4.3.4G (DEPP 4.1.7G).
[63] DEC 4.3.10G (DEPP 4.1.5G).
[64] DEC 4.3.12G (DEPP 4.1.13G).
[65] *See* 9.4.
[66] DEC 4.3.14G (DEPP 4.1.13G).

notices that result from settlement. Accordingly, DEC Appendix 1 1.2.1G (DEPP 5.1.4G) now ring-fences the settlement process from the RDC entirely. Settlement decisions will now be made by Enforcement. There must be two "settlement decision makers" of at least director of division level. It is anticipated that one of the settlement decision makers will be the Director of Enforcement. DEC 1.2.1G (DEPP 5.1.4G) provides that neither Enforcement nor the firm may disclose to the RDC any such admissions or statements made by the other.

On consultation there was a suggestion that the RDC should have a role in approving or ratifying settlements. However, this was rejected on the ground that either the RDC will effectively only be "rubber stamping" settlement and would not add to the process, or it could reject the proposed settlement, leaving the procedure open to the objections which it has faced in the past. In order to ensure consistency between settlement decisions made by Enforcement and contested cases decided by the RDC, regular discussions will be held both at a level of principle and also where there are potential points of disagreement on completed cases.[67]

## 9.4 Warning notices

### 9.4.1 Role of Enforcement

The warning notice stage marks the beginning of the transmission of the responsibility for enforcement decisions from Enforcement to the RDC though, as has been observed, Enforcement has hitherto retained a significant influence on the decision-making process and to a lesser extent will continue to do so post Review. Once the investigation is complete, Enforcement reach a decision, having regard to FSA policies as set out in ENF as to whether enforcement action is justified. If so, an investigation report setting out the facts as found by Enforcement, together with any response from the firm to the preliminary findings letter (a sweep-up part of the investigation process), Enforcement's case review paper and a draft warning notice, is sent to the RDC. There follows a meeting between Enforcement and the RDC panel. A decision is reached as to whether the warning notice

---

[67] Policy Statement 05/11, paragraph 2.8.

should be issued and, if so, in what terms. It is rare for the documents underlying the investigation report to be provided to the RDC, which casts some doubt on the degree to which the RDC can make a decision which is truly independent of Enforcement, a shortcoming which was highlighted in the *Legal and General* case.

### 9.4.2 Content of a warning notice

Warning notices are governed by the provisions of Section 387 FSMA 2000, as supplemented by DEC (DEPP).[68]

A warning notice must:[69]

(a)  state the action the FSA proposes to take;
(b)  be in writing;
(c)  give reasons for the proposed action;
(d)  give details of rights of access to evidence which either supports or undermines the FSA's case;
(e)  specify a reasonable period (which may not be less than 28 days) within which the firm may make representations to the FSA.[70]

The warning notice is not a pleading as such, and DEC (DEPP) does not provide, for example, for the lodging of a defence or the making of requests for further and better particulars. Such matters may be raised informally with enforcement staff but, subject to the RDC's discretion to extend the time limit for making written representations and the timetable for making oral representations, the service of the warning notice initiates a highly structured process which will not, in practice, be delayed by requests from the recipient of the warning notice for further factual information or for specification of how the FSA puts its case or implements its policy. The legislation reserves such processes for the Tribunal. The process will not be delayed by the existence of parallel proceedings.[71]

---

[68]  Made pursuant to Section 395(1) FSMA 2000 and which the FSA must follow: Section 395(9) FSMA 2000; DEC 1.1.2G (DEPP 5.1.4G).
[69]  Section 387(1) FSMA 2000.
[70]  Section 387(2) FSMA 2000. The period of 28 days may be extended by the FSA: Section 387(3) FSMA 2000. In computing the number of days, no account is to be taken of any day which is a public holiday in any part of the UK.
[71]  See *R v Immigration Appeal Tribunal ex parte Khan (Mahmud)* [1983] 2 AER 420; *R v Civil Service Appeal Board, ex parte Cunningham* [1992] 1 CR 816.

The statutory duty to give reasons will, like the duty to give reasons imposed by other statutes or at common law, be satisfied if the warning notice outlines (albeit briefly) the relevant issue and why the FSA resolved the issue in the way it did.

Whilst there is no required or standard form for a warning notice, its usual content is:

(a)  a statement of the action to be taken;

(b)  a summary of the findings of fact of the FSA's Enforcement Division (in cases where a preliminary findings letter has been provided during the investigation, this summary is likely to follow quite closely the contents of that preliminary findings letter);

(c)  a recitation of the rule(s) alleged to have been breached;

(d)  a description of how the FSA applies its policy to the breach;

(e)  a statement of the rights available to the person to whom the warning notice is directed; that is, to make representations to the RDC, and the date by which such representations should be made; access to evidence; ultimate recourse to the Tribunal and mediation;

(f)  a notification that the warning notice and its contents are confidential and may not be published.[72]

The warning notice must set out the action which the FSA proposes to take.[73] In addition to the generality of this requirement, there are certain specific requirements depending on the nature of the enforcement action. A warning notice of a prohibition order must set out the terms of the prohibition.[74] A warning notice to impose a financial penalty on, or publish a statement about, an approved person must set out the amount of the proposed financial penalty or set out the terms of the proposed statement.[75] A warning notice to impose a financial penalty on, or publish a statement about, a person who has engaged in market abuse must set out the amount of the proposed financial penalty or set out the terms of the proposed statement.[76] A

---

[72] Section 391(1) FSMA 2000.
[73] Section 387(1)(a) FSMA 2000.
[74] Section 57(1) FSMA 2000.
[75] Section 127(2) and (3) FSMA 2000. It cannot do both: Section 123(3) FSMA 2000.
[76] Section 127(2) and (3) FSMA 2000. It cannot do both: Section 123(3) FSMA 2000.

warning notice to impose a financial penalty on, or publish a statement about, an authorised person in respect of a contravention of FSMA 2000, or rules or regulations made under FSMA 2000, must set out the terms of the proposed statement or the amount of the proposed penalty.[77] A warning notice in connection with the payment of restitution must specify the amount which the FSA proposes to require the person concerned to pay.[78]

### 9.4.3 Service of warning notice

The warning notice is sent to the firm both by hand and by first-class post. [79] If the warning notice identifies another party and, in the opinion of the FSA, is prejudicial to the other party, it is also sent at the same time and in the same manner to that party.[80] A decision as to whom a third-party notice should be sent is also made by the RDC. It will invite representations as to the substance of the alleged notice and the prejudice which might be caused by publication of a decision notice or final notice in similar terms. The notice affords an opportunity for the third party to make written and oral representations.

The warning notice, though in practice drafted by Enforcement, is signed off by the chairman of the RDC Panel assigned to the case.

Though there is no statutory or manual provision requiring it, the warning notice (and any associated third-party notice) is accompanied by a copy of the Investigation Report prepared by the FSA's enforcement staff and by a disclosure list[81] identifying the material upon which the RDC relied in coming to its decision (Part 1 material) and identifying material which undermines the FSA's case (Part 2 material). This suggests that the RDC has read and probed the material which has been presented to them by Enforcement. However, it has more usually been the case that the RDC has relied simply upon the investigation report, and it is the author's experience that reference to

---

[77] Section 207(2) and (3) FSMA 2000.
[78] Section 385(2) FSMA 2000.
[79] The provisions governing the service of notices are found in the Financial Services and Markets Act 2000 (Service of Notices) Regulations 2001 (SI 2001/1420) as amended by the Enterprise Act 2002 and the Financial Services and Markets Act (Service of Notices) (Amendment) Regulations 2005 (SI 2005/274).
[80] Section 393(1) FSMA 2000.
[81] Served pursuant to Section 394(1).

materials contained in the disclosure lists in oral representations has made it apparent that the underlying materials have not been read. It is anticipated now that the RDC office will play a significant role in analysing, for the RDC, the evidence provided by Enforcement. The recipient of the warning notice now routinely receives the materials referred to in the disclosure list. If written representations have been made by the firm, Enforcement may provide a written reaction to the representations. There is no obligation upon them to do so and, a fortiori, no time limit by which their response should be provided. Indeed, there is no obligation to share their commentary with the firm. In practice, it is provided, though frequently at a very late stage of the process.

Although the investigation report forms part of the material relied upon by the RDC, the reasons for the FSA's proposed action are contained in the warning notice and the FSA's covering correspondence states that representations should be directed to the content of the warning notice rather than the investigation report. Given that the reasons expressed in the warning notice may, expressly or impliedly, have been influenced to varying degrees by the Investigation Report, there is no basis for restricting the scope of the representations[82] in this way, and material within the investigation report should be as open to comment as material in the warning notice.

### 9.4.4 Publicity

Neither the FSA nor the firm nor any third party may publish the notice or any details concerning it.[83] This statutory prohibition does not, directly, carry a criminal penalty. Insofar as the notice contains any confidential information in respect of which the FSA is a "primary recipient", disclosure by it or by any person obtaining the information directly or indirectly from such primary recipient, without the consent of the person from whom the primary recipient obtained the information or the person to whom the information relates, may amount to a criminal offence.[84] Publication in breach of the prohibition by an authorised person or by an approved person

---

[82] There is no statutory or DEC basis for the restriction.
[83] Section 391(1) FSMA 2000.
[84] Sections 348 and 352 FSMA 2000.

will enable the FSA to take disciplinary action.[85] The prohibition may cause difficulties in the context of due diligence exercises in a commercial transaction or in ensuring compliance with listing rules. The FSA does not have a discretion to permit publication; it does have a discretion, however, as to whether it will take action in respect of a breach of Section 391 FSMA 2000.

## 9.5   Access to FSA material

### 9.5.1   *General right*

Section 394 FSMA 2000 confers on the recipient of a warning notice to which Section 394 relates, and a third party prejudiced by it, the right to have access to the material on which the FSA has relied when making the decision to give the warning notice and to any material ("secondary material") which, in the opinion of the FSA, might undermine that decision.[86] Section 394 applies only to warning notices issued in relation to a proposed:

(a)   cancellation of Part IV permission (Section 54(1));
(b)   prohibition order (Section 57(1));
(c)   withdrawal of approval (Section 63(3));
(d)   disciplinary action against an approved person (Section 67(1));
(e)   cancellation of a person's approval as a sponsor (Section 88(4)(b));
(f)   public censure of a sponsor (Section 89(2));
(g)   disciplinary action for breach of the Listing Rules (Section 92(1));
(h)   penalties for market abuse (Section 126(1));
(i)   disciplinary action against an authorised person (Section 207(1));
(j)   revocation of authorisation (Section 255(1));
(k)   revocation of recognition as a recognised overseas scheme (Section 280(2));
(l)   disapplication of recognition as a designated professional body (Section 331(3));

---

[85]  Sections 66, 205 and 206 FSMA 2000.
[86]  Section 394(1) FSMA 2000.

(m)     disqualification from acting as an auditor or actuary of an authorised person (Section 345(2)).[87]

These are generally cases in which the warning notice is given on the FSA's own initiative rather than in response to an application or notification.[88]

### 9.5.2   Limitations

The FSA is not obliged to afford access rights in respect of "excluded material" or material which:

(a)     relates to a case involving a person other than the person to whom the warning notice is directed; *and*
(b)     was taken into account by the FSA only for purposes of comparison with other cases.[89]

Clearly this is designed to protect the confidentiality of those involved in other cases. Arguably, if the FSA has used other cases as a yardstick for its action in the instant case, its comparative exercise should be subject to scrutiny. Where the action in another case used as a comparator has resulted in a final notice, the contents of which have been made public under Section 391(4) FSMA 2000, there is no disadvantage to the firm. However, where other cases have led to no action, or to private warnings under ENF 11.3 (EG 7.10 et seq.), and given that the FSA's action in previous cases is a factor which is required to be taken into account under the enforcement policy, inaccessibility to such material can disadvantage the firm in attempting to address the propriety of proceedings or the type and level of penalty.[90] Issues relating to confidentiality should be adequately catered for in FSMA 2000's provisions relating to confidentiality.

"Excluded material" means material the disclosure of which is prohibited by Section 17 of the Regulation of Investigatory Powers Act 2000 (protection of information relating to interception of

---

[87]  Section 392(a) FSMA 2000.
[88]  DEC 2.4.1G (DEPP 2 Annex 1: Note).
[89]  Section 394(1) FSMA 2000.
[90]  *See* ENF 11.4.1G; ENF 12.3.3G; ENF 13.3.3G; ENF 14.4.2G; ENF 14.6.2G; ENF 14.7.4G (EG 8, EG 9, EG 10 and EG 11).

communications made pursuant to the Interception of Communications Act 1985) or communications and items subject to legal professional privilege as defined in Section 413 FSMA 2000.[91]

Where access to "excluded material" is refused on the ground that it is subject to legal professional privilege, the FSA must give written notice of the existence of the material and of its decision not to allow access to it.[92]

The FSA may refuse access to particular material to which it would otherwise have to provide access if, in its opinion, such access would not:

(a)   be in the public interest; or
(b)   would not be fair,

having regard to the likely significance of the material to the person to whom the warning notice is directed and to the potential prejudice to the commercial interests of another caused by the material's disclosure.[93] Where access is refused on this ground, the FSA must provide written notice of the refusal and the reasons for it.[94]

### 9.5.3   Practice

The statutory right is of access to the documents, though if a request for access is made, the FSA may, within a reasonable period after the request is made, provide facilities for the inspection and photocopying of the material to be disclosed or provide a photocopy of the material. The FSA will provide the first photocopy of the material free of charge, but will charge for subsequent copies it provides to the same firm.[95]

Almost invariably the appropriate course will be to request Section 394 access which will enable informed decisions to be made as to whether representations should be made to the RDC, or settlement

---

[91]   Section 394(7) and Section 413 FSMA 2000.
[92]   Section 394(4) FSMA 2000.
[93]   Section 394(3) FSMA 2000.
[94]   Section 394(4) FSMA 2000.
[95]   DEC 2.4.6G (no provision in DEPP).

broached with Enforcement and, in either case, as to whether the strategy is to contest liability in whole or in part, and/or mitigate the terms of the warning notice and the penalty, and to prepare accordingly. In obtaining a copy of the material, there may be some concern as to the subsequent disclosability of the material in civil proceedings. However, this is unlikely to be an overriding concern. Insofar as the materials emanate from the firm against whom the warning notice is directed, or have been provided to that firm during the course of the FSA's investigation, they will be disclosable in any event. These materials will include not only source documents, but also correspondence with the FSA, the warning notice, the Investigation Report, and the list of Section 394 materials.[96] Documents sourced from third parties may be vulnerable to third-party disclosure orders, and the FSA may be obliged to disclose confidential information in certain civil proceedings under Section 349 FSMA 2000.[97]

In providing the warning notice, the FSA (in its accompanying letter) indicates the material considered by the RDC and the material to which it has had access. The frequent format of the correspondence is that it states that the RDC has considered the Investigation Report prepared by Enforcement and has had access to all the evidential material referred to in the Report. It was a cause of much concern that the RDC was unlikely to have been provided with a copy of the underlying documents, therefore, to have considered them before deciding upon the issue of a warning notice. There was almost total, if not total, reliance on the information as presented by Enforcement, rather than an independent scrutiny of the evidence. This is not necessarily inconsistent with the requirement in Section 395(2) FSMA 2000 that the decision which gives rises to the warning notice should be taken by a person not directly involved in establishing the evidence on which the decision to issue the warning notice is based. It was another consequence of the administrative nature of the process, which leaves close independent scrutiny to the Tribunal and leaves little room for effective forensic challenge at the RDC stage. This raises issues about the degree to which there could be informed,

---

[96] And, of course, any decision notice and final notice.
[97] *See* Section 349 FSMA 2000 and Regulation 5 of the Financial Services and Markets Act 2000 (Disclosure of Confidential Information) Regulations 2001 (SI 2001/2188). These permit, *inter alia*, the disclosure of material in civil proceedings arising under or by virtue of FSMA 2000 and any other civil proceedings to which the FSA is, or is proposed to be, a party.

independent decision making and, to the extent that was lacking, the worth of the RDC stage. It also highlighted the importance, in appropriate cases, of making representations to the RDC on the documentary evidence and of directing the RDC to documents which they should read in order to understand the defence case.[98]

The covering letter which accompanies a warning notice also indicates that the RDC had regard to the advice and recommendation of Enforcement. Enforcement did not, however, not regard such advice and recommendation as constituting either material, or material relied on, by the RDC for the purposes of meeting its disclosure obligations in Section 394 FSMA 2000. It also took the view that the document comprising the advice and the recommendation of the enforcement staff to the RDC would be a "protected item" under Section 394(4) FSMA 2000 and may be subject to public interest immunity.[99]

The suggestion that the advice and recommendation of enforcement staff is not "material" is difficult to comprehend. There was no basis in Section 394 FSMA 2000 for restricting "material" to evidence obtained by the FSA, and a document comprising the advice and recommendation would clearly amount to material. It seems equally clear that such a document will have been relied on (to a greater or lesser degree, probably a greater degree) by the RDC when reaching its decision.

The Review has resolved a number of these issues. Although it reiterated that the RDC was not an independent body or a Tribunal, it has to be and be seen to be separate from Enforcement. Whilst the FSA believes that the previous procedure was sufficient to meet the requirements of FSMA 2000 and fairness, it recognised the perception of unfairness as expressed in the consultation prior to publication of the Review. The Review looked for a means which eradicated any "justifiable" sense that firms had been dealt with unfairly but which maintained an efficient and effective method of

---

[98] This was an issue in *FSA v Legal & General Assurance Company Limited*, 18 January 2005, paragraph 210 where the RDC was criticised for accepting, without more, the conclusions of an expert report, and drawing conclusions therefrom which the expert was not prepared to draw.

[99] As to the grounds on which public interest immunity may be raised.

dealing with enforcement action. As indicated above, it was recommended (and has been accepted) that all substantive communications between Enforcement and the RDC (whether oral or written) should be disclosed to the firm. Further, the RDC will rely upon lawyers in the RDC independent of Enforcement to advise it. This will include finalising warning notices and drafting decision notices. It will also include an independent view of the evidence to be placed before the RDC to support the request for a warning notice. This would assist the RDC in taking an impartial and objective view of the case, enabling a greater degree of challenge than hitherto.[100]

In relation to secondary material Section 394 FSMA 2000 leaves much discretion in the hands of the FSA. It must determine, under Section 394(1)(b), whether the information might undermine its decision. It determines whether material should be held back because it relates to another person and was used for comparison only. For the purposes of Section 394(3), Enforcement alone decides whether it is in the public interest, or fair, to refuse access. Judicial challenge to the exercise of this discretion is virtually impossible. In relation to protected items[101] and decisions in relation to the public interest and fairness, Enforcement is at least obliged to give notification that it is holding back from giving disclosure and its reasons for doing so. Representations as to disclosure can then be made accordingly.

The more difficult issue is the existence of secondary material which is not disclosed because it is not deemed to undermine the FSA's decision[102] or because public interest immunity is relied upon by the FSA (though public interest immunity is not referred to in FSMA 2000). A party subject to regulatory proceedings may never become aware of the existence of material withheld on either of these bases, or of the reasons for it being withheld.

---

[100] Enforcement Process Review, paragraph 6.14–6.17.
[101] Section 394(7) FSMA 2000.
[102] Or deemed to support the defence. Note that there has been no change here corresponding to the amendment of the Criminal Procedure and Investigations Act 1994.

# 9.6   Representations

## 9.6.1   Timing

The warning notice must contain a statement informing the firm of its right to make representations to the RDC.[103] FSMA 2000 provides for a minimum of 28 days to make such representations. The RDC may extend the period and, whilst it may do so on its own initiative, the practice is for such extensions to be requested by the firm. If an extension is sought by the firm, it should be applied for within 14 days of receiving the notice. The request will be considered by the RDC (in practice, the chairman or deputy chairman allocated to the case) and a decision will be communicated promptly to the firm. Extensions are usually limited to two or three weeks and more lengthy extensions are permitted only in highly complex cases.

The wording of Section 387(3) FSMA 2000 permits further extensions to be allowed. However, there is no provision within DEC (DEPP) for further extensions; DEC 4.4.4G (DEPP 3.2.16G), which provides for applications for an extension to be made within 14 days of receiving the warning notice, suggests that further extensions cannot, or will not, be allowed. Further extensions will, in practice, be allowed where there is good cause; the adoption of a strict policy of never entertaining applications beyond 14 days from the warning notice or further extensions could be contrary to the scope of the discretion given in Section 387(3).

## 9.6.2   Nature of representations

Representations may be written, oral or both.[104] The representation process is not a judicial process; it is an opportunity to say why the proposed action should not be taken. Typically, the exercise will analyse Enforcement; evidence, its shortcomings and the application of the FSA's enforcement and penalty policies to it. Some question whether the process is worth participating in. The better view is that, even in a contested case where the parties are far apart, it is. The exact limits of the process are not defined but it is not, realistically, a forum

---

[103] Section 387 FSMA 2000; DEC 4.4.1G; DEC 4.4.2G (DEPP 3.2.15G).
[104] DEC 4.4.6G; DEC 4.4.7G. There is no provision allowing written and oral representations, but the practice has developed of permitting both (DEPP 3.2.15G).

for mounting any substantial challenge to the facts alleged by the FSA, even if the timetable were to permit the preparation for such a challenge, because witness evidence will not be heard. The representation process is particularly useful where the facts are not in contest, or where there is an issue as to the interpretation of a rule or the application of a policy, or where liability is accepted or where an opportunity to mitigate is required. If there is evidence which unquestionably and fundamentally damages the FSA's case, the representations will, again, provide a useful forum for airing it. Whilst there is no obligation to make representations, and those under enforcement must consider the value and the cost of doing so, there are implications in not making representations. If no response or representations are received, the RDC may regard as undisputed the allegations or matters in the warning notice and a decision notice may be given on that basis.[105] Failure to respond or make representations does not affect the firm's right to refer the decision notice to the Tribunal,[106] and should not prejudice a person's position before the Tribunal, but it would be prudent where no representations are to be made, to preserve expressly the firm's position in the event that the matter reaches the Tribunal. Making representations can be a positive step to securing an early and acceptable disposal of the matter if that is the firm's strategy.

Written representations must be sent to the FSA at the address stated in the warning notice.[107] Warning notices state the date by which written representations should be received.

If the firm wishes to make oral representations, it should notify the FSA in writing at the address stated in the warning notice at least five business days before the end of the period for representations specified in the notice. Although not provided for in DEPP, where the period has been extended, the notification must be given five business days before expiry of the extended period. The notification should specify the matters on which the firm wishes to make oral representations, include an estimate of how long the representations are expected to take, and state the names of the representatives (legal or otherwise) who will attend to make the oral representations.

---

[105] DEC 4.4.13G (DEPP 2.3.2G).
[106] DEC 4.4.13G (DEPP 2.3.2G).
[107] DEC 4.4.6G (no special provision in DEPP).

### 9.6.3   Meeting the RDC

The RDC office is responsible for scheduling the firm's meeting with the RDC and will inform the firm of the date (typically three weeks after receipt of any written representations or of the closing date for such representations). DEC does not provide for consultation as to the date of the meeting and it is prudent, therefore, to indicate inconvenient dates when requesting to make oral representations. It is very difficult to rearrange the date once set.

In notifying the date of the hearing, the RDC office identifies the panel with a short biography of each member. Any written representations are considered before the meeting and no written material is permitted to be provided at the meeting unless good reason is shown why it was not submitted earlier and at the discretion of the chairman. The person may, however, table a script or outline on which the oral representations are to be based.

The RDC may, and does, limit the duration of oral representations.[108] Where written representations have been received, it is expected that oral representations should last no longer than an hour. A request may be made for longer and it is assumed that, for good reason, a reasonable extension will be permitted. Again, this should be raised at the outset with the RDC office when the hearing arrangements are being planned.

The meeting with the FSA is held in private.[109] In addition to the panel, members of the RDC office attend to keep a record, and the proceedings are transcribed.[110] Enforcement are in attendance; they may be, and usually are, in attendance prior to the arrival of the firm and its representatives.

The panel endeavours not to interrupt the oral representations (save to seek clarification or expansion of a particular point) though it is now anticipated that before or at the start of a meeting the RDC will

---

[108] DEC 4.4.10G permits the decision maker to limit the type, length and content of any representations (DEPP 3.2.18G).

[109] DEC 4.4.10G (DEPP 3.2.17).

[110] A copy of the tape is available freely, but a transcript will be provided only on payment.

indicate what it considers most important. The representations must be relevant to the matters specified in the warning notice,[111] but should include matters which, for example, have not but should have been addressed in the warning notice. On conclusion of the oral representations, the panel may ask questions about the oral and written representations and will invite questions from Enforcement arising out of the representations. No representations tended to be made by Enforcement in the presence of the party subject to the proceedings either before or in response to the firm's representations prior to the Review. Following the Review, it will now be expected of Enforcement that it will participate in the oral representation process (DEPP 3.2.18G(2) and (4)), which it is anticipated will have the effect of focusing areas of difference between the two parties. When any questioning and debate is concluded, the RDC will invite the firm to make any closing remarks that may be appropriate (for example, to summarise briefly its case or to emphasise any key points).

The parties are then invited to withdraw. It was the practice for the RDC to request Enforcement to remain after the withdrawal of the firm and its representatives and to participate in subsequent discussions. The firm was not informed what further information, if any, was provided by Enforcement to the RDC in the firm's absence. The Review has recognised the concern of practitioners in this regard and the perceived threat to the appearance of separation of function and transparency. Its recommendations, which are now being put into practice, serve to enhance the distance between Enforcement and the RDC at the decision-making stage. Once the representations have concluded, further contact between Enforcement and the RDC is debarred (DEPP 3.2.21G). It is arguable that the inability of Enforcement to liaise with the RDC after oral representations is artificial and a retreat from the position, as stated in its latest form by the Review, that the RDC is not an independent body or a Tribunal but part of the FSA. The FSA does not concede that the previous practice was inconsistent with FSMA 2000 but were prepared to modify the practice as it often left those subject to it with a sense of unfairness. The failure to concede is questionable because it is difficult to

---

[111] As advised in the standard FSA letter.

reconcile the previous practice with the duty to ensure the separation between the investigation and the decision maker.

Where there are several parties to a warning notice or third parties potentially prejudiced by a warning notice, there will not be automatic cross-filing of written representations (though the parties are free to exchange their written representations if they wish) and it is the practice for consent to be sought for an exchange. Oral representations will be made separately, though frequently on the same day. It is not the practice to permit parties to attend the oral representations of other parties.

## 9.7 Decision notices

Section 387(4) FSMA 2000 requires the RDC to decide, within a reasonable period, whether to give a decision notice. A decision to enforce (whether on the same or different terms from the warning notice) will be contained in a decision notice; where no action (including a private warning) is to be taken, a notice of discontinuance will be served.[112]

### 9.7.1 Content of decision notice

Section 388 FSMA 2000 sets out the requirements for decision notices.[113] A decision notice must:

(a) be in writing;
(b) provide the FSA's reasons for the decision to take the action to which the notice relates;
(c) state whether the notice is one to which rights of access to FSA materials apply under Section 394 FSMA 2000;[114]
(d) if Section 394 applies, describe its effect and state whether any secondary material[115] exists to which the person concerned must be allowed access;

---

[112] DEC 2.3.1G (DEPP 3.2.26G).
[113] *See* also DEC 2.3.2G (DEPP 1.2.2G).
[114] *See* Section 392(b) for a list of the decision notices to which Section 394 applies. These correspond to the warning notices to which Section 394 applies by virtue of Section 392(a). *See* 9.5.1.
[115] That is, material undermining the FSA's decision.

(e)    inform the person concerned of any right to have the matter referred to the Tribunal and the procedure on such a reference.[116]

The terms of the decision notice may differ from the terms of the warning notice, both as to factual content and penalty. However, if the decision notice was preceded by a warning notice, the action to be taken under the decision notice must be action under the same Part of FSMA 2000 as the action proposed in the warning notice.[117] Accordingly, a decision under Part XIV FSMA 2000 to impose a fine may be changed to impose a different fine or a public censure. It may not cancel or vary the firm's permission under Part IV or order restitution under Part XXV.

In the *Legal & General* case[118] the RDC was criticised for failing to include in the decision notice any answer to Legal & General's submission to certain parts of its defence. Whilst recognising that the RDC's decision had to be concise and to the point, and that the decision notice is not a judgment, it was useful for any decision to refer to the competing cases of the parties, if only in very brief terms. There was, otherwise, no indication that the RDC had considered a party's representations and the basis upon which they had been rejected. The Review concluded that parties were entitled to know the basis upon which their representations have been rejected.[119] This is both fair and will possibly aid a settlement process, which may continue beyond the issue of the decision notice. In recognising the concern, the Review recommended that decision notices should in future set out how the RDC has dealt with the key points made by the subject of the regulatory action. Issues of principle, however, arise. This is an administrative process and the formulation of a document which seeks to recite and respond to the arguments advanced by the parties will soon become judicial in nature and will, inevitably, cause delay. The RDC is a limb of the FSA; it will not wish to leave anything to chance in the Tribunal process.

---

[116] For these purposes, "matters" is to be read broadly to include the FSA decision, the imposition of a penalty and the surrounding facts, and not simply the particular facts recorded in the Decision Notice: *FSA v Legal and General Assurance Company Ltd*, 18 January 2005, paragraph 12.
[117] Section 388(2) FSMA 2000.
[118] *FSA v Legal & General Assurance Company Limited*, 18 January 2005, paragraph 213.
[119] Enforcement Process Review, paragraph 6.16.

### 9.7.2   Further decision notices

The RDC may issue a "further decision notice" taking different action in respect of the same matter provided it does so before it takes action in relation to the original decision notice and the person concerned consents in writing.[120] DEC (DEPP) provides for Enforcement to recommend such further action to the RDC.[121] If the RDC considers such further action to be inappropriate, the original decision notice stands; this is so even if the person concerned has consented to the further decision notice. If the RDC considers that the further notice is appropriate, and the consent of the person concerned is obtained, a further decision notice is given, superseding the original decision notice.[122] The person's right to refer the matter to the Tribunal is maintained.[123]

### 9.7.3   Publicity

Neither the FSA nor the person to whom the decision notice is given may publish the notice or any details concerning it.[124]

## 9.8   Notice of discontinuance

Section 389 FSMA 2000 makes provision for notices of discontinuance. If the FSA decides not to take the action proposed in the warning notice or the action to which the decision notice relates, it must issue a notice of discontinuance to the person to whom the warning notice or the decision notice was given.[125] The notice must identify the proceedings being discontinued.[126] Furthermore, the notice must state that, if the person to whom the notice is addressed consents, the FSA may publish such information as it considers appropriate about the matter to which the discontinued proceedings relate. In some circumstances the FSA must give a copy of a notice of discontinuance to a third party, such as where the third party has been given a copy

---

[120] Section 388(3) and (4) FSMA 2000 and DEC 2.3.7G (DEPP 2.3.5G).
[121] DEC 2.3.6G (DEPP 2.3.5G(1)).
[122] DEC 2.3.6G(4) (DEPP 2.3.5G(4)).
[123] DEC 2.3.6G(5) (DEPP 2.3.5G(5)).
[124] Section 391(1) FSMA 2000.
[125] Section 389(1) FSMA 2000; DEC 2.3.8G (DEPP 3.2.26 G).
[126] Section 389(3) FSMA 2000.

of the warning notice or the decision notice as a person whose interests may be affected. In such instances, the copy must be accompanied by a statement that the FSA may, if the third party consents, publish information about the matter as far as is relevant to the third party. No guidance is provided as to how this is to work in practice. Whilst Section 391(2) and (3) is widely drawn to permit the FSA to be exclusive arbiter of what it publishes, it clearly embraces conditional or restricted consent, allowing the person concerned or the third party the right to negotiate the terms of any publication before consent is given. No guidance is provided for when there is a conflict between the person subject to the notice and a third party as to whether publication should take place. In the vast majority of cases consent of both parties is likely to be required. Again, in most cases, parties will prefer to avoid publicity. But where the existence of the investigation has already been made public, there may be a desire to give public finality by indicating that the investigation has been completed without enforcement.

## 9.9 Final notice

### 9.9.1 Content of final notice

The decision notice is required to inform the person against whom the enforcement action is taken of his right to refer the matter to the Tribunal and the procedures on such a reference.[127] A reference to the Tribunal must be made before the end of the period of 28 days beginning with the date on which the decision notice is given or such other period as Tribunal rules provide.[128]

Where the matter is not referred to the Tribunal, the FSA must, on taking the action to which the decision notice relates, give the person concerned (and any third party to whom the decision notice was copied) a final notice.[129] Upon a reference being made the matter is deferred pending the Tribunal's decision and directions and, if an appeal is made under Section 137 FSMA 2000, pending the

---

[127] Section 388(i)(e) FSMA 2000.
[128] Section 133 FSMA 2000. The Financial Services and Markets Tribunal Rules also provide for references to be made within 28 days of the date on which the notice was given (Rule 4(2)).
[129] Section 390(1) FSMA 2000.

determination of that appeal. Where the Tribunal or the appellate court gives directions to the FSA as to the action which it is appropriate to take on the matter, the FSA, on taking action in accordance with such a direction, must issue the person concerned (and any third party to whom the decision notice was copied) with a final notice.[130]

The content of the final notice depends on the action proposed by the FSA or the direction given under Section 133 FSMA 2000. A final notice about a statement, for example, relating to market abuse, will set out the terms of the statement and how and when it will be published.[131] A final notice about a penalty must state the amount of the penalty, how and by when it should be paid, and how it will be recovered if not paid by the date stated in the notice.[132] A final notice requiring a payment or distribution under Section 384 FSMA 2000 must set out to whom, how and where such distribution should be made.[133]

There are no other statutory requirements. But final notices typically specify:

(a)   the penalty;
(b)   the relevant regulatory provisions;
(c)   the reasons for the FSA's action;
(d)   the facts and matters on which it relies;
(e)   enforcement policy relevant to the breach;
(f)   relevant conduct following the investigation;
(g)   a comparison with previous cases;
(h)   directions (if a fine is imposed) regarding manner of payment and consequences of default;
(i)   the FSA's intention regarding publicity.

### 9.9.2   Publicity

The FSA must publish such information about the matter to which the final notice relates as it considers appropriate.[134] However, the FSA

---

[130] Section 390(2) FSMA 2000.
[131] Section 390(3) FSMA 2000.
[132] Section 390(5) FSMA 2000.
[133] Section 390(6) FSMA 2000.
[134] Section 391(4); DEC 5.2.1G.

may not publish information if publication would, in its opinion, be unfair to the person with respect to whom the action was taken or prejudicial to the interest of consumers.[135]

Section 391(7) FSMA 2000 and DEC (DEPP) provide that the manner of publication will be determined by the FSA according to the circumstances of each case.[136] In practice, the publication takes the form of a release on the FSA's website comprising a summary of the case, comment from a senior member of FSA staff, and a copy of the final notice. The person concerned (and a third party to whom the notice is copied) is given 24 hours' notice of the publication and an opportunity to comment, though the statement is the FSA's and, whilst comments are listened to, there is no obligation on the FSA to accept any comments made or changes suggested. However, it is important to review the terms of the press release to ascertain whether it conflicts with the terms of the (often hard-negotiated) final notice.

Neither a decision to publicise nor as to the content of the publication are within the jurisdiction of the Tribunal. Any challenge on these issues should be made by judicial review and an application for injunctive relief on the usual principles. In practice, any challenge to the FSA's decision to publish, or the content of the publication, is likely to prove extremely difficult.

## 9.10 Settlements

### 9.10.1 *The roles of the RDC and the executive*

The foregoing describes the enforcement process at its most formal. Frequently the investigation process or the issue of a warning notice may prompt early without prejudice informal settlement discussions. These may take place with Enforcement at any stage in the enforcement process. Neither party may subsequently rely on admissions or statements made in the context of the discussions, or documents recording such discussions should the settlement process falter.[137]

---

[135] Section 391(6) FSMA 2000.
[136] Section 391(1) FSMA 2000.
[137] DEC Appendix 1, paragraph 1.2.1G (DEPP 5.1.4G).

Accordingly, such material will not be admissible before the Tribunal. However, an issue of concern to practitioners was that the fact and content of such discussions was available to the RDC, who were obliged to consider and, if appropriate, approve any settlement proposal. It would meet with Enforcement and set parameters for settlement. Even where no settlement proposal was ultimately agreed on, the RDC would be kept informed of the discussions. If the settlement discussions broke down, the same RDC panel would (if such representations had not already been considered) consider the written and oral representations of the person concerned prior to determining whether to issue a warning notice. There was apprehension that the RDC members could not put the firm's settlement attempts out of their minds and that the firm would not have an independent hearing before the RDC. The settlement process was also laboured, with Enforcement having to report every material development with a view to ensuring that the RDC might ultimately approve it.

These concerns were recognised in the Review. It recommended that, in future, such decisions should be made by the FSA by means of two decision makers of at least director of division level (one of whom would usually be the Director of Enforcement). The Review regarded this change as an integral part of the desire for increased separation and transparency between Enforcement and the RDC. Such a change would enable true without-prejudice discussions between Enforcement and the firm.[138] Their recommendation was, therefore, that the FSA could decide settlements and issue a statutory notice arising therefrom, leaving the RDC to decide contested cases. This recommendation received mixed views on consultation.[139] It was, however, accepted: the FSA thought that the concept of increased separation between Enforcement and the RDC would immediately be breached if the RDC became involved in settlement discussions where the case is not ultimately settled. It was also acknowledged that executive decision making in this area would allow the party concerned to have direct access to the decision makers during negotiations or mediation, rather than the indirect access hitherto. The much-expanded provisions for settlement are found at DEC Appendix 1 (DEPP 5). The core provisions confirm that discussions

---

[138] Enforcement Process Review, paragraph 7.5 to 7.8.
[139] Policy Statement 05/11 paragraphs 2.5–2.8.

regarding settlement may take place before the giving of a warning notice, before a decision notice, or even after a referral of the matter to the Tribunal. The FSA and the firm should agree that discussions will take place on a "without prejudice" basis, and that neither party may subsequently rely on admissions or statements made in the context of the discussions, or documents recording the discussions. Further, neither party may disclose to the RDC any admissions or statements made by the other party.[140] The terms of any proposed settlement must be in writing and must include a statement of the facts and breaches upon which it is based, together with a statement as to the proposed action. It is contemplated that even where a matter is settled, there will still be a decision notice and a final notice[141] though the decision as to whether the settlement is accepted and whether or not a statutory notice is issued is to be made as indicated above by two members of the FSA's executive of at least director of division level, usually including the Director of Enforcement.[142] The decision makers may decide to reject the settlement, in which case they may invite FSA staff and the firm to enter into further discussions to try to achieve an outcome that the decision makers would be prepared to accept.[143] If settlement discussions conclude in a final notice there will be a parallel agreement that the recipient will not, nevertheless, take the matter to the Tribunal.

### 9.10.2 Third-party rights on settlement

A practical difficulty arises where third parties or multiple parties are involved. It is possible that the firm settles but a third party is not prepared to accept the wording of the settlement or the decision and final notices following from it. Prior to the Review, representations by third parties were considered by the RDC as an overall part of the settlement process. The Review recommended that the consideration of representations by third parties should be by FSA staff in line with representations on settlement heard by the firm. Involving the RDC in this process would mean that the RDC would become linked with the underlying settlement decision. The practice now will be that the firm will be present when the third party makes its representations. If

---

[140] DEC Appendix 1 1.2.1G (DEPP 5.1.4G)
[141] DEC Appendix 1 1.2.2A G(1) (DEPP 5.1.6G) (DEPP 5.1.1G(2)).
[142] DEC Appendix 1 1.2.2A G(2), (3) and (4) (DEPP 5.1.1G(3)).
[143] DEC Appendix 1 1.2.4 G(1) (DEPP 5.1.8G(1)).

the executive is minded to make changes to the statutory notice as a result of third-party representations and these are not acceptable to the firm, then the settlement would fall away and the RDC would have to decide the case afresh.[144]

This recommendation has now been implemented.[145]

### 9.10.3 *Discounts for early settlements*

The FSA has always taken into account the cooperation shown by a firm with an investigation in determining the level of penalty to be imposed as part of the enforcement process. The Review concluded that settlement should be further encouraged and proposed a structured scheme for discounts of penalty depending upon the stage at which settlement was reached. The Review suggested four stages:

(a)   Stage 1, described as the "early settlement" phase, embraced the position before the drafting of detailed documents but after sufficient work had been done to satisfy the FSA that settlement could be achieved on a sound basis;

(b)   Stage 2 extended to all activity from the conclusion of the "early settlement" phase up to the written representations phase;

(c)   Stage 3 covered the period from the consideration of and response to written and oral representations up to the issue of a decision notice;

(d)   Stage 4 related to settlement after the decision notice stage.

Various practical difficulties were identified in the consultation stage.[146] Some consultees regarded the scheme as a penalty for those who contest cases and as unfair pressure to settle early. It was also suggested that the FSA would need to make available the evidential basis of its case in order that an informed decision on settlement could be taken. These issues were overruled largely on the basis that the purpose of the scheme was to provide a rough and ready means of achieving settlement. The discounts now to be applied are: Stage 1 (30 per cent); Stage 2 (20 per cent); Stage 3 (10 per cent); and Stage 4 (0 per cent). The provisions for discount for early settlement are now

---

144   Enforcement Process Review, paragraph 7.12.
145   DEC Appendix 1 1.13.1G (DEPP 5.1.9 G(3)).
146   Policy Statement 05/11 paragraphs 2.9 to 2.13.

included in ENF 13.7, and will become part of DEPP. It is envisaged that the settlement agreement will include a statement as to the appropriate penalty discount in accordance with the discount procedure.[147] It will not usually be appropriate to seek to move from the percentage figures stipulated. The only exception is that "back tracking" (i.e. treating the discount as referable from an early stage of the proceedings) is permissible where there has been a substantial change in the nature or seriousness of the disciplinary action and that an agreement could have been reached at an earlier stage if the action had commenced on a different footing.[148] It is apparent that this is workable only in relation to financial penalties.

---

[147] ENF 13.7.4G (DEPP 6.6.3G; DEPP 6.6.4G).
[148] ENF 13.7.4G (4) (DEPP 6.6.4G(2)).

# Chapter 10

# The Role of Mediation

**David Scott**
Partner

**Oliver Kerridge**
Associate
Freshfields Bruckhaus Deringer

## 10.1   Introduction

Mediation is a dispute resolution process which is frequently used in litigation to help the parties reach settlement. It involves a neutral third party who acts as a mediator. Unlike a Judge, the mediator does not have the power to impose a result on the parties and cannot determine the outcome of the dispute. Instead, the mediator helps the parties to negotiate an agreed settlement by facilitating discussions between them. If the parties reach a deal at the end of the mediation, they enter into a settlement agreement, which is binding on them and enforceable as a contract.

Another important characteristic of mediation is that it is entirely voluntary. In other words, it is up to the parties whether they enter the mediation process.[1] Equally, because the mediator has no power to impose an outcome, each party is free to walk away from the mediation. All information exchanged at or in connection with the mediation is without prejudice and therefore not admissible in any subsequent proceedings, whatever the forum.[2] So, mediation is a voluntary, without prejudice procedure which is flexible and can be adapted by the parties to fit their needs.

---

[1] The court in civil litigation does have the power to impose ADR on an unwilling party and has indicated that it will do so in certain cases. Similarly, the courts have the power to impose costs penalties on parties who refuse to mediate.
[2] A term to this effect will almost always be found in mediation agreements.

However, whilst a mediation with the FSA bears some of the ordinary features of the mediation process, there are also certain characteristics that are different. For a start, although the mediation process itself is private, the likely outcome of the mediation with the FSA will involve details becoming public. This is because the focus of the mediation is likely to be about the size of the fine being imposed and what will be said about the circumstances giving rise to the penalty in the final notice that the FSA will publish once agreement has been reached. Whilst firms will, inevitably, endeavour to persuade the FSA, at the mediation, that no penalty should be imposed at all, a firm going into a mediation with the FSA must be realistic about the range of possible outcomes. The authors are not aware of any case where the FSA has been persuaded at a mediation that no penalty is appropriate, although in one case a penalty was reduced to a private warning. Of course, the mediation does not need to result in a settlement, but firms should appreciate that a mediation with the FSA is likely to be focused upon reducing the penalty, and any agreement reached will subsequently be published.

This chapter considers the rules under which the FSA's mediation scheme operates. It will then consider some of the advantages and disadvantages of mediation and some practical points which practitioners and firms should bear in mind when considering whether to agree to enter into the mediation process.

## 10.2   Mediation – the rules

### 10.2.1   The rules of the scheme

#### 10.2.1.1   The scope of the scheme[3]
Attracted by the flexibility of the process and by the possibility of settling cases more quickly and cost efficiently than if they went through the full enforcement process, the FSA developed a pilot mediation scheme which came into force on 1 December 2001. In February 2004, the FSA decided to continue with the scheme and at

---

[3] The rules are set out in Appendix 1 to the decision-making section of the FSA Handbook ("DEC").

the same time introduced changes which have widened the scope and availability of mediation in enforcement cases. Further changes were introduced in 2005 as a result of the FSA's Enforcement Process Review which is discussed in more detail in Chapter 9.

Mediation is now available in all enforcement cases except where the FSA is contemplating bringing a criminal prosecution or in cases involving disciplinary action for late submission of a report to which ENF 13.5 applies.[4] However, there are two exceptions. Cases involving the following can only be mediated if the FSA consents:[5]

(a)     an allegation of unfitness and impropriety based on judgments about dishonesty or lack of integrity; or

(b)     the exercise of the FSA's own initiative powers on a variation or cancellation of permission.

### 10.2.1.2     *Settlement discussions and mediation under the scheme*

Informal settlement discussions may take place at any time during the enforcement process.[6] Nevertheless, the rules provide that:

> "The period following the issue of the warning notice is ... a natural point for mediation if the parties consider that the involvement of a neutral mediator is required to facilitate progress in any settlement discussions."[7]

Mediation is an option that is only available to a firm after the warning notice has been issued and before the decision notice is issued.[8] If a firm wishes to mediate before the warning notice or after the decision notice, mediation will only be available if the FSA consents.[9] Otherwise, it appears from the wording of the rules of the scheme that, provided the case falls within the scope of the scheme and the FSA's express consent is not required, the FSA will be obliged to

---

[4] This is as a result of the feedback it received during the review. *See* DEC Appendix 1, paragraph 1.4.1.

[5] *See* DEC Appendix 1, paragraph 1.4.2.

[6] *See* DEC Appendix 1, paragraphs 1.1.1 and 1.2.1.

[7] *See* DEC Appendix 1, paragraph 1.3.3.

[8] Note that where the FSA enforcement staff have recommended enforcement action, mediation will be available where settlement discussions are, in the opinion of either party, unlikely to lead to an agreed settlement: DEC Appendix 1, paragraph 1.1.1.

[9] DEC Appendix 1, paragraph 1.4.3.

mediate if the firm elects for mediation.[10] This right to mediate contrasts with the position under the Civil Procedure Rules ("CPR"), where a party may ask the court to order a mediation, but otherwise cannot compel the other party or parties to enter into mediation.

Importantly, a firm may elect to mediate only once during the enforcement process. This does not mean that the firm and the FSA cannot continue without-prejudice negotiations once the mediation has finished, as the gap between the parties may have narrowed on the day and could be closed by further negotiation, either with or without the assistance of the mediator. It simply means that the firm will have only one opportunity to compel the FSA to engage in the formal mediation process. Therefore, this means that the firm needs to make an important tactical decision. On the one hand, if it mediates after the FSA enforcement staff have presented their case and the RDC has decided to issue a warning notice, then the view might be that it is very hard to persuade the FSA that no penalty should be imposed. On the other hand, seeking a mediation before the FSA enforcement staff have prepared and presented their case to the RDC runs the risk of the mediation taking place in a vacuum and without the firm knowing precisely how the FSA enforcement staff view the case. One possible way of dealing with this dilemma would be to adjourn an early mediation rather than abandon it. This would enable the firm to suggest to the FSA, at a later stage, that the mediation process could be resurrected and pursued further. However, this is not an attractive proposition for the FSA and it would probably be difficult in practice to resurrect a mediation after anything other than a short period.

### 10.2.1.3 *The mechanics of the scheme*
To initiate the mediation, the parties send a joint mediation notice in a form agreed between them to the mediation provider. If the mediation takes place between the service of the warning notice and the

---

[10] "Mediation will be available in all other enforcement cases falling within the scope of the RDC"; *see* DEC Appendix 1, paragraph 1.4.2. "In a case falling within the scope of the scheme . . ., mediation will take place where an election to mediate is made after the warning notice has been issued and before the FSA issues a decision notice"; *see* DEC Appendix 1, paragraph 1.4.3. "We will mediate in all appropriate enforcement cases following the issue of the warning . . . notice and prior to the issue of the decision . . . notice . . . [W]e are proposing to amend the scheme to reflect [this] option"; FSA Consultation Paper 199, paragraphs 8.26 and 8.27.

decision notice, the parties also have to inform the secretary of the RDC.[11] At the time of writing, the mediation provider selected by the FSA is A Commercial Initiative for Dispute Resolution ("ACI"). ACI has published its Mediation Procedure and the Explanatory Notes for the FSA's mediation scheme on its website.[12] The Procedure and Notes complement the rules in DEC Appendix 1 and set out how ACI will run the mediation.

Once the parties send the mediation notice to the mediation provider, the provider will liaise with the parties in order to deal with the following matters.

*Appointment of mediator*
Unless the parties agree otherwise, there will be a sole mediator.[13] The mediator is appointed from a panel of suitable mediators maintained by ACI. ACI will recommend up to three mediators to the parties, who then endeavour to agree who should be appointed.[14] If the parties cannot agree within seven days of the recommendation, ACI will appoint one of the mediators whom it recommended.

The mediator has to be an experienced commercial mediator and accredited by or registered with a recognised mediation organisation. Experience in the financial services sector is desirable but not compulsory.[15] In accepting an appointment, the mediator has to confirm to the parties that he has no conflict of interests in doing so.[16]

*Date for mediation*
The parties will agree this with ACI, along with a timetable for the whole mediation process.[17] The length of time from the appointment of the mediator to the date of the mediation hearing will depend on the circumstances of the case, the parties' requirements, their availability and that of the mediator. In theory, the mediation could take

---

[11] DEC Appendix 1, paragraph 1.6.1. The scheme stipulates that: "The mediation notice will commit each party to use their best endeavours to progress the mediation in a timely manner"; paragraph 1.6.2.

[12] *See* www.aci-adr.com / FSAschemeACIdocumentsfor.htm.

[13] ACI Mediation Scheme for FSA Enforcement Cases, Mediation Procedure, paragraph 3.5.

[14] ACI Mediation Scheme for FSA Enforcement Cases, Mediation Procedure, paragraph 3.3.

[15] DEC Appendix 1, paragraph 1.7.2(4).

[16] DEC Appendix 1, paragraph 1.7.2(5).

[17] DEC Appendix 1, paragraph 1.7.3.

place straight after the appointment of the mediator, but in practice there is likely to be a period of between two and four weeks before the mediation actually takes place.

### Duration of mediation

The rules provide that most mediations should last no longer than one full day, but acknowledge that more time may be necessary in complex cases. If the mediation requires more time than has been allotted to it, the parties may ask ACI to set up a further day or days.[18]

### Venue

The mediation can take place anywhere that is acceptable to the parties and the mediator.[19] Typically, it will take place at the FSA's offices.

### Mediation agreement

The mediation takes place in accordance with a mediation agreement which is signed by the parties, the mediator and ACI.[20] The parties are able to tailor the agreement to meet their specific requirements, but the rules of the scheme stipulate that the mediation agreement will always provide that:

(a)    the mediation will be on a "without prejudice" basis and confidential; and

(b)    the parties who attend the mediation will have authority to settle (as to which, *see* DEC Appendix 1 paragraph 1.7.9 discussed further below).[21]

### Confidentiality

The FSA recognises that confidentiality is a key element of the mediation process. Confidentiality in this context means that matters referred to in the mediation cannot be referred to publicly and that matters disclosed by one party to the mediator in confidence will not be disclosed to the other party without the disclosing party's consent.[22] However, confidentiality is limited in that:

---

[18]  DEC Appendix 1, paragraph 1.7.4.
[19]  DEC Appendix 1, paragraph 1.7.6.
[20]  DEC Appendix 1, paragraph 1.7.7(2).
[21]  DEC Appendix 1, paragraph 1.7.7.
[22]  DEC Appendix 1, paragraph 1.7.8(1).

(a) the mediator is not required to keep confidential any information which he receives and which indicates potentially criminal conduct (in which case he may choose to terminate the mediation[23]);

(b) the terms of the settlement will, if approved by the FSA's executive decision makers, be incorporated in a decision notice and, subsequently, a final notice which will, ordinarily, be made public;[24]

(c) FSA enforcement staff may, in exceptional circumstances, notify other individuals within the FSA of any matters requiring urgent regulatory action to be taken in order to protect the interests of consumers or the integrity of the market;[25]

(d) the FSA and ACI may publish information on the operation of the scheme on an anonymous basis.[26]

*Who can attend the mediation?*
There are no restrictions on who from the firm can attend the mediation, and the firm can, as in a normal commercial mediation, attend with lawyers and any other advisers. However, the FSA cautions in the rules that: "it is important to preserve the informality of the mediation process".[27] This is intended to ensure that mediations remain outcome focused and do not resemble a court or tribunal hearing.

*Conduct of the mediation*
Although there is no set procedure in a mediation, it usually commences with an opening plenary session with all the parties and the mediator in attendance. This session will typically be started by the mediator making a number of statements about mediation in general and the structure for the day ahead. If the mediation agreement has not already been signed by the parties, it will be signed at this stage. The parties are then invited to take it in turns to make a short presentation to each other and to the mediator. These presentations can be conducted by the lawyers instructed or by the client or by a factual or expert witness or any combination of these. Depending on the tone of

[23] DEC Appendix 1, paragraph 1.7.8(2)(a).
[24] DEC Appendix 1, paragraph 1.7.8(2)(b).
[25] ACI Mediation Scheme for FSA Enforcement Cases, Mediation Procedure, paragraph 7.1.3.
[26] DEC Appendix 1, paragraph 1.7.8(2)(c) and ACI Mediation Scheme for FSA Enforcement Cases, Mediation Procedure, paragraph 7.1.4.
[27] DEC Appendix 1, paragraph 1.11.1.

the plenary session, the mediator may ask one or two questions or invite, but not require, either party to respond to what the other has said. Once that has been done, the parties will usually retire to their separate rooms and the mediator will then commence the exploratory process of talking to each party in turn. At the outset, these discussions will concentrate on legal and factual issues but, as the day progresses, the focus will turn to what the scope for an agreement might be.

However, there is no set pattern for a mediation and it may be that the parties and/or the mediator think it would be useful to have a further plenary session at some stage during the day or that there might be a point at which it is useful for the mediator to sit down for a joint session with clients only. The essence of a mediation, however, is that it is an entirely voluntary process and, therefore, no party need do anything with which they feel uncomfortable.

The parties, of course, have the right to choose whether solicitors and/or counsel should attend the mediation. There is no right answer to this, and a lot will depend on the size and importance of the dispute, the complexity of the legal and factual points involved and how well the firm thinks it can deal with these on its own. However, in the vast majority of cases, clients will find it useful to have at least their solicitors present in order to advise on the legal points in dispute, to help present the legal and factual arguments both to the other side and the mediator, to assist in the presentation of various settlement propositions and, hopefully, to help document the settlement agreement.

*Authority to settle*
As already mentioned, one of the key requirements of a mediation, which is acknowledged by the rules,[28] is that those who attend the mediation on behalf of each party have full authority to agree settlement terms. The firm will therefore need to ensure that an individual who has the necessary authority to enter into a settlement attends the mediation.

However, this requirement is modified in relation to the FSA. As discussed in Chapter 9 (at 9.10), it is for the executive decision makers

---

[28] DEC Appendix 1, paragraph 1.7.9(1).

to approve settlements and make statutory notice decisions following settlements being agreed in principle with the FSA enforcement staff. The same settlement approval and decision-making procedure applies in cases where settlement is achieved as a result of a mediation. Despite this, the rules specify that the FSA will be represented at the mediation only by the FSA enforcement staff who initially recommended the disciplinary action.[29] It is not compulsory for either of the executive decision makers to attend. The FSA Handbook merely states that one or both of the executive decision makers *may* attend the mediation and if their attendance is impracticable the FSA will endeavour to ensure that they are available for consultation during the mediation.[30] There is therefore no obligation for someone from the FSA who has full authority to settle to be present at the mediation. If the executive decision makers do not approve the settlement, the case will return to the point it had reached in the enforcement process prior to the mediation. As we will see below, this may cause some real problems for the firm when mediating with the FSA.

*Documents for the mediation*
Each party attending the mediation has to produce a short position statement, usually seven days before the mediation, setting out the issues in dispute and any documents that are referred to. The ACI Mediation Procedure also provides that the parties will agree a paginated bundle of documents and highlight certain documents which may assist the mediator (such as a chronology, the investigation report, the firm's response, the warning notice, the firm's response (where applicable), the decision notice and, finally, a list of issues between the parties).[31] However, the parties and the mediator are equally free to dispense with the requirement to produce documentation before the mediation.[32] In practice, the occasions on which documents are not produced are likely to be rare.

---

[29] DEC Appendix 1, paragraph 1.7.9(2).
[30] DEC Appendix 1, paragraph 1.7.9(3). Other schemes require the presence of those who have full authority to agree settlement terms. *See*, for example, Section 6 of the Centre for Effective Dispute Resolution's Model Mediation Procedure 7 Agreement (February 2004) and Section 2.4 of the Chartered Institute of Arbitrators' Cost-Controlled Procedure For The Mediation Of Disputes (2003).
[31] ACI Mediation Scheme for FSA Enforcement Cases, Mediation Procedure, paragraphs 4.4 and 4.5.
[32] DEC Appendix 1, paragraph 1.7.10.

*Costs of the mediation*

The ACI's costs, including the mediator's fee, will be split equally between the FSA and the firm. The legal and any other costs incurred by each of the FSA and the firm in relation to the mediation are the separate responsibility of the parties.[33] Additional details about the costs of the mediation process are contained in Part 2 of the ACI's Mediation Procedure.

# 10.3 Mediation – practical issues

## 10.3.1 Introduction

Although mediation has been available since 1 December 2001, uptake has been slow. The FSA has sought to address this by increasing the flexibility and scope of the process. The FSA hopes that firms will see the advantages of mediation and will engage in the process in greater numbers. This would, of course, help the FSA to deliver faster enforcement outcomes.

So, what are the advantages and disadvantages of the mediation process for firms? If firms do not proceed to mediation, what are the alternatives to that process? If they do, and reach agreement with the FSA, how should they document the settlement agreement? Those issues are considered in this section in an attempt to give some practical guidance.

## 10.3.2 Mediation with the FSA – the advantages

For a firm, the mediation process is relatively quick and cost effective if the mediation results in a settlement. The gain can be measured both financially and in terms of management time. A mediation which concludes in settlement (or enables a settlement soon after) makes it possible for senior management to concentrate on their usual tasks rather than spending time dealing with the case as it progresses through the RDC process and possibly thereafter through proceedings before the Financial Services and Markets Tribunal (*the Tribunal*). For the FSA, resolving cases quickly uses the limited resources of the

---

[33] DEC Appendix 1, paragraph 1.7.11.

Enforcement Division economically and thereby satisfies the statutory requirement to use its resources in the most efficient and economic way.[34]

Where the mediation does not result in a settlement of the dispute, it may seem that the firm has spent time and money for little or no gain. However, this may not be the case. Frank and frequently face-to-face discussions with the FSA's enforcement staff during the mediation tend to clarify the matters of greatest concern to the FSA in a way that the investigation report or the warning notice will rarely, if ever, achieve. This "dry run" may therefore prove to be of assistance to the firm when it is preparing its written representations or presenting its case orally before the RDC. The debates and discussions that can take place at a mediation may also give a valuable insight into what points are likely to come to the fore in any subsequent tribunal proceedings.

This dialogue with the enforcement staff that have investigated the case and have led the case through the enforcement/RDC/tribunal process may be direct, through the plenary sessions chaired by the mediator. Alternatively, the dialogue may be indirect, with the mediator engaging in shuttle diplomacy as he or she tries to find a compromise acceptable to both sides. While there may have been opportunities along the way for a discussion in relation to the matter under investigation, a mediation gives the firm a valuable and worthwhile opportunity to explain its points to the FSA orally and to explore and debate the issues and concerns that the enforcement staff have there and then. Typically, many of the facts will not be in dispute. The majority of the time during the course of the day is likely to be spent on a few particular points, putting them in their proper factual context, discussing what the fair and reasonable conclusions to draw from those facts may be, the appropriate level of the fine, what remedial action may be due, and the wording of the proposed final notice.

This face-to-face debate with the FSA is an opportunity that does not exist if the firm goes directly to oral representations before the RDC and, subsequently, the Tribunal. It is true that there is nothing to stop the firm and the FSA from meeting to discuss the matter at any stage,

---

[34] *See* Section 2(3)(a) FSMA 2000 and www.fsa.gov.uk/pages/About/Aims/Principles/index.shtml.

even during the RDC process or the tribunal process. However, it is unlikely that such a meeting, were it to take place, would be scheduled for a whole day, nor would it have the benefits that can be gained from having an experienced mediator to facilitate the process. The importance of this should not be underestimated – all too often, without-prejudice negotiations between two parties break down as each becomes increasingly entrenched. A skilled mediator can often overcome such attitudes and guide the parties towards agreement or at least an understanding of each other's main concerns. This can be very positive and beneficial. On some occasions, however, there is a danger of feeling a pressure to settle on the day, even if that means accepting an outcome that the firm regards as not entirely satisfactory.

### 10.3.3   Mediation with the FSA – the disadvantages

Mediating with the FSA presents three principal difficulties for firms. The first is the fact that the FSA is a public body that has specific regulatory obligations and responsibilities and so a mediation with the FSA will always be different to mediation in the normal commercial context. The second difficulty is a result of the FSA's decision-making process and the fact that there is no certainty that either of the FSA's executive decision makers will be present at the mediation. Finally, if firms decide to mediate before they receive a warning notice, firms may not understand the FSA's findings well enough to address them and the FSA enforcement staff may be tempted to propose an unrealistically high fine from which to start negotiations.

#### 10.3.3.1   The status of the FSA
A firm involved in FSA enforcement proceedings has to be aware that it is not dealing with a commercial adversary. The FSA is a statutory regulator, subject to various checks and balances and, ultimately, accountable to Parliament. A statutory regulator that has regulatory objectives (such as maintaining confidence in the financial system and securing the appropriate degree of protection for consumers) will not be able to make concessions in the same way that a commercial litigant can, and this means that the likelihood is that a "deal" in the ordinary commercial sense cannot be struck.

The role of precedent in the FSA's decision-making process is also important in this context. Whilst there is no formal system of precedent akin to that in the courts, a "wider implications" framework exists in which decisions have to be taken. Enforcement decisions reached by the FSA, even after a mediation, are ordinarily publicised in a final notice. This is seen by the FSA as a key mechanism for sending out its regulatory messages. The FSA's decisions will therefore be held up to public scrutiny and can be compared and contrasted with one another. These are important elements of FSA accountability and the FSA will therefore be conscious of them when it enters a mediation.

Therefore, it is clear that there are important differences between a mediation with the FSA and a mediation with, say, a market counterparty, where the dynamics and priorities would almost certainly be very different. However, this does not mean that a deal cannot be done. It is always important to understand the opponent and their position. In the same way, firms that enter a mediation process with the FSA need to understand and be aware that the very nature of the FSA makes it inevitable that its approach to the mediation will differ from that of a typical commercial organisation.

### 10.3.3.2  *The FSA's decision-making process*

Prior to the implementation of the recommendations of the Enforcement Process Review which is discussed more fully in Chapter 9, mediation discussions took place with the FSA's enforcement staff, but any final agreement had to be approved by the RDC which was not represented during the mediation process. However, the involvement of the RDC without any of its members being present at the mediation proceedings raised practical difficulties. First, concerns were raised that should the mediation negotiations fail, the RDC's objectivity at a later stage in the enforcement process could be tainted, given that it, as the FSA's decision maker, would have knowledge of any without-prejudice admissions that had been made during the mediation process. Second, given that the RDC was not required to be present during the mediation and, in practice, was informed in confidence on the progress of the mediation by the FSA's enforcement staff, firms complained that they did not have direct access to the FSA's decision maker. There was, in short, a perception of unfairness and with good reason.

The Enforcement Process Review aimed to achieve greater clarity as to the distinct and separate roles of the RDC and the Enforcement Division. Therefore, it is now clear that the role of the RDC is to be the FSA's decision maker in cases where settlement cannot be reached between the firm and the Enforcement Division. The Review recommended that executive decision makers be responsible for approving settlements and issuing subsequent statutory notices in all settlement cases including mediated settlements.[35] A fixed-scale discount scheme was also introduced in order to encourage early settlement. For example, if a firm settles with the FSA prior to the warning notice stage it will receive a discount of 30 per cent on the fine that the enforcement staff would have recommended to the RDC.

However, there are still certain problems:

(a)  By the time that the mediation takes place, the FSA enforcement staff will have already assessed the evidence and presented the case to senior management for their input prior to making a recommendation to the RDC. The FSA enforcement staff will therefore have already formed a view of the facts and the appropriate penalty. The firm may therefore find it difficult to persuade or convince the FSA enforcement staff and the executive decision makers, through the submissions and the points that it makes during the mediation, that they should change their assessment of the case. Of course, minor changes to the sanction proposed may be achievable (such as a small reduction in the level of the fine or minor alterations to the wording of the final notice), but it can readily be seen that more major changes are likely to be harder to achieve.

(b)  That difficulty is likely to be compounded by the fact that the new rules do not oblige the executive decision makers to be present at the mediation. Thus, it could be the case that they will not hear, and therefore cannot be influenced by, what is said during the course of the mediation. If that is the case, then the firm has two hurdles to overcome. First, it has to persuade those

---

[35] *See* the Enforcement Process Review Report and Recommendations, paragraph 7.5.

attending the mediation of the merits of a particular point and what consequences should flow from it. Second, it has to hope that those people that have been persuaded will, in turn, be able to persuade the executive decision makers of the same points. In theory, either or both executive decision makers could be present but, in reality, it is very unlikely that two FSA directors of division level or above will be present at a day-long media- tion. If neither are present at the mediation, then there is little reason to believe that, in practice, the position will improve, if at all, on the situation prior to the Enforcement Process Review. The firm will be mediating with opponents that:

(i)     are not present;
(ii)    have the power to decide whether or not to approve any settlement proposal; and
(iii)   do not communicate either with the mediator or the firm and so do not hear the arguments that are actually advanced at the mediation but instead receive them through the filter of the enforcement staff.

(c)   It is only once a warning notice has been issued that a firm will know precisely what has been alleged against it and what sanc- tion the RDC considers is appropriate. However, under the new fixed-scale discount scheme, firms are encouraged to settle before the warning notice is issued and therefore prior to consideration of the matter by the RDC. There are two prob- lems with this. If the firm has not seen a warning notice or draft investigation report, it may not understand the FSA's findings well enough in order to be able to address them properly. Furthermore, if the FSA enforcement staff are unrealistic in their own expectations, for example by proposing an unreason- ably high fine, then firms might settle at a 30 per cent discount to the unreasonably high fine thereby creating a precedent of some sort, which will be unhelpful for firms that face enforce- ment action in the future. The effectiveness of the mediation process will therefore depend on the FSA enforcement staff setting penalties at a proper level before mediations are commenced and clearly presenting their findings to the firm before the mediation so that the firm has a proper opportunity to consider its position and how to respond to those points at the mediation.

There are some possible solutions. The first and second problems could be resolved by choosing executive decision makers who have had no prior involvement in the matters in issue and by ensuring that one of them attends the mediation. If neither of them attend the mediation, the firm should ask to speak to them directly rather than relying on the FSA enforcement staff to relay the progress of the mediation to them.

This still leaves the third issue, namely that if firms are to initiate mediations before the warning notice stage, the views of the FSA enforcement staff, both as to facts and penalty, may not have been fully presented to the firm and will not have been independently scrutinised. The first part of this problem can be solved relatively easily by asking the FSA enforcement staff to prepare a draft warning notice setting out their findings and which can then form the basis of the mediation. However, the draft warning notice will not have had the benefit of the RDC's consideration and input and so it will still be possible for the enforcement staff to propose an unreasonably high fine. At present, the FSA's mediation rules offers no solution to this problem and the firm will have to bear this in mind when considering whether or not to mediate and whether or not to accept a settlement offer from the FSA.

To date, relatively few mediations have taken place. Whether an increasing number of firms opt to mediate in the future and whether such mediations are successful remains to be seen.

### 10.3.4   *Documenting the settlement*

When agreement is reached at the end of a mediation, it may be tempting to consider that the mission has been accomplished. However, one stage remains: the settlement needs to be documented in a formal settlement agreement. What should the parties bear in mind when drafting the agreement?

It is generally desirable for the settlement agreement to be finalised and signed at the mediation rather than afterwards for the simple reason that if the agreement is not finalised at that stage, there is a danger that the deal will be lost. One of the parties may change their mind, the parties may differ as to precisely what was agreed, or there may be a dispute over a term that was not discussed but which is important and needs to be documented. In particular, with an FSA mediation, it would be possible for the parties to agree on the level of penalty only to then have quite different views about the language used in the final notice. Any or all of these points can lead to further negotiation, time and costs and, possibly, may prevent the agreement being documented and signed. If it is not possible to finalise the agreement at the mediation, the parties should document as accurately as possible the heads of terms that have been agreed and then produce the settlement agreement and final notice as soon as practicable afterwards.

Some of the key items that firms may wish to insert into settlement agreements with the FSA are set out below:

(a)   The agreement should be expressed to be in full and final settlement of the regulatory action.
(b)   The FSA should agree not to issue any further warning notices against the firm[36] relating to the facts and matters connected with the decision and/or final notices. However, the FSA is likely to want to keep open the possibility of reopening the matter or starting a new action if new information comes to light.
(c)   The agreed timing of the press release (if any) to be issued by the FSA with the final notice. The press release is often crucial in terms of publicity and reputation for the firm and it should aim to see the press release at least 24 hours in advance so that it can prepare its own release and brief relevant staff so that they are ready for any press enquiries. Although the firm may wish to comment upon the wording of the FSA's draft press release, the FSA is unlikely to allow this. Indeed, the FSA may not be willing to allow the firm to see the press release in advance of its publication.
(d)   The FSA is likely to insist that the firm should not dispute the findings of fact in the final notice in any future proceedings. It is important for the firm to limit its agreement to findings of fact and not to agree any expression of opinion (such as references to "serious breach" or "fundamental disregard for compliance").

---

[36] This may also include the current and/or former employees of the firm, depending on the nature of the enforcement proceedings.

(e) The settlement agreement should be confidential between the parties (and their legal advisors, if any). This will almost always be subject to both the final notice and the press release being made public.

On a practical note, it may be useful to draft the heads of a settlement agreement and the boilerplate clauses in advance of the mediation and to have secretarial services on standby so that the agreement can be documented even if the mediation runs on into the evening. Alternatively, the draft can be saved on a laptop computer which can then be taken to the mediation. This may enable the parties to document and sign the agreement at the mediation rather than afterwards.

## 10.4   Conclusion

Firms need to remember that a mediation with the FSA will never be the same as a mediation with a commercial party. This is an inevitable and unavoidable consequence of the FSA being a statutory body with statutory functions. Nevertheless, a mediation in which the firm may also have to accept and contend with the fact that neither of the executive decision makers are present at the mediation and so do not hear directly from either the firm or the mediator, is one where the prospects of an outcome that is genuinely regarded as satisfactory for both parties are significantly reduced. Additionally, the introduction of a fixed-scale discount scheme which encourages firms to settle prior to consideration of the case by the RDC may encourage firms to mediate at too early a stage in order to receive the maximum discount.

Notwithstanding the observations and comments made above, the mediation scheme is a welcome addition to the FSA's decision-making process and is useful for firms that wish to achieve a settlement but have found that they cannot reach, or believe that they will not be able to reach, an acceptable compromise with the FSA without the independent assistance of a mediator. Firms can gain from the process, even if settlement is not reached in the end.

# Chapter 11

# Disciplinary Sanctions and Other Enforcement Options

**Andrew Carnes and Saima Hanif**

4–5 Gray's Inn Square

## 11.1   Introduction

The mechanisms of the disciplinary and enforcement decision-making process are dealt with in Chapter 9. This chapter deals with the sanctions and other enforcement measures that may be imposed through the Regulatory Decisions Committee ("RDC") and describes the principal enforcement remedies available to the Financial Services Authority ("FSA").[1]

In order to navigate the route to the most favourable outcome for a defendant in FSA enforcement proceedings, a practical under-standing of the FSA enforcement rules, guidance and policy is required. The focus of the FSA's enforcement action is directly aligned to its statutory objectives.[2] Whilst the FSA will often concentrate its resources upon the most serious and high-profile cases, a range of enforcement tools enables the FSA to deal effi-ciently and effectively with smaller firms and individuals where their misconduct is sufficiently serious to merit enforcement action. A risk-based approach means that the FSA will use a range of enforcement measures or, if appropriate, supervisory action to achieve its statutory objectives.

The FSA will, in reality, be judged by the public largely on the number of successful enforcement cases it brings and the levels of penalties

---

[1] Where appropriate Reference is made to other chapters where topics may receive additional consideration and to relevant sections of the Enforcement Chapters of the FSA Handbook at http://fsahandbook.info/FSA/handbook.jsp?doc=/handbook/ENF.

[2] *See* Sections 3–6 FSMA 2000.

imposed. It is likely that the FSA will be under public pressure to demonstrate an upward trend in the level of enforcement activity and penalties. It will be engaged from time to time in major cases which attract significant public attention and political scrutiny.[3] These cases are necessarily more problematic because they often involve a number of potential defendants, are complex to investigate and prosecute, and are subject to external pressures from the political and public arenas, particularly where there has been loss to retail investors. These cases exert pressure on the FSA's senior management in a way which often requires defendants and their advisers to approach their resolution in a very different way to less high-profile cases.

In addition, the rapidly changing nature of the financial services markets means that the FSA's attention may focus on new areas. A good recent example of this has been the increasing attention that hedge fund managers are receiving from regulators. In early 2005, the FSA undertook specific work to review and understand the risks posed by hedge funds to the statutory objectives of the FSA. This led to the publication of a discussion paper in July 2005. A "Feedback Document" was issued in March 2006, which stated that the FSA's "current policy thinking is not to proceed with any specific changes to the rules applied to hedge fund managers." Two immediate priority areas for the Hedge Fund Managers Supervision Team were identified: the risk associated with asset valuations and the use of side-letters. The "next steps" identified by the FSA demonstrate that it is adopting an approach that is based on risk assessment and controls. As the document states, it intends to "stimulate improvements in valuation arrangements and the governance framework, policies and procedures surrounding the calculations of those valuations." As the hedge fund market seeks to attract more individual investors the FSA's scrutiny is likely to intensify. The hedge fund market has traditionally fed on volatile markets. If the markets enjoy periods of stability these funds may struggle to make their projected returns for investors or be tempted to adopt over-optimistic valuations where the managers' remuneration is linked to them. This is clearly an area to watch; solvency and investor litigation are beginning to emerge and regulatory intervention is more likely.

---

[3] For example, investigations concerning split capital investment trusts, pensions/endowment misselling and structured products such as precipice bonds.

Where possible, this chapter identifies and discusses cases of relevance or general interest to the way in which the FSA approaches enforcement. However, it is important to bear in mind that each case depends on its own facts, thereby making it difficult to draw anything from the cases other than very general principles. It is not suggested that the cases be used as any form of precedent, but they are of assistance in assessing the FSA's broad approach towards enforcement. Furthermore, the FSA has said that in determining whether to bring disciplinary actions and the appropriate level of financial penalty, its approach in previous similar cases is a relevant factor.[4]

The sanctions or other enforcement tools at the FSA's disposal include:[5]

(a)    private warnings;
(b)    public censures and public statements;
(c)    fines or financial penalties;
(d)    variation of permission or approval;
(e)    cancellation of permission or approval;
(f)    prohibition of individuals;
(g)    prosecution of criminal offences;
(h)    injunctions;
(i)    restitution orders; and
(j)    insolvency proceedings.

Some enforcement methods are only available to the FSA when used against authorised firms and approved persons. The ambit of other enforcement powers is more extensive as they may also be used against individuals or entities outside the regulated community.[6]

---

[4] ENF 11.4.1(5) and ENF 13.3.3(7).
[5] The scope of this Chapter excludes restitution and less-frequently exercised enforcement tools and related provisions (e.g. those in relation to collective investment schemes (ENF 16)); disqualification of auditors and actuaries (ENF 17); disapplication orders against members of the professions (ENF 18); directions against incoming ECA providers (ENF 19); and unfair terms and consumer contracts (ENF 20).
[6] For example, restitution orders, injunctions, criminal prosecutions and penalties for market abuse.

## 11.2 The FSA's approach to enforcement[7]

The Financial Services and Markets Act 2000 ("FSMA 2000") prescribes the FSA's powers. Within that statutory framework the FSA formulates its own policy, rules and guidance. The starting point for an understanding of the FSA's approach to disciplinary sanctions lies in an appreciation of its underlying policy.

The FSA's policy on the exercise of its enforcement powers is set out in the Enforcement Manual within the FSA Handbook, which is referred to as ENF. The approach taken by the FSA to the exercise of its enforcement powers is driven by a desire to maintain an open and cooperative relationship between the FSA and those whom it regulates and to ensure that it exercises its powers in a way that is transparent, proportionate and consistent with its stated policies.[8] The exercise of its discretion as to which enforcement mechanism to use or sanction to deploy will depend very much on the circumstances of each particular case.[9] The FSA acts in pursuance of its regulatory objectives, having a range of enforcement powers capable of being tailored to the particular enforcement situation.

Since the last edition of this book, perhaps the two most significant events have been the decision in the *Legal and General* case, and the resulting enforcement process review. Both of these events merit further consideration in light of their importance to the enforcement process as a whole.

### 11.2.1 *Legal and General case (18 January 2005)*

The Tribunal finally delivered its long-awaited judgment on the 18 January 2005. The FSA's central case was that Legal and General's procedures for the sale of its Flexible Mortgage Plans to 41,000 "low-risk" customers between 1997 and 1999 were defective, that these defects led to actual misselling, and that the level of this misselling

---

[7] ENF 1.3.
[8] ENF 1.3.1.
[9] ENF 1.3.3–5.

was significant. Legal and General denied these allegations and referred the case to the Tribunal. Legal and General did not accept that its procedures were defective or that any misselling resulted from procedural defects.

The Tribunal upheld the FSA's case that Legal and General's sales procedures were defective and found that "these procedural defects will have caused or contributed to missales". However, the Tribunal also found that the FSA was not justified in its approach of extrapolating from a sample review of 250 sales to arrive at a conclusion that there was a pattern of general misselling, but it did state that "common sense indicates that there will have been a fair number of missales beyond the eight that have been established". The Tribunal also commented on aspects of the FSA's enforcement procedures, noting that "if Legal and General was not cooperating in securing a review which could be used effectively for enforcement, it was for the FSA to impose a suitable exercise". In addition, criticisms were made of the FSA's enforcement procedure. It is probably fair to say that the case was a victory for both sides: the FSA's essential allegation of misselling was upheld, but the Tribunal found that it was not as extensive as the FSA had claimed.

At the subsequent hearing in May 2005, the Tribunal imposed a financial penalty of £575,000 on Legal and General, a reduction from the original penalty of £1.1 million imposed by the Regulatory Decisions Committee ("RDC").

The Tribunal decided that there would be no order for costs, despite the fact that there had been some criticism of the FSA's procedures. The Tribunal held that Legal and General earned no discount because it did not promptly acknowledge fault. The Tribunal in this case appears to have taken the approach therefore, that a firm which asserts its innocence will pay a higher fine even if it is in the end found guilty of charges which are significantly reduced in scope from those originally proposed. In reaching its decision on this issue, the Tribunal appears to have adopted a restrictive view of what is unreasonable because, despite the criticisms and shortcomings identified by the Tribunal in the FSA's handling of the matter, the Tribunal still held that the FSA had not acted unreasonably so Legal and General was left to pay its own costs.[10]

### 11.2.2   The Strachan Review

Following the Tribunal judgment in the *Legal and General* case, the FSA commissioned a thorough internal review of its enforcement process to ensure it was both fair and efficient. The review, carried out by a team led by David Strachan, made 44 recommendations in its published report, which broadly fell into three categories:

(a)   increasing transparency;
(b)   improving the quality of inputs to the process; and
(c)   providing a more attractive incentive to settle.

All of the report's recommendations were accepted by the FSA. The changes recommended are discussed in detail in Chapter 7 above, but some of the key changes are summarised below.

These changes make the process more transparent, give the firm or individual and the FSA Enforcement Division equal access to the decision-making body (the Regulatory Decisions Committee ("RDC")), and establish a clear divide between the role of the executive in settlement discussions and the RDC in hearing a contested case. Changes to the RDC's working arrangements are already underway, for example the FSA has held seminars for stakeholders to emphasise that the RDC is an administrative process as opposed to a

---

[10] On the issue of costs, it seems that the approach taken by the Tribunal is very much in line with that adopted by the courts. In the case of *Baxendale-Walker* v *Law Society* [2006] EWHC 643 (Admin), the Court of Appeal held that regulators of professional bodies should not, in the absence of bad faith, be ordered to pay any costs of a professional who had committed a disciplinary offence. The court held that where a regulator brought proceedings in the public interest in the exercise of a public function which it was required to perform, the principles applicable to an award of costs differed from those in relation to private civil litigation. Absent dishonesty or a lack of good faith, a costs order should not be made against such a regulator unless there was good reason to do so. That reason had to be more than that the other party had succeeded. In considering an award of costs against a public regulator, the court had to weigh the financial prejudice to the professional against the need to encourage public bodies to exercise their public function of making reasonable and sound decisions without fear of exposure to undue financial prejudice, if the decision was successfully challenged.

court. The RDC now takes its own legal advice from its appointed lawyers and thus has no need to obtain legal advice and support from enforcement. In its budget for 2006/07, the FSA earmarked £2 million to fund improvements to the enforcement process recommended by the Strachan Review.

Among the other new measures being introduced to achieve the recommendations in the review are that Enforcement staff no longer have private access to the RDC. Any discussions between the RDC and Enforcement – usually before the issue of a warning notice – are now minuted and disclosed, and any documents submitted to the RDC by Enforcement are provided to the firm or individual concerned, which will help to ensure there is clarity about the case to be met and transparency of communications between the RDC and Enforcement.

In terms of the process, the FSA has sought to improve the quality of inputs to it by strengthening the legal review conducted within Enforcement before a case goes to the RDC by boosting Enforcement's resources, by creating a legal support staff for the RDC and by reverting to the practice of providing "preliminary findings letters", amongst other measures. The FSA also appears keen to increase the number of negotiated settlements, based on its proposals for the establishment of a tiered level of "discounts" on financial penalties, depending on how early cases are settled, offering a discount of up to 30 per cent of the financial penalty which would otherwise have been imposed. The effect of the Strachan review is that proper Chinese walls have now been instituted between Enforcement and the RDC.

As a result, the general view is that the RDC is likely to be more interventionist during hearings, and will be seen to be exercising an independent judgment. However, the RDC is not a court or tribunal and it will, subject to the requirements of fairness, determine its own procedure. The downside of these new measures is that it may take longer to progress to a decision notice.

## 11.3   Disciplinary action

### 11.3.1   *The FSA's general approach to disciplinary action*

FSA disciplinary proceedings primarily apply to authorised persons and approved persons,[11] although private warnings may in some circumstances also be given to non-authorised persons and financial penalties for market abuse may be imposed on any person.

The objective of the FSA is to use discipline to ensure an effective and proportionate use of its powers to enforce regulatory requirements in support of its statutory regulatory objectives. The FSA currently pursues a themed approach to enforcement, concentrating on areas which it perceives to be of greatest risk to consumers and the market.[12] The disciplinary measures available to the FSA under FSMA 2000 are:

(a)   public statements and public censures; and
(b)   financial penalties.

Other measures described in this chapter may be used in conjunction with these disciplinary measures; for example variation or cancellation of Part IV Permission or withdrawal of a firm's authorisation, the withdrawal of an individual's status as an approved person or the prohibition of an individual from performing some or all functions in relation to a regulated activity.

The considerations in relation to enforcement action for market abuse are in a separate section of the Enforcement Manual (*see* 11.7 below).[13]

### 11.3.2   *Criteria for determining whether to take disciplinary action*

The criteria for determining whether to take disciplinary action are set out in detail in the Enforcement Manual[14] and include a wide range of factors within the following broad categories:

---

[11] ENF 11.1.
[12] Past themes have included anti-money laundering controls and breaches of the financial promotion rules, with the FSA bringing a number of enforcement cases in both of these areas.
[13] Section 123 FSMA 2000 and ENF 14 and ENF 15.
[14] ENF 11.4.

(a)  the nature and seriousness of the alleged breach;[15]
(b)  the conduct of the firm or the approved person after the breach;[16] and
(c)  the previous regulatory record of the firm or approved person.[17]

The FSA will also consider whether it has issued any guidance in relation to the relevant behaviour and, if so, whether that guidance has been followed, the approach that it has taken in previous similar cases and whether any action is proposed by other regulatory authorities.[18]

### 11.3.3  *Disciplinary action against approved persons and the Statements of Principle for Approved Persons*[19]

Section 66 FSMA 2000 enables the FSA to take action against an approved person if it appears to the FSA that he is guilty of misconduct and that taking action is appropriate. An approved person is guilty of misconduct if he:

(a)  has failed to comply with the statements of principle for approved persons issued under Section 64 FSMA 2000; or
(b)  has been knowingly concerned in a contravention by the relevant firm of a requirement imposed on it by or under FSMA 2000.

The action that can be taken against an individual under Section 66 is the imposition of a penalty or the making of a public statement in relation to the misconduct.

The FSA emphasises that the responsibility for ensuring compliance with a firm's regulatory obligations rests primarily with the firm itself and has stated that it will only bring disciplinary action against an approved person where there is evidence of personal culpability on the part of that approved person. Personal culpability arises where

---

[15]  ENF 11.4.1(1).
[16]  ENF 11.4.1(2).
[17]  ENF 11.4.1(3).
[18]  ENF 11.4.1(4)–(6). The FSA's approach in cases which may involve other national or international regulatory authorities is considered further in Chapter 13 below.
[19]  ENF 11.5.

the behaviour was deliberate or where the approved person's standard of behaviour was below that which would be reasonable in all the circumstances. The onus remains on the FSA throughout to prove that the approved person has committed an act of misconduct.[20]

The FSA may not begin proceedings against an individual under Section 66 if more than two years have passed since the FSA first became aware of the misconduct.

Proceedings are often brought against individuals for breaches of the Statements of Principle for Approved Persons. Statements of Principle 1–4 apply to the conduct of all approved persons, but Principles 5–7 apply only to the conduct of those approved persons performing a *significant influence function* (a defined term). Those holding significant influence functions within the organisation broadly comprise those individuals who have senior management responsibility for key aspects of the business.

The application of Principles 5–7 to approved persons holding significant influence functions exposes them to disciplinary action for management failings. The FSA's approach on this has to be seen in the light of express provisions within the Enforcement Manual and the provisions on the standard of reasonable care applicable in such circumstances. Disciplinary action will not be taken against an approved person performing a significant influence function simply because a regulatory failure has occurred in an area of business for which he had responsibility. A breach will be considered to have occurred only if that person has breached Statements of Principles 5–7 and only if his conduct was below the standard which would be reasonable in all the circumstances.[21] An approved person will not be in breach if he has exercised due and reasonable care when assessing information, has reached a reasonable conclusion and has acted on it.[22]

---

[20] Section 66(4). Beginning proceedings, for these purposes, means issuing a warning notice.

[21] *See* the case of *David John Maslen* 10 April 2006: a penalty of £350,000 was imposed on Mr Maslen for being knowingly concerned in the contravention of Principle 5 by Deutsche Bank AG ("Deutsche"). In setting the penalty, the FSA took into account the fact that disciplinary action had been taken against Mr Maslen by Deutsche which resulted in a reduction of his 2004 bonus, and a reduction in his role and responsibilities as Head of European Cash Trading. In addition, Deutsche Bank was fined separately.

[22] ENF 11.5.6(3).

At the time of writing, instances of proceedings against individuals who have not been engaged in deliberate wrongdoing have been rare. Recent cases concerning significant failures in compliance/control arrangements and money laundering procedures have led to enforcement proceedings against the firm rather than individuals concerned. The case of *Carr Sheppards Crosthwaite Limited*,[23] in which the firm was fined £500,000 for compliance failings which had exposed clients to the risk of loss, underscores the FSA's approach to date of disciplining firms rather than individuals. However, commentary from the FSA suggests that this approach is likely to change and the FSA will begin to concentrate enforcement proceedings on individuals within senior management who have been held responsible for failing to ensure adequate systems of internal control or appropriate training and competence within a particular firm.

### 11.3.4 Disciplinary action against firms and the Principles for Businesses

The FSA has power to take disciplinary action against a firm which contravenes requirements imposed on it by or under FSMA 2000. It can issue a public censure under Section 205 or impose a financial penalty under Section 206. However, it cannot both impose a financial penalty on a firm and withdraw its authorisation under Section 33.

The FSA can bring disciplinary proceedings against firms for breaches of specific rules in the FSA Handbook and/or for breaches of the Principles for Businesses.[24] The FSA often chooses to allege breaches of the principles rather than contravention of specific rules. Its stated policy is to do so where:

(a)  there is no detailed rule which prohibits the behaviour in question, but the behaviour clearly contravenes a Principle; or

---

[23] Final Notice 19 May 2004.
[24] City Index Ltd was fined for both types of breach (22 March 2005): it was required to pay a fine of £35,000 for breaching the Conduct of Business ("COB") and Senior Management Arrangements, Systems and Controls ("SYSC") rules, and Principles 3 and 7 of the FSA's Principles for Business. The breach arose out of City Index's communication of a financial promotion which failed to include a fair description of the nature of the investment offered, or an adequate description of the commitment required and risks involved with contracts for differences and spread betting. Financial promotions have been targeted as one of the FSA's themed enforcement initiatives, resulting in a number of cases on this topic.

(b)    where the firm has committed numerous breaches of rules
       which individually may not merit disciplinary action but which
       cumulatively indicate the breach of a Principle.[25]

In February 2007, the FSA published its Business Plan for 2007/08
which sets out its priorities for the coming year. The plan focuses
on the organisation's move towards "more principles based regulation" ("MPBR"). The FSA's view is that senior management of
firms, not the FSA, have the responsibility to assure that the firm
abides by the principles and rules in the Handbook. As such the
regulator's position is that the shift to MPBR means that senior
management will have more scope to decide for themselves how
the firm should comply and therefore more scope to shape compliance to the overall needs of the business. Central to this change
appears to be an intention significantly to increase the freedom of,
and the responsibilities on, senior management of regulated institutions to determine their own approach to regulatory compliance
issues.

In respect of any guidance, the FSA's view appears to be that whilst
following the guidance does not necessarily mean that firms will
achieve the results required under the outcomes-focused rules, they
will stand a very good chance of doing so, and hence that should
provide a certain degree of assurance to firms. The FSA has also been
at pains to emphasise that it will recognise industry guidance.
Indeed, at a seminar in January 2007, the FSA stated that:

> "Industry owns the guidance, not the FSA. We review it, but we
> do not own it. It is up to industry to decide if or when the guid-
> ance needs to be changed – either because the business has
> changed, or because industry has developed more effective
> methods of achieving the right results."

The FSA has also indicated that it will be receptive, and hence will
review any guidance that industry may produce so that firms can get
some assurance.

---

[25] ENF 11.6.3.

The shift to MPBR also implies a shift to more principles-based supervision. This implies supervisors exercising more judgment about firms.

This ability to rely on the Principles provides the FSA with flexibility due to the breadth of conduct that is potentially covered by them. It also avoids the FSA becoming embroiled in technical arguments about whether a specific alleged rule breach has been proved. In practice the FSA places very considerable reliance on the Principles when bringing disciplinary action against firms.[26] The FSA has tended to favour alleging breaches of Principles rather than, or as well as, specific rule breaches, even where specific rules could arguably have been said to have covered the misconduct in question.[27]

### 11.3.5    The FSA's standard of reasonable care[28]

In many circumstances, the FSA is required to show that a firm has failed to exercise the appropriate standard of reasonable care in order to establish a breach of a Principle or rule. In order to retain flexibility it will consider all the circumstances of the case, although regard is had to the following particular matters:

(a)    what information the firm knew at the time of the behaviour, and what information it ought to have known;

(b)    what steps the firm took to comply with the rule or Principle, and what steps it ought to have taken; and

(c)    the standards of the regulatory system that applied at the time of the behaviour.

---

[26] An example of this can been seen in the decision to impose a financial penalty on Deutsche Bank: Deutsche Bank entered into two transactions ("the Scania transaction" and "the Cytos transaction"). In respect of the Scania transaction, the FSA felt that the manner and size of trading had a material effect on the price of the Scania shares, but that potential investors would not have known that it was Deutsche's activity that was affecting the share price during the period of trading, hence Deutsche was fined £3.5 million for breaching Principles 2 and 5 of the Principles, and an additional amount of £2,363,643 in respect of the loss avoided in relation to the transaction. In respect of the Cytos transaction, the trader had bought shares to ensure that they opened at a higher price than they had closed the previous day. Deutsche was criticised for failing to ensure that internal procedures were followed, and for failing to prevent the matter escalating; a penalty of £500,000 was imposed in respect of the breaches of Principle 2.

[27] *See,* for example, Final Notices relating to *Cantor Index* (30 December 2004) and *AXA Sun Life plc* (21 December 2004).

[28] ENF 11.7.

These considerations will also apply to approved persons where it is necessary to consider whether they have taken reasonable care.

### 11.3.6 Disciplinary action for breaches of the money laundering rules[29]

In deciding whether to take disciplinary action in respect of a potential breach of the FSA's money laundering rules, the FSA will have regard to whether a firm has followed the relevant provisions of the Joint Money Laundering Steering Groups Guidance Notes for the financial sector.[30] This has been a fertile area for FSA enforcement action, even where there has been no evidence that systems and controls failings have allowed money laundering actually to occur.

### 11.3.7 Financial penalties[31]

There are express statutory powers to impose financial penalties on a firm[32] or approved person[33] or, in the case of market abuse[34] or breaches of listing requirements,[35] on any other person. The principal rationale for the imposition of financial penalties is deterrence and to achieve high standards of regulatory conduct. A firm is prohibited from entering into arrangements that have the effect of indemnifying a person against any financial penalty.[36]

The FSA is required under FSMA 2000 to issue statements of its policy relating to the imposition of financial penalties on firms and

---

[29] ENF 11.9.

[30] In April 2004 Raiffeisen Zentralbank Osterreich was fined £150,000 for breaching Rule 2.1.1 and Rule 3.1.3 of the FSA's Money Laundering Sourcebook. Specific reference was made to the fact that the firm's practices did not adhere to the Guidance Notes. *See* also the following cases as examples of enforcement proceedings and penalties concerning control failings and inadequate procedures in the context of money laundering: *The Governor and Company of the Bank of Ireland* Final Notice 31 August 2004 (fine of £375,000); *The Governor and Company of the Bank of Scotland* Final Notice 12 January 2004 (fine of £1,250,000); *Abbey National plc* Final Notice 9 December 2003 (fine of £2,000,000); *Northern Bank Ltd* Final Notice 4 August 2003 (fine of £1,250,000); *Royal Bank of Scotland* Final Notice 12 December 2002 (fine of £750,000).

[31] ENF 13.

[32] Section 206.

[33] Section 66(3).

[34] Section 123(1).

[35] Sections 91(1) and (2).

[36] *See* GEN 6 for the detailed rules.

approved persons,[37] and the FSA must have regard to these statements in deciding whether to impose a financial penalty.

In the interests of retaining flexibility and exercising its powers proportionately, the FSA does not operate a tariff of penalties for different types of breach (there is one exception to this in relation to late regulatory reporting, *see* 11.3.8 below).

The FSA's policy[38] in relation to approved persons must have regard specifically to:

(a)   the seriousness of the conduct in question;
(b)   the extent to which the misconduct was deliberate or reckless; and
(c)   whether the person on whom the penalty is to be imposed is an individual.

The factors which the FSA has stated it will consider to be relevant in determining the amount of financial penalty to impose are not exhaustive, but include:

(a)   The seriousness of the misconduct or contravention.[39] The FSA says that the following factors may be relevant:

   (i)     the seriousness of the misconduct or contravention in relation to the nature of the Statement of Principle or requirement breached;
   (ii)    the duration and frequency of the misconduct or contravention, including, in relation to a firm, whether the misconduct or contravention was identified by persons exercising a significant influence function;[40]
   (iii)   whether the misconduct or contravention demonstrated serious or systemic weaknesses in the management

---

[37] Sections 69 and 210.
[38] Section 69(2); *see* also Section 210(2) for firms.
[39] ENF 13.3.3(1).
[40] *See* Final Notice relating to *Bradford and Bingley plc* (22 December 2004) as an example of where a failure to follow up on warning signs about potential misselling was viewed as an aggravating factor. A financial penalty of £650,000 was imposed.

systems or internal controls relating to all or part of the firm's business;[41]

(iv)    the impact of the misconduct or contravention on the orderliness of financial markets and public confidence in those markets;[42] and

(v)    the loss or risk of loss caused to consumers or other market users.[43]

(b)    The extent to which the contravention or misconduct was deliberate or reckless. In determining whether a contravention was reckless the FSA will have regard to matters such as:

(i)    a failure to comply with the firm's procedures;

(ii)    whether a firm or person made a decision beyond their field of competence; and

(iii)    whether there was an apparent failure to give consideration to the consequences of the behaviour alleged.[44]

(c)    The size, financial resources and other circumstances of the firm or individual on whom the penalty is to be imposed:

(i)    the FSA may take into account verifiable evidence[45] of serious financial hardship or financial difficulties or issues of solvency that may arise in relation to the firm;

(ii)    the size of a firm may be relevant to the degree of seriousness of a contravention. For example, a systemic failure in

---

[41] This was one of the factors taken into account when imposing a penalty of £900,000 on ABN AMRO Equities(UK) Ltd on 15 April 2003 for improper trading (the relevant misconduct in fact occurred prior to the implementation of FSMA 2000). The FSA noted that the fact that there had been three breaches in a six-month period illustrated the lack of a robust compliance environment on the firm's trading floor, which resulted from the absence of sufficient compliance resources and inadequate compliance procedures, policies and training.

[42] *Evolution Beeson Gregory* Final Notice (12 November 2004). *See* in particular paragraphs 48(iii) and (v).

[43] Braemar Financial Planning Limited was fined £182,000 for systemic failings in its sales process for pensions unlocking (11 September 2006). The failings resulted from advisers not taking reasonable steps to ensure that recommendations were suitable for their customers. The FSA was clearly of the view that this was a high-risk business which was only suitable for a limited number of people, and not the public more generally. Behind the decision was a strong desire to protect vulnerable consumers from high-risk products which they would be unlikely to understand. Of note is the fact that the firm received a 30 per cent discount under the Executive Settlement Process, to reflect the fact that it had agreed to settle at the earliest opportunity.

[44] Deliberate or reckless behaviour is plainly an aggravating factor and will inevitably lead to a higher financial penalty being imposed.

[45] *See* footnote 59 below.

a large firm may risk damaging a larger number of consumers than an equivalent breach in a smaller firm, and so be viewed as more serious;

(iii)    the FSA may consider the size of a firm and its resources in relation to mitigation when assessing the reasonableness of a firm's response after a contravention has been identified.

(d)    The amount of profits accrued or loss avoided. The FSA will have regard to the fact that a person should not benefit from misconduct and that the penalty should act as an incentive for persons to comply with regulatory standards.

(e)    Conduct following a contravention. This is often critical; an appropriate response may significantly mitigate an accused's position and reduce the financial penalty that would otherwise be imposed. Relevant factors include:

(i)    the degree of cooperation of the firm or approved person in the context of the investigation;[46] and

(ii)    any remedial steps taken including the identification and compensation of those consumers who may have suffered loss.[47]

(f)    Disciplinary record and compliance history. The previous disciplinary record and compliance history of a firm or approved person can be taken into account when deciding the appropriate level of penalty.[48] Where a firm or individual has committed similar contraventions in the past, the FSA may conclude that it is appropriate to impose an increased penalty. The age of any prior breach will be taken into account, although a long-standing

---

[46] For example, in *Lincoln Assurance Ltd* (16 April 2003), the FSA imposed a financial penalty of £485,000 for various breaches of the PIA and LAUTRO Rules, and the SIB principles. The FSA expressly recognised the extent of the cooperation demonstrated by Lincoln once the failings had been drawn to its attention, and this was said to be appropriate justification for reducing the level of financial penalty.

[47] This was a key mitigating factor in determining the appropriate penalty against *Royal & Sun Alliance Life and Pensions Limited and Royal & Sun Alliance Linked Insurances Ltd* (25 March 2003), who were in breach of the PIA and LAUTRO rules, and the SIB principles arising from its sale of RSA's Homeplan mortgage endowment customers. RSA subsequently implemented a redress procedure, which ensured that no customer suffered loss in relation to the issue of short-term contracts.

[48] In a matter involving a mishandling of mortgage endowment complaints by *Friends Provident Life and Pensions Ltd* (15 December 2003), the FSA made reference to the fact that Friends Provident had been the subject of formal disciplinary action on one previous occasion.

matter could still be relevant. Private warnings are not taken into account.

The issue of remedial action is considered in detail in Chapter 6. The FSA attaches considerable importance to firms cooperating with its investigations and has issued guidance on the types of factor that the FSA will consider to demonstrate cooperation.[49] Mere compliance with the obligations on firms and approved persons to be open and cooperative with the FSA is insufficient to gain credit for cooperation; the FSA says that there must be "evidence of active cooperation". On occasion FSA enforcement staff have said that whilst firms and individuals are perfectly entitled to withhold privileged material from the FSA, they cannot expect credit for cooperation if they do so. If the FSA decides to take this stance in a particular case, its appropriateness is likely to depend on the particular circumstances and firms and individuals should take great care with any decision to waive privilege, and should consider taking legal advice before doing so.

A further indication of the FSA's approach arose in a misselling case involving Allied Dunbar Assurance plc (Final Notice March 2004), in which Allied Dunbar initially gave a robust defence to the FSA's criticism of its procedures. Allied Dunbar subsequently accepted those procedures were defective and, in its Final Notice, the FSA said that it found Allied Dunbar's initial robust response to be an aggravating factor. A firm or individual is, therefore, frequently required to make a judgment as to whether to defend its or their position vigorously and risk losing the benefit of any credit for cooperation, or to challenge the FSA's findings in the hope of obtaining a more favourable outcome if the FSA can be persuaded that those findings cannot be supported (in whole or in part) on the evidence but run the risk of being found to have aggravated the misconduct or contravention by a perceived failure to cooperate.

The types of factor that the FSA says it will consider when deciding whether credit should be given for cooperation include:

---

[49] *See* "The benefits to firms and individuals of cooperating with the FSA" on the "Enforcement in focus" section of the FSA website.

(a)   what the firm did to investigate the nature or source of a problem;

(b)   whether a firm instructed independent third parties to carry out a review;

(c)   whether a firm promptly paid redress to consumers;[50]

(d)   did senior management actively participate in the efforts to address and remedy the issue;[51]

(e)   did the firm voluntarily provide material that had not been requested and of which the FSA might not otherwise have been aware; and

(f)   did the firm or individual quickly agree the facts and seek to agree a basis on which enforcement action could be concluded.

If the FSA is satisfied that a firm or individual has cooperated, it may decide either that a matter which might otherwise have resulted in enforcement action can be addressed on a supervisory basis or, if enforcement action does occur, that a lesser penalty should be imposed. There is no set amount by which financial penalties are reduced as a result of cooperation, nor is the extent of the reduction made public in individual cases.

The FSA may permit a firm or person to pay a financial penalty by instalments in order to avoid financial hardship or solvency issues

---

[50]   A final notice was published against Abbey National plc (25 May 2005) requiring it to pay a financial penalty of £800,000, for mishandling customers' mortgage endowment complaints between October 2001 and September 2003, and providing the FSA with inaccurate and potentially misleading information in response to an FSA letter. The FSA considered that there was sufficient mitigation in the Abbey's willingness to cooperate with the FSA's investigation and the remedial action proposed (e.g. to review all mortgage endowment complaints rejected since 1 January 2000 and to pay redress where a complaint had been unfairly rejected) for a fine of this magnitude to be sufficient. The decision notice was explicit that without the level of cooperation, the financial penalty would have been substantially higher.

[51]   Citigroup Global Markets Ltd (28 June 2005) was required to relinquish profits in the amount of £9,960,860 and an additional penalty of £4 million was also imposed. The penalty arose out of a trading strategy executed on the European government bond markets, whereby Citigroup was judged by the FSA to have breached Principles 2 and 3 of the Principles for Business. By way of mitigation, Citigroup enhanced its escalation policies, and introduced a web-based training module to focus specifically on escalation. In addition, all staff henceforth would receive annual refresher training courses in relation to market conduct. On the basis of this, the FSA was satisfied that senior management within the bank had taken the matter raised by the trading in question very seriously, and had fully engaged to address the FSA concerns, ensuring that the correct remedial actions were taken. This was clearly a factor upon which the FSA placed considerable weight. This case is also of interest because no action was taken against any of the individuals as the FSA felt that the matter of regulatory concern was the serious corporate failings of Citigroup, demonstrating the FSA's willingness in this case to focus on corporate failings rather than individual culpability.

depending on the overall circumstances of the case.[52] The period within which the full payment of the penalty must be made will not generally exceed one year from the date of the final notice. This time period may also enable defendants to argue a reduction in financial penalties proposed if the financial penalty concerned is expected to be paid within that period of time.

### 11.3.8  Financial penalties in specific cases

#### 11.3.8.1  Late submission of reports[53]
There is a separate and more prescriptive regime for the imposition of financial penalties for the late submission of reports in relation to a firm's regulatory reporting obligations. Where the period of delay is no more than 28 business days the FSA will, in the majority of cases, impose a financial penalty fixed by reference to an indicative scale of penalties. This is the only circumstance in which the FSA imposes such an indicative scale. The FSA reserves the right to impose higher penalties than those indicated on the scale if there are aggravating factors (such as deliberate, reckless or repeated contravention). The FSA may also bring disciplinary action in serious and persistent cases.

#### 11.3.8.2  Breaches of prudential requirements[54]
Where there are breaches of prudential requirements the FSA will have regard to the impact that a financial penalty may have upon the firm's customers. This is particularly important in relation to mutual organisations (such as building societies). Long-term insurers are prohibited from paying financial penalties from a long-term insurance fund.[55]

### 11.3.9  Public censures and public statements[56]

The FSA may issue a public censure or public statement against a firm, an approved person, or a person who is not an approved person

---

[52] In *F T Investments & Insurance Consultants* for example (7 August 2002), the IFA was a small partnership of only two persons, and was permitted to pay a £4,000 fine in 18 monthly instalments.
[53] ENF 13.5.
[54] ENF 13.6.
[55] ENF 13.6.3.
[56] Sections 205, 66(3)(b), 123(3) and 91(3).

or a firm. The purpose of public censures and statements is not only punitive in terms of the reputational impact on the person concerned, they also serve to identify to the markets the standards of conduct expected of firms and individuals and demonstrate that those standards are being enforced. Censures and public statements also promote public awareness of the standards of behaviour expected and thereby increase consumer protection as well as promoting and maintaining confidence in the financial system.[57]

The criteria considered by the FSA in determining whether to issue a public censure or public statement are set out in the Enforcement Manual.[58] The factors may include:

(a)   whether the firm or approved person has made a profit or avoided a loss. If so, this may militate in favour of a financial penalty;
(b)   the seriousness of the breach or misconduct concerned;
(c)   whether the firm or approved person has admitted the breach or misconduct, cooperated with the FSA and compensated consumers;
(d)   the firm's or approved person's disciplinary record or compliance history;
(e)   the FSA's approach in previous similar cases; and
(f)   the means of the firm or approved person, although it will only be in exceptional circumstances that the FSA will agree to issue a public statement rather than impose a financial penalty if a financial penalty would otherwise be the appropriate sanction. Such exceptional circumstances include where an approved person can present verifiable evidence that they would suffer serious financial hardship if the FSA imposed a financial penalty and where a firm can present verifiable evidence[59] that it may be unable to meet other regulatory requirements (e.g. financial resource requirements) if the FSA imposed a financial penalty at what it would consider to be an appropriate level.[60]

---

[57]   ENF 12.2.2.
[58]   ENF 12.3.3.
[59]   It is important that advisers present such evidence, preferably from a source other than the accused, at an early stage.
[60]   Such examples are rare; *see* Final Notice *The Underwriter Insurance Company Limited* (29 November 2004). *SFI Group plc* (11 December 2003) is another example, in a case involving Listing Rule breaches.

### 11.3.10 *Private warnings*

Private warnings are used in circumstances where formal disciplinary action is not considered appropriate. They are quite commonly
used by the Enforcement staff of the FSA. They constitute a warning
that the person in question came close to being the subject of formal
disciplinary action. Private warnings tend to be used where the
matter giving rise to concern is relatively minor in nature or degree,
or the firm or approved person concerned has taken full and immediate remedial action.[61]

The FSA generally uses private warnings in the context of firms and
approved persons, but their use may extend to non-authorised
persons in the context of the market abuse regime or in circumstances
where the FSA may otherwise consider making a prohibition order
against a non-authorised person.

A private warning will state[62] that:

(a)  whilst no determination of misconduct has been made, the FSA
     has had cause for concern arising from the conduct;
(b)  the FSA does not presently intend to take formal disciplinary
     action, having regard to all the circumstances of the case;
(c)  the private warning will form part of the firm's or approved
     person's compliance history and may be taken into account in
     deciding whether the FSA brings disciplinary action in the
     future;[63] and
(d)  the FSA requires the firm or approved person[64] to acknowledge
     receipt of the warning letter and invites comment upon it.

The age of a prior private warning will be considered in assessing
its relevance to determining whether or not to take subsequent

---

[61] The FSA may also raise concerns in correspondence that does not constitute a formal private
   warning, but which will also form part of the firm's compliance history. Correspondence of
   this nature normally arises out of supervision visits during which minor breaches have been
   identified.
[62] ENF 11.3.4.
[63] But if disciplinary action is brought in respect of a subsequent breach, prior private warnings
   will not be relied upon in determining whether a breach has occurred or in determining the
   level of sanction to be imposed.
[64] Private warnings to approved persons may also be notified to that person's employer.

disciplinary action in relation to another matter. Where there has been more than one private warning, the cumulative effect of those warnings may be considered in deciding whether they are indicative of the compliance culture of the firm or its management.

## 11.4   Other action against individuals

### 11.4.1   *Withdrawal of approved person status*

The FSA may withdraw approval from an approved person if it considers that the person is not a fit and proper person to perform the function to which the approval relates. The procedure for withdrawing an approval requires the issue of a warning notice to the approved person and interested parties (i.e. their employers), followed by a decision notice which is subject to a right of referral to the Financial Services and Markets Tribunal in the event that the approved person or interested party wishes to challenge it. The Tribunal will consider the matter afresh and review all material, including, where relevant, material that was not available to the FSA at the time of its decision.[65]

There is no definitive list of the matters which the FSA may take into account in considering whether to withdraw a person's approval, but the FSA's policy and a number of the factors that it considers relevant are set out within the Enforcement Manual.[66] Important amongst those factors will be the criteria for assessing the fitness and propriety of approved persons which include:

(a)   honesty, integrity and reputation;
(b)   competence and capability (taking account, where appropriate, of the particular controlled function carried out by the approved person); and
(c)   financial soundness.

---

[65] *See* FSMT Decision in *Rayner and Townsend* v *FSA*, 6 August 2004 para. 94.
[66] ENF 7.5.1 to 7.5.5. In a matter involving a Christopher John Liston, the main factor relied upon by the FSA in deciding to withdraw Mr Liston's approval was the fact that he had been convicted of criminal offences, involving both dishonesty and fraud, resulting in a custodial sentence. The FSA took the view that this was relevant and important to the performance of any controlled function and concluded that Mr Liston was not a fit and proper person to perform an investment adviser function (8 September 2003).

Other factors to which the FSA may have regard in deciding whether to withdraw a person's approval include:

(a)    the extent to which that person has failed to comply with the Principles or been knowingly concerned in a contravention of a requirement imposed under FSMA 2000;

(b)    the length of time since the occurrence of any matters indicating unfitness;

(c)    the severity of the risk that the person concerned poses to consumers and the financial system; and

(d)    that person's previous disciplinary history.[67]

Regard also may be had to the cumulative effect of factors which when considered on their own may not be sufficient to show that the person is not fit and proper.[68]

The FSA will generally publicise a final notice relating to a withdrawal of approval unless this would prejudice the interests of consumers.

### 11.4.2   *Prohibition of individuals*

The FSA may make a prohibition order if it appears to it that an individual is not fit and proper to perform functions in relation to a regulated activity carried on by an authorised person. This power may be used against both approved persons and individuals who are not approved persons but are employed by an authorised person.[69] The order may relate to any specified regulated activity or all such activities and will be tailored to meet the facts of the particular case.[70]

An individual who acts in breach of a prohibition order is guilty of a summary offence and liable to be fined.[71] However, it will be a

---

[67]   ENF 7.5.2(6).

[68]   *See* Final Notice of 18 May 2004 relating to *Richard Bernard Charles* as an example of conduct involving lack of honesty and integrity and of competence and capability in a controlled function; *see* also Final Notice of 15 April 2003 relating to *Michael Ackers*, as an example of withdrawal of approval as a consequence of allegations of market misconduct and breach of Principle 3.

[69]   Such orders may also be made in respect of persons who are exempt persons under Part XX FSMA 2000.

[70]   Section 56.

[71]   Section 56(4).

defence for the accused to show that he took all reasonable precautions and exercised all due diligence to avoid committing the offence. An authorised person must take reasonable care to ensure that it does not permit a function to be performed in relation to the carrying on of a regulated activity by a person who has been prohibited from performing that function.[72]

If a prohibition order is proposed, the FSA must give the individual concerned a warning notice through the usual RDC procedures, setting out the terms of and reasons for the proposed prohibition followed, if appropriate, by a decision notice. A right of referral to the Financial Services and Markets Tribunal exists in the normal way.[73]

In deciding whether to make a prohibition order in relation to an approved person, the FSA will consider a similar range of factors to those which it will consider in deciding whether to withdraw an approved person's approval.[74] It will also consider whether its regulatory objectives can be adequately achieved by withdrawing the person's approval or by disciplinary sanctions instead. Similar factors will also be considered for prohibition orders against non-approved persons who are employed or were formerly employed by an authorised person, save that failures to comply with the Statements of Principle and their being knowingly concerned in contraventions of requirements imposed under FSMA 2000 will only be considered insofar as the relevant conduct occurred when the individual was an approved person. Prohibition orders are sought in the most serious of cases where the individual concerned presents a sufficient risk to consumers or the market. In the case of approved persons, withdrawal of approval would normally be the sanction considered by the FSA, although the FSA will proceed straight to a prohibition order if

---

[72] Section 56(6). If a firm has failed to search the register to ascertain whether or not an individual whom it employs is prohibited or not, it exposes itself to the possibility of liability under Section 71 FSMA 2000 in an action for damages by a private person who suffers loss as a result of the contravention.

[73] ENF 8.3.

[74] *See* 11.4.1 above. In a matter involving Rupert Bruce, a prohibition order was made in February 2004, despite the relevant incidents having occurred in 1996 and 1997. An aggravating feature in the case, which concerned allegations of mispricing and misuse of confidential information, was that the FSA stated that his subsequent conduct demonstrated "a continuing lack of openness and honesty in his dealings with regulators". *See* also *Michael Harding* Final Notice 21 January 2005.

*A Practitioner's Guide to FSA Investigations and Enforcement*

the concerns are sufficiently serious. The FSA is likely to consider making a prohibition order against approved persons only in the more serious cases of lack of fitness and propriety.[75]

If a prohibition order is made against an individual, that individual can apply to the FSA to have the order varied or revoked. The FSA will consider all relevant circumstances at the time of the application, including (but not limited to) criteria set out in the Enforcement Manual.[76] The FSA will generally not grant applications to vary or revoke a prohibition order unless it is satisfied that the concerns that gave rise to the original order have been adequately addressed. The usual warning notice and decision notice procedure applies, with the right of referral to the Financial Services and Markets Tribunal if the person does not accept the FSA's decision.[77]

Once a final notice relating to a prohibition order has been issued the FSA will generally publicise its decision. Additionally, the FSA is obliged to keep a public record of individuals against whom a prohibition order has been made once the final notice has been issued.[78]

## 11.5 Other action against firms

### 11.5.1 Variation of Part IV Permission on the FSA's own initiative

The FSA may use its own initiative power to vary or restrict a firm's Part IV Permission to:

---

[75] ENF 8.5.
[76] ENF 8.9.2.
[77] The FSA will be obliged to answer to the Tribunal if serious allegations affecting the fitness of individuals are based largely on inference, as demonstrated by the case of *Manchanda v FSA* (15–17 May 2006). The applicant applied to the FSA for two approvals to control a mortgage broker and to perform the functions of a director of it. Both were refused by the FSA. The case turned on the applicant's role at RBG Resources plc ("RBG") a metal and minerals trading company which suffered losses of more than $400 million as a result of extensive frauds. In essence, the controversy was over the inferences to be drawn from the facts, which were largely agreed. The Tribunal concluded that the applicant was a fit and proper person; they did not consider that on the material they had seen, he had any knowledge of the frauds or that his professional conduct was open to serious criticism.
[78] Section 347(1)(g), ENF 8.12.1 to 8.12.5.

(a)  remove a regulated activity from the firm's Part IV Permission;
(b)  vary the description of a regulated activity;
(c)  vary a requirement imposed under Section 43 FSMA 2000;
(d)  limit the number and category of customers that a firm can deal with; and
(e)  limit the number of specified investments a firm can deal in.

The FSA may also impose requirements that a firm take or refrain from taking specified action. For example, in *Oak Financial Services*,[79] in addition to removing various regulated activities from the Part IV Permission, the FSA also imposed requirements that Oak Financial Services:

(a)  advise all its clients in writing that it no longer had professional indemnity insurance in place and was no longer permitted by the FSA to carry on a regulated activity; and
(b)  provide the FSA with a copy of the written advice sent to all clients for its regulated activities.

In *Woodward's Independent Financial Advisers*[80] the FSA varied the firm's Part IV Permission to impose a requirement that the firm appoint external consultants, at its own expense, to review its past pension transfer and opt-out business.

The FSA can seek to vary a Part IV Permission where it appears to the FSA that:

(1)  a firm is failing or is likely to fail to satisfy the threshold conditions in relation to its regulated activities;
(2)  the firm concerned has failed during a period of at least 12 months to carry on a particular regulatory activity to which the permission relates; or
(3)  it is desirable to vary the permission in order to protect the interests of consumers or potential consumers in relation to such regulated activity.

---

[79] 26 March 2003.
[80] 4 April 2002.

The FSA has a duty to ensure that firms satisfy the threshold conditions at all times in accordance with its published policy. This policy focuses upon the FSA's regulatory objectives and emphasises the responsibilities of the firm's management to manage the firm. In supervising and monitoring a firm, the FSA will normally take early steps to ensure that the management are aware of its concerns and that they have adequate time to respond to those concerns before taking the significant step of varying the firm's permission.

However, where there are serious concerns in relation to a firm that present immediate risks, the FSA will take urgent and immediate action. The FSA is likely to take action without protracted discussion with a firm's senior management where:

(a)   there is a likelihood of significant loss or risk of loss or other adverse effects to consumers;
(b)   the firm may be involved in financial crime;
(c)   the firm has submitted inaccurate and misleading information to the FSA which gives rise to a concern that it may not be able to meet its regulatory obligations; or
(d)   the firm's controllers or the firm itself have such serious problems that the firm's ability to meet its threshold conditions is in doubt.

### 11.5.2   Cancellation of Part IV Permission on the FSA's own initiative

The FSA has power to cancel a firm's Part IV Permission on its own initiative. This power applies to all firms that have a Part IV Permission and the grounds upon which the power may be exercised are the same as those which apply to the variation of a Part IV Permission. Where there is a need to take urgent action against a firm, the FSA will normally use its own initiative power to vary a firm's Part IV Permission rather than seek to cancel its Part IV Permission, as a variation of a Part IV Permission becomes effective immediately, whereas a cancellation only becomes effective on completion of the statutory decision-making procedure and any subsequent referral to the Tribunal.

If the FSA decides that a firm should cease all regulated activities, it may first vary the firm's Part IV Permission so that the firm cannot carry out any regulated activities. If it does this, the FSA will then have a *duty* to cancel the firm's Part IV Permission once it is satisfied that it is no longer necessary to keep that permission in force. However, it may decide to postpone cancellation of the permission in order to maintain the firm's status as an authorised person and enable its activities to be monitored and, if necessary, controlled, for example during a wind-down of its activities.

Trends in the exercise of the FSA's own initiative powers remain difficult to discern, but as a matter of practice they are used in urgent and clear-cut cases where failure to act may significantly undermine the FSA's regulatory objectives. In considering whether to cancel a Part IV Permission, the FSA may also have regard to the findings of any other investigations to which the firm is subject. A final notice was issued to Reynolds and Dodd in August 2003, informing the firm of the cancellation of its Part IV Permission. The FSA specifically relied on the fact that the firm had been the subject of an investigation by the Law Society involving serious allegations of dishonesty, which had resulted in the immediate suspension of the firm's practising certificate. The FSA concluded that the firm was therefore failing to satisfy the threshold conditions, in that it was failing to conduct its business with integrity and in compliance with proper standards.

### 11.5.3 Intervention against incoming firms

The FSA also has a power to intervene against incoming firms[81] and may exercise this power in support of overseas regulators.[82] The grounds for exercising the power against an incoming firm include the contravention of a requirement imposed by FSMA 2000, the provision by the firm of false or misleading information to the FSA, or that it is in the interests of actual or potential customers that the power be exercised.

The FSA's policy in this area is similar to its policy in relation to the exercise of its own initiative powers to vary a permission[83] and it will have particular regard to the views of the firm's home state regulator

---

[81] Section 194.
[82] Section 195.
[83] ENF 4.4.

when it is considering action against an incoming firm.[84] The procedure for the exercise of this power broadly follows the supervisory
notice procedure before the RDC.

# 11.6   Injunctions

The FSA can apply to the court under FSMA 2000 to seek an injunction against a person in cases of regulatory breach,[85] market abuse[86]
and at the request of the home state regulator of an incoming
European Economic Area ("EEA") firm.[87]

The FSA has power to apply to court for an injunction against any
person, whether authorised or not, in connection with contraventions
of a "relevant requirement".[88] An injunction can be obtained to
prevent an anticipated or ongoing contravention of a relevant requirement by a firm and/or to require a person to remedy or mitigate the
effects of such a contravention.[89] An injunction may also be sought by
the FSA under Section 380 FSMA 2000 against a person who has been
knowingly concerned in the contravention of a relevant requirement,
as well as those who have directly contravened the requirement.[90]

The court may make an order restraining a person whom the court is
satisfied may have contravened a relevant requirement or been
knowingly concerned in such a contravention from disposing of or
dealing with his assets.[91] In cases where a breach of a relevant
requirement has not yet occurred, but the FSA can demonstrate that
there is a reasonable likelihood that a person will contravene a relevant requirement and dissipate assets belonging to investors, the FSA
can ask the court to grant a freezing injunction under its inherent
jurisdiction.

---

[84] ENF 4.4.3.
[85] Section 380, for "relevant requirement" *see* Section 380(6) FSMA 2000.
[86] Section 381.
[87] Section 198; ENF 6.2.1 to 6.2.6.
[88] Section 380. A "relevant requirement" means, in broad terms, a requirement imposed by or
    under FSMA 2000 or one which is imposed under another Act but which the FSA has power
    to prosecute under FSMA 2000.
[89] Section 380(2) and (5).
[90] Section 380(2).
[91] Section 380(3).

Similar powers exist in FSMA 2000 in relation to injunctions in cases of market abuse (*see* 11.7.7 below).[92]

The FSA's policy in relation to the use of injunctions recognises the serious consequences for those concerned, and takes into consideration a wide range of factors[93] which include:

(a)  the nature and seriousness of the contravention or expected contravention of a relevant requirement;
(b)  whether the losses suffered by consumers are or are likely to be substantial;
(c)  whether the number of consumers who have suffered or may suffer losses is significant;
(d)  whether the conduct has stopped or is likely to be repeated; and
(e)  whether remedial steps have been taken by the persons concerned.

The FSA will also consider a range of other factors such as cost, the availability of alternative measures and whether other authorities can more adequately deal with the matter.

The FSA considers it generally appropriate to publish details of its successful applications to the court for injunctions (subject to any court order preventing such publication). However, it may decide not to publicise, or not to publicise immediately, where publication could damage confidence in the financial system or undermine market integrity.[94]

## 11.7  Sanctions for market abuse

Sanctions for market abuse may be imposed on any person, whether regulated or not. The FSA may decide that any person should be the subject of a financial penalty or public statement if the FSA believes that person is or has been engaged in market abuse or has required or encouraged another to engage in conduct which, if that person had

---

[92]  Section 381 FSMA 2000; ENF 6.4.1 to 6.4.6.
[93]  ENF 6.6.2.
[94]  ENF 6.11.1.

engaged in the conduct himself, would have amounted to market abuse.

The power to impose a financial penalty in cases of market abuse is provided for in Section 123(1) FSMA 2000. However, the FSA may not impose a penalty on a person if, having considered representations made in response to a warning notice, there are reasonable grounds for the FSA to be satisfied that the person reasonably believed that his behaviour did not fall within the definition of market abuse, or that the person took all reasonable precautions and exercised all due diligence to avoid behaving in such a manner.[95] If the FSA is entitled to impose a penalty for market abuse on a person it may, instead, publish a statement to the effect that he has engaged in market abuse.[96]

The FSA is required by FSMA 2000 to issue a statement of policy on the imposition and amount of penalties under the market abuse regime.[97] That statement of policy must indicate the circumstances in which the FSA is to be expected to regard a person as:

(a)  having a reasonable belief that his behaviour did not amount to market abuse; or
(b)  having taken reasonable precautions and exercised due diligence to avoid engaging in market abuse.

Of particular interest are the rights of third parties in market abuse cases, an issue that was expressly considered by the Financial Services and Markets Tribunal in the case of *Sir Philip Watts v FSA*, 25 July 2005. This was a preliminary hearing held under Rule 13 of the Financial Services and Markets Tribunal Rules 2001,[98] which raised an important point regarding the rights of third parties in market abuse cases brought by the FSA. The specific issue was the meaning of Section 393 of the FSMA 2000.

The case arose out of Shell's announcement in January 2004 relating to its oil reserves, which prompted action by the FSA and the

---

[95]  Section 123(2).
[96]  Section 123(3).
[97]  Section 124. The statement of policy is found in ENF 14.
[98]  Under Rule 13, a Tribunal is empowered to direct that any question of fact or law which appears to be in issue in relation to the reference be determined at a preliminary hearing.

Securities and Exchange Commission in the US. On 29 July 2004, without admitting or denying the findings or conclusions, Shell agreed to the FSA issuing a final notice stating that Shell had breached the market abuse provisions of FSMA 2000 as well as the Listing Rules. The FSA levied a financial penalty of £17 million on Shell, the largest ever financial penalty imposed by the FSA.

Shell's former Chairman, Sir Philip Watts, upon learning of the proposed settlement, asserted his rights as a third party under Section 393 FSMA 2000. He asserted that even if he was not explicitly identified in the proposed FSA notice (which he was not), he was entitled to the statutory rights of a third party if he was identifiable by reference to publicly available sources as the individual responsible for the matters complained of. The FSA disagreed that the applicant was a third party for the purposes Section 393, and refused to supply copies of the notices to him in advance.

Hence on 16 September 2004, the applicant filed a Reference pursuant to Section 393(11) FSMA 2000, a provision which gives a person who alleges that a copy of the notice should have been given to him but was not, the right to refer the alleged failure to the Tribunal.

The Tribunal stated the purpose of Section 393 was to ensure fairness where there was some wrongdoing alleged on the part of a third party who was not himself the subject of action by the FSA. In particular, the construction of Section 393(4) was crucial. Section 393(4) provides that if any of the reasons given in a decision notice identify a person (the third party) other than the person to whom the decision notice is given and, in the opinion of the Authority, is prejudicial to the third party, a copy of the notice must be given to the third party. The dispute turned on how a third party was "identified" for the purposes of Section 393(4).

The crux of the applicant's case was that the duty to give a copy of the notice to a third party was not confined to instances where the third party was named or otherwise identified in the decision notice itself; the test proposed was whether the reasons related to an external matter which itself identified the third party.

The Tribunal did not accept the applicant's submissions. It agreed with the FSA that Section 393(4), properly construed, afforded third-party rights to a person who was identified in the decision notice, and not, as the applicant argued, to a person who also could be identified in the "matter" to which the reasons in the decision notice related by looking at external sources. The Tribunal did not consider that fairness required third-party rights to be accorded where the identification of the individual concerned arose externally to the notice.

However, the Tribunal also made it clear that it did not accept the FSA's suggestion that in interpreting Section 393(4) the fundamental requirement as regards identification is that "the third party must be picked out, referred to or singled out in the notice." In the Tribunal's view, the word "identifies" should stand without elaboration, until there has been more experience of working through the problems which the provision could throw up in practice. Nor did the Tribunal accept the FSA's argument that whilst identification could be effected by reference other than by an express naming of him, for example "all of the Company's directors", Section 393(4) would not apply unless the individual was identified in the notice either by name or job description. The Tribunal did not accept this limitation: identification did not necessarily have to occur by express naming, job description or some collective reference.

### 11.7.1 Factors relevant to determining whether to take action in market abuse cases

The FSA has a discretion in market abuse cases as to whether it should seek to impose a penalty or issue a public statement. There is a range of factors which the FSA will consider, which includes:[99]

(a) the nature and seriousness of the suspected behaviour, including whether it was deliberate or reckless, its duration and frequency, its impact on prescribed markets and public confidence in those markets, the amount of benefit gained or loss avoided and the risk of loss to consumers or market users;

---

[99] ENF 14.4.2.

(b)   the conduct of the person concerned after the behaviour was identified, including:

  (i)    how quickly and fully the behaviour was brought to the attention of the FSA or another relevant regulator,

  (ii)   the degree of cooperation shown during the FSA's investigation, and

  (iii)  the remedial action taken, such as to compensate those who suffered loss, take appropriate disciplinary action and prevent similar problems arising in the future;

(c)   the degree of sophistication of the users of the market in question and the size and liquidity of the market;

(d)   whether the action taken by other regulatory authorities, such as a recognised investment exchange or the Takeover Panel, is adequate to address the FSA's concerns;

(e)   the action taken by the FSA in previous similar cases;

(f)   the impact, having regard to the nature of the behaviour, that any financial penalty or public statement may have on the financial markets or the interests of consumers;

(g)   the likelihood of a repetition of that type of behaviour if no action is taken; and

(h)   the disciplinary record and general compliance history of the person in question, both in relation to market conduct and more generally.

### 11.7.2   *The FSA's choice of powers in market abuse cases*

The FSA may issue a public statement rather than impose a financial penalty for market abuse where it considers that such a statement is more appropriate than a financial penalty. In deciding this, the FSA will have regard to a number of factors, including:[100]

(a)   whether a person has made a profit or avoided a loss as a result of the behaviour. If they have, this will militate in favour of a financial penalty;

(b)   if the behaviour is serious in nature or degree; the more serious the behaviour the more likely the FSA is to consider that a financial penalty is appropriate;

---

[100]  ENF 14.6.2.

(c)    if the person has admitted the behaviour and fully cooperates with the FSA and pays compensation. This may make a public statement more likely;

(d)    the need for the FSA to take a consistent approach in similar cases;

(e)    the person's compliance history;

(f)    the impact of a financial penalty on the person concerned. In exceptional cases, where a person has inadequate means to pay a financial penalty, the FSA may impose a reduced penalty of a public statement instead.

Section 123(2) FSMA 2000 prevents the FSA from imposing a financial penalty if there are reasonable grounds for it to be satisfied that a person suspected of market abuse had a reasonable belief that his behaviour did not amount to market abuse or had taken reasonable precautions and exercised due diligence to avoid engaging in market abuse. In considering these issues, the FSA will take into account a range of factors, which include but are not limited to the following:[101]

(a)    whether the person concerned took reasonable precautions to avoid engaging in market abuse;

(b)    whether, and if so to what extent, the behaviour in question was analogous to behaviour described in the Code of Market Conduct as amounting to or not amounting to market abuse;

(c)    whether the FSA has issued any guidance in relation to the behaviour in question and, if so, whether that guidance was followed;

(d)    whether, and if so to what extent, the behaviour complied with the rules of any relevant prescribed market or other regulatory requirements;

(e)    the level of knowledge, skill and experience to be expected of the person concerned;[102] and

(f)    whether, and if so to what extent, the person can demonstrate that the behaviour was engaged in for a legitimate purpose and in a proper way.

---

[101] ENF 14.5.1.

[102] On 10 February 2004 the FSA issued a final notice against Robert Middlemiss imposing a financial penalty. Interestingly, in considering whether Mr Middlemiss had failed to observe proper standards of behaviour, the FSA referred not only to the Code, but also to the fact that his behaviour was below the standard to be expected not only of an investor, but that of a Chartered Accountant who was employed as a Company Secretary of an AIM listed company, as Mr Middlemiss was.

In deciding whether the person concerned took reasonable precautions to avoid engaging in market abuse the FSA will consider factors such as the extent to which the person followed internal consultation and escalation procedures, whether expert legal or other professional advice was sought and followed, and whether guidance was sought from relevant market authorities or the Takeover Panel.

### 11.7.3 *Determining the level of financial penalty in a market abuse case*[103]

In determining the level of financial penalty to be imposed in a particular case, the FSA will consider broadly similar factors to those which it considers in determining whether to take action in market abuse cases, described in 11.7.1 above.

A degree of caution must be exercised in drawing conclusions from the levels of financial penalty that the FSA has imposed in market abuse cases at the date of writing as the number of cases has so far been limited. Arguably, the FSA has not yet been particularly ambitious in terms of the cases it has brought. Most have been familiar insider-dealing type cases.[104] Other cases have been fairly clear examples under the misleading statements and practices or market distortion limbs of the market abuse provisions (*Shell* Final Notice 24 August 2004; *Evolution Beeson Gregory* Final Notice 12 November 2004; and *Indigo Capital/Bonnier* Final Notice 21 December 2004). Cases involving, for example, complex trading strategies have to date been the subject of disciplinary proceedings largely brought by exchanges (e.g. the International Petroleum Exchange). The FSA was unsuccessful in what has probably been the most complex market abuse case that it has pursued to date.[105]

---

[103] ENF 14.7.

[104] *See Peter Bracken* Final Notice 7 July 2004, *Michael Thomas Davies* Final Notice 28 July 2004, *Robin Mark Hutchins* Final Notice 13 December 2004, *Jason Smith* Final Notice 13 December 2004. For an FSMT decision on market abuse *see Arif Mohammed* v *FSA*, 9 March 2005.

[105] Reference should be made to (1) *Davidson* (2) *Tatham* v *FSA* (2, 6 and 7 March 2006), famously referred to as the "plumber case". The case was spread over two months, and in a judgment running to some 77 pages, the Tribunal unanimously decided that the applicants were not guilty of market abuse. Indeed the Tribunal considered the hypothetical scenario of whether the penalties were appropriate, assuming that the applicants had engaged in market abuse. The Tribunal stated that whilst it would have regarded the alleged behaviour as serious, it would not have regarded it as deliberate or reckless. The

The FSA's objective is to impose penalties which not only deprive the wrongdoer of the benefits of the misconduct but also act as a significant deterrent to others.[106] Even though early admission of wrongdoing, cooperation and the prospect of financial hardship operate as mitigating features, the FSA have been quick to identify aggravating features, such as in the case of *Davies* (Final Notice 28 July 2004), where the position of trust occupied by the individual concerned was found to be an aggravating feature of the conduct alleged.

The *Shell* case[107] stands out as the highest financial penalty imposed for any form of misconduct. The penalty would have been higher still but for the cooperation afforded by the company once the misconduct came to light. The scale of the misstatement, a failure by management to respond to warning signs and the effect of the conduct of the company upon the markets were the principal aggravating features in this case.

### 11.7.4 *The relationship between market abuse and breaches of the FSA Principles*[108]

Principle 5 of the FSA Principles for Businesses requires a firm to observe proper standards of market conduct. Behaviour which

---

Tribunal concluded that in its view, an appropriate penalty would have been a published statement. In short, the Tribunal considered that the evidence presented by the FSA did not come up to proof under judicial scrutiny. It is also instructive to mention *(1) Timothy Edward Baldwin (2) WRT Investments Ltd* v *FSA* (5 April 2006), where following a three-day hearing, the Tribunal determined that on the evidence before them the individuals were not guilty of market abuse. The case turned on the timing and purchase of certain shares, with the FSA contending that the timing could not be explained in the absence of insider information. The Tribunal's decision was based on the credibility of the witnesses before them – it was very fact specific. Of particular interest is the Tribunal's decision not to award costs against the FSA for their conduct prior to referring the matter to the Tribunal on the basis that the investigations prior to the reference could not be characterised as unreasonable. However, the Chairman of the Tribunal expressly stated that they were not laying down any general rule to the effect that no award of costs would be based on conduct prior to the FSA's decision where the decision itself was reasonable. This approach to costs was endorsed in the plumber case. The Tribunal criticised the decision-making process, in particular the fact that there was no dedicated legal function independent of the Enforcement Decision to assist the Committee in its decision making. In addition, it felt that the Committee's approach to the law of market abuse was unreasonable. Finally, the Tribunal decided that it was unreasonable of the committee not to have mitigated the financial penalties more than they did. Costs were therefore awarded against the FSA.

[106] For example, *Peter Bracken* (7 July 2004) £2,824.45 profit, £15,000 fine; *Michael Thomas Davies* (28 July 2004), £420 profit, £1,000 fine.

[107] Final Notice *Shell Transport and Trading Company plc and the Royal Dutch Petroleum Company N.V.* (24 August 2004).

[108] ENF 14.8.

constitutes market abuse will also constitute a breach of Principle 5; however, conduct which constitutes a breach of Principle 5 will not necessarily constitute market abuse (for example, because it does not involve behaviour in relation to a market which is a prescribed market for the purposes of the market abuse regime). The FSA's stated policy is that where conduct appears to fall within the market abuse regime it will bring proceedings for market abuse rather than breach of Principle 5 (and conversely, where it is clear that the market abuse regime does not apply the FSA will bring proceedings for breach of Principle 5). Where it is unclear or arguable where the principal mischief lies, the FSA may elect to bring proceedings for both market abuse and, in the alternative, Principle 5.[109]

### 11.7.5 Market abuse cases involving other UK regulatory authorities[110]

Conduct which may give rise to proceedings for market abuse may also involve potential action by other regulatory authorities. In relation to behaviour which occurs on a recognised investment exchange, the FSA will confer with the relevant exchange to decide what action is appropriate and whether the exchange has adequate powers to address the misconduct. It is possible that proceedings will be brought both by the FSA for market abuse and by the relevant exchange for breaches of its rules.

In cases involving conduct in the course of a takeover bid, the FSA will refer to the Takeover Panel and give due weight to its views. The FSA considers that the use of the Takeover Panel's informal powers will often be sufficient to address the relevant concerns, but the FSA is likely to consider that the exercise of its own powers is appropriate in a range of circumstances, including where:

---

[109] On 1 August 2006, the FSA published its Final Notice against both Mr Jabre and GLG. The Final Notice confirms a financial penalty of £750,000 on both Mr Jabre and GLG. This is the largest fine that the FSA has imposed on an individual. GLG was fined in respect of market abuse and a breach of Principle for Businesses 5 (market conduct). The Final Notice is of interest in itself since it reflects one of the recommendations of the Enforcement Process Review, namely that Decision Notices should set out how the RDC has dealt with the key points made by the subject of regulatory action.

[110] ENF 14.9.

(a)   the Takeover Panel is unable to investigate properly due to lack of cooperation by the relevant person;

(b)   the behaviour falls within the "misuse of information" limb of market abuse;[111]

(c)   the person concerned has deliberately or recklessly failed to comply with a Takeover Panel ruling;

(d)   the Takeover Panel asks the FSA to use its powers to impose a financial penalty;

(e)   the behaviour extends to securities outside the Takeover Panel's jurisdiction;

(f)   the behaviour threatens the stability of the financial system.

Exceptional circumstances would have to prevail for the FSA to use its enforcement powers during the course of a takeover bid.[112]

### 11.7.6   Market abuse cases involving overseas regulatory authorities[113]

In cases where there is an international context to the market abuse alleged, the FSA will work together with the relevant overseas regulator or other enforcement agency and coordinate its enforcement action.[114]

### 11.7.7   Injunctions and restitution orders in market abuse cases

The FSA may apply to the court[115] for an injunction restraining conduct which constitutes market abuse and for the making of a restitution order.[116] The FSA also has an administrative power to require restitution for market abuse.[117]

---

[111] Section 118(2)(a).

[112] The FSA is only able to take enforcement action under Section 143 FSMA 2000 in respect of a breach of the takeover code or the SARs at the request of the Takeover Panel unless such behaviour also constitutes a breach of the FSA rules, in which case it is obliged to consult with the Takeover Panel.

[113] ENF 14.11.

[114] For example Final Notice 24 August 2004 *Shell Transport and Trading Company and Royal Dutch Petroleum Company N.V.*

[115] Section 381.

[116] Section 383.

[117] Section 384(5).

On application by the FSA to the court for an injunction or a restitution order in respect of market abuse, the court also has power to impose a financial penalty of such amount as it considers appropriate.[118]

## 11.8 Listing rule breaches

This chapter does not deal in detail with the provisions of the UKLA Rules or breaches of the Combined Code.[119] Guidance on the criteria considered by the UKLA when deciding whether to bring disciplinary action, and if so in what form, can be found in the UKLA Guidance Manual, Chapter 8.[120] The UKLA will consider all of the relevant circumstances of the alleged breach. Factors relevant to the imposition of sanctions and the level of financial penalties are similar to those within the Enforcement Manual. It is important to note that in respect of UKLA breaches, penalties can only be imposed on the issuer and its directors who were knowingly concerned in the breach.[121] However, under Section 88 FSMA 2000 the UKLA also has power to cancel a person's approval as a sponsor and, under Section 89, to publicly censure sponsors.

In some cases where potential breaches of UKLA Rules or the Combined Code have been identified, a range of enforcement action will be available, including action for breaches of the FSA Principles (where a regulated firm is involved), civil law remedies and the criminal law.[122] The approach will be tailored to the particular circumstances of each case. In the Shell case (above) in which Shell was fined £17 million for market abuse by the FSA, no separate penalty was imposed for UKLA Rule breaches. In the *SFI* case[123] the FSA only considered it appropriate to censure the company for failing to take reasonable care to ensure an announcement of its preliminary financial results was not

---

[118] FSMA 2000, Section 129(1).

[119] UKLA Rules, Guidance and Combined Code are to be found on the FSA's website.

[120] *See* UKLA Guidance Manual 8.8.

[121] Section 91(1); *see* also *Sportsworld Media Group plc* (29 March 2004) where the FSA fined the former CEO £45,000 for listing rules breach and *Universal Salvage PLC* (19 May 2004) where the CEO was fined £10,000.

[122] *See* for example the criminal proceedings currently being brought against certain former directors of AIT Group Plc under Section 397 FSMA 2000 in respect of allegedly misleading public announcements.

[123] *SFI Group plc* (11 December 2003); *see* also *The Big Food Group plc* (26 April 2002).

misleading or false due to SFI's financial circumstances. In the *Marconi* case,[124] the FSA made a public statement regarding Marconi's contravention of the UKLA Rules on a failure to notify the Company Announcements Office of the change in its expectations as to its performance. The FSA made it plain that they did not allege, nor was there any finding of, bad faith on the part of Marconi or its officers.

---

[124] *Marconi plc* (11 April 2003).

# Chapter 12

# Challenging FSA Decisions – the Financial Services and Markets Tribunal

**Charles Flint QC and Javan Herberg**
Blackstone Chambers

## 12.1 Introduction

The creation of the Financial Services and Markets Tribunal ("the Tribunal") by Part XI of the Financial Services and Markets Act 2000 ("FSMA 2000") is one of the most important reforms to the enforcement aspect of financial services regulation. In contrast to the internal tribunal and appeal systems operated by the Self-Regulating Organisations ("SROs"), which the Financial Services Authority ("FSA") replaced and consolidated, the Tribunal is wholly independent of the regulator and its members are appointed by the Secretary of State for Constitutional Affairs.[1] Persons affected by regulatory decisions of the FSA have a right of reference to the Tribunal which, as an independent and impartial tribunal complying with the provisions of Article 6 of the European Convention on Human Rights ("ECHR"), has full jurisdiction to adjudicate in a public hearing on the appropriate action in respect of the matter referred, with a right of appeal thereafter on a point of law to the Court of Appeal.

The Tribunal therefore has a most important role as the statutory check upon the wide regulatory powers of the FSA, which include powers to impose unlimited financial penalties and make prohibition

---

[1] The previous statutory tribunal constituted under the Financial Services Act 1986 to hear references from decisions of the Securities and Investments Board ("SIB"), the Financial Services Tribunal, perhaps had a greater degree of institutional separation from the regulator than the SRO tribunals from the SROs, but it was effectively operated by the Treasury, which was the primary donee of the regulatory powers delegated to SIB.

orders. In practice these powers of the FSA will rarely be amenable to judicial review because the Tribunal is effectively the specialist court for all financial services regulation. The decision of the Court of Appeal in *R (Davies)* v *FSA* [2004] 1 WLR 185 makes clear that only in the most exceptional circumstances would it be right to make an application for judicial review instead of pursuing the statutory right of referring the matter to the Tribunal.[2]

The Tribunal therefore has a significant part to play in assisting in the meeting of the market confidence objective imposed on the FSA by Section 3 FSMA 2000, namely to maintain confidence in the financial system. That confidence depends in significant part on the knowledge that decisions of the regulator may be challenged before an independent tribunal applying settled law and principles. The early stages of the Tribunal's development were clouded by the controversy arising from the conduct of the first market abuse case referred to the Tribunal, *Davidson and Tatham* v *FSA* (FIN/2003/0016 and 0020), in which the Tribunal was obliged to recuse itself on grounds of apparent bias. However, in the important decision of *FSA* v *Legal & General Assurance Society Ltd* (judgment of 13 January 2005), the Tribunal demonstrated a readiness in an appropriate case to investigate and set aside a decision of the FSA on the merits. This has been followed in a number of recent cases in which the Tribunal has declined to confirm decisions of the FSA:

(a) In *Manchanda* v *FSA* (FIN/2995/0014-5), the Tribunal found the applicant seeking authorisation to have discharged the burden of showing that he was fit and proper, notwithstanding FSA concerns as to his involvement in a corporate fraud.

(b) In *Baldwin* v *FSA* (FIN/2005/0011; 24 January 2006), the Tribunal found that the applicant had not traded on inside information, the relevant share trades having been undertaken innocently, contrary to the FSA's view.

(c) In *Davidson and Tatham* v *FSA* (FIN/2003/0016 and 0020; 16 May 2006), the Tribunal overturned the FSA's finding of market abuse in respect of a share placement on AIM and linked spread bet, holding that the applicants had no knowledge of the scheme which in any event did not in law amount to market abuse.

---

[2] *See* further, Chapter 13 below.

These decisions demonstrate an independence of judgment on the part of the Tribunal, as required by FSMA 2000, and a proper requirement that the FSA should be in a position to adduce cogent evidence in order to uphold serious allegations of impropriety. An applicant who wishes to refer a decision or supervisory notice can thus be assured of a full hearing on the merits by an independent tribunal.

## 12.2  Constitution of the Tribunal

### 12.2.1  Constitution of the Panels

The Tribunal's constitution and powers derive primarily from Part IX FSMA 2000 (Sections 132 to 137) and Schedule 13, together with rules made thereunder, the most important being the Financial Services and Markets Tribunal Rules 2001 (SI 2001/2476) made under Section 132(3) ("the Tribunal Rules").[3] Parts II and III of Schedule 13 effectively place the constitution of the Tribunal in the hands of the Secretary of State for Constitutional Affairs. He is responsible for appointing a panel of persons who may serve as chairmen of the Tribunal (the "Panel of Chairmen");[4] appointing one of their number as "President of the FSMT",[5] presiding over the discharge of the Tribunal's functions; and appointing another as deputy president.[6] Paragraphs 2(5) and 3(2)–(3) set out minimum qualifications for the president and members of the Panel of Chairmen respectively. The president of the Tribunal is currently Sir Stephen Oliver QC, who is also president of the VAT and Duties Tribunals and the presiding special commissioner.

The Secretary of State for Constitutional Affairs is also responsible for constituting a lay panel of "persons who appear to him to be qualified by experience or otherwise to deal with matters of the kind that may be referred to the Tribunal" ("the Lay Panel") (paragraph 3(4) of Schedule 13). This wording does not contain any requirement that such persons have experience from within the financial services

---

[3] Particular matters which the Rules may cover are set out in paragraph 9, Schedule 13 FSMA 2000.

[4] Paragraph 3(1).

[5] Paragraph 2(1) and (2).

[6] Paragraph 2(3).

industry; indeed, the wording of paragraph 3(4) ("experience or otherwise") makes it plain that no experience of any particular kind is a prerequisite. But a review of the members appointed to the lay panel (who are listed on the Tribunal's website[7]) shows that financial services experience is, as might be expected, the norm.

The terms upon which members of the Panel of Chairmen and Lay Panels hold and vacate office lie with the Secretary of State, in accordance with their terms of appointment.[8] This sits alongside a power conferred by paragraph 4(2) to remove "on the ground of incapacity or misbehaviour". It may be inferred from paragraph 4(2) that it was contemplated by Parliament that the terms of appointment would not contain a discretionary power to dismiss (since there would then be no need for paragraph 4(2)). Rather, what appears to have been contemplated was that the appointment would be for fixed terms (which may be renewed[9]), and that removal would be confined to the circumstances in paragraph 4(2). This would accord with the ordinary principles of judicial independence, and would buttress compliance with Article 6 of the Convention, considered below.

### 12.2.2 Composition of particular tribunals

From the Panel of Chairmen and Lay Panels, members are selected to sit as members of the Tribunal hearing particular references "in accordance with arrangements made by the President" ("the Standing Arrangements").[10] The only restriction on these arrangements is that they must provide that at least one member be selected from the Panel of Chairmen[11] (although more than one member of the chairman's panel may sit[12]). There is no requirement in FSMA 2000 that any members of the Lay Panel be appointed, or that there be any fixed

---

[7] www.financeandtaxtribunals.gov.uk.

[8] Paragraph 4(1) of Schedule 13. The Secretary of State has powers to determine remuneration of members of the Chairmen and Lay Panels, to appoint staff and remunerate for the Tribunal, and to defray expenses of the Tribunal: paragraphs 5 and 6, Schedule 13 FSMA 2000.

[9] Paragraph 4(3)(b) of Schedule 13.

[10] Paragraph 7(1) of Schedule 13.

[11] Paragraph 7(2) of Schedule 13.

[12] As was the case on the *Davidson and Tatham* (Ref FIN/2003/0016), where two chairmen sat on the first (recused) tribunal, on the basis that the case was the first involving market abuse, and was relatively complex. *See* also, *Eurolife Assurance Co Ltd* v *FSA* (decision dated 4 September 2002); *Thomas* v *FSA* (decision on preliminary issues, dated 17 September 2004).

overall number of tribunal members. Nevertheless, the general (though not invariable[13]) expectation and practice is that tribunals will be constituted by a chairman sitting with two lay members. The Standing Arrangements were presented by the president to a meeting of the Panel of Chairmen on 24 September 2001.[14]

Tribunals can appoint "one or more experts to provide assistance" if it appears that the matter involves "a question of fact of special difficulty".[15] Such a question might be expected to involve the workings of a specialised sector or aspect of the financial markets, although since the lay member(s) may well have specialised knowledge, and since the parties may call their own expert evidence in the usual way, it is anticipated that this power will be rarely used.

### 12.2.3 Independence and impartiality, and compliance with Article 6

The arrangements contained in Schedule 13 are directed to ensuring that the Tribunal complies with the requirements of Article 6 of the European Convention on Human Rights ("ECHR") (as incorporated into domestic law by the Human Rights Act 1998), embodying due process requirements. During the passage of FSMA 2000 through Parliament and thereafter, there was intense debate as to whether various enforcement actions available to the FSA which might be referred to the Tribunal (in particular, market abuse and, separately, other disciplinary action) would be likely to amount to the "determination of a criminal charge" for the purposes of Article 6 so as to fall

---

[13] In the *Davidson* reference (above), there were four members in total on the first (recused) tribunal: two chairmen and two lay members.

[14] These provide:

> "In the ordinary course of events it is proposed that chairmen should be allocated references in rotation. The chairman will take up the reference file at the very start and, so far as this is possible, see it through to its conclusion. There are bound to be exceptions, e.g. late notice or unavailability, to this ordinary method of distribution. Cases arising in Scotland will, most likely, be allocated to Gordon Coutts and cases arising in Manchester will usually be allocated to Colin Bishopp. The choice of members will, to an extent, be dictated by their particular expertise. Subject to that, it is hoped that they too will be allocated to references on a rotational basis. Chairmen will probably sit alone for directions hearings but one or two members will be appointed for most references."

[15] Paragraph 7(4) of Schedule 13.

within the Article's criminal limb (and hence the enhanced protections that apply in criminal cases) or whether they were the "determination of civil rights and obligations" for Article 6 purposes, in which case a lesser level of protection would apply.[16]

The issues raised by the debate are many,[17] but for these purposes, a number of points or conclusions can be summarised:

(a)  FSMA 2000 was drafted to ensure that those facing FSA enforcement action had protection which at least complied with the "civil" limb of Article 6 (i.e. that such persons would receive (through the availability of a reference to the Tribunal) a fair and public hearing within a reasonable time by an independent and impartial tribunal established by law and with full jurisdiction, with judgment (subject to some exceptions) pronounced publicly).

(b)  In relation to the independence and impartiality of the Tribunal, this standard is in any event identical for the "civil" and "criminal" limbs of Article 6. It is secured by the Schedule 13 arrangements described above, and by the institutional separation of the Tribunal from the FSA. Whilst particular arrangements or events might still breach the Article 6 requirements (for example, if the Secretary of State were to adopt terms of appointment for tribunal members which entitled him to remove members on the basis of disagreement with particular decisions), it would appear that the overall structure complies with these Article 6 requirements.

(c)  Parliament declined to extend to the FSA disciplinary actions the protection that results or arguably results from an Article 6 "criminal" classification, save in proceedings involving market

---

[16] *See*, by way of example, the First Report of the Joint Committee on Financial Services and Markets chaired by Lord Burns (HL Paper 50, HC 328); its Second Report (HL Paper 66, HC 465), both of which contain useful appendices and further references; Waters, D and Hopper, M, (2001) Regulatory Discipline and the ECHR – A Reality Check. In *Regulating Financial Services and Markets in the Twenty-First Century* (eds Ferran, E and Goodhart, CAE) Hart Publishing, Oxford; Beazley, T, Holding the Balance – Effective Enforcement, Procedural Fairness and Human Rights. In *Regulating Financial Services and Markets in the Twenty-First Century* (eds Ferran, E and Goodhart, CAE) Hart Publishing, Oxford; Page, A, Regulating the Regulator – A Lawyer's Perspective on Accountability and Control. In *Regulating Financial Services and Markets in the Twenty-First Century* (eds Ferran, E and Goodhart, CAE) Hart Publishing, Oxford.

[17] Reference should be made to Chapter 7 and 8 for example.

abuse. In the latter case, whilst the government did not accept that the power to fine for market abuse did involve the determination of a criminal charge within the meaning given to that phrase for the purposes of the European Convention on Human Rights, it nonetheless ensured that FSMA 2000 extends "criminal" protections (in particular, the prohibition on the use of compelled interviews, and the legal assistance scheme contained in Sections 134–136 FSMA 2000, both referred to further below) to those alleged to have committed market abuse. It should be emphasised, however, that a penalty for market abuse is not a criminal offence under FSMA 2000.[18] The only question is whether the penalty should be *classified* as criminal under the autonomous meaning of that term in the Convention.

(d)     In these circumstances, it may be of little more than academic interest as to whether the market abuse regime is indeed correctly classified as "criminal" in some or all cases, unless the "criminal" protections enshrined in FSMA 2000 are in some way deficient.[19] In *Davidson and Tatham*, the Tribunal concluded (at paragraphs 174 to 182) that the market abuse charges in that case were criminal for the purposes of Article 6, but did not, in consequence, hold that the FSMA 2000 protections were in any way deficient or that domestic "criminal" protections applied (*see* paragraphs 183 to 200).

In relation to other FSA disciplinary or other enforcement action, there has not yet been any authoritative determination as to the classification of any such powers, and whether the "criminal" protection should have been extended to any of them, although decisions on the former SRO tribunals and the general domestic and Strasbourg case-law on Article 6 post-FSMA 2000 strongly suggests that a "civil" classification will be defensible for all or nearly all such disciplinary powers.[20]

---

[18] Confirmed in *Davidson and Tatham* v *FSA* (FIN/2003/0016; interlocutory decision of Dr A N Brice, 30 July 2004), at paragraph 28.

[19] As to which, *see* 12.4.5 (legal assistance) and 12.4.2 and 12.5 (disclosure).

[20] *See*, in particular, *R (Fleurose)* v *Securities and Futures Authority* [2001] EWCA Civ 2015; [2002] IRLR 297; *SFA* v *Crisanti, Ezra and Archer* (published decision of the SFA Tribunal, chaired by Beldam LJ, dated August 2001). In *Ernest Rayner and John Townsend* v *FSA* (Decision of the FSMT, FIN/2003/017 and 018), the Tribunal held (at paragraph 95) that a prohibition from carrying out a controlled function and withdrawal of approval to perform the investment adviser function were held not to be regarded as involving a criminal charge or offence for the purposes of Article 7, although it does not appear that the Tribunal heard full argument on the point.

In individual cases, a failure by the Tribunal to comply with the standards of independence and impartiality required by Article 6 is likely to amount to a breach of the domestic common law duty to ensure a fair trial free of the taint of actual or apparent bias.[21] In such a case, the Tribunal has the inherent power to take action to ensure a fair trial, if necessary by the recusal of some or all of its members, as in the reference of *Davidson and Tatham*.[22]

## 12.3 Jurisdiction of the Tribunal

### 12.3.1 Functions conferred by FSMA 2000

The Tribunal has "the functions conferred on it by or under" FSMA 2000.[23] Those functions include the determination of matters referred to it in respect of decisions made by the FSA:

(a) determining an application for permission to carry on regulated activities under Part IV, or varying an authorised person's permission under Section 53;

(b) exercising disciplinary powers against an approved person under Section 66;

(c) imposing financial penalties on a listed company or its directors for breach of the listing rules under Section 91 or censuring sponsors under Section 89;

(d) imposing financial penalties for market abuse under Section 123;

(e) censuring or imposing disciplinary measures on an authorised person under Sections 205 or 206.[24]

In addition, the Treasury has by Section 300(1) a power to confer further functions upon the Tribunal with respect to disciplinary powers of investment exchanges or clearing houses. In essence, what

---

[21] *See*, for example, *In re Medicaments and Related Classes of Goods (No.2)* [2001] 1 WLR 700, where the House of Lords pointed out that the Article 6 duty to be independent and impartial is one that has been long recognised by English common law.

[22] FIN/2003/0016 and 0020. *See* the short decision of the first Tribunal recusing itself dated 14 June 2004.

[23] Section 132(2).

[24] For a more comprehensive list, *see* in the commentary to Section 132 in Lomnicka E and Powell J *Encyclopaedia of Financial Services Law*. Sweet & Maxwell, London at 2A-274. In addition, references may be made in cases covered by the Electronic Commerce Directive (Financial Services and Markets) Regulations 2002, SI 2002/1775; *see* Reg 12(4).

appears to be contemplated is that the Tribunal might be constituted as an appeal body from the disciplinary proceedings of some or all such bodies, but only where the conditions set out in Section 300(2) are satisfied. These are (in essence) that it is desirable to exercise the power to promote consistency with Tribunal decisions on market abuse and other disciplinary references, and to promote compliance with Convention rights. This power has not, however, been exercised.

The central role of the Tribunal is, by Section 133(4) and subject to certain qualifications referred to below, to "determine what (if any) is the appropriate action for the [FSA] to take in relation to the matter referred to it". The FSA is thus maintained as the formal decision-maker even in respect of a matter referred to the Tribunal; the Tribunal decides what action the *FSA* should take; it does not take action itself. Thus when it has determined a reference, the Tribunal must (by Section 133(5)) remit the matter to the Authority with such directions (if any) as the Tribunal considers appropriate for the giving of effect to its determination, together with (by Section 133(8)) any recommendations as to the Authority's regulating provisions or its procedures. The FSA must act in accordance with the Tribunal's determination and any directions which it gives (Section 133(10)), although any recommendations made are not binding upon it.

### 12.3.2  A Tribunal with full jurisdiction

In respect of all matters referred, it is clear that the Tribunal, by virtue of Section 133(4), has full jurisdiction to make its own *de novo* determination as to what is the proper decision on the matter referred. As the Tribunal pointed out in the reference *Hoodless and Blackwell* v *FSA* (published decision, 3 October 2003, at paragraph 4): "these references are not a review of the decisions taken by FSA. The role of the Tribunal is to consider the matter afresh in the light of all the evidence made available to us".[25] On the other hand, this does not mean that

---

[25] *See* also *Davidson and Tatham* v *FSA* (FIN/2003/0016 and 0020; interlocutory decision of Dr A N Brice, 30 July 2004) at paragraph 27, where the Chairman rejected the applicant's attempt to call into question proceedings before the Regulatory Decisions Committee of the FSA, and the final decision of the Tribunal dated 16 May 2006 at paragraphs 201 to 203. A limited exception would be where the applicant contends that the FSA should bear the costs of the reference on the ground that the decision the subject of the reference is "unreasonable": paragraph 13, Schedule 13 FSMA 2000. *See* further *David Thomas* v *FSA* (Tribunal decision on

the reasoning of the FSA, as expressed in the Decision Notice, will be irrelevant to the issues, and it may be necessary for the Tribunal to review that reasoning, and the evidence which supported it, in order to make its own determination.[26] Section 133(3) provides that the Tribunal may take into account fresh evidence, whether or not that evidence was available to the FSA at the time it made the decision.

In the draft Bill the Tribunal had been referred to as an Appeal Tribunal, and its powers were accordingly circumscribed. As enacted, Section 133 has the effect that the Tribunal is not confined as an appellate body to reviewing the basis of the decision on the evidence available to the FSA at the time it took its decision, still less confined to reviewing whether the decision had been reasonably made. The power to receive further evidence was necessary to make clear that an applicant could deploy evidence not taken into account by the FSA when making its decision, as well as to allow either party to deploy evidence which had subsequently become available.

### 12.3.3    Fresh evidence and fresh grounds?

As the Tribunal has full jurisdiction, the question arises whether on a reference an applicant runs the risk not only that the case may be decided against him on fresh evidence, but also that the decision challenged may be supported on different grounds, of fact or law, from those set out in the FSA's decision notice or supervisory notice, or even attract a greater penalty. On the latter point it is clear that Section 133 does not prevent the Tribunal from directing that a greater penalty be imposed than that imposed by the decision notice or supervisory notice, although it was noted in *Parker* v *FSA*[27] at paragraph 178 that the Tribunal should be slow to increase the penalty for fear of serving as a disincentive to meritorious appeals. However, the recent decision in *Philippe Jabre* v *FSA* (FIN 2006/0006) illustrates that an applicant runs a serious risk that the case may be decided against him on different grounds and evidence from that considered by the

---

preliminary issues, 17 September 2004), where the Tribunal addressed (at paragraphs 32–68) the consequences of the FSA being in breach of a time limit in making the decision which was then referred to the Tribunal.

[26] *FSA* v *Legal and General Assurance Soc. Ltd,* at paragraph 206.

[27] This decision is undated within 2006 and unreferenced on the Tribunal website, an unhelpful feature of some Tribunal decisions.

Regulatory Decisions Committee of the FSA ("RDC") and even that a different statutory power may be invoked from that relied upon in the Decision Notice.

The powers of the Tribunal are limited, under Section 133(6), to directing the FSA to take action only to the extent that the FSA itself had power, when issuing the decision notice under Section 388, to take such action.[28] In effect Section 388(2) prevents the FSA, and hence the Tribunal on the reference, from taking action under a different part of FSMA 2000 from that in respect of which the warning notice was issued. Thus, Section 133(6) contains no express restriction on the Tribunal deciding that action should be taken on grounds different from those set out in the decision notice, *provided that* the basis of the finding falls under the same part of FSMA 2000.

Section 133 does not clearly determine the extent to which it is open to the FSA to put forward a different case, in fact or law, from that which formed the basis of the decision notice which has been referred. The point was addressed in *Philippe Jabre v FSA* (FIN 2006/0006), where the Tribunal held (in particular at paragraphs 23–37) that the starting point was that the phrases "the subject-matter of the reference" and "the matter referred", the phrases used in Section 133(3) and (4), refer to the full circumstances, evidence and allegations before the Regulatory Decisions Committee, not simply to the issues arising out of the decision referred. Hence, provided that the case sought to be put by the FSA before the Tribunal is a case in fact or law which was before the RDC, even if not embodied by the RDC in its decision, and even if the point is inconsistent with the decision, then the FSA is entitled to advance that case before the Tribunal, and seek a different or more severe order or penalty than that contained in the Decision Notice. It is only if a new allegation is unconnected to the factual context that gave rise to the original decision that it cannot be raised for the first time by the FSA in the Tribunal.[29]

As noted above, it is clear that the Tribunal has jurisdiction to determine that the contravention found by the Authority may be

---

[28] *See*, similarly, the restriction contained in Section 133(7) in respect of supervisory notices.
[29] *See Jabre*, paragraph 29, and *Parker v FSA* there referred to.

supported by new evidence, under Section 133(3), so that the appropriate action to be taken in respect of the contravention is to impose a penalty, even if the contravention could not be proved on the basis only of the evidence which was available to the Authority when it made the Decision Notice.

Thus the powers of the Tribunal are only limited, under Section 133(6), to directing the FSA to take action to the extent that the FSA itself had power, when issuing the decision notice under Section 388, to take such action. In effect Section 388(2) prevents the FSA, and hence the Tribunal on the reference, from taking action under a different part of FSMA 2000 from that in respect of which the warning notice was issued. Interestingly, and this is likely to be fortuitous rather than the result of deliberate legislative intent, this means that an approved person who makes a reference in respect of a decision made under Part V is considerably more exposed that an authorised person who makes a reference in respect of disciplinary measures made under Part XIV. The latter, which applies to firms, confers powers only to impose a financial penalty, or make a statement of censure, and Section 206(2) expressly provides that the FSA may not in respect of the same contravention require an authorised person both to pay a penalty and withdraw authorisation. On the other hand Part V, under which action may be taken against approved persons, contains powers to impose penalties, make a prohibition order or withdraw approval, and there is no restriction on the power of the FSA taking more than one measure in respect of the same contravention.

## 12.4   Procedure before the Tribunal

### 12.4.1   *Making of a reference*

The Tribunal's jurisdiction is engaged by the making, by a person affected by relevant FSA enforcement action, of a reference to the Tribunal under Section 133(1). The reference must be made within 28 days of the date of the decision notice or supervisory notice,[30] or such

---

[30] Since time runs from the date of the decision notice or supervisory notice, not from knowledge of that date, difficulties may arise in third-party notice situations (*see* 12.6) where a third party who contends that he has been prejudicially identified and has a right to refer the

other period as provided by rules made under Section 132.[31] In fact, the Tribunal Rules provide (at Rule 4(2)) for an identical period of 28 days for any reference not covered by Section 133(1)(a). Section 133(2) and rules 10(1)(d) and 4(6) of the Tribunal Rules permit an applicant to seek a reference out of time, which may be done by seeking an extension of the time for filing the reference on the face of the proposed reference document.[32]

The reference must be made by way of written notice signed by or on behalf of the applicant (Rule 4(1)) and copied to the FSA. It must contain the information identified in Rule 4(3), the most significant being Rule 4(3)(e), "the issues concerning the Authority notice that the applicant wishes the Tribunal to consider". It is submitted that this provision may be complied with by a general statement of the grounds for reference (analogous to short form grounds of appeal in a civil case), rather than by a detailed statement of the applicant's case, which awaits the applicant's reply, referred to below.[33]

One important consequence of the filing of a reference is that the FSA's proposed action, if embodied in a *decision* notice, is effectively stayed: by Section 133(9) the FSA may not take the action specified in a decision notice until the reference and any appeal against the Tribunal's determination have been finally disposed of (nor may it take action before that, during the period allowed for making a reference). This

---

matter to the Tribunal may not even know of the decision or supervisory notice until after the time for making a reference has expired because he may not have been served with it. This is presumably a circumstance in which the Tribunal would be willing to exercise its power to extend time for the making of a reference.

[31] Note that by virtue of Section 417(3) FSMA 2000, any provision of FSMA 2000 authorising or requiring a person to do anything within a specified number of days must not take account of any day which is a public holiday in *any part of* the UK. The sensible – but non-literal – interpretation of this provision would read it as directing that account be taken only of public holidays in the part of the UK with which the applicant is concerned.

[32] As was done in *Theophilus Folagbade Sonaike v FSA* (FIN/2005/0021, 13 July 2005) at paragraph 4, where the Tribunal granted a one-day extension where the Notices had come to the applicant's notice one week before the deadline, and there was no prejudice to the Authority in extending time.

[33] There is no express power in the Rules to permit an applicant to amend a reference notice: the power to amend contained in Rule 10(1)(f) of the Tribunal Rules is confined to "response documents" which by Rule 2(1) are defined as the Statement of Case and Reply. It is not easy to imply into the general power in Rule 9(1) to give directions relating to "the reference" a power to amend the reference, particularly given the express power contained in Rule 10(1)(f). In theory, it would be possible for a reference to be withdrawn by the applicant, with the Tribunal then giving permission for a new reference to be filed out of time.

provision does not, however, have effect in relation to *supervisory* notices, which can have effect in advance of the decision of the Tribunal and will do so if, for example, the FSA has specified that the decision embodied in the supervisory notice shall have immediate effect. In these circumstances, the Tribunal has a power by Rules 10(1) and 10(6) of the Tribunal Rules to suspend the effect of a notice (or prevent it taking effect) until the reference has been finally disposed of (including any appeal). However, the power may only be exercised where the Tribunal is satisfied that to do so would not prejudice both "the interests of any person (whether consumers, investors or otherwise) intended to be protected by the ... notice" and "the smooth operation or integrity of any market intended to be protected by that notice".

The Tribunal has on several occasions declined to suspend the immediate effect of a supervisory notice varying Part IV permission to remove regulated activities from its scope. In *HPA Services* v *FSA* (FIN 2003/0004, decision of Stephen Oliver QC dated 5 March 2003), the Tribunal chairman noted that the FSA had been aware of the absence of PII cover (which led to the notice) for a long time, but held that this did not undermine the urgency of the case; rather, it indicated that the applicant had been given every opportunity to cure the problem. He suggested (at paragraph 15) that relevant factors for the Tribunal would include the circumstances leading to the issue of the notice, the applicant's case as to why the decision to issue the notice had been made (without finally deciding this), and whether the notice had come "out of the blue" or had resulted from a fair amount of correspondence. This approach was endorsed in *Eurosure Investment Services Ltd* v *FSA* (FIN 2003/0015, decision of Dr A N Brice dated 10 September 2003), where the chairman held that she was not satisfied that suspension of the notice would not prejudice consumers, and that the giving of immediate effect to the notice was necessary and proportionate.[34]

A reference may be withdrawn without the permission of the Tribunal at any time before the hearing[35] of the reference.[36] Thereafter, permission from the Tribunal is required.

---

[34] *See* also *Theophilus Folagbade Sonaike* v *FSA* (FIN/2005/0021).

[35] The hearing does not begin until the hearing actually commences, not when it is listed: *Eurolife Assurance Co Ltd* v *FSA* (decision of 4 September 2002).

[36] Rule 14(1) of the Tribunal Rules.

## 12.4.2   Statements of Case and general disclosure obligations

By Rule 5 of the Tribunal Rules, the FSA must file its written Statement of Case within 28 days of its receipt of notice from the Tribunal of the reference. It must include "all the matters and facts upon which the [FSA] relies to support the referred action", and must be accompanied by the FSA's primary list of documents, which are those "on which it relies in support of the alleged action" and "the further material which in the opinion of the [FSA] might undermine the decision to take that action".[37] Exceptions to the inclusion of items on the list are set out in Rule 8 (such as documents whose disclosure is prohibited by Section 17 of the Regulation of Investigatory Powers Act 2000; third-party documents relevant only for comparison purposes; or documents in respect of which an application has been made to the Tribunal under Rule 8(4) for non-disclosure on grounds of public interest[38] or fairness). Disclosure of items on the list must follow upon request,[39] unless the item is a "protected item" within the meaning of Section 413 of FSMA 2000, which relates to legally privileged material, considered below at 12.5.2. The disclosure obligations which these provisions impose are considered further in 12.5 below.

The applicant's Reply is then due within 28 days of receiving the Statement of Case or any amended Case.[40] It must include the grounds on which the applicant relies in making the reference, and identify all matters contained in the Statement of Case which are disputed, and the reasons for disputing them. It must be accompanied by a list of documents on which the applicant relies; there is no general obligation to disclose documents which may undermine the applicant's case.

Both Statement of Case and Reply (collectively referred to as "response documents") may be amended with permission of the Tribunal (Rule 10(1)(f)), and further information or supplementary statements may be ordered. Time for filing response documents or amendments may be extended: Rule 10(1)(d) (but subject to the

---

[37] Rule 5(3). This parallels the FSA's disclosure obligation in respect of warning notices contained in Section 394 FSMA 2000.

[38] This would appear to accommodate without prejudice material, which is not expressly protected from disclosure.

[39] Rule 8(7).

[40] Rule 6.

guidance set out in Rule 10(2) and (3)). Response documents may be struck out at any stage as scandalous, frivolous or vexatious, or for want of prosecution (Rule 26(3)).

Following receipt of the applicant's Reply, the FSA must consider whether there is any further material which "might reasonably be expected to assist the applicant's case" as disclosed by the Reply. If so, this material should be disclosed. This is considered further at 12.5.1 below.

### 12.4.3 Other Tribunal directions and powers

The Tribunal has, by Rule 9, a general power to give directions to enable the parties to prepare for the hearing of the reference, to assist the Tribunal to determine the issues, and to ensure the just, expeditious and economical determination of the reference. Directions may be given on the Tribunal's initiative or on application of any party, may be made orally or in writing, and may be varied or set aside after having given the parties an opportunity to make representations. The Tribunal has shown itself ready and willing to deal with the usual procedural incidents of litigation, such as extensions of time for filing response documents, permitting the service of a rejoinder where it is appropriate for a Reply to be answered, and ordering that further information be provided in respect of pleaded allegations in response documents which require clarification or supplementation. The Tribunal has given guidance as to the preparation of a chronology and core bundle in complex cases.[41]

Directions will, in particular, be considered on the pre-hearing review, held before the chairman alone (Rule 9(11)).[42] Rule 10 sets out a number of specific forms of direction which may be given by the Tribunal, although the list is not exhaustive. These include a power to:

---

[41] *Townrow* v *FSA* (decision of 12 January 2006) at paragraphs 106 to 107.
[42] Under Rule 29, the Chairman sitting alone has power to do anything which the Tribunal can do, other than make the determination on a reference, or set a reference aside.

(a) fix hearings (including preliminary issues on questions of fact or law: Rule 13[43]);
(b) conjoin references or order that they be heard together;
(c) order a party (by Rule 10(1)(g)) to provide further "specific" disclosure of documents in its custody or control;
(d) require statements of (agreed) relevant issues and facts;
(e) require lists of witnesses;
(f) provide for witness statements and statements of expert witnesses;
(g) make provision for oral evidence to be given.

The Tribunal may summon any person (not merely a regulated person) to attend and give evidence or produce documents: paragraph 11(1), Schedule 13 to FSMA 2000 and Rule 12 of the Tribunal Rules; it is an offence for a person to refuse or fail to attend without reasonable excuse. It is also an offence for anyone to alter, suppress, conceal, destroy or refuse to produce a document as required: paragraph 11(3), Schedule 13. The Tribunal also has a coercive power vis-à-vis the parties for breaches of the Tribunal Rules or directions given: it may make a costs order, dismiss the whole or part of the applicant's reference, or strike out the whole or part of the FSA's case, or debar it from contesting the reference (Rule 27). The exercise of the power to dismiss a reference would have to be exercised in accordance with the applicant's Article 6 right to a fair hearing.[44]

### 12.4.4 Procedure at the hearing

The Tribunal has a general power to regulate its own procedure, at the hearing as well as generally (Rules 19(1) and 26(2)). Usually the FSA will open its case first, on the basis that the burden of justifying the regulatory action taken will, in general, be on the FSA. Thus the FSA's Statement of Case is the first substantive pleading. Subject to the Tribunal's directions, the parties are entitled to give evidence (which may be on oath: paragraph 11(2), Schedule 13); call witnesses; question any witnesses; and address the Tribunal on the evidence and the subject

---

[43] *See* for example *Thomas v FSA* (decision on preliminary issues, 17 September 2004); *Sir Philip Watts v FSA* (FIN/2004/0024, 7 September 2005) (preliminary issue relating to power to refer under Section 393(11) FSMA 2000); *Jabre v FSA* (FIN/2006/0006, preliminary decision on market abuse).

[44] *See* for example Lester, A & Pannick, D (eds) *Human Rights Law and Practice* (2nd ed., 2004, Butterworths Law, UK) at paragraphs 4.6.16–4.6.19.

matter of the reference. Witnesses' statements will normally stand as evidence in chief, in accordance with modern court practice. A person referring a decision may have an adverse inference drawn against him if he does not give evidence, but this will not be automatic.[45]

Rule 19(3) provides that evidence may be admitted whether or not it would be admissible in a court of law, and whether or not available to the FSA when taking the referred action. This is likely to be found to be compatible with the requirements of Article 6 (whether under its civil or criminal limb), since Article 6 does not generally require that procedures or principles applicable to proceedings in the civil or criminal courts are adopted by other tribunals simply because civil or criminal rights are in issue in proceedings before those other tribunals, provided that the substantive standards required by Article 6 are met. Exercising this broad power the Tribunal is unlikely to refuse to admit evidence, including expert evidence, which has some relevance to the issues.[46] The Tribunal has held that it is entitled to admit in evidence the findings of another tribunal (the Solicitors' Disciplinary Tribunal) not just as evidence of the decision of that tribunal but as evidence of the underlying facts as found by it, although it held that it would also have regard to other evidence adduced by the applicant on the same issues.[47] It has held, however, that it is not bound by the finding of a County Court, at least in a case where fraud is alleged.[48]

The Tribunal has jurisdiction, as part of its power to regulate its own procedure, to hear an issue as a separate or preliminary issue, or (in the course of a hearing) to entertain a submission of no case to answer. But the Tribunal has shown itself reluctant to permit the latter, rightly holding that if a submission of no case were permitted,

---

[45] *See Piggott v FSA* (FIN/2006/0008, 2 January 2007), at paragraphs 17–19, referring to *Wisnlewski v Central Manchester Health Authority* [1998] EWCA Civ 596.

[46] *See FSA v Legal & General Assurance Society Ltd*, at paragraph 13. In *Manchanda v FSA* (FIN/2995/0014-5) at paragraph 19 the Tribunal was prepared to admit witness statements adduced by the FSA although the witnesses were unavailable and there were "serious doubts" about their reliability. It placed "very little weight" on the contents.

[47] *Allen Elliott v FSA* (FIN/2004/0001; decision of 11 July 2005). Perhaps confusingly, the Tribunal held that it would be an abuse of process to allow the applicant to mount a collateral attack on the findings of the Solicitors' Disciplinary Tribunal, but also held that it would have regard to evidence adduced by the applicant going to the same issues: see paragraph 36.

[48] *See George Piggott v FSA* (FIN/2006/0008), 2 January 2007) at paragraphs 42–46.

the applicant should be put to his or her election, so that (if unsuccessful) he or she would not be entitled to call any evidence.[49]

### 12.4.5  Legal assistance

The parties are entitled to be represented at the hearing by any person, whether legally qualified or not,[50] unless prevented by the Tribunal for good and sufficient reason.[51]

A separate regime for legal assistance has been created in Sections 134 to 136 FSMA 2000 in respect of those facing a market abuse penalty. This was included by the government out of recognition of the strength of the argument (although not conceded) that a market abuse allegation might in some or all cases represent a "criminal charge" for the purposes of Article 6. Because Article 6(3) requires the provision of legal assistance for those without sufficient means to pay for it, FSMA 2000 confers a broad power on the Secretary of State for Constitutional Affairs to establish and administer an assistance scheme "in connection with proceedings before the Tribunal" (Section 134(1)), in favour of an individual who has referred an FSA decision to impose a penalty or publish a statement in respect of that individual's alleged market abuse. A detailed scheme has been created by the Financial Services and Markets Tribunal (Legal Assistance) Regulations 2001, SI 2001/3632, and the Financial Services and Markets Tribunal (Legal Assistance – Costs) Regulations 2001, SI 2001/3633.

Section 136 provides a mechanism whereby the Secretary of State can recover the costs of the legal assistance scheme from the FSA, and thence from the financial services industry. The FSA is entitled to make rules requiring payment to it by authorised persons or classes of authorised persons.

### 12.4.6  Hearings to be in public

The rules governing public access to Tribunal hearings and publicity for Tribunal decisions are also heavily influenced by Article 6 of the

---

[49] *Davidson and Tatham* v *FSA* (FIN/203/0016 and 0021; 16 May 2006), at paragraphs 205 to 208, applying *Benham Ltd* v *Kythira Investments Ltd* [2003] EWCA 1794, and the Tribunal decision in *Baldwin* v *FSA* (FIN/2005/0011; 24 January 2006) at paragraphs 26 to 28.
[50] Rule 18(1).
[51] Rule 18(2).

Convention, which provides (both under the "civil" and "criminal" limbs) that "everyone is entitled to a fair and *public* hearing" (emphasis added), with judgment pronounced publicly, subject to exclusion of the press and public in limited categories of exceptional case. These include "in the interest of morals, public order or national security", "where the protection of the private life of the parties so require" or "to the extent strictly necessary in the opinion of the court in special circumstances where publicity would prejudice the interests of justice".

Under the Tribunal Rules, the presumptive position is that all hearings shall be in public.[52] The presumption applies to all hearings, interlocutory and final, save that it does not apply to:

(a)   the determination of a reference, or of any particular issue, without an oral hearing under Rule 16(1) (i.e. where the parties have agreed in writing; where the issue concerns an application for directions; or where the Tribunal determines the reference without a hearing pursuant to Rule 14(3)[53]); or

(b)   the hearing of an application made without notice to the other party.

Subject to these exceptions, the presumption that the hearing be in public may only be displaced if the Tribunal so directs under Rule 17(3). This imposes stringent criteria: the Tribunal may only so direct either:

(a)   upon the application of all the parties; or
(b)   on the application of any party, if the Tribunal is satisfied that:

> "a hearing in private is necessary, having regard to the interests of morals, public order, national security or the protection of the private lives of the parties, or any unfairness to the applicant or prejudice to the interests of consumers that might result from a hearing in public".

*In addition* to either (a) or (b) above, the Tribunal must be satisfied that a hearing in private would not prejudice the interests of justice. It

---

[52] Rule 17(2).
[53] Although even then, the Tribunal must consider whether it is possible to make a public pronouncement of the whole or part of its decision: Rule 16(2) and (3). *See Greenfields Financial Management Ltd* v *FSA* (FIN/2005/0022; 3 October 2005) where judgment was given without an oral hearing where the reference was unopposed.

must also consider whether only part of the hearing should be held in private.[54] Therefore, the exceptions, whilst closely mirroring the exceptions contained in Article 6(1) of the Convention, are if anything more tightly drawn in imposing the "interests of justice" requirement as a further cumulative condition. Furthermore, the exceptions have so far been tightly interpreted. In *Eurolife Assurance Co v FSA* (FIN 2002/001, decision of 23 May 2002), the Tribunal rejected an application for a private hearing of a reference made by Eurolife of an FSA notice under Section 12A of the Insurance Companies Act 1982 directing that Eurolife cease to be authorised to effect contracts of insurance on the grounds that it appeared to the FSA that it had not fulfilled the criteria of sound and prudent management. The Tribunal held that a private hearing was unlikely to be "necessary" having regard to unfairness to the applicant merely because of the risk of damage to reputation; only the suffering of disproportionate damage could be unfair within the test. The Tribunal also commented that *even if* it had found that a hearing in private was necessary for reasons of unfairness, and that it would not prejudice the interests of justice, it still retained a discretion whether or not to order a private hearing, although it noted "if the two conditions are established, we think the normal course would be to accede to the application".[55]

Even where the hearing has been held wholly or partly in private, the Tribunal must consider whether the ordinary rule that its decisions be publicly pronounced either orally or by being published[56] can be upheld. The Tribunal must ensure that any restriction on public pronouncement is the minimum necessary consistently with the need for the restriction, and must consider anonymising, editing or part-publishing it.[57]

The Tribunal has power (which would presumably only be exercised where it has agreed that the hearing be held in private) to require that the Tribunal register[58] shall include no particulars about the

---

[54] Rule 17(5).
[55] Paragraph 27.
[56] Rule 20.
[57] Rule 20(2) and (3).
[58] As defined in Rule 2: the register of references and decisions kept in connection with the Tribunal's functions, and which is open to inspection.

reference.[59] The criteria for making such an order are the same as for holding the hearing in private, save that the "interests of justice" criterion is not present.

### 12.4.7 *Form of decision*

Paragraph 12, Schedule 13 FSMA 2000 provides that a decision of the Tribunal must be recorded in a document containing a statement of reasons for the decision, must state whether it was unanimous or by a majority, and be signed and dated by the chairman. Rule 22 of the Tribunal Rules contains a power for a Tribunal to review its decision determining a reference, and to set it aside if it is satisfied that it was wrongly made as a result of error on the part of the Tribunal staff, or if new evidence has become available since the conclusion of the hearing, the existence of which could not have been reasonably known or foreseen.

Quite apart from the statutory obligation upon the FSA to implement decisions of the Tribunal, Section 133(11) FSMA 2000 provides that an order of the Tribunal may be enforced as though it were an order of the County Court.

### 12.4.8 *Costs*

Paragraph 13, Schedule 13 FSMA 2000 (read together with Rule 21 of the Tribunal Rules) gives the Tribunal a power to award costs incurred in respect of the whole or part of the proceedings, but only where "the Tribunal considers that a party to any proceedings has acted vexatiously, frivolously or unreasonably". Further, the FSA may be ordered to pay costs if its decision the subject of the reference is found by the Tribunal to be "unreasonable".[60] In either case, it appears that the costs are limited to (at most) the cost of the "proceedings" (i.e. costs incurred from the submission of the reference). In *Baldwin* v *FSA* (FIN/2005/0011; decision of 5 April 2006), the Tribunal

---

[59] Rule 10(1)(p) and 10(9). *See Theophilus Folagbade Sonaike* v *FSA* (FIN/2005/0021, 13 July 2005), where the Tribunal rejected an application to exclude from the register the details of a reference of Supervisory Notice pending full hearing of the reference, noting that "mere embarrassment falls far short of satisfying the criteria set out in the rule" (at paragraph 12).

[60] The decision as to unreasonableness is a primary one for the Tribunal, rather than an issue of *Wednesbury* unreasonableness: *see Baldwin* v *FSA* (above) at paragraphs 5 to 8.

held (*see* paragraphs 19 to 26) that the first of these two powers to award costs may be triggered not only by vexatious, frivolous or unreasonable conduct *during the reference proceedings*, but also at earlier periods (at least when sought against the FSA), such as during the course of the FSA investigation leading to the warning and decision notices (although the Tribunal also found (at paragraph 26) that such prior conduct would only be relevant if it had "some bearing" on the reference proceedings). This conclusion has a potentially dramatic effect of opening up the FSA's entire conduct throughout the investigation phase to scrutiny by the Tribunal at the costs stage, by contrast with the Tribunal's primary remit which, as noted above (at 12.3.2), is limited to a *de novo* consideration of the FSA's decision. The FSA sought to challenge this aspect of the *Baldwin* decision in *Davidson and Tatham* v *FSA* (FIN/2003/0016 and 0021; costs decision 11 October 2006),[61] but the Tribunal did not find it necessary to pronounce on the issue. Therefore, it may well be that the decision will be revisited in future. Certainly, the distinction between prior conduct that has a bearing on the proceedings and that which does not is by no means easy to draw.

The costs jurisdiction has thus far only been exercised in the case of *Davidson and Tatham* v *FSA*, where the Tribunal awarded costs on three occasions during the course of the Reference:[62]

(a)  The Tribunal ordered that half of the costs thrown away in connection with an abortive hearing of the reference which was terminated by the recusal of the Tribunal for apparent bias be met by the FSA. The chairman held that the FSA had acted unreasonably within paragraph 13, Schedule 13 where the chairman of the FSA's Regulatory Decisions Committee (who was otherwise unconnected with the reference) had had a conversation with a member of the Tribunal about the case. Half of the costs only were awarded because the recusal was partly because of the actions of the member of the Tribunal (Decision, paragraph 17). The chairman commented (at paragraph 18) that such applications should

---

[61] The decision in *Baldwin* itself was not challenged, the FSA having won the costs application on the facts.

[62] FIN/2003/0016 and 0021; at the interlocutory stage, the decision of Dr A N Brice, chairman, dated 30 July 2004; at the substantive stage, decision of the Tribunal dated 11 October 2006.

ordinarily be considered at the end of the full Tribunal hearing, but on the facts entertained it at an earlier stage because the matter was a discrete one, and payment of costs might assist the applicant with funding the rehearing of the reference.

(b)  Limited costs were awarded against one of the applicants in respect of a late application to widen the scope of his reference.

(c)  The Tribunal awarded costs in favour of both applicants on the substantive hearing of the reference, on the basis that the FSA's decision notice was unreasonable. The Tribunal had regard to the FSA's approach to the evidence and the facts (as disclosed by the decision notice and the minutes of the relevant meetings of the Regulatory Decisions Committee of the FSA), the FSA's approach to the law, and the levels of penalty imposed by the decision notice, finding in each respect that the FSA's approach and/or decision was unreasonable.[63] Although the Tribunal expressed the view that the matters which it had found as being unreasonable were unlikely to re-occur in the future as the decision making in this case took place before the Strachan report and consequent changes to the FSA's decision-making process, it is by no means clear that the Tribunal's reasoning is so confined. The sweeping views which it expressed as to the FSA's substantive decision making, based in part upon limited minutes of the relevant decisions, is, it is suggested, not easily confined in the way proposed.[64]

If not agreed, costs and expenses are to be assessed (if not fixed by the Tribunal) by a costs official of the court on a basis determined by the Tribunal.

## 12.5  Disclosure of documents: further questions

The disclosure obligations contained in the Tribunal Rules have been summarised above. However, there are difficult questions as to the

---

[63]  However, the Tribunal rejected an alternative contention that the FSA's conduct in not withdrawing the disputed decision during the course of the Tribunal proceedings was unreasonable: Judgment at paragraph 76.

[64]  For a more developed, and robust, view of penalty in a market abuse case, and the suggestion that the treatment of penalty in *Davidson and Tatham* was "hypothetical" and should (by inference) be confined to its own facts, *see James Parker v FSA* at paragraphs 147 to 178, particularly at 167.

extent to which these translate into practical obligations to disclose, particularly for the FSA.

### 12.5.1 Disclosure of unused material

As noted above, under Rule 7 the authority has an obligation, following the filing of the Reply, to disclose any further material "which might be reasonably expected to assist the Applicant's case as disclosed by the Applicant's Reply" which has not been previously disclosed. That language mirrors the wording of Section 7(2) of the Criminal Procedure and Investigations Act 1996, which imposes a duty of secondary disclosure on a prosecutor (just as the primary duty to disclose under Rule 5(3) mirrors Section 3(1) of the 1996 Act). As the Tribunal commented in the case of *Davidson and Tatham* v *FSA* (interlocutory decision of Dr A N Brice, 30 July 2004 at paragraph 30), "thus it appears that the disclosure already provided to the applicant under the Rules meets the criminal standard of disclosure." It considered that it was therefore not necessary for this purpose to determine whether or not a penalty for market abuse amounted to a criminal charge for the purposes of Article 6 (although on the substantive hearing of the reference the Tribunal found that it was, as noted at 12.2.3 above).

The position is therefore that Rules 5(3) and 7 impose a duty equivalent to the "golden rule" of full disclosure recently referred to (in the criminal context) by Lord Bingham in *R* v *H* (2004) UKHL3, [2004] 2 AC 134 at paragraph 14: "Fairness ordinarily requires that any material held by the prosecution which weakens its case or strengthens that of the defendant, if not relied on as part of its formal case against the defendant, should be disclosed to the defence".

### 12.5.2 Exceptions to disclosure

The requirement of disclosure will be subject to any claim for public interest immunity, which would be judged by reference to the same principles as apply in criminal cases.[65] In addition the requirement of secondary disclosure imposed by Rule 7(1) is subject to an exemption,

---

[65] *See* for example Archbold (2006) at paragraph 12-26 and following. See other exceptions to disclosure listed in Rule 8.

by virtue of Rule 8(8), from the duty to disclose any document that is a "protected item".

"Protected item" is defined under Section 413 of FSMA 2000, which provides protection for documents equivalent to the common law protection for legal advice privilege (Section 413(2)(a)) and litigation privilege (Section 413(2)(b)). It has been said (*see Re L* [1997] AC 16 at page 25 per Lord Jauncey) that "Litigation privilege . . . is an essential component of adversarial procedure". Although the FSA is a public body it is also a party to the Tribunal proceedings, with a right to invoke legal privilege. There is no doubt that Section 413 would exempt the FSA from the requirement to disclose items subject to legal advice privilege, so that communications between the FSA and its professional legal advisers (including in-house legal advisers) made in connection with giving legal advice would be protected, and thus exempt from the duty of secondary disclosure under Rule 7.[66]

In relation to litigation privilege, on the wording of Section 413(2)(b) and (3), material obtained by the FSA, or a legal adviser acting on its behalf, for the purposes of a reference to the Tribunal would, in general, be covered by the protection of Section 413. By virtue of Section 413(3)(b) the material must be made in connection with or in contemplation of legal proceedings and for the purposes of those proceedings. Thus it appears clear that pre-existing material obtained by the FSA after a reference was in contemplation, but not made for the purposes of that reference, would be subject to the requirement of secondary disclosure under Rule 7.

In relation to statements or material obtained by the FSA from witnesses or potential witnesses for the purposes of the Tribunal proceedings, Section 413 would appear to entitle the FSA to invoke litigation privilege. There is an argument (at least in a market abuse

---

[66] *See*, however, the narrow view of the Court of Appeal in *Three Rivers DC* v *Bank of England (No. 5)* [2003] QB 1556 on the issue of who may be within the class of persons comprising "the client", whose communications or preparatory materials created for the purposes of seeking legal advice will attract privilege. *See* further the House of Lords in *Three Rivers DC* v *Bank of England (No. 6)* [2004] 3 WLR 1274, where the House of Lords declined to review the Court of Appeal's holding, although noting the strength of criticism expressed in relation to it (per Lord Scott at paragraphs 20–22, 46–48). The Court of Appeal's decision could be of relevance in circumstances where the FSA holds third-party material prepared for the purpose of litigation.

case which on the finding of the Tribunal in *Davidson and Tatham* v *FSA* is "criminal" in at least some cases) that this position is anomalous. Given the overriding principle of full disclosure by a prosecutor in a criminal case, where, typically, unused material which falls within the statutory tests will be disclosed even if a plea of privilege might be maintained, it can be argued that the FSA, as a public body acting in the role of a quasi-prosecutor in a market abuse case, should owe the same duty of disclosure as a prosecutor, given that the statutory duty is framed in closely similar terms. Thus, for example, statements of witnesses whom the FSA elects not to call at the hearing, or draft statements, would be disclosable if capable of undermining the FSA's case or assisting the applicant. Section 413, the argument would run, must be read restrictively in the light of Article 6 of the ECHR so as to protect the applicant's right to a fair trial. On the other hand, even assuming that market abuse is correctly classified as criminal for the purposes of Article 6, it does not follow (and is not the case) that Article 6 requires that all protections attaching to a criminal trial must be followed (as the Tribunal noted in *Davidson and Tatham* v *FSA*, at paragraphs 183–4). What is required are the minimum guarantees of fairness set out in Article 6 as elaborated by the case law. It is at least arguable that those guarantees do not require an unrestricted obligation to disclose material otherwise subject to privilege. This issue is one which will require ventilation before the Tribunal before a clearer answer can be given. As a matter of practice, the FSA do frequently voluntarily disclose (on the basis of a waiver of privilege) unused statements which may be considered to undermine its case or assist the applicant, which may explain why the issue has not yet needed to be determined.

Protection was in the past routinely claimed by the FSA for the internal advice and recommendations given to the RDC in connection with the issuing of a Warning and Decision Notice. However, in light of the recommendations to the FSA's Enforcement Process Review ("the Strachan Review", July 2005), the FSA altered its procedures so that all legal submissions made by Enforcement to the RDC are disclosed to the applicant. Therefore, no question of privilege arises. The RDC now has its own legal advice function, but its legal advice to the RDC is not disclosed either to Enforcement or to the applicant; it is suggested that such advice is properly treated as privileged. Difficult questions may remain, however, as to material held by Enforcement which is *not* disclosed to the RDC. There is, as yet, no authority on whether the RDC process amounts to "legal proceedings" so as to found a claim for litigation privilege.

## 12.6 Third-party rights

Under Section 393 FSMA 2000, a person other than the person to whom a decision notice is given who is (in short summary) identified in the reasons contained in the notice and to whom, in the opinion of the FSA, it is prejudicial, is entitled to be served with a copy of the notice. Such a person ("a third party") has the right to refer to the Tribunal the decision in question (as far as it is based on a reason which identifies him adversely) or the expression of any opinion by the FSA about him. The third party may refer whether or not the subject of the notice does so, and may also (by Section 393(11)) refer a *failure* by the FSA to serve him with a copy of the notice in circumstances where he contends it should have done so.

The wording of Section 393 gives rise to a number of questions, some of which have been answered in *Sir Philip Watts* v *FSA* (FIN/2004/0024, decision of William Blair QC and Dr Nuala Brice dated 7 September 2005). The Tribunal there held (*see* in particular paragraphs 49 to 54) that the requirement in Section 393(4) that the reasons contained in the notice must "relate *to a matter* which identifies a person" (emphasis added) does not mean that the Section affords third-party rights to a person who is only identified in the "matter" to which the reasons in the decision notice relate, by reference to external sources. The third party must be identified in the decision notice (or other notice referred) in order to engage the Section. On that basis, the Tribunal rejected Sir Philip's reference because he was not referred to in the relevant decision notice addressed to Shell, but only in external documents and commentary not the responsibility of the FSA.

The Tribunal also considered (at paragraphs 56 to 59) what might amount to an "identification". It declined to place any formal gloss on the word "identifies", holding that it should be considered on a case-by-case basis, although it approved the concession that a person could be identified by job description or by a collective reference (e.g. "all the directors") as well as by name, indicating further that in its view there might be other methods of identification. This leaves for the future the difficult question of precisely what may constitute an identification (and, if identified, whether it is prejudicial). For example, it is an open question as to whether there is an identification where an individual is not referred to, but a transaction to which he was a party is identified and impugned. The position is complicated by the fact that even if a third party is not identified in a decision notice, it may be obvious that, if the decision notice is referred by the recipient to the Tribunal, the third party will be prejudicially identified at that stage, in what is (presumptively) a public hearing. Yet the section provides no mechanism for third-party rights at that stage. Therefore, it is suggested that (as the Tribunal recognised) the decision in *Sir Philip Watts* v *FSA* is unlikely to be the last word on the subject.

By virtue of Rule 15, the Tribunal Rules apply to such a third-party reference as they do in the case of a reference by the subject of the decision notice. The Tribunal determines what is the appropriate course of action for the FSA to take in respect of the referred matter in the same way.

## 12.7 Appeals

Under Section 137(1) an appeal may be brought, with permission and on a point of law only, to the Court of Appeal from "a decision of the Tribunal disposing of a reference". The use of that language, in contrast to "any decision of the Tribunal", indicates that an appeal will not lie against an interlocutory decision, but only against the final decision of the Tribunal adjudicating on the substantive reference.[67] Accordingly, where a party is aggrieved by an interlocutory decision, the usual course will be for the point to be taken (if still relevant) as a ground of appeal at the end of the proceedings unless, possibly, the decision is so fundamental that judicial review may lie notwithstanding the alternative remedy.[68] The appeal route has not, in practice, been used.

---

[67] Although the determination of a preliminary issue which substantially disposes of the reference may be treated as the hearing of the reference: Rule 13(2) of the Tribunal Rules. It is an open question as to whether a decision on costs of the reference is (or is part of) a "decision ... disposing of the reference" so as to permit a statutory appeal. It is submitted that the better view is that it is, since a costs decision constitutes a part of the final disposal, even if determined at a separate hearing subsequent to the main determination.

[68] *See* Chapter 13 below.

An appeal may be made either by the FSA or by the applicant to the reference. Under Rule 23 of the Rules an application for permission to appeal must be made within 14 days after the decision is sent to the party making the application. If the application is refused by the Tribunal then the applicant has a further 14 days in which to seek permission to appeal from the Court of Appeal.

Where the Court of Appeal allows an appeal, it may remit the matter to the Tribunal or itself make a determination (Section 137(3)). In the former case, Rule 25 applies to the remitted hearing, requiring the Tribunal to give further directions within 28 days. In the latter case, there appears to be a lacuna in the Act and Rules, in that there is no express duty cast upon the FSA to adopt the decision of the Court of Appeal (as there is with a decision of the Tribunal; *see* 12.3.1 above). Presumably, the existence of such a duty must be taken to be implied.

# Chapter 13

# Challenging FSA Decisions – the Courts and Other Avenues

**Andrew Lidbetter**

Partner
Herbert Smith LLP

## 13.1    Introduction

The Financial Services and Markets Act 2000 ("FSMA 2000") set up
the Financial Services and Markets Tribunal to provide a mechanism
for challenging a wide range of Financial Services Authority ("FSA")
decisions. Anyone who wishes to challenge an FSA decision which
falls within the jurisdiction of the Tribunal will normally be expected
to mount that challenge in the Tribunal (*see* 13.7.4 below). Where a
matter falls outside the jurisdiction of the Tribunal (and possibly in
certain other exceptional circumstances) the route for challenge to
FSA enforcement decisions will be judicial review.

There are also circumstances when a civil claim against the FSA might
be possible in respect of enforcement action. Finally, there is the possibility of a complaint to the FSA Complaints Commissioner.[1]

## 13.2    Judicial review

Judicial review is the mechanism through which the courts examine
administrative action by public bodies such as the FSA. It is a supervisory jurisdiction which reviews administrative action rather than
operating as an appellate jurisdiction. This means that a successful
judicial review will not have the effect of reversing the decision made
by the FSA, but rather it is most likely that the decision would be

---

[1] Note that the FSA falls outside of the list of bodies that comes within the jurisdiction of the
Parliamentary Ombudsman.

quashed and remitted to the FSA to be re-made. This leaves a risk that the FSA may reach the same result but follow a different process or take into account something it had previously failed to consider. In the FSA context therefore, an aggrieved party may be better off having a complete re-hearing and determination on the merits by the Tribunal rather than the more limited review mechanism.

Judicial review is available only in respect of decisions by public bodies and only where those decisions are public law decisions or public law actions. As a body created by statute the FSA is a public body.[2] Further, enforcement and supervisory decisions by the FSA will fall within the ambit of public law functions and hence potentially are reviewable.[3]

However, circumstances in which a challenge by judicial review can properly be brought against the FSA are likely to be rare. At the time of writing this chapter there had been only a handful of judicial review applications against the FSA. Broadly most have failed because the courts held that they concerned matters that could have been dealt with by the Tribunal. An important general principle is that where there is an alternative remedy to judicial review, that alternative remedy should be exhausted first (*see* 13.7.4 below). If that test is passed, it must then be demonstrated that one of the grounds for judicial review exists.

## 13.3   The grounds for judicial review

The grounds under which a public law decision by a public body may be open to judicial review have evolved through case-law and cases set in the context of one area of administrative activity will be relevant in another. For example, cases from an immigration context may

---

[2] Note that the self-regulating organisations and recognised investment exchanges under the Financial Services Act 1986 were subject to judicial review, for example *R v Lautro ex parte Ross* [1993] QB 17 and *R v London Metal Exchange ex parte Albatros Warehousing BV* (2000) LTL 31/3/2000. By contrast the Insurance Ombudsman Bureau operated in contract rather than public law and so could not be the subject of judicial review (*R v Insurance Ombudsman ex parte Aegon Life Insurance Limited* [1994] CLC 88 and Lloyd's of London), for example *R (on the application of West) v Lloyd's of London* [2004] EWCA Civ 506.

[3] By contrast, employment decisions are an example of an area where judicial review is not usually available, for example *R v Berkshire Health Authority ex parte Walsh* [1985] 1 QB 152.

be equally relevant for the financial services enforcement context. A consideration of how these grounds may apply to decisions by the FSA forms the bulk of this chapter.

There are various ways in which the grounds for judicial review can be classified. However, a commonly used classification is the tripartite distinction in *CCSU* v *The Minister for the Civil Service*[4] between the heads of illegality, irrationality and procedural impropriety. Within each of the heads there are a number of grounds which are capable of being characterised in more than one way. For example, where a statute lays down a procedure which a public authority needs to go through, then a failure to follow the wording of the statute could fall under the illegality head or alternatively under the procedural impropriety head.

Cases can be brought against financial services regulators by applicants seeking to rely on all three heads and there are certainly instances where the same decision has been challenged under more than one head. For example, in *R* v *Financial Intermediaries, Managers and Brokers Regulatory Association ex parte Cochrane*[5] the applicants sought to challenge a decision of the FIMBRA Appeals Tribunal, arguing that the penalty imposed for breach of FIMBRA's rules was so harsh that it was irrational and also that the Appeals Tribunal had been motivated by "unconscious" bias, an aspect of procedural impropriety. In *R* v *London Metal Exchange ex parte Albatros Warehousing BV*[6] the applicants sought judicial review on the grounds of:

(a) procedural impropriety, alleging that the Appeal Committee was biased and because the London Metal Exchange had tried to adduce new evidence of fact during the disciplinary hearing; and
(b) irrationality, both because of an alleged failure to take into account a material consideration and also because the sanctions were grossly disproportionate.

---

[4] [1985] AC 374.
[5] [1990] COD 33.
[6] (2000) LTL 31/3/2000.

Similarly, a breach of Section 8 FSMA 2000, which states that the FSA must "make and maintain effective arrangements for consulting practitioners and consumers", could give rise to a challenge based on illegality and procedural impropriety.

# 13.4 Illegality

## 13.4.1 Breach of a domestic or European legal provision

Where a public body acts outside of the terms of a domestic or European legal provision it will be tainted by illegality.

For example, in *R* v *Secretary of State for Trade ex parte R*[7] the court held that the power of the Secretary of State under Section 105 of the Financial Services Act 1986[8] to investigate the affairs of an "investment business" did not entitle him to investigate transactions which took place before the material provision came into force.

Another example is *R* v *Securities and Investments Board ex parte Independent Financial Advisers Association*[9] where the applicant sought, *inter alia*, a declaration that the decision of the Securities and Investments Board ("SIB") to issue guidance promulgating a scheme of self-assessment by independent financial advisers ("IFAs") in relation to the provision of advice on pension transfers and opt-outs was ultra vires and unlawful. The applicant argued that the guidance was in fact mandatory and not merely directory and therefore was ultra vires, SIB not having power to order IFAs to pay compensation to investors. The court rejected this contention; it held that although the guidance may have given the impression of a claim to greater power than SIB possessed, this impression would not have deceived the regulatory bodies to whom the guidance was addressed.

FSMA 2000 sets out the general duties of the FSA. These are that it must (as far as is reasonably possible) act in a way which is compatible with its four regulatory objectives:

---

[7] [1989] 1 WLR 372.
[8] The predecessor legislation to FSMA 2000.
[9] [1995] BCLC 872.

(a)   market confidence;
(b)   public awareness;
(c)   the protection of consumers; and
(d)   the reduction of financial crime (Section 2 FSMA 2000).

In addition Section 2 sets out criteria to which the FSA must have regard in discharging its functions, such as proportionality, facilitating innovation and facilitating competition.

Actions of the FSA which are incompatible with these objectives or criteria may therefore be reviewed for breaching domestic legislation.

FSMA 2000 permits those carrying out an investigation to require the provision of evidence. Such powers are not untrammelled since they are subject to public law principles. The powers are initially restricted by the wording of the legislation. By analogy, challenges have been brought alleging that notices requiring provision of documents issued by Inland Revenue officers pursuant to the Income and Corporation Taxes Act 1998 were too wide in requesting categories of documents rather than specific documents. The Court of Appeal held that the relevant statutory wording was in fact wide enough to encompass descriptions of classes of documents (*R* v *O'Kane ex parte Northern Bank Limited*[10]).

In addition to looking at breaches of primary legislation as illegality, it is possible to characterise a breach of delegated legislation or a regulator's own rules as an aspect of illegality, *see* for example *R* v *Investors Compensation Scheme ex parte Bowden.*[11]

---

[10] [1996] STC 1249. The notice was originally struck down for a failure to comply with the wording of the particular legislation, since the notices purported to require the production of conjectural and not actual documents. However, the Court of Appeal in *R* v *Commissioners of Inland Revenue ex parte Ulster Bank Limited* [1997] STC 832 considered *ex parte Northern Bank* and found that the wording in Section 20(8D) which referred to documents "specified or described" was, by virtue of the word "described", appropriate to cover classes or categories of documents. The particular tax legislation did not require the description permissible in a notice to exclude classes or categories of documents that were not known to exist or to be in the possession or power of the recipient of the notice, and which were to that extent conjectural.

[11] [1996] 1 AC 261. The case concerned a challenge to the Investors Compensation Scheme's restrictive interpretation of its own rules. The court found that the decision was a reasonable one and within the rules.

A breach of those articles of the European Convention on Human Rights which have been incorporated into UK law by the Human Rights Act 1998 can also be analysed under the illegality head. So, for example, an allegation that the exercise of search and seizure powers violated respect for a person's home under Article 8 could be based on illegality (*see* 13.8 below for a discussion of the impact of human rights law in the FSA regulatory context).

### 13.4.2 Error going to jurisdiction (including error as to a precedent fact)

An alternative way of analysing an illegality is as an error going to jurisdiction, for example *R v Monopolies and Mergers Commission ex parte South Yorkshire Transport Limited*,[12] where the House of Lords in the event found no error of law in the Monopolies and Mergers Commission's interpretation of the term "a substantial part of the United Kingdom".

Traditionally it has not been possible simply to commence judicial review proceedings arguing that a regulator got the facts wrong. However, *E v Secretary of State for the Home Department*[13] illustrates the gradual development of "mistake of fact" as a separate ground of review in administrative law. Although *E v Secretary of State for the Home Department* was set in the immigration context, it potentially has application across the full range of regulatory activities including in relation to the FSA.

## 13.5 Irrationality/abuse of power

### 13.5.1 A decision which is so unreasonable that no reasonable authority could ever have come to it (Wednesbury unreasonableness)

In *Associated Provincial Picture Houses v Wednesbury Corporation*[14] Lord Greene MR said that if a decision is so unreasonable that no reasonable

---

[12] [1993] 1 WLR 23.
[13] [2004] EWCA Civ 49.
[14] [1948] 1 KB 223.

authority could ever have come to it then the courts can intervene. He added, however, that to prove a case of that kind would require something overwhelming. The cases have tended to bear out the difficulty of proving that something is *Wednesbury* unreasonable. It requires something more than mere unreasonableness. As an example, in *R v SIB ex parte Independent Financial Advisers Association* (above), judicial review of SIB's guidance to self-regulating organisations ("SROs") concerning a proactive review of pensions misselling was generally found not to be *Wednesbury* unreasonable, notwithstanding that it imposed great costs on firms and imposed liability regardless of fault. The only criticism which was upheld was that IFAs should not be required to take any steps which would invalidate their insurance cover.

Generally, when considering an allegation of *Wednesbury* unreasonableness the courts will look more closely where fundamental human rights are involved than when the question before them is, for example, one of economic policy. In addition, where matters of economic judgment or policy are involved and a decision has been made by an expert regulator such as the FSA who has been given a wide statutory ambit, the courts will acknowledge this role and will think carefully before intervening in the substance of a decision.[15]

### 13.5.2  Failure to take account of a relevant consideration or taking into account an irrelevant consideration

When making an enforcement decision the FSA must take account of all relevant considerations and not take into account any irrelevant considerations. For example, in *R (on the application of Norwich and Peterborough Building Society) v Financial Services Ombudsman Service Ltd*[16] a building society applied for judicial review of the Ombudsman's decision arguing (unsuccessfully) that he had failed to take into account a material consideration by misapplying the Banking Code when making his decision.

---

[15] *R (on the application of Yukos Oil company) v Financial Services Authority and London Stock Exchange* [2006] EWHC 2044.
[16] [2002] EWHC 2379.

### 13.5.3   Bad faith

A public authority must not act in bad faith. For example, where a county council decided not to advertise in *The Times Educational Supplement* because of *The Sunday Times* having published an article criticising a councillor, the decision was tainted by bad faith (*R v Derbyshire County Council ex parte The Times Supplements Ltd*[17]).

### 13.5.4   Improper purpose

Where a power is granted to a public body for one purpose it must not be exercised for a different purpose. For example, where a local authority decided to avoid a particular company's products in order to put pressure upon its parent companies to withdraw their interests from South Africa (*R v Lewisham LBC ex parte Shell UK Limited*[18]) or where a transaction by a local council was for the improper purpose of circumventing its restrictions on borrowing and spending (*Credit Suisse v Allerdale Borough Council*[19]) the decisions were tainted by an improper purpose.

### 13.5.5   Abuse of power/substantive legitimate expectation

An undertaking or promise by a public authority may lead to a legitimate expectation which must not be thwarted (*R v Liverpool City Council ex parte Liverpool Taxi Fleet Operators' Association*[20]). Such a legitimate expectation that a particular policy will be applied can arise even where the claimant is unaware of the existence of the relevant policy.[21]

This could also be viewed as abuse of power. This is relevant, for example, in the context of a far-reaching request for evidence. In *R v Secretary of State for Trade ex parte Perestrello*,[22] authorised officers served a notice pursuant to statutory powers[23] that required an individual to produce

---

[17] (1991) 3 Admin LR 241.
[18] [1988] 1 All ER 938.
[19] [1996] 4 All ER 129.
[20] [1972] 2 QB 299.
[21] *R (Rashid) v Secretary of State for the Home Department* [2005] EWCA Civ 744.
[22] [1981] 1 QB 19.
[23] Section 109 of the Companies Act 1967, predecessor legislation to the Companies Act 1985.

various categories of documents including "all accounting records of the company such as to disclose the financial position of the company" and "all files of correspondence relating to the affairs of the company". In the particular circumstances of that case, the court took the view that the notices were "unreasonable and excessive in the circumstances". However, it would take a strong case on the part of an applicant before a court would hold that there has been abuse of power by a regulator. For example in *R v Inland Revenue ex parte Banque International a Luxembourg SA*[24] the court rejected an argument that a far-reaching request for documents by the Revenue amounted to abuse of power. The overall principle is that the breadth of the notice has to be considered in the context of the scale of the investigation. In that case the investigation was into complicated tax avoidance schemes involving some £150 million of tax.

One area where substantive legitimate expectation or abuse of power may be raised is where an officer of a public authority makes a statement or otherwise leads someone to act in a particular way and then the public authority effectively reneges on its position. For example, in *R v IRC ex parte Unilever*[25] the Revenue had for many years allowed Unilever to submit late tax relief claims which the court said had given rise to a legitimate expectation. To depart from that practice without clear and general advance notice was so unfair as to amount to an abuse of power.

Such an argument could be relevant where FSA supervisors have agreed to a particular course of conduct, for example a business practice, but then as a result of policy shift or consumer pressure the FSA decides to take action.

The FSA publishes rules and guidance in its Handbook. Guidance in the Handbook is not binding on those to whom FSMA 2000 applies and does not need to be followed in order to achieve compliance. However, if a person acts in accordance with general guidance, then the FSA has said it will proceed as if that person has complied with the relevant rule. If the FSA were to depart from this it may be reviewable as an abuse of power.

---

[24] [2000] All ER (D) 863.
[25] [1996] STC 681.

The Handbook also contains evidential provisions which are not binding but simply indicative in nature. Compliance with an evidential provision creates only a rebuttable presumption of compliance with the binding rule to which it refers. The FSA is therefore not bound by those evidential provisions.

In order for abuse of power to arise the following four specific elements need to be satisfied:

(a) the representation or expectation sought to be relied upon must be clear, unambiguous and unqualified;
(b) the applicant must be within the class of persons entitled to rely upon the representation, or alternatively it must be reasonable for the applicant to rely upon it;
(c) there must usually be reliance upon the representation to the detriment of the applicant, although in recent cases reliance has not been considered essential;[26] and
(d) there must be no overriding public interest which would entitle the public authority to renege on its representation. Public bodies will be permitted to resile from a representation where it is a proportionate response having regard to a legitimate aim pursued in the public interest.[27]

### 13.5.6  Improper delegation

Generally a public law function must be exercised only by the body to whom those functions have been given and the decision making should not be delegated to someone else unless there is an express power to delegate.

Thus, for example, a delegation by the Director of Public Prosecutions ("DPP") to non-qualified lawyers of the power to review prosecutions in order to decide whether there was sufficient evidence to proceed was invalid because the statute clearly contemplated that the

---

[26] R v *Department for Education and Employment ex parte Begbie* [2000] 1 WLR 1115; R (*Nadarajah and Abdi*) v *Secretary of State for the Home Department* [2005] EWCA Civ 1363.
[27] R (*Timothy Rex Bamber*) v *Commissioners of Her Majesty's Revenue and Customs* [2005] EWHC 3221.

discretion would only be delegated to a member of the Crown Prosecution Service who was a lawyer.[28]

### 13.5.7 Fettering of discretion

A public authority must not adopt a rigid policy, thereby fettering its discretion. Although a public authority can have a policy, it must consider particular cases rather than always following its stated policy blindly. Thus, for example, a blanket policy to restrict access to a solicitor by a person remanded in custody was unlawful (*R v Chief Constable of South Wales ex parte Merrick*[29]).

### 13.5.8 Proportionality

Proportionality is a European law concept. It requires remedies or measures to be proportionate to the aim that is sought to be achieved or the state of affairs they are intended to address. The administrative process should be in proportion to the outcome of the process. The conventional view has been that proportionality is simply a facet of irrationality/*Wednesbury* unreasonableness within the domestic context (*see R v Secretary of State for the Home Department ex parte Brind*[30]).

## 13.6 Procedural impropriety

### 13.6.1 Infringement of express procedural rules

An FSA decision should not infringe express procedural rules.

FSMA 2000 sets out at Part XIV the procedure which the FSA must follow if it wishes to institute disciplinary proceedings against an authorised person. If the FSA proposes to either publish a statement that an authorised person has contravened a requirement under FSMA 2000, or to impose a penalty, it must give the authorised person

---

[28] R v *The Director of Public Prosecutions ex parte Association of First Division Civil Servants, The Times* 24 May 1988.
[29] [1994] 1 WLR 663.
[30] [1991] 1 AC 696.

a warning notice which sets out the terms of the statement or states the amount of the penalty (Section 207). If the FSA then decides to publish a statement or impose a penalty it must give the authorised person a decision notice, at which stage the authorised person may refer the matter to the Financial Services and Markets Tribunal (Section 208). FSMA 2000 requires that the warning and decision notices must be in writing, give the FSA's reasons for the proposed action, give the person access to the material upon which it relied in making the decision (Section 394) and in relation to warning notices provide a reasonable period for representations to be made to the FSA. A failure to comply with these procedural requirements will amount to procedural impropriety.

An example of a judicial review of express procedural requirements is *Seifert* v *Pensions Ombudsman*.[31] Section 149(1) of the Pension Scheme Act 1993 obliges the Ombudsman to give trustees or other persons against whom allegations are made an opportunity to comment on any allegations contained in the complaint or reference. The court at first instance criticised the Ombudsman for failing to disclose a particular letter. However, the Court of Appeal accepted that the letter had introduced a new and relevant matter to a limited extent, but said that it was followed by the Ombudsman's provisional determination which should have alerted the others concerned to the true nature of the dispute, or at least put them on enquiry.

### 13.6.2 Failure to comply with common law obligations to provide a "fair hearing"

The right to a fair hearing is made up of the right of a person to know the case against him or her and an adequate opportunity to make representations. The content of the requirement of a fair hearing in relation to FSA enforcement matters varies from case to case. The extent of the rights which must be afforded to comply with natural justice will depend on a number of factors including a consideration of what is at stake, for example loss of livelihood.

---

[31] [1997] 1 All ER 214.

It is unlikely that regulators will have to give an opportunity to some-one to make representations as to why an investigation should not be started against him. In *Norwest Holst Limited* v *Secretary of State for Trade*[32] it was held that, as long as the minister acted in good faith, it was not incumbent upon him to disclose the material he had before him or the reasons for his enquiry when initiating an investigation. A similar approach was adopted in the Lloyd's context in *Moran* v *Lloyd's*.[33]

A further example of a case concerning natural justice in a financial services regulation enforcement context is *R* v *Life Assurance Unit Trust Regulatory Organisation ex parte Ross*.[34] The applicants had been served with a copy of an intervention notice by LAUTRO. They contested the procedure by which restrictions could be placed on members but where Mr Ross and others were not given an opportu-nity to make representations challenging the notices even though they were directly affected by them. The Court of Appeal held that on the face of it, there should have been an opportunity to make repre-sentations. The application for judicial review was refused because the Court of Appeal held that the powers given to SROs for the protection of investors must on occasion, as in this case, require urgent action and the entertaining of representations may not be compatible with the urgency. However, even if the urgency of the case has the effect that representations need not be entertained prior to serving such an intervention notice, there should be an opportunity to challenge the notice subsequently.

The position of third parties affected by notices issued by the FSA is specifically dealt with in Sections 392–394 FSMA 2000 (see the Financial Services and Markets Tribunal decision in *Sir Philip Watts* v *FSA*, 25 July 2005).

### 13.6.3  *Procedural legitimate expectation*

Procedural legitimate expectation arises where someone has been given an expectation of being able to make representations prior to a

---

[32] [1978] Ch 201.
[33] [1981] 1 LIR 423.
[34] [1993] QB 17.

decision being made. For example, taxi drivers had a legitimate expectation of consultation prior to the issue of licences in circumstances where such consultation had been expressly promised (*R v Liverpool Corporation ex parte Liverpool Taxi Fleet Operators' Association*[35]). The expectation can be derived from an express promise or representation or an implied representation based upon past action. The promise must be clear and unambiguous and the claimant must have made full relevant disclosure prior to obtaining it. The expectation can be overridden where there is a clear public interest.

### 13.6.4 Infringement of the rule against apparent bias

Normally in cases where decision-makers have a direct personal or proprietary interest in the outcome of a matter, they will automatically be disqualified from adjudicating upon the issue. However, where they have an indirect interest the courts should:

(a)  ascertain all the circumstances which have a bearing on the suggestion that the tribunal is biased; and

(b)  ask whether the circumstances would lead a fair-minded and informed observer to conclude that there is a real possibility that the tribunal is biased.[36]

Although this automatic disqualification normally applies only in cases where the judge has a pecuniary interest, it was extended in a case where the judge had a non-pecuniary interest in one of the parties thereto which was held to be sufficient to amount to an interest in the outcome of the proceedings.[37]

In *R v Secretary of State ex parte Perestrello*,[38] the applicant alleged that Department of Trade and Industry Inspectors investigating business dealings had acted with the appearance of bias. The application failed on the basis that the Inspectors could not be expected to avoid all appearances of bias: they were acting in their policing capacity and

---

[35] [1972] 2 QB 299.
[36] *Porter v Magill* [2001] UKHL 67, [2002] 2 AC 357.
[37] *R v Bow Street Metropolitan Stipendiary Magistrate ex parte Pinochet Ugarte (No. 2)* [1999] 2 WLR 272.
[38] [1981] QB 19.

must therefore suspect some wrongdoing before even starting their investigation.

### 13.6.5 *Reasons*

Reasons should be given where:

(a)   the statute requires it; or
(b)   a decision without reasons is insufficient to achieve justice; or
(c)   the decision on its face appears aberrant.[39]

For example, the General Medical Council was required to give reasons for its decision not to restore a doctor's name to a register of general practitioners. Although the relevant legislation did not expressly or impliedly impose on the Council a duty to state reasons for its decisions, this did not exclude an obligation to give reasons where the common law would require reasons to be given.[40] The duty to give reasons is a universal principle applying to any tribunal having to reach a judicial or quasi-judicial conclusion. Any such tribunal should ask itself whether its decision was clear and whether it had been explained in such a way that the parties could clearly understand why they had won or lost.[41] The position is influenced by the fact that there is an obligation in Article 6 of the European Convention on Human Rights at least to give a short statement of the reasons for a decision which determine civil rights.

## 13.7   Procedural issues

The Civil Procedure Rules ("CPR") set out a specific pre-action protocol that must be followed, if appropriate, before starting judicial review proceedings. This protocol envisages the prospective claimant sending a letter before action, detailing the relevant facts and the grounds of its claim, and the prospective defendant responding to that letter within a period normally of 14 days.

---

[39]   *R v Ministry of Defence ex p. Murray* [1998] COD 134.
[40]   *Stefan v GMC* [1999] 1 WLR 1293.
[41]   *Robert Phipps v GMC* [2006] EWCA Civ 397.

Judicial review proceedings are a two-stage process. An applicant for judicial review must first obtain permission from the court before going on to make the substantive application. The permission requirement is designed to weed out hopeless cases.

### 13.7.1  Standing

An applicant must have a "sufficient interest in the matter to which the application relates" (Section 31(3) of the Supreme Court Act 1981). The courts have interpreted the test of "sufficient interest" quite widely although "busy bodies" will be excluded. Investors are likely to have standing to seek judicial review in respect of a decision made by the FSA against firms with which they have invested funds, for example a decision to close an investigation without disciplinary action or without requiring remedial action.

### 13.7.2  Delay

The CPR require that a claim form for judicial review should be filed promptly and in any event within three months from the date when grounds for the claim first arose. This time limit may not be extended by agreement between the parties. In some cases the courts have held that even when applications were made within three months, they were not made sufficiently promptly and the cases were rejected on the grounds of delay.[42] The court does, however, have the power to extend time.

### 13.7.3  Procedures generally

The claim form must be served on the defendant and any person the claimant considers to be an interested party within seven days after the date of issue. Any person served with the claim form who wishes to take part in the judicial review must file an Acknowledgement of Service not more than 21 days after service of the claim form.

The court will generally consider the question of permission without a hearing. Where there is a hearing, neither the defendant nor any

---

[42] And note also the effect of Section 31(6) of the Supreme Court Act 1981 which allows the court in cases of undue delay to refuse to grant the relief sought if it may prejudice the rights of any person or be detrimental to good administration.

other interested party need attend a hearing on the question of permission unless the court directs otherwise; but sometimes, depending on the case, the defendant will attend. Where a decision on permission is made without a hearing, the court must give its reasons for the decision when it serves the Order. The claimant may not appeal the decision but may request the decision to be reconsidered at a hearing. A request for any reconsideration must be filed within seven days of service of the reasons given by the court.

Following the grant of permission, a defendant and any other person served with the claim form who wishes to contest the claim or support it on additional grounds, must file detailed grounds for contesting the claim or supporting it on additional grounds, and any written evidence, within 35 days after service of the Order giving permission.

In general, applications for judicial review tend to be dealt with by way of written evidence rather than oral evidence, and cross-examination is usually permitted only where there is a direct conflict of evidence or an allegation of bad faith. The general presumption is that a right to disclosure of relevant documents is not available in judicial review proceedings (in contrast to private law proceedings) unless the court orders otherwise.

### 13.7.4   *Alternative remedies*

An important general principle for the FSA is that where there is an alternative remedy rather than judicial review, that alternative remedy should be exhausted first. Indeed, where the alternative remedy is a statutory appeal, the appeal mechanism has the effect of excluding judicial review for decisions which fall within the ambit of the appeal. This is of importance in the FSA context because FSMA 2000 provides that a large number of matters may be referred to the Financial Services and Markets Tribunal. In *R (on the application of Davies and Others) v Financial Services Authority*[43] it was confirmed not only that the FSA has a wide discretion in selecting the most appropriate statutory route for dealing with conduct

---

[43] [2003] EWCA Civ 1128.

which it wishes to stop or prevent reoccurring, but also reaffirms the importance of exhausting all alternative remedies, such as recourse to the Financial Services and Markets Tribunal, rather than resorting to judicial review proceedings. If the Tribunal has jurisdiction in relation to the matter complained of, it is only in exceptional circumstances where there is very good reason for not proceeding to that Tribunal that a prospective claimant may be able to apply for judicial review.[44]

The alternative remedy point does not prevent someone initiating an application for judicial review, but it will be a reason for the court refusing permission or relief.[45]

### 13.7.5 Remedies available in judicial review proceedings

The remedies which can be granted are mandatory orders (which require that certain action be taken), prohibiting orders (which prohibit certain actions), quashing orders (which quash the decision and remit it back to the public body to be re-taken), declarations, injunctions and, occasionally, damages. Damages can normally only be awarded where there is also a private law cause of action (*see* 13.9 below). There is no general right to damages where a judicial review application is successful.

## 13.8 Human rights aspects

The Human Rights Act 1998 ("HRA 1998") has imported many of the rights protected by the European Convention into domestic law. In addition, Section 3 of the Act imposes an obligation of statutory interpretation by saying that as far as possible legislation must be read in a way which is compatible with the Convention rights.

The most relevant rights for present purposes are Article 6, Article 8 and Article 1 of the First Protocol.

---

[44] *See*, for example, *R (on the application of G)* v *Immigration Appeal Tribunal* [2004] EWCA Civ 1731.
[45] *R (Cookson & Clegg)* v *Ministry of Defence* [2005] EWCA Civ 811.

Article 6 lays out the right to a fair and public hearing within a reasonable time by an independent and impartial tribunal established by law in order to determine a person's civil rights and obligations. This is primarily a procedural right, but it is absolute and may not be derogated from under any circumstances.

Article 8 enshrines the right to respect for privacy of private life, home and correspondence. However, this right is qualified by allowing interference with this right in accordance with the law and if necessary in a democratic society in the interests of national security, public safety or the economic well-being of the country, for the prevention of disorder or crime, for the protection of health or morals, or for the protection of the rights and freedoms of others.

Article 1 of the First Protocol, which relates to the protection of a person's property, has a similar qualification. A person may be deprived of his possessions if it is in the public interest and subject to the conditions provided for by law and by the general principles of international law.

Apart from Article 6 then, the other relevant rights provide only limited protection against the actions of the FSA, as there is a strong possibility that their actions (provided they are reasonable) will be seen as being justified in the public interest.

It appears that the FSA has gone to considerable lengths to comply with Human Rights and public law principles when designing certain aspects of its rules and procedures such as, for example, the use of separation of functions in disciplinary decision making and the use of additional protections in market abuse proceedings.

## 13.9   Civil remedies

There is very limited opportunity for bringing a civil claim against the FSA due to the express statutory exemption from liability in damages contained in paragraph 19 of Schedule 1 to FSMA 2000. This states that "neither the Authority nor any person who is, or is acting as, a member, officer or member of staff of the Authority is to be liable in damages for anything done or omitted in the discharge, or purported discharge, of the Authority's functions".

However, this exemption does not apply if the act or omission is shown to have been in bad faith, or if damages are claimed under the HRA 1998. If bad faith can be shown, then there is the possibility of bringing normal civil claims in negligence or for breach of statutory duty or for misfeasance in public office against a public body. However, as discussed below, it is difficult to bring a successful action against the FSA in any of these ways.

### 13.9.1 Human Rights Act 1998 claims

Section 6 of the HRA 1998 makes it unlawful for a public authority to act in a way which is incompatible with a Convention right. Possible Convention rights that may be in issue when dealing with the FSA include (*inter alia*) Article 6 (the right to a fair trial), Article 8 (the right to privacy) and Article 1 of the First Protocol (the right to protection of property).

Individuals can challenge acts of a public authority which they believe are incompatible with Convention rights in the domestic courts rather than having to go to the European courts.

If it is found that a public authority has violated any of the Convention rights, Section 8 HRA 1998 gives the court discretion to award such relief or remedy as is necessary to award "just satisfaction" to the injured party, taking into account any other relief or remedy granted. There is no guidance in the Act as to how the Section should be applied, other than to say that the courts must take into account the principles followed by the European Court of Human Rights.

The case of *Anufrijeva* v *London Borough of Southwark*[46] provided guidance on how the courts should use this discretion. Lord Woolf advocated an equitable approach, emphasising the words "just satisfaction". The court singled out damages claims in respect of maladministration, saying that in these cases damages awarded should be modest in order to prevent a drain on public resources. The court went on to note that the cost of the claim would most likely be

---

[46] [2003] EWCA Civ 1406.

disproportionate to the possible damages available and suggested that the permission procedure for such claims should be more stringent in order to avoid this situation.

*R (Greenfield)* v *Secretary of State for the Home Department*[47] provided further guidance, concentrating in particular on violations of Article 6. These were distinguished from other breaches of the HRA 1998 as a violation of Article 6 would not necessarily mean that the trial had reached a wrong decision or that the outcome would have been different if there had been no violation. The court noted that the European Court of Human Rights very often considers a finding of a violation of Article 6 sufficient for just satisfaction. The court would therefore be slow to award compensation and would only do so in cases where there was a clear causal connection between the violation and the loss suffered by the claimant. The court took the clear view that in considering damages awards under the HRA 1998, UK courts should be guided by Strasbourg precedent rather than domestic precedents or analogies as the purpose of the HRA 1998 was to give victims access to the same remedies as they could get in Strasbourg without the delay and expense, rather than to enable victims to claim more favourable remedies domestically.

### 13.9.2   Negligence

A public authority can be sued in negligence just as any individual can, and the same elements need to be shown (i.e. that there was a breach of a duty of care and that the breach caused damage to the claimant). In examining whether there is a duty of care, the *Caparo*[48] three-limbed test is used (foreseeability, proximity and whether it is fair, just and reasonable to impose a duty). In theory then there is little to distinguish a negligence action against a public authority from one between two private individuals. However, in practice there are important issues relating to the imposition of liability on public authorities including fears about creating a precedent leading to a flood of claims against public authorities, creating a defensive culture amongst officials which may impede their ability to carry out their duties effectively.

---

[47] [2005] UKHL 13.
[48] *Caparo Industries plc* v *Dickman* [1990] 2 AC 605.

The leading cases are *Barrett* v *Enfield LBC*[49] and *Phelps* v *Hillingdon LBC*.[50] It is clear that the courts will not become involved in matters that it regards as non-justiciable (primarily matters of policy which are best dealt with by the authority or officer whose power they are under). If the matter is one which is regarded as justiciable, there may be a further problem with finding a sufficient level of foreseeability and/or proximity between the authority and the claimant for there to be a duty of care as the duty of a public authority is to the public at large rather than to particular individuals.[51] There may, however, be a relationship of sufficient proximity if there is some prior interaction involving the authority and the individual concerned.[52]

Specific cases involving regulatory bodies analogous to the FSA confirm the problem of a lack of proximity. *Yuen Kun Yeu* v *A-G of Hong Kong*[53] and *Davis* v *Radcliffe*[54] both concerned financial services regulators who were being sued by investors/consumers who had suffered damage after depositing money with the companies under the regulation of these bodies. In both cases the courts found that there was not a sufficiently close and direct relationship between the regulatory body and the consumer for a duty of care to exist. The factors that led to these decisions included the fact that the duty of care alleged would have been owed to a wide and unascertained class of individuals – all deposit makers or potential deposit makers. Most importantly, however, the court discussed the delicate policy decisions that such regulators were faced with, so that it could not be said that they owed their duty primarily to any one group, but rather were under a duty to balance the competing interests of the consumer and the financial services industry. Lord Goff stated in *Davis* that "the very nature of the task, with its emphasis on the broader public interest, is one which militates strongly against the imposition of a duty of care . . . in favour of any particular section of the public." This is a broad statement

---

[49] [2001] 2 AC 550.
[50] [2001] 2 AC 619.
[51] For example, in *Capital and Counties plc* v *Hampshire CC* [1997] QB 1004 it was held that there was not sufficient proximity between the fire brigade and the individual owners of premises for a duty of care to exist.
[52] For example in *Swinney* v *Chief Constable of Northumbria* [1997] QB 464 the police had the individual informer's name brought to their attention as someone who needed protection and confidential treatment, thus creating a duty of care.
[53] [1988] AC 175.
[54] [1990] 1 WLR 821.

clearly intended to be of general application, emphasising the unwillingness of the courts to impose a duty of care on regulators where there is no prior relationship. Both of these cases were cited with approval by Lord Steyn in *Three Rivers DC v Bank of England (No. 3).*[55]

Although protection of consumers is a specific statutory objective of the FSA, this is unlikely to make the courts more willing to impose a duty of care, as protection of the public at large is a common function for many public authorities, as Lord Goff's comment in *Davis* shows.

The combination of the paragraph 19 Schedule 1 exemption and the unwillingness of the courts to impose a duty of care on regulators means in practice that a successful action for negligence against the FSA would be unlikely.

### 13.9.3   Breach of statutory duty

In a claim against a public authority or official for breach of statutory duty the court will examine the particular statute to ascertain whether it intended to give rise to a private law cause of action. The claim must fall within the ambit of the statute, so that the damage suffered should be of a type that the legislation was trying to prevent, and the claimant should fall within the category of people that the legislation was aimed at protecting or benefiting.

A claim for breach of statutory duty is less likely to be successful if there are alternative remedies. This is because the existence of alternative remedies makes it less likely that the statute intended to confer a cause of action in the courts.[56] Similarly if the statute is intended for the benefit of the public at large rather than for any one identifiable category of individuals, it seems less likely that it was intended for an individual to have a private law cause of action arising from that statute.[57]

---

[55] [2000] 3 All ER 1.

[56] For example, in *Richardson v Pitt-Stanley* [1995] QB 123 the Court of Appeal found no cause of action for breach of the statutory duty on employers to insure against employers liability, mainly because there were civil remedies and criminal penalties available to enforce the duty.

[57] A view endorsed by Lord Browne-Wilkinson in X v *Bedfordshire County Council* [1995] 2 AC 633.

If there is a cause of action the standard of liability will depend upon how the statutory duty is expressed. If it is an absolute duty then the court may impose strict liability, but this will not be appropriate if the duty is only to take reasonable care, employ reasonable endeavours or to do what is reasonably practicable.

### 13.9.4 Misfeasance in public office

This area of law has been re-examined and clarified by *Three Rivers DC* v *Bank of England (No. 3)*.[58]

There are two alternative limbs to the tort. The first is known as "targeted malice" – where public power is exercised with the specific intention of injuring a person. This is quite a narrow and extreme situation.

The second limb is wider as it covers the situation where a public officer performs an unlawful act or omission, which amounts to an abuse of his power, in bad faith. For this second limb it must be shown that the officer knew (although subjective recklessness is also sufficient) that the act was beyond his power (i.e. unlawful) and that it would probably cause the claimant injury. Carrying out the act without an honest belief that it was lawful would be sufficient to satisfy the bad faith requirement. However, inadvertent acts or omissions or oversights, even those amounting to serious negligence, will not be sufficient to satisfy the bad faith requirement. Misfeasance requires a deliberate abuse of power.[59]

## 13.10 Complaints Commissioner

### 13.10.1 Introduction

FSMA 2000 (paragraph 7, Schedule 1) requires the FSA to establish an arrangement for the investigation of complaints against the FSA. Accordingly, two Complaints Schemes were introduced with effect from 3 September 2001: the Main Scheme and the Transitional

---

[58] [2001] 2 All ER 513.
[59] *Ashley* v *Chief Constable of Sussex* [2006] EWCA Civ 1085.

Scheme. The Main Scheme deals with complaints about the way in which the FSA has carried out, or failed to carry out, its role under FSMA 2000.[60] An independent person (the "Complaints Commissioner") is responsible for the conduct of the investigation in accordance with the Complaints Scheme.

The Complaints Scheme provides that there may be two distinct stages for each complaint. In the first stage, the FSA itself will investigate any complaint that meets the requirements of the Complaints Scheme and take whatever action it thinks appropriate to resolve the matter. A complaint will normally only proceed to the second stage if the complainant is dissatisfied with the FSA's determination of his complaint or how it has been handled. This second stage consists of an investigation of the complaint by the Complaints Commissioner.

### 13.10.2  Role of the Complaints Commissioner

The Main Scheme provides a procedure for enquiring into complaints of maladministration by the FSA arising from the way in which it carried out its statutory functions.[61] Such complaints will generally be likely to include:

(a)    mistakes or lack of care;
(b)    unreasonable delay;
(c)    unprofessional behaviour;
(d)    bias; and
(e)    lack of integrity.[62]

---

[60] The Transitional Scheme deals with investigation of complaints about the FSA, and the self-regulating organisation under pre FSMA 2000 legislation.

[61] The Complaints Commissioner will not investigate complaints made by customers of regulated firms (in this instance a complaint should be directed to the firm itself), complaints made about the actions of the Financial Ombudsman Service and the Financial Services Compensation Scheme (both of these organisations have their own independent assessors to deal with this), complaints made about the way in which a complaint about a firm regulated by one of the former self-regulating organisations was handled (i.e. the PIA Ombudsman Bureau, the Investment Management Regulatory Organisation ("IMRO") or the Securities and Futures Authority ("SFA") Complaints Bureau – any complaints should be directed to the Financial Ombudsman Service), complaints made about the FSA's rule making, issuing of statements of principle and codes of practice, complaints regarding the FSA's employment relationships and any commercial or contractual disputes involving the FSA.

[62] The Main Scheme rules are contained in the Redress Section of the FSA Handbook.

In nearly all the circumstances, the Complaints Commissioner will normally expect a complainant to give the FSA an opportunity to deal with the complaint at first instance. When the FSA decides not to investigate a complaint, it must inform both the complainant and the Complaints Commissioner and provide reasons for their decision not to investigate. The Complaints Commissioner will then decide whether to investigate the complaint and there will be no need for the complainant to contact the Complaints Commissioner directly.

Alternatively, if an individual, company or organisation is dissatisfied with the time taken by the FSA to investigate a complaint (i.e. if the complaint is not handled within eight weeks of receipt by the FSA), the outcome of the FSA's internal investigation or the way in which it has been handled, a complaint may also be made directly to the Complaints Commissioner. The Complaints Commissioner can consider complaints from anyone directly affected by the way in which the FSA has carried out its function and will include private individuals, regulated firms, employees of regulated firms, listed companies and those authorised to deal with a complaint on someone's behalf (e.g. lawyers).

### 13.10.3 Procedure

Any complaint may be made in writing to the Complaints Commissioner and should be acknowledged within five working days of receipt. Within the next 10 working days, the Commissioner will consider whether the complaint is one which she is able to investigate and if so, the complainant will be informed and provided with a timetable for the completion of the investigation. If the Complaints Commissioner cannot undertake an investigation into the complaint he or she must provide written reasons for this decision.

Any subsequent investigation into the complaint will involve obtaining all relevant paperwork and information from the FSA and any other party involved, including the complainant. The Complaints Commissioner may choose to interview individuals where he or she feels that it would be helpful to do so. Following the completion of the investigation, the Complaints Commissioner will provide a preliminary report setting out his or her provisional findings supported by reasons and, where appropriate, the steps he or she would recommend the FSA take to remedy the situation. This may include the payment of compensation to the complainant. The Complaints Commissioner may also decide to publish all or part of his or her final report and at this stage the Complaints Commissioner should notify both the FSA and the complainant of his or her intention to do so and the reasons for that decision.

The complainant, the FSA and any other individual referred to in the report will be given an opportunity to comment both on the preliminary report and the decision to have it published. The deadline for comments will be decided by the Complaints Commissioner. The report will then be finalised and sent to both parties.

Where the Complaints Commissioner has upheld a complaint and made a recommendation to the FSA, the FSA will consider whether to accept the recommendations and will inform both the complainant and the Complaints Commissioner of their decision to do so. Any reasons for the decision reached by the FSA should be provided. Finally, the Complaints Commissioner will consider whether the response from the FSA, or any part of it, should be published. Again, the Complaints Commissioner should provide any reasons for a decision to publish the response to both parties.

There has been an increase in the workload of the Complaints Commissioner, with 126 new complaints and enquiries received during 2005/06. A large proportion of these have related to the FSA's supervision and enforcement functions.

Where the Complaints Commissioner upholds a complaint the recommendations made include:

(a)   an apology to the complainant;
(b)   changes to procedures; and
(c)   an ex-gratia payment by the FSA to the complainant.

The vast majority of those recommendations are accepted by the FSA, illustrating the effectiveness of the role of the Commissioner.

### 13.10.4   *Timing and costs*

The Complaints Commissioner will aim to complete the investigation of a complaint within 20 working days of confirming that the complaint is one he or she is able to investigate and the majority of cases are dealt with within this timescale. However, the overall time taken to complete the investigation will depend on the nature of the complaint and the extent of the enquiries the Complaints Commissioner has to make.

Any complaint made to the FSA should be made within 12 months from the date on which the complainant first became aware of the circumstances giving rise to a complaint. If a complaint is made any later than this, both the FSA and the Complaints Commissioner will only investigate the complaint if there are reasonable grounds for the delay.

Any complaint made to the Complaints Commissioner is free, but where a complainant chooses to employ professional help this cost will not be met by the Complaints Commissioner even if the complaint is valid.

# Chapter 14

# Interface with Other Investigations and Proceedings

**Angela Hayes**
Partner
Lawrence Graham LLP

## 14.1 Introduction

Action by the Financial Services Authority ("FSA") is often not the only front on which a firm or individual must defend itself. Often, at the same time that firms are facing an FSA investigation, they have to deal with parallel investigations and proceedings, or threatened proceedings, arising from the same facts and circumstances.

A firm with activities and a presence outside the UK may have attracted the attention of overseas financial services regulators or criminal authorities, for example in market abuse cases.[1] Fraud and money laundering investigations are also often multi-jurisdictional. Within the UK, concurrent investigations by other regulatory or prosecuting bodies may have to be dealt with, for example, where there has been fraud there may be investigations by the police or the Serious Fraud Office ("SFO"). Individuals involved may face disciplinary proceedings before the FSA and also before a relevant professional body, such as the regulators of the accounting and actuarial professions.[2] There may also be civil proceedings (or the threat of

---

[1] This may become increasingly common with the implementation of the Market Abuse Directive in the EU.

[2] For example, in two notable recent public-interest cases, Equitable Life and Independent Insurance, certain in-house individuals that are qualified accountants have been under investigation by the accountants' Joint Disciplinary Scheme ("JDS"). The JDS is now in run-off phase in respect of its existing caseload. It is being replaced by the new Accountancy Investigation and Discipline Board under the Financial Reporting Council which is already dealing with new cases. Where the FSA is investigating breaches of the Listing Rules in relation to the publication of financial information, Finance Directors, Audit Committees and other senior in-house accountants also often come under scrutiny.

proceedings) by aggrieved investors or counterparties who have suffered a loss that they are looking to the firm to compensate. Individual directors can also be the target of investor action. A firm may also have to respond to customer complaints put to the Financial Ombudsman Service ("FOS").

Therefore, firms and individuals must sometimes be prepared to handle multiple concurrent investigations and proceedings both in terms of manpower and strategically. This can be particularly taxing for the individuals involved, where legal representation separate from that of their employing authorised firm may be required. Individuals can struggle to fund this if the authorised firm is unwilling or unable to provide support and if Director's and Officer's liability insurance is unavailable or does not provide for interim payment of legal costs.[3] Firms and individuals may find themselves involved in satellite proceedings with insurers to enforce insurance cover.

This chapter does not seek to address the powers of the various other regulators and prosecuting agencies that may be involved, but simply to provide some guidance about the practical issues that can arise in the following main areas:

(a) FSA powers to share information and cooperate with other regulators and bodies;
(b) responding to multiple investigations and proceedings;
(c) what the impact of an FSA disciplinary/enforcement finding or a Tribunal finding will be on parallel proceedings, such as criminal proceedings or third-party civil claims against an authorised firm;
(d) the respective roles of the FSA and the Financial Ombudsman Service ("FOS") and "wider implications" cases.

---

[3] The difficulties for directors and officers in meeting defence costs should be alleviated in part by reforms to Section 310 Companies Act 1985 introduced by the Companies (Audit, Investigations and Community Enterprise) Act 2004 that came into force on 6 April 2005.

## 14.2    FSA powers to share information and cooperate with other regulators and bodies

### 14.2.1    *The FSA's ability to pass on information*

The FSA has a specific duty to cooperate, as it considers appropriate, with other bodies in the UK and abroad that have functions similar to the FSA, or in relation to the prevention or detection of financial crime (Section 354, Financial Services and Markets Act 2000 ("FSMA 2000")). Cooperation may include the FSA passing on information that it has gathered in the course of carrying out its regulatory functions.[4] The FSA has made it very clear that it regards such cooperation between regulatory bodies as a matter of critical importance, particularly in international efforts to combat market abuse, fraud and financial crime. A prime example of this approach is the FSA's active role in the International Organisation of Securities Commissions ("IOSCO"). In 2002, IOSCO adopted a Multilateral Memorandum of Understanding, the first global information-sharing arrangement between securities regulators, as a benchmark for international cooperation. In February 2005, IOSCO announced a new initiative giving multilateral cooperation the highest importance. This initiative was spurred by recent financial scandals where lack of real cooperation in some jurisdictions had a material adverse impact.

However, for the FSA there is a tension between its duty and wish to cooperate and other provisions of FSMA 2000 that on the face of it greatly restrict the FSA's ability to share confidential information that it has obtained with others. Section 348 FSMA 2000 provides that the FSA cannot disclose confidential information without the consent of the person from whom the information was obtained and, if different, of the person to whom it relates. In this context, "confidential information", put broadly, is information that relates to the business or affairs of any person and was received by the FSA for the purposes of, or in the discharge of, any of its functions.[5] However, the FSA is

---

[4] Insofar as the FSA is not restricted from disclosing the information.
[5] Under Section 348(2) FSMA 2000, confidential information is defined as:

> "information which (a) relates to the business or other affairs of any person; (b) was received by the primary recipient for the purposes of or in the discharge of any function

released from this restriction in respect of information covered by Section 349 FSMA 2000.

Section 349 provides that the FSA is permitted to disclose confidential information if that disclosure is made for the purpose of facilitating the carrying out of a public function and is permitted by regulations made by the Treasury. The relevant regulations have come to be known as the "Gateways Regulations".[6] They permit the FSA to disclose confidential information to numerous public bodies and officials both in the UK and abroad to assist them in discharging public functions. However, the pattern of permissive gateways under the Gateways Regulations is complex because a distinction is drawn between confidential information that the FSA receives in carrying out functions as a competent authority for the purposes of the EU single-market directives ("single-market directive information") and the Markets in Financial Instruments Directive, and information that the FSA receives during the course of its functions outside the ambit of those directives. This is because the directives impose their own specific restrictions, that in turn must be implemented in UK legislation, on the disclosure and use of confidential information.[7]

The FSA (and any person who has obtained confidential information from the FSA, known as "secondary recipients") can disclose any confidential information for the purposes of any criminal investigation or proceedings whatever, whether in the UK or elsewhere and for the purposes of facilitating a determination whether any criminal investigation or proceedings should be initiated (or ended). This is not limited to criminal proceedings where the FSA is prosecutor or has a direct interest. Similarly the FSA can disclose confidential information

---

of the Authority, the competent authority for the purposes of Part VI or the Secretary of State under any provision made by or under this Act; and (c) is not prevented from being confidential information by subsection (4)".

Section 348(4) provides that information is not confidential information if (a) it has been made available to the public by virtue of having been disclosed in any circumstances in which, or for any purposes for which disclosure is not precluded by this section; or (b) it is in the form of a summary or collection of information so framed that it is not possible to ascertain from it information relating to any particular person.

[6] Financial Services and Markets Act 2000 (Disclosure of Confidential Information) Regulations 2001 (SI 2001/2188).

[7] Amendments to the Gateways Regulations to implement changes arising from the Markets in Financial Instruments Directive are made by SI 2006/3413.

for the purposes of certain civil proceedings, including proceedings to which the FSA is, or is proposed to be, a party, and proceedings under specified statutes including the Company Directors Disqualification Act 1986 and the Insolvency Act 1986.[8]

Disclosure of directive information is permitted to be made to a long list of bodies and officials set out in Schedule 1 to the Gateways Regulations for the purposes of specified functions set out there. The list includes:

(a)    central banks and monetary authorities;
(b)    financial services regulators both within and outside the EEA;
(c)    investment exchanges and clearing houses;
(d)    the Department of Trade and Industry;
(e)    the Takeover Panel;
(f)    the Office of Fair Trading;
(g)    the Competition Commission;
(h)    the Financial Services Compensation Scheme ("FSCS") manager;
(i)    designated professional bodies;
(j)    the Pensions Regulator (previously known as the Occupational Pensions Regulatory Authority ("OPRA"));
(k)    the Charity Commissioners;
(l)    inspectors, investigators, officials, auditors and actuaries authorised to act under FSMA 2000 and under various statutes related to financial services and the Companies Acts.

Disclosure of other confidential information can be made for additional specified purposes and to additional bodies, including to the Pensions Ombudsman and the Financial Ombudsman Service.

### 14.2.2   *Disclosure to the FSA by other bodies*

The FSA makes considerable use of information passed to it by other regulators and public bodies. For example, overseas regulators pass a great deal of information to it about market misconduct. In the UK FOS is a valuable source of information about potential breaches of FSA rules. In passing on information to the FSA the regulator/body

---

[8] Full details of the legislation in respect of which the FSA can disclose information for use in proceedings are set out at Regulation 5(5) of the Gateways Regulations.

may have the power to impose specific limitations on the use that the FSA can make of the information. In the case of information passed to the FSA by the Inland Revenue, the use restrictions are set out in FSMA 2000 itself (Section 350).

The extent of the ability of the Serious Fraud Office ("SFO") to pass on information to other agencies has been the subject of recent litigation arising from the SFO's investigation into alleged price fixing in the generic pharmaceuticals industry. The SFO's investigation has been attacked as a tactical use of the SFO's compulsory powers to gather information for use in parallel civil proceedings brought by the Department of Health. However, it is clear that the SFO does prima facie have power under the Criminal Justice Act 1987 (Section 3) to pass on information gathered to any government department or other authority or body discharging functions on behalf of the Crown. There are also explicit gateways under the Criminal Justice Act 1987 for the SFO to pass information to FSA inspectors appointed under FSMA 2000. In *R (Kent Pharmaceuticals Limited) v Director of the Serious Fraud Office* it was held that, to enable any objections to be raised, generally the owner of the documents should be informed before his confidential material is passed on.

### 14.2.3   Cooperation within the UK

The ability to share information with other bodies within the UK is a key aspect of cooperation. This has been dealt with at 14.2.1 above. The other key issue that the FSA has recognised is the need to divide up responsibility where there are a number of prosecuting or investigating agencies within the UK that have overlapping remits. The FSA sought to address this in relation to the SFO, the DTI and the Crown Prosecution Service in agreeing and publishing guidelines on the investigation of cases of interest or concern to the FSA and other prosecuting and investigating agencies.[9]

---

[9] ENF 2 Ann 1G. At the time of writing, the FSA is consulting on replacing its Enforcement and Decision Making Manuals (ENF and DEC) with a more streamlined Decision Procedure and Penalties Manual (DEPP) backed up by a new regulatory guide, the Enforcement Guide (EG). Draft consultation text, that is subject to change, has been published in CP 07/02. In the rest of this chapter references to ENF will be followed by the equivalent reference in draft DEPP or EG. In the case of this footnote the reference is EG Annex 2.

The purpose of the guidelines is to set out broad principles which the agencies involved agree should be applied by them:

(a)   to assist in deciding which agency should investigate in a partic-ular case where there is overlapping remit;
(b)   to facilitate cooperation where more than one agency is investi-gating;
(c)   to prevent undue duplication of effort wherever possible by reason of the involvement of more than one agency; and
(d)   to prevent the subjects of proceedings being treated unfairly by reason of the unwarranted involvement of more than one agency.

The aim is that the agencies will endeavour to ensure that only the agency or agencies with the most appropriate functions and powers will commence particular investigations. However, the view is expressed in the guidelines that in certain cases "concurrent investi-gations may be the most quick, effective and efficient way for some cases to be dealt with".

The guidelines set out a list of indicative factors that would tend towards action being taken by the FSA and a further list of indicative factors that would tend towards action being taken by one of the other agencies. For example, it is a factor tending towards action by the FSA if any possible relevant criminal offences are technical or in a grey area, whereas regulatory contraventions are clearly indicated. Similarly where the balance of public interest is in achieving repara-tion for victims and prosecution is likely to damage the prospects of this, this will weigh in favour of the FSA taking action. On the other hand, where criminal proceedings may be indicated for which the FSA is not the statutory prosecutor or where serious or complex fraud is the predominant issue, this will tend towards action being led by an agency other than the FSA.

It is considered to be best practice for the agencies involved or inter-ested in an investigation to continue to liaise during the course of an investigation so that the position of the respective agencies can be kept under review, particularly where there are material develop-ments in an investigation that might cause other agencies to recon-sider the purpose or scope of their own investigation. This is also appropriate because it is recognised that where concurrent investigations are taking place, action by one agency can prejudice the investigation or subsequent proceedings brought by another agency. Notwithstanding this, the SFO has shown itself unwilling to request the FSA to hold off interviewing individuals who could become co-defendants in criminal prosecutions in respect of serious fraud where the SFO is conducting a parallel investigation, even though the ultimate impact (as those individuals are likely to be provided with transcripts of the interviews of their potential co-defendants if FSA disciplinary action proceeds) could well be an application for a subsequent criminal trial to be split, leading to significant additional expense that might not otherwise have been necessary. This issue, arising from the *Wickes* case,[10] is discussed in more detail at 14.3.1.2 below.

According to the guidelines, the agencies recognise that in making a decision whether to commence proceedings it is relevant for them to consider whether commencement of proceedings might prejudice ongoing or potential investigations or proceedings brought by other agencies and whether, in the light of any proceedings being brought by another party, it is appropriate to commence separate proceedings against the person under investigation. Section 14.3 below discusses the unfortunate fact that, from the perspective of a defendant or respondent, there is likely to be little that can be done to prevent multiple investigations and proceedings going ahead concurrently if the FSA and the other agencies involved decide that is appropriate.

### 14.2.4   Cooperation with overseas regulators

*14.2.4.1   Power to assist overseas regulators*
This topic was touched upon in Chapter 8 above in the context of criminal investigations.

The FSA has power under Section 169 FSMA 2000, at the request of an overseas regulator, to exercise its general compulsory power to

---

[10] For a discussion of the two criminal trials in which former directors of Wickes Plc were prosecuted, and the implications of the trial judge's ruling that a defendant's statement to the SFO under Section 2 Criminal Justice Act 1987 can be put in evidence by a co-defendant with the likely result of the trial being severed, *see* for example 'Compulsory Questions' by Nigel Hood in *New Law Journal*, 25 July 2003.

require information from authorised firms and those connected with them (Section 165) or to appoint investigators.[11] Where the overseas regulator making the request is a competent authority purporting to act in pursuance of a Community obligation[12] the FSA is obliged to consider whether the exercise of its powers is "necessary" to comply with the Community obligation.

If the request comes from a regulator outside the EU, or where the FSA decides that the exercise of its power is not necessary to comply with a Community obligation, the FSA can make its cooperation conditional upon the overseas regulator making a contribution towards the FSA's costs. The FSA will first consider whether it is able to assist without using formal powers, for example by requesting that information to be supplied voluntarily. Where that is not possible, the FSA will take into account the following factors:

(a) whether in the country or territory of the overseas regulator concerned, corresponding assistance would be given to a UK regulatory authority;

(b) whether the case concerns the breach of a law, or other requirement, which has no close parallel in the UK or involves the assertion of a jurisdiction not recognised by the UK;

(c) the seriousness of the case and its importance to persons in the UK (the FSA may give particular weight to this factor);[13]

(d) whether it is otherwise appropriate in the public interest to give the assistance sought.[14]

### 14.2.4.2 *Conduct of interviews in support of an overseas regulator*
The FSA-appointed investigator can permit a representative of the overseas regulator to attend and take part in any interview conducted for the purposes of the investigation, if the FSA so directs. The FSA is

---

[11] Investigators so appointed will have the same powers as an investigator appointed as a result of Section 168(1) FSMA 2000, which means that not only do they have the power to require the person who is the subject of the investigation to attend and answer questions and provide information and documents, but also a person who is neither the subject of the investigation nor connected with the person under investigation. This can be done provided the investigator is satisfied that the requirement is "necessary or expedient" for the purposes of the investigation.

[12] An obligation imposed by EU legislation.

[13] ENF 2.8.7G; EG 5.15.

[14] Section 169(4) FSMA 2000.

only entitled to give such a direction if it is satisfied that any information obtained by the overseas regulator as a result of the interview would be subject to safeguards equivalent to those contained in Part XXIII FSMA 2000, in particular the restrictions on the disclosure and use of confidential information.

The FSA's statement of policy on this is set out in an annex to Chapter 2 of the FSA's Enforcement Manual.[15]

The FSA investigator determines the venue and timing of the interview, of which the interviewee will be notified in advance in writing. It is the FSA investigator who will generally decide which documents or other information may be put to the interviewee and whether it is appropriate for the interviewee to have sight of those documents before the interview takes place. The representative of the overseas regulator will be obliged to give the FSA proper opportunity to inspect any documents that the overseas regulator wishes to ask questions about. If the interviewee wishes to be represented or accompanied by a person from or familiar with the overseas regulator's jurisdiction, then those wishes should be accommodated if practicable, but the FSA reserves the right to proceed with the interview if it is not possible to find such a person within a reasonable time or for them to attend at a suitable venue.

Although the FSA's statement of policy emphasises that it is the FSA that will have control of and lead the interview process, it is also apparent that the representative of the overseas regulator will in practice play a very significant role in interviews. This is not surprising as the representative is likely to be better briefed on the detail of the matters under investigation and the local regulatory requirements alleged to have been breached. According to the FSA's policy, the FSA's investigator will have the conduct of the interview under the control of the FSA. The FSA may permit the overseas regulator representative to assist in the preparation of the interview and to attend and ask questions of the interviewee. The FSA investigator should still retain control of the interview throughout. This will include explaining the procedure of the interview, giving appropriate warnings

---

[15] DEPP Chapter 7 and EG 5(f).

(including of the possible consequences of refusing to answer questions and the uses to which any answers that are given can and cannot be put) and asking the preliminary questions. The FSA investigator will determine the length of the interview and when there should be any breaks during the course of it and will have the responsibility for making a record of the interview. As is usual for the FSA, all compulsory interviews will be tape recorded and although the FSA will not provide the overseas regulator with transcripts of tapes of interviews, unless specifically agreed to, copies of the tapes will normally be provided.

The FSA investigator has a right to intervene at any stage during questioning by the representative of an overseas regulator. It is the FSA investigator who has the power, if he considers it appropriate, to suspend or terminate the interview or to ask the overseas representative to leave. In doing so the investigator will have to bear in mind the terms of the specific FSA direction including any agreement that the FSA has made with the overseas regulator as to the conduct of the interview.

The FSA will pursue a policy on publicity similar to the policy that relates to its own investigations.

## 14.3 Managing responses to multiple investigations and proceedings

### 14.3.1 Parallel criminal proceedings

#### 14.3.1.1 The problem
One of the most challenging situations that individuals in the financial services sector, and firms with which they are associated, may face is where a criminal investigation has been launched by the police or by the SFO in circumstances where the firm and/or individuals within it are also the subject of an FSA investigation. For example, as mentioned in 14.2.3 above, where the SFO is investigating the circumstances of a serious fraud in which approved persons within an authorised firm are suspected of involvement, this does not prevent the FSA commencing its own investigation into whether those individuals are fit and proper persons to be involved in regulated activities.

Individuals who are the subject of the criminal investigation will often have been suspended or dismissed from the authorised firm involved. Nevertheless, the firm may need the continued cooperation of the individuals involved to enable it to respond fully to the regulatory investigation.

Information provided to the FSA by an individual or firm in the course of an FSA investigation may, whether through that investigation process or subsequent disciplinary proceedings, or through cooperation of the FSA with the criminal investigators, become disclosed to the criminal prosecutor and directly or indirectly to potential co-defendants. The potential impact of such disclosure on a subsequent criminal trial (and perhaps the outcome for the individual concerned) is shown particularly starkly where an individual may have exercised his right not to answer questions in an interview under caution by criminal investigators but the FSA's own interview of the individual is conducted using the FSA's compulsory powers. If transcripts of FSA interviews are requested by the SFO or provided by the FSA to a potential co-defendant (where that potential co-defendant is also the subject of FSA disciplinary proceedings) then the individual's defence to the criminal offence has become disclosed to the prosecutor and co-defendants at a time when that could not have been required in the criminal process. It could give potential prosecution witnesses and potential co-defendants (who may be running "cut-throat defences") an opportunity to fabricate evidence tailored to meet the defence disclosed. It cuts across the privilege against self-incrimination to which an individual is entitled as against the prosecutor in the criminal process. Early in the proceedings, it could disclose to the prosecution where they need to strengthen their case to meet the matters raised in defence.

Although a transcript of interview obtained by the FSA using compulsory powers cannot be relied upon by a prosecutor in a subsequent criminal trial as evidence against the interviewee,[16] it can be put in evidence by the prosecutor against co-defendants or by co-defendants in support of their defence. This means that the contents of the transcript will still be before the jury, leading to prejudice

---

[16] Unless the interviewee himself puts that transcript in evidence because he wishes to rely upon it.

unless a successful application for a split criminal trial can be made (*see* the discussion of *Wickes* at 14.3.1.2 below).

Publicity given to the result of a disciplinary hearing might also have an influence on a jury in a criminal trial.

### 14.3.1.2   *Can a regulatory investigation or proceedings be stayed?*

As has been made clear above, the fact that there is an existing criminal investigation does not prevent the FSA, or any other regulator, from investigating the same subject matter and launching its own regulatory proceedings. A firm or individual in this situation could ask the FSA to agree to stay proceedings if there are grounds to suggest that the defence in criminal proceedings could be prejudiced. If the FSA refuses, that refusal could be the subject of a judicial review application. However, where such applications to stay disciplinary proceedings pending criminal proceedings have been made in the past, the court has made clear that, whilst it does have jurisdiction to intervene to prevent a serious injustice occurring:

> "it will only do so in very clear cases in which the applicant can show that there is a real danger and not merely a notional danger that there will be a miscarriage of justice in the criminal proceedings if the court did not intervene".[17]

It will be difficult to persuade a court that this hurdle has been overcome.

The court's decision in *R v Solicitors Disciplinary Tribunal ex parte Gallagher*[18] is equally relevant to FSA disciplinary proceedings (or indeed proceedings by other regulatory bodies). In that case a solicitor faced disciplinary proceedings before the Solicitors Disciplinary Tribunal and there was also an ongoing criminal investigation which resulted in the solicitor being charged with offences involving dishonesty arising from the same subject matter. The solicitor applied for a judicial review of the Tribunal's decision to continue with disciplinary proceedings when the criminal investigation was ongoing. The court reviewing the decision held that each case depended upon

---

[17] *R v BBC ex parte Lavelle* [1983] 1 All ER 241.
[18] 30 September 1991 unreported.

its own facts and if it appeared that to allow proceedings to go forward would "muddy the waters of justice", then it would be appropriate to adjourn the disciplinary proceedings or to take some other course to avoid that result.

The court said that an example of where a tribunal might well consider that to proceed would muddy the waters would be a situation where the Tribunal was about to make a finding and order a day or two before criminal proceedings began. In those circumstances it might be appropriate to reserve judgment pending the hearing of the criminal proceedings. In the *Gallagher* case the criminal trial was not due to be heard for over a year, so arguments by Gallagher that the proceedings might reveal his defence to a co-defendant and to the prosecution, and that material published in the press might prejudice a jury, were considered by the court to be too remote to justify a stay. They were matters that could be dealt with by the judge at the criminal trial instead. There was also to be weighed against a stay the interests of co-defendants in the disciplinary proceedings and a public interest that complaints against solicitors should be disposed of quickly. It is easy to see that similar arguments would weigh in any application to stay FSA disciplinary proceedings pending a criminal trial.[19] However, leaving matters for the trial judge in this way is an approach that may lead to the collapse or disruption of a subsequent criminal prosecution with the consequential waste of taxpayers' money.

Since *Gallagher*, there has been the incident of the *Wickes* trial mentioned above. In *Wickes*, the trial judge ordered that a criminal trial had to be split (meaning that certain co-defendants would have to have a separate trial before a different jury) where evidence obtained under compulsory powers from one co-defendant (in this case an interview of Mr Rosenthal by the SFO using its compulsory powers under Section 2 of the Criminal Justice Act 1987) was sought to be used in the criminal trial by another party and so would be before the jury. A co-defendant (Carson) wished to rely in his defence and in cross-examination on an extract of the transcript of Rosenthal's compulsory interview. When the Judge agreed that this evidence

---

[19] The authorities discussed at 14.3.2 below in relation to attempts to stay parallel civil proceedings are also relevant in addressing the court's likely attitude.

could be admitted, Rosenthal applied to be tried by a different jury as otherwise he would be obliged to explain in the witness box the answers he had given under compulsion. Section 2 of the Criminal Justice Act 1987, like the compulsory powers under FSMA 2000, gives the interviewee the protection that answers obtained under compulsion will not be used as prosecution evidence against him in a criminal trial. The Judge agreed that in the circumstances the trial of Rosenthal would have to be severed. Similar principles would apply if a co-defendant attempted to rely on the contents of another co-defendant's compulsory FSA interview as evidence against that other co-defendant.

One would expect that the SFO would want to avoid a *Wickes* situation arising in the future. However, recent attempts to persuade the FSA and the SFO that compulsory interviews by the FSA should not proceed against a number of individuals under FSA investigation who are the target of an SFO investigation, and so likely co-defendants in a subsequent criminal trial, have failed. This was the case even though disclosure by the FSA at warning notice stage would be likely to furnish those co-defendants with material rendering a split trial appropriate, as in *Wickes*.[20]

### 14.3.1.3 *Refusal to answer questions*
The discussion above shows that FSA disciplinary proceedings are likely to continue in parallel to a criminal investigation. The remnant of protection against self-incrimination available to an individual questioned under compulsory powers in an FSA investigation is the restriction on the use to which the transcript can be put, namely that it cannot be used as evidence in a prosecution against that individual unless the individual concerned himself chooses to bring the transcript into play as evidence in criminal proceedings. However, the limitations on that protection, in that the transcript can still come before the court deployed against a co-defendant, have been discussed above.

---

[20] Though the SFO has shown itself willing to comment that publication of an FSA final notice against individuals could be prejudicial to a future criminal trial and unfair to the defendants, and in particular circumstances the FSA's Regulatory Decisions Committee has been persuaded to hold off reaching a decision that would need to be published in such circumstances.

Not infrequently, individuals in this situation ask what would happen if an individual employed, or formerly employed, by an authorised firm simply refused to answer the FSA's questions put under its compulsory powers where the circumstances concerned amounted to a criminal offence.

A similar conclusion is likely to be reached to that in *R v Institute of Chartered Accountants in England & Wales ex parte Taher Nawaz.*[21] Mr Nawaz refused to provide information, relating to his audit activities, to the Institute's Investigating Committee in breach of Institute rules requiring him to do so. He had been practising as an auditor without being registered as such with the Institute, which was a criminal offence under the Companies Act 1985. The Investigating Committee declared him guilty of failing to respond properly to an information requirement. Mr Nawaz applied for judicial review of this decision. The Court of Appeal held that by virtue of his contract of membership with the Institute, he accepted the Institute's rules, including the duty to provide information, and so waived reliance on any privilege against self-incrimination. It was held that it was in the public interest to uphold the Institute's power to require information to be provided under compulsion. The FSA's position in face of such a challenge will be even stronger because its powers are derived from statute, not merely a membership contract. A similar challenge to the FSA, subject to the particular facts of the case, would be likely to result in a similar conclusion.

The FSA has shown its willingness to force uncooperative individuals to attend interview (*see* discussion of contempt of court in Chapter 7 and police assistance in arrests in Chapter 8). It can be seen, therefore, that a refusal to answer FSA questions where the FSA acts under its compulsory powers is a high-risk strategy, but it is not to be discounted when an individual truly considers that his answers would be incriminating. It is an area in which the boundaries of protection of rights to a fair trial under the Human Rights Act 1998 remain to be tested fully.

---

[21] [1997] 16 PNLR 433.

### 14.3.2 *Parallel civil or regulatory proceedings*

*14.3.2.1 Can regulatory proceedings be stayed pending a civil case?*
There have been attempts to stay regulatory proceedings to enable a
defendant to concentrate on a civil case.

One of the most recent decisions illustrating the likely approach of the
court to an application to stay proceedings by the FSA, to enable civil
proceedings to be dealt with first, is *R (on the application of Nicholas
Land) v Executive Counsel of the Joint Disciplinary Scheme.*[22] This was
Ernst & Young's attempt to have an investigation by the Accountants
Joint Disciplinary Scheme ("JDS") into their audit of Equitable Life
stayed pending the civil proceedings brought against them by
Equitable Life in the English court, further proceedings in Greece and
the non-statutory Penrose Inquiry. The court adopted the summary of
the relevant general principles set out by Mr Justice Dyson in a previous ruling in *Hipps,*[23] an earlier case in which a stay of JDS proceedings
had been sought. Mr Justice Dyson was summarising previous judgments of the court that have set the court's approach, in particular the
leading cases of *Brindle* and *Smith.*[24] The principles are as follows:

(a)   the court considers afresh whether a stay should be granted,
      rather than reviewing the reasonableness of the regulator's deci-
      sion to pursue its regulatory investigation;
(b)   the jurisdiction to stay one of two concurrent sets of proceedings
      must be exercised sparingly and with great care;
(c)   unless the party seeking the stay can show that if a stay is
      refused there is a real risk of serious prejudice which may lead
      to injustice in one or both of the proceedings, a stay must be
      refused;
(d)   if the court is satisfied that, absent a stay, there is a real risk of
      such prejudice then the court has to balance that risk against the
      countervailing considerations. Those considerations will almost
      always include the strong public interest in seeing that the disci-
      plinary process is not impeded;

---

[22] Administrative Court, [2002] NLJR 1617.
[23] *R v Executive Council of the JDS, Ex-parte Hipps* [1996] New Law Transcript 296069202.
[24] *R v Institute of Chartered Accountants of England and Wales, ex parte Brindle* [1994] BCC 297; *R
v Chance, ex parte Smith* [1995] BCC 1095.

(e)     in a case where the balancing exercise is carried out, the court will give great weight to the view of the person or body responsible for the decision as to the factors militating against the stay and the weight to be given to them, but the court is the ultimate arbiter for what is fair;

(f)     each case turns on its own facts. Accordingly, only limited assistance can be derived when comparing the facts of a particular case with those of other cases where a stay was granted (as in *ex parte Brindle*) or where a stay was refused (as in *ex parte Smith*).

The main lines of argument run on behalf of Ernst & Young were:

(a)     that the continuation of the JDS inquiry would delay, impede and prejudice the claimants in their defence in the Commercial Court proceedings and of the inquiry itself;

(b)     it was argued that Equitable Life could gain substantial and unfair advantage in the Commercial Court proceedings from the generation of documents in the inquiry;

(c)     the personal demands of the JDS inquiry on individuals concerned (one had suffered recent personal tragedies); and

(d)     the risk of a decision by a JDS Disciplinary Tribunal influencing a Commercial Court Judge.

The Judge considered that the similarity of subject matter of the Commercial Court litigation, the Penrose Inquiry and the JDS inquiry reduced the burden added by the JDS inquiry. The Judge clearly considered that Ernst & Young, as a very large firm, was able to devote considerable resources to dealing with litigation and that the court's view might well have been different if the individuals concerned did not have that support. Considerable weight was also given to the views of the JDS Executive Counsel, in particular as to estimates of the likely requirements the JDS would put upon the audit partners involved and the time that would be needed to deal with them. The court was also unwilling to speculate as to the likely progress of the civil proceedings or the Penrose Inquiry. At the time of this judgment, a summary judgment application by Ernst & Young in the High Court proceedings was pending which, if successful, could have removed or significantly reduced Ernst & Young's involvement in the civil proceedings.

The Judge did not see any substance in an argument that concurrent proceedings raised a risk of inconsistent decisions. The Judge considered that this risk existed even if civil and disciplinary proceedings are sequential because the disciplinary tribunal is not bound by a decision of the civil court on issues of fact and vice versa. There was also thought to be no substance in a suggestion that a decision of the JDS Disciplinary Tribunal might influence a Commercial Court Judge, there being no justification for any suggestion that a Commercial Court Judge would decide the claims before him otherwise than on the evidence before him. The stay application was declined. However, the Judge stressed that a decision made at that particular point in time to refuse a stay was not final and that changing circumstances might later make a stay necessary when formerly it was not.

### 14.3.3    Practicalities

Chapter 4, in discussing internal investigations that a firm should undertake when it is faced with a regulatory problem, summarises the practical issues that a firm needs to address in preparing to deal with FSA investigations. These include gathering and preserving evidence, document handling and storage, the approach to retaining legal privilege in documents and the need to minimise the risk that new, potentially unhelpful, material might be generated by a firm in the course of dealing with the investigation process.

Where a firm faces multiple concurrent investigations or proceedings, those concerns and issues can also be multiplied. It will be vital that very clear records are kept of information and documents that have been supplied to different investigating agencies conducting concurrent investigations. Where there are differences in the information and documents that may have been supplied to different agencies, for example in response to compulsory requests, there must be a clear and legally privileged record of why the differences in disclosure have arisen and the judgments that have been made by individuals in the firm managing the responses and the lawyers. This is important to avoid mistakes being made at a later date.

Great care should be taken to ensure that, as far as possible, a consistent message is given in responding to multiple investigations on particular issues of fact. This can be difficult if individuals have to undertake multiple separate interviews by different regulators or agencies (who will possibly be focusing on slightly different issues) and also prepare witness statements in civil proceedings. Although a court or regulator should be capable of distinguishing between minor and insignificant differences in accounts of events as distinct from material conflicts of evidence, it is important to avoid discrepancies wherever possible. Consequently the process of preparation for interviews and responses to disclosure requests where there are multiple strands of investigation can be extremely time consuming. It is, however, time well spent that will reduce queries at a later date and reduce the capacity of investigators and prosecutors to attack credibility.

Nevertheless, it is important that any in-house team that is tasked with responding to investigations and proceedings is kept as narrow as is practicable, to avoid leaks of confidential information and to reduce the chances of unhelpful documents being created in the course of responding to multiple investigations and proceedings.

## 14.4 Impact of FSA and Tribunal findings on parallel proceedings

### 14.4.1 Introduction

A notable feature of some recent FSA investigations has been that the FSA has shown itself willing to reach an agreed settlement without requiring the firm or individual involved to admit breach. For example this has happened in two major cases, the *Shell* market abuse case (where the FSA did publish its own adverse findings as to the facts and breaches) and the investigation into split capital investment trusts (where the FSA explicitly stated that it was not making findings against firms participating in the settlement or their employees). This shows a willingness by the FSA to act in a way that reduces the chances of significant collateral damage that a firm that has already paid hefty fines or consumer redress could suffer if there are claims against it in the courts. In both the *Shell* case and the investigation into alleged misconduct in the split capital investment trusts sector, the possibility of claims by aggrieved investors both in the UK and in the US weighed heavily.

### 14.4.2 *Findings of fact or breach by the FSA or by the Tribunal*

Most FSA disciplinary proceedings settle. The impact of admissions of fact by a firm in reaching an agreed settlement is discussed at 14.4.3 below.

Where a firm does not reach an agreed settlement with the FSA and the firm has contested a finding of breach, a firm may nevertheless decide not to refer the FSA's adverse decision to the Tribunal. In this case the FSA will issue a final notice setting out findings of fact and breach. These are findings of the FSA in its administrative decision-making capacity and although those findings will bind the firm (or individual) concerned as against the FSA, the findings can still be contested in other proceedings provided the firm has not made admissions of fact or breach to the FSA (*see* 14.4.3 below).

On the other hand, the firm or individual may refer the matter to the Tribunal and the Tribunal may make an adverse finding, notwithstanding that the firm or individual concerned has argued before the Tribunal that there was no regulatory breach. Again, the Tribunal's finding will bind the firm (subject to appeal) as against the FSA. Although the finding of the Tribunal is likely to be given weight in other regulatory or civil proceedings, the finding of the Tribunal will not prevent the firm from re-litigating the issues against other parties, for example in civil proceedings brought by investors or in proceedings by other regulators. This view is based on the legal authorities described below.

There is old Court of Appeal authority, in *Hollington v F Hewthorn and Co. Ltd*,[25] but which nevertheless remains good law, that judgments in civil proceedings are not admissible in subsequent proceedings as evidence of the facts upon which the judgment was based. This authority has been reconfirmed in more recent cases, for example in a case where the Secretary of State brought civil proceedings under the Company Directors Disqualification Act 1986 seeking a disqualification order against the managing director of the company.[26] By the time that case came to trial the managing director had been dismissed

---

[25] [1943] KB 587.
[26] *Secretary of State for Trade and Industry v Bairstow* [2003] EWCA Civ 321.

by the company and had brought wrongful dismissal proceedings that were unsuccessful both at a first instance hearing and before an appeal court. The Court of Appeal in the disqualification proceedings held that the factual findings and conclusions of the judge in the wrongful dismissal case were not admissible in the disqualification proceedings as evidence of the facts found in the wrongful dismissal case. This principle has also been applied to findings of inspectors appointed under the Companies Act 1985 and in a number of other cases. There has been some contrary authority, for example in a 1907 case[27] the Court of Appeal held that a finding by the General Medical Council that a dentist was guilty of misconduct was admissible as evidence of misconduct in civil proceedings relating to the dissolution of his partnership.

It seems fairly clear that a claimant in civil proceedings will not be able to rely on findings by the FSA as to fact or breach, or even findings by the Tribunal, as evidence in the civil proceedings about the relevant facts and circumstances. The facts and the question of breach will fall to be litigated and determined afresh. Nevertheless adverse findings by the FSA or the Tribunal are likely to be given considerable weight by a civil court and may be persuasive before a jury in a criminal trial.

### 14.4.3   *Admissions by firms about breach or the facts*

Most proceedings brought by the FSA result in an agreed settlement, even though that settlement usually involves adverse findings by the FSA. As part of that agreed settlement process, the FSA may require a firm or individual concerned to admit that there has been a breach or admit particular facts, although as discussed at 14.4.1 above, the FSA has shown flexibility about this. The FSA may also require as part of the settlement that the firm agrees not to make any statements in public to the effect that it has not been in breach.

In cases where admissions have been made to the FSA which are recited in the FSA's public findings, it will be difficult, in practice, for the individual or firm concerned credibly to take a different position in other proceedings. For this reason firms and individuals should

---

[27] *Hill* v *Clifford* [1907] 2 Ch 236.

avoid making formal admissions of fact or breach during an FSA investigation or disciplinary process and, if admissions must be made tactically in the course of attempting to reach a settlement, then this should only be done under the cloak of "without prejudice" discussions. Efforts should be made to ensure that any publicised findings by the FSA are stated expressly to be without admission or are otherwise clearly stated to be the opinion of the FSA.

Even where an adverse finding has been made by the FSA in circumstances where a firm has made admissions of fact or breach, third-party claimants will still have to prove that the breach committed by the firm has caused the loss that they seek to recover. For example, a finding by the FSA that there has been a rule breach may give private persons a right of action for breach of statutory duty under Section 150 FSMA 2000. However, even if breach cannot be contested, the private person still has the hurdle of demonstrating that the breach has caused the financial loss that the individual suffers, applying legal principles about causation of loss, remoteness of damage and scope of duty. It may still be possible, therefore, for the firm to defend civil claims under Section 150 as these other legal hurdles can often be difficult to overcome.

There is also a question about the extent to which a court will take into account any compensation that a firm has already provided voluntarily to a private person concerned. Although there is no clear legal authority on the point, the court is likely to give credit for compensation paid, whether by the firm concerned or by any other party that may be responsible for indemnifying a customer in respect of its losses.

It is always preferable to avoid making admissions at all, where possible, to avoid encouraging third-party legal action, such as claims relying upon Section 150. This leaves a firm with more control over how it may choose to remediate in appropriate cases.

## 14.5  Interface between the FSA and FOS

The Financial Ombudsman Service is a body set up under FSMA 2000 to provide a means by which disputes between individual consumers and financial firms can be resolved by an independent person with a minimum of formality. It provides a single Ombudsman service for disputes relating to investments covered by FSA regulation.[28] Where firms fail to resolve a complaint under their internal complaints-handling procedures, complainants have the option of referring the dispute to FOS or taking civil court proceedings.

The Ombudsman makes a determination of a customer complaint by reference to what is, in the opinion of the Ombudsman, "fair and reasonable in all the circumstances of the case". His decision may, therefore, not be legally correct and the procedure that the Ombudsman follows in reaching a decision will not necessarily have the rigour of a court, the Tribunal or even the Regulatory Decisions Committee ("RDC"). For example, no particular rules must be applied about evidence that may or may not be admitted and firms that are party to a complaint may not be given access to all relevant material to enable them to respond to a complaint effectively.

Authorised firms are under a duty to cooperate with the Ombudsman in providing information and documents and attending hearings. The Ombudsman also has compulsory powers to require provision of information or documents if this is "necessary" to determine a complaint, which could be used against recalcitrant firms. An issue may arise for firms about the use that the Ombudsman will make of information provided by them, which will generally be confidential and may be commercially sensitive. The Ombudsman may disclose the information to other parties and use it at a hearing of the complaint (which may be held in public) and can pass it to other regulatory or statutory bodies. It is sometimes a particular concern that complainants may not take care with a firm's confidential information that is put into their hands. It may also be a concern that the Ombudsman can pass information to the FSA. This may well happen if the information suggests that there may have been breaches of FSA rules or raises doubts about whether individual approved persons involved, or indeed firms, are not fit and proper (*see* discussion of the Memorandum of Understanding with the FSA below).

---

[28] Precise details of FOS jurisdiction can be found in the complaints-handling section of the FSA Handbook (DISP) and on the FOS website.

Although FOS's role is not to set regulatory standards, but merely to provide a low-cost adjudication route for individual customer claims, FOS determinations have in some cases had a major impact on industry practice and costs. For individual firms the financial impact may also be severe if there are likely to be a large number of claims on similar facts. Therefore, firms need to decide at an early stage whether they wish to acquiesce and cooperate in the FOS process and allow the flow of claims to run its course with the FOS, or whether an alternative route for dealing with claims may be better, for example bringing legal proceedings on a "test" case or agreeing with the FSA a restitution process. Submissions can then be made to the Ombudsman that it will be more appropriate for customer complaints to be dealt with by that alternative route. The Ombudsman has a discretion in that respect. Where a firm decides to cooperate in the FOS process it is vital that it is consistent in the way that it deals with all similar cases and is vigilant to ensure that the Ombudsman is also consistent in approach.

A Memorandum of Understanding ("MOU") between the FSA and FOS was drawn up when FOS was first established and has been updated and revised since. The MOU contemplates FOS referring "wider implications" cases, where a regulatory response may be needed, to the FSA for consideration. "Wider implications" cases within the MOU are cases where there is a widespread issue, or issues, which could give rise to significant consumer detriment or have a possible detrimental effect on the financial resources of firms in a market sector. The FOS publishes on its website examples of cases that it has referred to the FSA under the "wider implications" procedure. One case involved a large firm where the FOS had noted that the firm rejected a steady stream of complaints into alleged misselling of an investment product. The complaints came from across the country, which suggested to FOS that the sales methods used were part of a firm-wide approach. In view of these wider implications, FOS notified the FSA. The FSA carried out an investigation into sales by the firm and found that it did not have sufficiently rigorous procedures and controls for the selling of the particular product. Ultimately, the firm agreed to pay a significant penalty for breach of FSA rules and to compensate some customers along the lines of compensation previously awarded by FOS in individual cases. Other customers remained entitled to refer their cases to FOS for individual consideration.

# Index

All indexing is to paragraph number